Created and Directed by Hans Höfer

INSIGHT GUIDES

CHINA

Editor: Manfred Morgenstern
Photograpers: Erhard Pansegrau,
Manfred Morgenstern and others
Text edited by: Ilse Wagner and Dieter Vogel

Translated by: Ann Adler, Barbara König
and Susan James

APA PUBLICATIONS

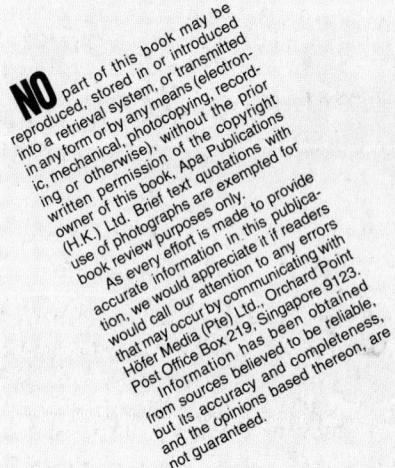
CHINA

Third Edition (Revised)
© **1994 APA PUBLICATIONS (HK) LTD**
All Rights Reserved
Printed in Singapore by Höfer Press Pte Ltd

Distributed in the United States by:
Houghton Mifflin Company
222 Berkeley Street
Boston, Massachusetts 02116-3764
ISBN: 0-395-66244-3

Distributed in Canada by:
Thomas Allen & Son
390 Steelcase Road East
Markham, Ontario L3R 1G2
ISBN: 0-395-66244-3

Distributed in the UK & Ireland by:
GeoCenter International UK Ltd
The Viables Center, Harrow Way
Basingstoke, Hampshire RG22 4BJ
ISBN: 9-62421-075-6

Worldwide distribution enquiries:
Höfer Communications Pte Ltd
38 Joo Koon Road
Singapore 2262
ISBN: 9-62421-075-6

ABOUT THIS BOOK

With the collapse of Communism in the former Soviet Union, China was left as the world's foremost guardian of Marxist thought. The question arose: would the winds of change blow as fiercely in Beijing as they had in Moscow? Or would there be a repeat of the repression seen in Beijing's Tiananmen Square?

Answers have been slow in coming, but the situation remains tantalizing. Free market reforms have so far failed to dent seriously the closed political system, but they have had an undoubted social impact. Luxury high-rise hotels financed by foreign capital, tower over Shanghai's slums. A headlong rush for wealth has created a rash of Chinese millionaires. A Japanese-owned department store in Beijing was so overwhelmed by Christmas shoppers that its escalators broke down.

Such fascinating changes make China an even more alluring destination for visitors. The attraction is based not only on an ancient and great culture or on the hospitality of its people, but also on the gaps in our knowledge of China, which arouse curiosity and the desire to travel there and see for ourselves. Of course, it is impossible to get to know China in one visit: there is too much variety in the Middle Kingdom, and most importantly, it is far too big. Therefore, the goal the publishers set for themselves was an ambitious one: to produce a book of a certain standard that would do justice to the attractions of the country, with the co-operation of several authors and photographers who are among the most knowledgeable experts on China. **Manfred Morgenstern**, the project editor, was responsible for developing the concept of the book and for bringing together the authors and photographers, most of whom he has got to know personally in nearly 15 years of work related with China. The first time Morgenstern went to the Middle Kingdom was in early 1977, a few months after the death of Mao. Countless trips to China followed, in which Manfred Morgenstern, a qualified sociologist, increased his knowledge of the history, culture and politics of China. As a travel journalist, tour guide and, over the last few years, as tour organizer, he has got to know almost all the regions of this enormous country.

Authoritative and Informative

The China experts **Helmut Forster-Latsch** and **Marie-Luise Latsch** have spent many years studying and researching in China. They have had the opportunity to make a special study of Chinese culture and the traditions of the ethnic minorities of China. Both have made names for themselves as authors of various textbooks and translators of Chinese literature and fairy tales.

Marie-Luise Beppler-Lie is particularly knowledgeable about the interior of China, Sichuan and the central regions of the Yangzi river. After studying Sinology in Frankfurt, she taught for three years at the Foreign Language Institute in Chongqing and trained a number of interpreters in the use of German. They now work in various travel bureaus all over China and many of them still remember "their" German teacher today. Marie-Luise Beppler-Lie also translates contemporary Chinese literature into German.

The past and present of north-western China, along the ancient Silk Road, is the

Morgenstern   *Forster-Latsch*   *Marie L. Latsch*   *Beppler-Lie*   *Grobe-Hagel*   *Klapproth*

hobby of **Karl Grobe-Hagel**. Editor of foreign political news for a major Frankfurt daily, he is also responsible for covering eastern Asia and China.

Eva Klapproth has taken over the job of describing the east of China. A suitable choice as she had studied for several years in Taiwan and at the famous Fudan University in Shanghai. Together with Helmut Forster-Latsch, she tries to publicize the writings of critical intellectuals from China in the West.

In this book, **Elke Wandel** has written about "her" city of Beijing, where she worked for several years as a teacher, and about Shandong province. She has also published an interesting book about the role of women in Chinese history.

Special thanks, too, go to **Tom Ots**, who contributed the section on Chinese medicine, although he is at present doing research in USA. He studied – and also practised – Chinese medicine for several years in Beijing and Nanjing.

Only the Best Shots

The photographic contributions are the supporting pillar of every Apa Guide, as they are not merely intended to accompany and illustrate the text, but to tell their own individual story as well. We had excellent pictures available, thus making our selection even more difficult. However, Manfred Morgenstern and Hans Höfer, the chairman of Apa Publications in hot and humid Singapore, were quite willing to share the task on this occasion.

Apart from these two who contributed some of their own photographic material, we would like to mention **Erhard Pansegrau**, who has already collaborated on the *Insight Cityguide: Beijing* as well as *Germany* and *The Rhine*. For 15 years, Pansegrau and his camera have been travelling the world, and his special affection for eastern Asia and China is unmistakable.

Mike Theiler worked as a photographer for a news agency in China for two years. Now based in Hong Kong, he travels throughout China and has been able to contribute interesting pictures of modern China.

The graphic artist, designer and photographer, **Bodo Bondzio**, who has been travelling in the Middle Kingdom since 1981, will no doubt be familiar to those who had already read *Insight Cityguide: Beijing*.

Peter Hessel, the second doctor in this team after Tom Ots, uses his leisure time to travel through China along the most unusual routes. His contribution mainly comprises pictures of the south-west of China.

Further photographs have been contributed by **Elke Wandel**, **Kosima Weber-Liu**, who has lived with her family for many years in Beijing where her husband is a photographer, and many other photographers who we came across when looking through the Apa archives in Singapore. The editor is also grateful to China Travel and Tourism Press in Beijing, who were able to provide rare photographs from the time of the Cultural Revolution.

Our special thanks to **Gisela Schneckmann** for her help in putting together the practical Travel Tips section.

—APA Publications

Wandel

Ots

Theiler

Bondzio

Hessel

Weber-Liu

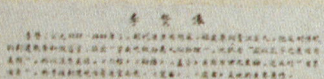

王夫之像

顾炎武像

CONTENTS

History & Culture

Towns & Places

Maps

TRAVEL TIPS

**For detailed Information
See Page 353**

ZHONGGUO –
THE MIDDLE KINGDOM

Zhonghua Renmin Gongheguo is the official name of the People's Republic of China, but in everyday language it is simply *Zhongguo* – the Middle Kingdom. In the Temple of Heaven in Beijing, the marble altar signifies the centre of the world, a place which only the Emperor was allowed to enter in order to communicate with heaven. According to cosmological view of the world held in ancient Chinese cultures, the Middle Kingdom lay precisely below the centre of the firmament. The peoples living on the dark peripheries of the earth's disk were regarded as barbarians.

The concept of centricity is prevalent in Chinese philosophy and ethics. The quest for harmony between opposite forces, for a state of balance, calmness, order and peace is central to the teachings of Confucius. Yet the history of China has been turbulent throughout, periods of peace and prosperity have alternated with times of change, chaos, famine and poverty, war and revolution.

Europeans have, for centuries, regarded China as an empire at the edge of the world. The ancient Greeks wrote about the *Serers*, which means the "bearers of silk". In subsequent centuries, other names were given to the distant Middle Kingdom which is still foreign to us. There was the name *Khitai*, which originated in Northern China when it was occupied by the Khitan in the 10th and 11th century. This name is still commonly used in Russian-speaking areas. The name China can presumably be traced back to the Qin Dynasty (221-207 B.C.) which was described as *Tschin*, *Tschina* or *Tzinistan* in the Indo-Germanic languages. The Chinese of the Qin and Han dynasties called the country *Daqin* and thus gave this empire their own name; the syllable *da* means big.

The 19th century was a period of humiliation for China; the central geo-political point had shifted. The imperialist powers of industrialised Europe had pushed China into a marginal existence and injured its self-esteem. From this situation arose national and revolutionary forces working towards building a modern and strong China. Will China move back towards the centre in future? Many people claim that the 21st century may become the age of the Pacific and this will no doubt allow modern China to play a leading role.

If one were to transpose the frontiers of China onto the European continent, the northern border would be at the height of the North Sea and the southern border would run through the African Sahel; from east to west the territory would reach from Portugal to the Ural. The Pacific coast forms the border to the eastern and south-eastern parts of China, while the north-western part of the country, the Province of Xinjiang, extends deep into Central Asia, and Heilongjiang in the north-east (what used to be Manchuria) is part of Siberia.

As a consequence, there are extreme climatic differences. On the south-eastern islands, winter is warm and people enjoy tropical fruits, while at the same time the northeast is paralyzed by Siberian frosts and people flee from the icy winds. Some parts of Tibet are regions with perpetual frost, while crops grow all year round in Taiwan, Guangdong and South Yunnan.

China has the highest mountains and deepest valleys in the world, deserts and fertile loess plains, dark pine forests and tropical rainforests, and rivers which are amongst the longest in the world. Almost a continent in itself, China is without doubt a country of extremes and superlatives.

The distance from the northern town of Mohe on the Heilongjiang, which forms the border to the Soviet Union, to the Zhengmu Reef on the Nansha Islands in the South China Seas is 3,420 miles (5,500 km). From the eastern border in the Pamir Mountains to the confluence of the Heilongjiang and the Wusulijiang (Ussuri) the distance is 3,230 miles (5,200 km). China covers an area of 3,691,500 sq miles (9,560,900 sq km). It is the third largest country in the world – after Russia and Canada – and roughly the same size as the whole of Europe.

China's border is 12,430 miles (20,000 km) long; its neighbouring countries are Korea, the People's Republic of Mongolia, Russia, Kazakhstan, Kyrgyzstan, Tajikistan, Afghanistan, Pakistan, India, Nepal, Sikkim, Bhutan, Myanmar (formerly Burma), Laos and Vietnam. The coastline in the east and south-east is more than 11,200 miles (18,000 km) long and stretches from the Bay of Bohai, east of Beijing, across the Yellow and East China Seas to the South China Sea.

Topography

With good reason China is occasionally called the land of mountains. Two thirds of its territory are mountainous, hilly or high plateaux. China's topography is characterised by its terraced structure with the land sloping downwards towards the north-east, east and south-east. The highest terrace is the Tibet-Qinghai-Plateau which is 13,120 ft (4,000 metres). It includes the Autonomous Region of Tibet, the Qinghai provinces and Western Sichuan. All the major rivers of China and South-East Asia rise in the Tibet-Qinghai-Plateau. The Huanghe (Yellow River) and the Changjiang (Yangzi River) flow eastwards through China, while the Zangbojiang (Bramaputra), the Nujiang (Salween) and the Lancang (Mekong) flow south and south-east, thereby passing through China's neighbouring countries.

The second terrace is formed by plateaux and terraces of heights averaging between 3,280 and 6,560 ft (1,000 and 2,000 metres); going from north to south they are the Tarim Basin, the Mongolian Plateau, the Central Chinese Loess Plateau, the Red Basin of Sichuan and the Yunnan-Guizhou Plateau.

The third terrace is formed of the plains and lowlands on the lower reaches of the large rivers; actually it is a large, wide strip of land, barely rising more than 1,640 ft (500 metres) above sea level, running along the coast from the north of China right down to the south. More than two-thirds of the population live here; it is China's agricultural and industrial heartland.

This terraced structure is the result of massive tectonic movements within the Chinese land mass, which to this day has not settled. As a result, earthquakes continue to strike in many regions of China. The 1976 earthquake in Tangshan, which claimed several hundred thousand lives, was the last major disaster.

Preceding pages: snow-covered peaks in the Himalayas. Left, the "Fiery Mountains" at the edge of the Taklamakan Desert.

China – land of mountains

China has the highest mountains in the world; nine of the 14 mountains which are higher than 26,260 ft (8,000 metres) are found in the Himalayas. The Shengmufeng (Mount Everest), on the border of Nepal, is the highest mountain in the world at 29,029 ft (8,848 metres). More than one hundred mountains are higher than 22,965 ft (7,000 metres), and more than a thousand reach a height of more than 19,685 ft (6,000 metres).

the Kongur (25,325 ft/7,719 metres) are the highest peaks in the Kunlun range. In summer the rivers which spring from the Qinghai Plateau are fed with water from the melting glaciers.

Farther north, again reaching from west to east, is the Tianshan Range; in English it means "Heavenly Mountains" (25,165 ft/ 7,000 metres). Between the Kunlun and Tianshan ranges lies the Tufan depression, 505 ft (154 metres) below sea level. Only the Dead Sea depression is lower than this. The

China's Regions

1000 km

Legend:
- Lowlands
- Basin
- Mountainous and Hilly Country
- Highlands
- High Mountain Region

The Himalayas is one of the youngest mountain ranges in the world; even today it grows between 0.13 and 0.5 inches (0.33 and 1.27 cm) every year. North of the Himalayas, the Kunlun mountains separate the Tibet-Qinghai Plateau from the Tarim Basin and the Taklamakan Desert. Its western-most point is in the Pamir Plateau and from there it extends eastwards for 1,553 miles (2,500 km). The Muztag (25,367 ft/7,723 metres), the Muztagata (24,757 ft/7,546 metres) and

two ranges enclose China's largest desert, the Taklamakan, which means: the desert one enters but never comes out of again.

The Greater Xingan Range in the north-east of China forms a natural border between the Manchurian lowland and the Mongolian steppe. It is also China's largest wooded area and therefore an important watershed. The range, which is between 124 and 186 miles (200 and 300 km) wide, reaches south-west from the banks of the Heilongjiang and is

746 miles (1,200 km) long. The highest elevation is only 6,821 ft (2,079 metres), but this mountain range has a great influence on the climate. The south-eastern summer monsoons pass here, so that the lowlands east of the mountains are very fertile, while the steppe west of the range remains dry all year round. A similarly important climatic divide is the Qinling Range which is 932 miles (1,500 km) long and reaches from the Gansu-Qinghai border through the Shaanxi province all the way to Henan. In summer it

the Lancang, Nujiang and others – flow through the deep valleys which run from north to south. The average height of the mountains is between 9,842 and 13,123 ft (3,000 and 4,000 metres), the highest peak, the Gongga, is 24,823 ft (7,556 metres). The peaks are covered in snow, dense forests line the lower edges of the slope, and tropical fruits and plants grow in the valleys.

In historical terms, the Yellow River (Huanghe) is no doubt the most important river in China. It rises in the Qinghai pro-

acts as a barrier to the heavy masses of humid air caused by the monsoon, in winter it stops the cold northerly winds from entering too far into Central China.

The group of mountain ranges running through eastern Tibet, west Sichuan and Yunnan are called Hengduan Mountains. The word *hengduan* means "barrier" and it is a fact that these ranges have, even in modern times, formed an insurmountable barrier between east and west. Large rivers – the Jinsha (the source river of the Yangzijiang),

Above, rice is the staple food of the Chinese; rice terraces in Sichuan.

vince, makes a sharp bend to the north near Lanzhou and farther on, near Baotou in Mongolia, it turns south again, forming the famous Huanghe knee. Along its course, it passes through the fertile loess plateau creating favourable conditions for the growth of human civilisation. It is not surprising that it was here in the valleys of the Yellow River and its main tributary, the Weihe, that the first Chinese states were formed. The loess, which was constantly threatened by erosion, as well as the wild Yellow River, called for large communities to work together in order to deal with the immense task of irrigating the land. It is because of this river that Chinese civilisation began. So it may not be a coincidence that the Chinese describe the loess as *huangtu*, yellow earth, and that the most important mythological emperor is called *Huangdi*, the Yellow Emperor.

In the upper reaches of the river, which is 3,395 miles (5,464 km) long, the water is crystal clear. Only as it passes through the Central Chinese Loess Plateau does it fill up with the yellow loess earth which erodes very easily because it is insufficiently

largest in the world, is the 3,915-mile (6,300-km) long Changjiang (Yangzi River). It divides the Middle Kingdom into North and South, a border which is also significant in cultural terms. In the North, there is predominantly cultivation of grain and sweet potatoes, while the South is dominated by wet and green rice fields. Even in this century, the river formed a barrier which was hard to overcome. Three large bridges across the Yangzi, constructed in the last decade at Chongqing, Wuhan and Nanjing have con-

vegetated. With 44 lbs (20 kg) of silt per cubic centimetre of water, the Huanghe transports more than one billion tonnes of sediments into its lower reaches every year. As the river bed widens in the north China lowland plain, the river deposits more than four million tons. Here the river bed grows by about 4 inches (10 cm) every year. In order to prevent floods, dykes are constantly being constructed or repaired; at some points the silt is dug from the river bed and used to fertilise the fields. The water level in the estuary is so low that there is no shipping route to the sea.

The largest river in China, and the third

tributed to the economic growth of China.

The Changjiang rises at the foot of the Geladondong (21,724 ft/6,621 metres high) in the Tanggula Mountains in Qinghai province. In its upper reaches its name is Tuotuo, then it is called Tongianhe, and from Yibin in Qinghai all the way to Sichuan it is called the River of Golden Sand (Jinshajiang). Changjiang is the name commonly used for the middle reaches, while the locals call the lower reaches of the river, from Yangzhou to the estuary, Yangzi. This is the name missionaries and colonialists were familiar with and, as a result, became established in Europe. Along a stretch of 127 miles (204 km), the river passes through the Three Gorges of the Yangzi. In the Qutang Gorge the river is only 330 ft (100 metres) wide. At this point the difference between deep and shallow water can be up to 197 ft (60 metres). In the Wu Gorge, which is the next one, the mountains rise from the banks and tower over the river at a height of 1,640 to 3,280 ft (500 to 1,000 metres).

Given the size of China, it is not unusual to find a variety of climatic conditions and extreme differences in temperature. The

horizontal gradient – 49 degrees of latitude lie between the northern and southern border of the country – and the vertical slope between the high plateaux in the west and the low plains in the east and south-east affect the climate, but the main determining factor is its position at the edge of the Asian continent and the vast Pacific Ocean. In winter, cold air masses form over the high pressure zones of the Asian continent and then move southwards; this causes the dry climate which is typical of the Chinese winter. The

Left, misty tropical landscape in Yunnan. **Above**, a message, carved onto bamboo for posterity.

only unpleasant aspect of this is the high dust content in the air blowing the loess in from the Gobi Desert. In summer, the climate is a maritime one. The summer monsoons bring the rains from the Pacific, so that the rainy season lasts from May until September and the rain zones move from south to north.

The north-east of China and northern Mongolia have short and warm summers, while the winters are long and cold. The growing season lasts for only three or four months. Immediately to the West lie the desert regions of Inner Mongolia and Xinjiang; they have hot and dry summers with occasional strong winds, the winters are cold and dry. In the Tibet-Qinghai Plateau which is, on average, 13,120 ft (4,000 metres) high, the winters are extremely cold, the short summers only moderately warm.

In Central China, summers are, without exception, hot and rainfall is high. North of the Yangzi, the main rainfall is in July and August. In the low plains of the Yangzi the winters are somewhat milder than in the loess plains north of the Qinling mountains. Here the growing period lasts for eight or nine months. One exception is the naturally sheltered Red Basin in Sichuan where the growth period lasts for up to 11 months.

The Chinese have designated the land according to the colour of its soil: there is black earth in North-East China, the desert and steppe soil is described as white, the loess earth in Central China is yellow, red earth is found south of the Yangzi, and the fertile marsh lands in the South are described as blue or green soil. This short list alone indicates that the fertile soil is to be found in the south and east of the country, while in the north and the west there are pastures or steppes, deserts and high plateaux. Only 40 percent of the total area of the country can be exploited for agriculture or forestry, the remaining 60 percent are barren land, and only 11 percent of the total land is suitable for farming. In order to feed the population which has exceeded one billion, agriculture needs to be constantly intensified. Herein lies one of the most serious problems of the Chinese economy: it seems impossible to provide enough food for the population without causing serious ecological damage.

揉着有点发红肿
下，瞧也不瞧她
了几天，班里语文测
着"警告分三分"
我轻声叹了一口
花猫好象直冲我
们的视平线
一会儿，她把
"扣分就扣
。

China has been the most highly populated country on earth ever since history has recorded figures and data, and it will probably remain so for the next few decades.

China's population was for the first time counted in the year A.D. 4. During the turbulent times under the usurper Wang Mang, between the Western and the Eastern Han Dynasty, the country had 57,671,400 inhabitants. There were 51 million people in A.D. 742 during the Tang Dynasty. Just before the invasion of the Mongols, around A.D. 1250, the 100 million mark was probably exceeded briefly for the first time. In 1662 an indirect census (calculated on the basis of the number of households) showed 111 million Chinese. By the middle of the 18th century, the number had doubled; in 1850 the figure of 400 million had been reached, and this had not been exceeded even in 1930.

The dramatic population explosion started after the Revolution. In 1953, after four years of peace, there were 582,603,000 people in China; thirty years later, this figure had increased by almost exactly half a billion. Today, China is the home of over 1.17 billion people (1992), which is equivalent to 20 percent of humanity – but only 7 percent of the world's agrarian areas are found in China.

Conurbations and empty spaces

If you take a map of China and draw a line from the northernmost tip of the province of Heilongjiang to the point were Myanmar (formerly Burma), Laos and China meet, you find that only one fifth of the Chinese land lies to the East of this line; however, 90 percent of the population in the People's Republic live in this area. Situated at the border of this imaginary line, and surrounded by a relatively unpopulated area, is the province of Sichuan with a population of 100 million inhabitants. Only below the famous rapids, where the Yangzi River enters the lowlands, does the wide and incredibly densely populated part of the country begin; here are the cities of Wuhan, Nanjing, Shanghai, all with a population over the one million mark. Here, too, is the great plain which reaches beyond Beijing, and in which not

one square mile of land has remained uncultivated. The vast "empty areas" in the north and west are hardly habitable. They include the largest deserts of Asia, the Gobi and Taklamakan; there is also Tibet, the highland most hostile to human life, where permanent settlements are only possible in the valleys, which themselves are 11,800 ft (3,600 metres) above sea level. Finally, there are the desert-like steppes of southern Mongolia and Xinjiang.

So what about the empty spaces? They only exist if you use the abstract calculation of "people per square mile". No space remains empty if it is at all habitable or can be used for nomadic cattle rearing. They have, however, up until modern times, hardly been inhabited by the Han Chinese, but by other ethnic groups: Eastern Turks and Mongolians, Tibetans and South-East Asians. If the Chinese showed serious intentions of inhabiting these areas, they would have to dispute these peoples' right to the land.

Village structures were replaced by communes and similar units during the "left-wing time"; the actual village settlements, however, remained. Urbanization is not only a result of migration in China, but also an administrative matter: if more than half the inhabitants of a settlement live on non-agricultural work, it is classed as a town; in the opposite case, it is a village.

The reforms carried out since the late 1970s have led to more far-reaching changes in China's demographic planning than anything which had happened before. Ever since farmers began to work independently, having

people, more than half of all agricultural workplaces will have disappeared by the year 2000.

In the cities, too, the jobs of 25 percent of the 100 million strong labour force are threatened; once businesses have undergone price reforms and are forced to show profitability, saturation with workers will, for economic reasons, no longer be viable. Dismissals will be the inevitable consequence. This is the reason why a re-structuring in the country is

many children (preferably sons) has once more become synonymous with a larger workforce and higher incomes; these measures create ties to the land. Yet the agricultural areas are not growing with the population, and agriculture is not profitable when one worker has less than a hectare to farm. Although possibilities for mechanization are very limited for the 800 million

Preceding pages: a modern Chinese girl; a rice field being ploughed; one day he will master the 3,000 characters of the Chinese script. **Left**, relaxing with a pipe. **Above**, Bai men in Yunnan province.

necessary. Leading Chinese social scientists have for a long time argued that the rural population should remain in the country, yet be employed in non-agricultural jobs. Industry and commerce should be developed in small and medium-sized towns in order to cover local needs; many villages (by Chinese definition) should be changed to towns. Otherwise there would, for every city the size of Shanghai (13 million inhabitants), be three or four equally sized cities in the course of one decade. This is unimaginable, especially in the light of unemployment in the cities. Emigration to the cities is no solution; rural life should remain equally attractive as life in the city. The great migration should definitely be avoided.

There seems to be one practical solution, considering that four fifths of the country in the West are hardly inhabited at all. Could this area not become the home for the surplus people? For the last two centuries, many have emigrated from the densely populated south and east of the country, but they tended to go to South-East Asia or the United States, where the possibilities for earning a good living and thus surviving were greater.

allow for a massive movement of people into the area.

Nationalities

Around 6.7 percent of the population of China are not Han Chinese, but members of national minorities – this amounts to more than 66 million people. The constitution guarantees them certain national rights and privileges. One of the most important is the right to use their own language; it has by no means

Living conditions are difficult in the steppes and deserts of Middle Asia, in the Tibetan Highlands and particularly in the wintry north. Even the immigrants (usually not voluntary) who at present live here voice their wishes to return home – since 1976 there have been demonstrations, particularly in Xinjiang. This is where hundreds of thousands of youngsters were sent, mainly during the Cultural Revolution; they have never really settled there, and can only be kept there by administrative measures.

In Inner Mongolia and the north-eastern provinces, the situation is different. The central government's nationalist policy will not

been realized in those parts of the country which are inhabited by national minorities. For many, being fluent in both the spoken and written standard Chinese is the only way of becoming educated and improving their social status. Schools for members of national minorities are not found everywhere, and universities teaching a minority language hardly exist.

This reflects an ancient concept, based on historical experience, that there is no other developed culture apart from the Chinese. In reality, the slow expansion of the Chinese nation from the original area on the Yellow River and its tributary Weihe up to the South

China Sea – i.e. over a sub-continent – is linked to an equally slow assimilation of non-Chinese peoples into the Han nation, who were technically and culturally far superior to the non-Chinese. The small minorities which continue to live in less easily accessible areas ("areas once flees to") have resisted the attraction of Chinese culture and civilisation, and paid the price of slow progress within their own cultures. To grant these minorities the right to live according to their own beliefs and traditions is, in the eyes

of the Chinese, a sign of goodwill, namely the renunciation of the expansionism of the old regime. National characteristics and traditions are, however, limited to the sphere of folklore.

The quest for sovereignty or greater territorial autonomy does not allow for unrestricted development of other advanced civilisations within the frontiers of the People's Republic of China. The minority rights were never intended to be applied in this way.

Left, girls from the Gejia tribe in Guizhou province. **Above**, Miao women with precious silver jewellery (Guizhou).

There are, however, two minority groups representative of high cultures: the Tibetans and the Uighurs (the first group living within an entirely autonomous system, the second belonging to the Islamic community influenced by the Turkish language and culture). Neither of the groups are willing to accept that assimilation with the Han Chinese would allow them to benefit from the world of culture and science. They refuse to acknowledge that the only way to achieve progress is to discard the common Tibetan or East Turkish heritage in favour of the Han Chinese.

For the first time in the history of their expansionist politics, the Han Chinese are confronted with this phenomenon, and they do not have any ready solutions. The bitterness of the ever recurring anti-Chinese demonstrations in Tibet has much to do with this. The privileges of the minorities are not sufficient to remove these conflicts; but for the small minorities they ensure, for the time being, their continued existence.

It is only in Tibet that the minority group constitutes a clear majority of the population (98 percent in this case). The arbitrary frontier line of the region of Tibet, which was drawn up at the Simla conference in 1913/14, can easily obscure the process of change. In 1913/14 a differentiation was made between "Outer Tibet" and "Inner Tibet"; the latter included the present-day province of Qinghai, the regions of Aba (Ngaba) and Gerze, one district of the province of Yunnan, and some smaller areas in the province of Gansu. In all these places the Tibetans are still the majority (in Qinghai, however, this only applies if the two large cities of the province are not included in the statistic). About half of the 3.9 million Tibetans live in Tibet, the other half live in those regions which used to be called "Outer Tibet".

In Xinjiang, the autonomous region of the Uighurs, they remain the largest existing ethnic group, but they make-up only 45 percent of the entire population; only when grouped together with the Kazakhs, Kirghiz, Salaries and others do they constitute an Islamic, Turkic-speaking majority – and this in an area where 30 years ago, 80 percent of the population fulfilled these criteria. The large cities have a majority of Han Chinese (except for Kashgar); Ürümqi, a city with over 1 million inhabitants and the capital of Xinjiang, is made up of 80 percent Han Chinese.

The Muslim Hui only make up one third of the population in their autonomous region of Ningxia, and they usually live in the economically less privileged parts of the country in the south. As regards religion, most of them can only satisfy the criteria used to classify a Hui (Chinese-speaking Muslim) with great difficulty. Several times, the author has met a Hui to whom the word

Although the Zhuang have given their name and the status of an autonomous region to Guangxi, they are nevertheless a minority (albeit, the largest non-Han nationality within China). They are also more assimilated than any of the other minority groups. It is quite obvious that the national characteristics of this minority are particularly predominant in rural or isolated mountainous areas.

Government policies largely resulted in the desired results of settlement, internal migration and cultural assimilation, yet it

"Mecca" did not mean anything.

In Inner Mongolia, the Han nationality has predominated for decades and now forms 80 percent of the population. On the other hand, more Mongols live in this region than in the neighbouring state to the north, the People's Republic of Mongolia. This territory belonged to China until 1912 and is considerably larger than Inner Mongolia. It is mainly the nomadic population who are Mongolians; almost all settled farmers and people living in towns are Han Chinese. In the process of changing from pasture to agrarian land, Inner Mongolia has attracted a Han Chinese population.

must be taken into account that related groups live across the border in Russia, Kazakhstan, Kyrgyzstan, Tajikistan, Mongolia, Korea, Vietnam, Laos, Thailand, Nepal, India, Bhutan, Pakistan and Afghanistan. The policies on national minorities are, therefore, to a large extent, aimed at border security.

Family planning and one-child families

Even a richer country might despair when faced with the necessity to feed, house, clothe and educate one fifth of humanity. The demographic pyramid clearly shows a decrease in growth amongst those in their late 20s now

– i.e. those born between 1966 and 1968 at the beginning of the Cultural Revolution – and those born after 1968. On the other hand, there is an increase in the birth rate amongst those born around 1973.

This indicates a particularly marked population growth immediately after the first years of the Cultural Revolution, and those born at that time will, in the course of the next 10 years, reach the legal marriage age of 23 to 25 years. A baby boom is inevitable, although official statistics show that 16 per-

cent of all young families do not wish to have more than one child. In rural areas, however, only 10 percent have indicated these intentions.

In the late 1980s, China set a target for the year 2000 of a total population of 1.2 billion. But with the population already over 1.17 billion by the end of 1992, the target was revised to 1.294 billion. The government has forecast that the population will then continue growing, until it reaches 1.5 to 1.6 billion by the middle of next century, when it should level off.

Even at the current level, China's population is hard to sustain; most Chinese experts have said China can only support a population of 800 million. This is a major reason for the great emphasis China has placed on birth control.

Although its original targets have proven overly optimistic, the one-child policy has greatly reduced the rate of population increase. According to a 1993 estimate, based on Chinese women bearing an average of five to six children in the 1950s, and two in 1993, the policy had prevented 200 million births by 1993.

Yet problems still remain; 30 percent of births are not planned. The State Family Planning Commission, one of the major government agencies, admits to the reasons for this. Firstly, attitudes have not changed in rural areas; to a farmer, his sons still provide the only security for old age, as there is no state pension scheme. Secondly, sex education is still a taboo topic, especially in conservative rural areas where the grandmother educates her grandchildren according to her own beliefs.

Education alone, however, is not enough to influence young families. Social pressure is used as well; this could be instruction by a family planning officer in the neighbourhood, or the threat – and even imposition – of fines. In the rural areas, the first child receives a private plot of land, just like an adult; the second child does not receive anything, and if a third child is born, the first child has to return everything.

In the cities, families prefer to have one child because living space is restricted. Considering that living space in Shanghai or Beijing is, on average, 4.2 sq yards (3.5 sq metres), it is not surprising that controlling measures are being accepted. After the birth of the second prohibited child, the parents suffer a reduction in earnings and other material punishments, and have to pay nursery school fees and doctor's charges which are outrageous by Chinese income levels. It may sound harsh, but what other choice does China have in the light of overpopulation?

Left, the tribes in Yunnan love these splendidly colourful costumes and jewellery. **Above**, Kazakh woman riding a horse (Xinjiang province).

STATISTICS ON MINORITIES

Minority	1953	1990	Settlement Area (Province)
1. Sino-Tibetan Languages			
1.1. Sino-Thai-Languages	19 049 940		
Zhuang	6 610 000	15 489 630	Guangxi, Yunnan, Guangdong, Guizhou
Buyi (Bouyei)	1 250 000	2 545 059	Guizhou
Dong	680 000	2 514 014	Guizhou, Hunan, Guangxi
Dai (Tai)	560 000	1 025 128	Yunnan
Li	320 000	1 110 900	Guangdong
Shui	140 000	345 993	Guizhou, Guangxi
1.2. Tibeto-Burman Languages	15 683 031		
Yi	3 250 000	6 572 173	Yunnan, Sichuan, Guizhou, Guangxi
Tibetan	2 800 000	4 593 330	Tibet, Sichuan, Qinghai, Gansu, Yunnan
Tujia	–	5 704 223	Hunan, Hubei
Bai	460 000	1 594 827	Yunnan
Hani	260 000	1 253 952	Yunnan
Lisu	170 000	545 856	Yunnan, Sichuan
Lahu	160 000	411 476	Yunnan
Naxi	160 000	278 009	Yunnan
Qiang	50 000	198 252	Sichuan
Jingpo	110 000	119 209	Yunnan
Achang	–	27 708	Yunnan
Pumi	–	29 657	Yunnan
1.3. Miao-Yoa Languages	6 433 573		
Miao	2 510 000	5 030 897	Guizhou, Yunnan, Hunan, Guangxi, Sichuan, Guangdong, Hubei
Yao	630 000	1 402 676	Guangxi, Hunan, Yunnan, Guangdong, Guizhou
2. Altai Languages			
2.1. Turkic Languages	7 074 944		
Uighur	3 640 000	7 214 431	Xinjiang, Hunan
Kasakh	450 000	1 111 718	Xinjiang, Qinghai, Gansu
Kirgiz	80 000	141 549	Xinjiang, Heilongjiang
Salar	30 000	87 697	Qinghai, Gansu
Uzbek	–	14 502	Xinjiang
Tatar	7 000	4 873	Xinjiang
2.2. Mongol Languages	3 953 521		
Mongol	1 500 000	4 806 849	Inner Mongolia, Liaonning, Jilin, Xinjiang, Heilongjiang, Hebei, Qinghai, Henan, Gansu
Dongxiang	150 000	373 872	Gansu, Xinjiang
Tu	–	191 624	Qinghai, Gansu
Dahur	44 000	121 357	Inner Mongolia, Xinjiang, Heilongjiang
2.3. Tungusic Languages	4 407 739		
Manchu	2 420 000	9 821 180	Liaoning, Heilongjiang, Jilin, Hebei, Beijing, Inner Mongolia
Xibo	20 000	172 847	Xinjiang, Liaoning, Jilin
Hezhe	500	4 245	Heilongjiang
Oluntschun	2 000	6 965	Inner Mongolia, Heilongjiang
3. Korean Languages			
Korean	1 120 000	1 920 597	Jilin, Heilongjiang, Liaoning, Inner Mongolia
4. Austric Languages			
4.1. Austro-Asian Languages	369 362		
Wa	270 000	351 974	Yunnan
Bulang	35 000	82 280	Yunnan
Benglong	3 000	12 295	Yunnan
4.2. Austronesian Languages	1 549		
Gaoshan	150 000	2 909	Taiwan, Fujian
In Taiwan and beyond	400 000		

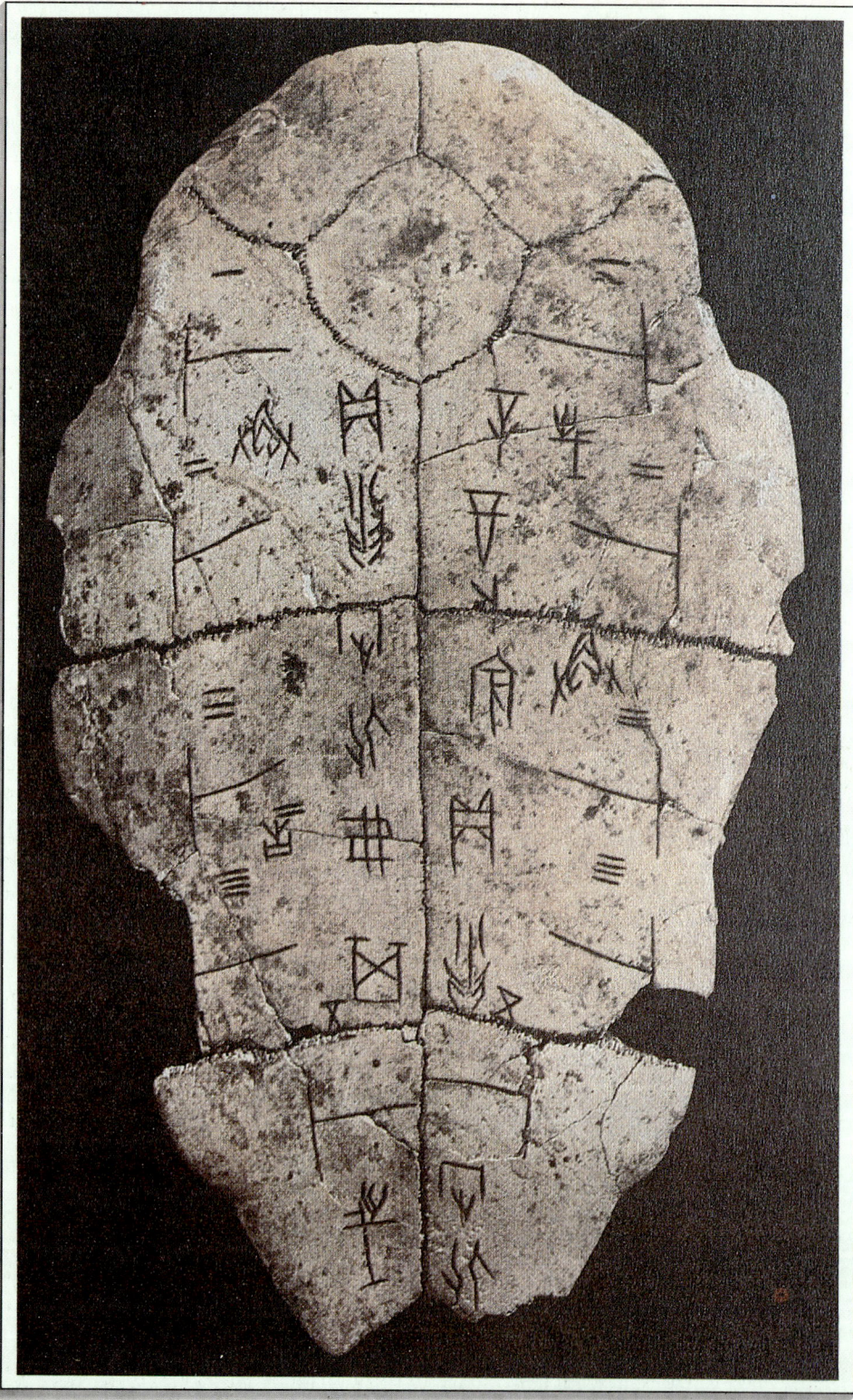

When the Chinese refer to their history, they might be speaking of times which are already legendary. After all, China's written history dates back approximately four thousand years. Archaeological material which has been found indicates that people were already living in the territory of today's China one million years ago. In the 1920s, fossilised remains of human species were discovered in Yuanmou (Yunnan province) and in Lantian (Shaanxi province). More than 400,000 years ago, Peking Man (*Sinanthropus pekinensis*) lived in Zhoukoudian, near Beijing; he was able to walk upright, produced simple tools and knew how to light fires. Yet the Peking Man marks a point at which there is a break in developments and little is known from then on until around 3000 B.C. The remains of various Neolithic civilisations date from this time, most importantly the matriarchal Yangshao civilisation and the patriarchal Longshan civilisation.

When the stone-age village of Banpo was discovered (in what is today known as Xi'an) it seemed obvious to conclude that the bend in the Yellow River with its fertile loess landscape had been the centre of ancient Chinese culture and civilisation. Discoveries made in recent years, however, suggest that neolithic civilisations were established in other areas – notably in Xinjiang, Manchuria, Sichuan and Guangdong.

To this day, there is a dispute as to the existence of the first dynasty recorded in Chinese historical writings – the Xia Dynasty (21st to 16th century B.C.). And it has not been proven conclusively if there really was an age of the Five Mythical Rulers. This is said to have been the age in which the foundations of Chinese culture, such as irrigation systems and rice plantations were developed. The Yellow Emperor Huangdi (allegedly ruled between 2490 and 2413 B.C.) is regarded as the forebear of the Chinese nation. Huangdi is alleged to have overpowered the other tribes with weapons made of jade, and his wife Leizu is thought to have invented the breeding of silkworms. The invention of the wagon, the boat and a precursor of the compass are all attributed to Huangdi. He is said to have been knowledgeable in astronomy and developed the first Chinese calendar. Under his rule, pictographic characters, the twelve-tone scale and various gauges were developed.

The Xia Dynasty was followed by the Shang Dynasty, a dynasty that grew out of the plains of northern China, on the river Huanghe (Yellow River) and in the basin of the Wei River. The Shang were an aristocratically-minded society, with the family as the basis to their social structure. The small towns were surrounded by walls or ramparts, the ruler's residence and religious buildings formed the centre. The Shang had already mastered the breeding of silkworms and the technique of spinning and weaving silk. They produced bronze of very high quality and used it to make weapons, tools, utensils and artefacts. Written evidence, such as inscriptions on oracle bones or bronze receptacles used for religious rituals have provided information on the Shang Dynasty.

The Zhou Dynasty

The Zhou Dynasty ruled from the 11th century B.C. until 221 B.C. when China was united under Qin Shi Huangdi. Originally, their settlements lay further west than those of the Shang (today the provinces of Shanxi and Gansu), but through contacts with the Shang, they increasingly assimilated to the Chinese. The rulers of the Zhou brutally overthrew the Shang, under the pretext that the Shang rulers had been corrupt and led a dissipated life, had disregarded their duties and therefore forfeited the mercy of the gods.

The Zhou took over the system which the Shang had developed and carried out considerable improvements. In order to administer their enormous territory, a system of fiefs, headed by a king, was established. He allocated land to the members of his clan, to the heads of tribes or to devout aristocrats.

In exchange, they had to pay the king a tax or support him in wars. The first capital of the Zhou Dynasty was Hao, situated near Xi'an.

In matters of religion, the Zhou followed the tradition of the Shang, and combined this with their old heavenly religion. Heaven was the first among the gods, the king was considered to be the son of heaven and acted as mediator between heaven and earth and the people. He alone was able to offer heaven the necessary ritualistic sacrifices. The Zhou banned human sacrifice, and it was no longer acceptable to consult oracle bones. The priests, who had been of great importance to the Shang and were the only people who knew how to read and write, had become superfluous. They became travelling teachers and earned their livelihood as advisers to the individual feifs. At the end of the 7th and beginning of the 8th century B.C., nomadic tribes and disgruntled feudal lords invaded the Wei valley, destroyed the capital in 771 B.C. and murdered the king. This was the end of the so-called Western Zhou Dynasty. The son of the murdered king founded the new capital of the Eastern Zhou Dynasty in Luoyang.

From this time on, the role of the ruler was limited to being a high priest and carrying out important ritual sacrifices. The Eastern Zhou Dynasty, which formally lasted until 221 B.C., can be divided into two main periods: the Spring and Autumn period (771-471 B.C.) and the time of the Warring States (476-221 B.C.). In the first period, the feudal lords and the landed gentry gained power and soon considered the land to be their own property which they were at liberty to inherit, sell or lease to the farmers. The kingdom was replaced by a system of allied and competing noble states. In the 6th century, the aristocracy was hit by a serious institutional crisis and the Zhou empire disintegrated into small splinter states.

From the 6th century onwards, the stronger states imposed their will on the weaker ones. At the beginning of the Warring States period, the number of states who were competing for supremacy had been reduced to seven. The time of Spring and Autumn as well as the Warring States period was one of important changes in the social structure. New social classes and groups emerged, commerce and trade between the individual states increased, and the question of unification of the empire became a central source of conflict.

These arguments were also reflected in the debates of the great philosophical schools. Confucianism and Taoism developed. This period is often described as the one during which one hundred schools competed with each other. The most successful turned out to be the legalistic one. The *legalists* fa-

voured a highly codified, positive system of law; it contained generally binding norms designed to strengthen the state economically and militarily and opposed feudal privileges.

Under the influence of the legalists, the feudal system in the state of Qin was replaced by administrative districts. The ruler of the belligerent border state of Qin was able to conquer the other states in the course of several campaigns because he had listened to his legalistic advisors and his troops were equipped with better weapons.

The first emperor of the Qin dynasty, Qin Shi Huangdi, united the Empire in the year

221 B.C. Xianyang (west of the present-day Xi'an) became the capital. The country was divided into prefectures and administered by specially chosen officials. To ward off the nomadic tribes, the Qin emperor launched a project to join together the already existing parts of a wall into one large wall (a predecessor of the wall exists today). Some 300,000 people were supposed to have worked on the construction of this wall. Members of the nobility were deprived of their power and forced to settle in the capital

where it was easier to control them. The Qin dynasty was in power for only a short time, yet its legacy was far-reaching. Measurements, weights and coins were standardized, and so was – most importantly – the Chinese script. Transport and communications were standardized, and all carriages had the same gauge. Qin Shi Huangdi was an extremely severe ruler. In 213 B.C., all non-legalistic books were burned, to publish other books meant risking the death penalty. It is alleged

Left, Qin Shi Huangdi, who created a uniform script. **Above**, sculpture with animal figures from the Tang tombs near Xi'an.

that 460 Confucian scholars were buried alive. Everyone suffered under the despotic Qin Shi Huangdi. Because so many were forced to work on his countless construction projects – amongst others a cemetery, the Great Wall and several palaces for the nobility – there was a shortage of labour in agriculture and the trades; as a result, there was an increasing number of famines, and soon after his death in the year 211 B.C., his son was overthrown by a peasants' revolt.

The leader of the revolt, Liu Bang, appointed himself First Emperor of the Han Dynasty in 206 B.C. The Chinese derived their name from this dynasty, and up to this day still describe themselves as the people of Han. Chang'an (Xi'an) became the capital of the Western Han Dynasty (206 B.C. - A.D. 8); this was followed by the Eastern Han Dynasty (A.D. 23-220) with Luoyang as its capital. During the reign of the first emperors of the Han Dynasty, (which lasted 400 years) the strict laws were relaxed to some extent; those who fought for or were related to the emperor's clan were rewarded with fiefs; it became possible to acquire land by purchase. Not only the nobility, but also merchants and civil servants could now be landowners.

Essentially, the system of government developed by the Qin Dynasty was taken over, except that the civil servants gained executive power. In 124 B.C. state examinations for civil servants were introduced. Theoretically, anyone could take part in these; in practice, however, it was only possible for children of the wealthy classes, as learning to write the script was difficult and time-consuming. The Han rulers relied heavily on the rich landowners who made good profits and had the time to learn the script and study the cultural history. This class is often described as the gentry. Every clan aimed to have as many members of its family as possible established in important government offices. Under Emperor Wudi (140-87 B.C.), Confucianism became the state doctrine. The educated upper class devoted itself to painting and the arts, new philosophical and historical works were also written. Paper was one of the most important inventions of the Han Dynasty; until then writing had been done on wood, bamboo or silk.

In the year 180 B.C., a new group appeared at the imperial court for the first time: the palace eunuchs, who were to play an important role until 1911. Originally they were hired to look after the emperors' wives and concubines, but they soon advanced to the status of advisors and played an important part in palace intrigues and power struggles.

The Han Dynasty was in its prime under the rule of Emperor Han Wudi (140-87 B.C.). It had always been an important challenge for the Chinese Empire to confront the nomadic tribes in the north and the west. Wudi succeeded in defeating the Huns who were nomads and had established a strong empire in the north. Now Wudi's empire stretched all the way to the western region to what is now Xinjiang. He conquered the Tarim Basin, Southern Manchuria and the area which is now North Korea. During the reign of the Han, there were numerous contacts with other cultures, which were imported by traders coming from far afield. Since the 1st century B.C., caravans had travelled along the Silk Road and had brought horses and gold in exchange for silk.

The military expansion to the south was also continued under the Han, and the peasants had, as usual, to carry the cost of the wars. Because of the increases in taxation, land ownership was concentrated amongst fewer and fewer families during the last 70 years of the dynasty. More peasants left the land, intrigues at court and corruption amongst civil servants were everyday occurrences, and the eunuchs meddled in power struggles too. There had also been a number of serious natural disasters. A peasants' revolt in the year 184, which was led by the Yellow Turbans, a secret sect, weakened the rule of the Han. When the emperor formally abdicated in 220, the country was run-down and the population decimated.

Amidst the chaos of war, which followed the fall of the Han Dynasty, Buddhism spread rapidly and found followers amongst the ordinary people. The largest and most famous Buddhist caves (Dunhuang, Luoyang and Yungang) date from this time. From the end of the Han Dynasty to the beginning of the Sui Dynasty in 581, various states fought each other. After the short period of the Three Empires, the Western and Eastern Jin Dynasty and the Dynasty of the Sixteen States were in power; then followed the time of the Southern and Northern Dynasties. This turmoil brought the Sui Dynasty to an end. It had only reigned for a short time, but had succeeded in uniting the country and establishing a new central government and consolidated the agriculture. The division into North and South China, which had lasted 400 years, finally came to an end. Ambitious projects were set up,

amongst them the building of the Emperor Canal which connected the rivers Haihe, Huanghe, Huaihe and Yangzi and enabled trade between north and south. The canal was used for transporting rice from the south. As a result, the fertile regions of South China gradually developed into an agricultural centre. At that time, 46 million people lived in China. Projects for new buildings, wars and the great extravagance of the emperor proved too much for the country – the situation was similar to that under the reign of the first Qin emperor. The Sui were soon overthrown by a people's revolt and the Tang Dynasty was founded in 618.

Prime of the Tang and rule of the Mongols

The dynasties of the Tang (618-907) and the Song (960-1279), which were only briefly interrupted by a renewed break-up amongst the Five Dynasties and Ten Empires, are regarded as particularly rich times in Chinese history. Important developments were taking place militarily, economically, politically and culturally. The first Tang emperors succeeded in re-establishing law and order. They practised an expansive style of

Chang'an was truly a cosmopolitan city, a multi-cultural metropolis.

Under the rule of Emperor Taizong, there was an economic upswing. A new system of land distribution and improved irrigation methods led to a greater yield of agricultural produce. The state founded numerous manufacturing industries. Courier systems and postal coaches boosted commerce and the Emperor Canal was completed. The arts and sciences flourished; even today, poems dating from the Tang Dynasty are regarded

foreign politics and invaded Central Asia, Korea and North Vietnam. They subjugated the Turkic people and assumed supremacy over Tibet. (The Tibetans, through their military skills, briefly occupied the Chinese capital Chang'an.) In the first half of the 8th century, Chang'an (which is Xi'an today) had approximately 2 million inhabitants, half of whom lived within the town walls. Based on the idea of a square world, the Tang capital was built like a chess board. One tenth of the population were foreigners and

Left, guarding soldiers. **Above**, ladies-in-waiting.

as unsurpassed. New administrative units, the *Dao*, were created with structures similar to the provinces. The military administration was separated from the civilian one. The imperial examination system for civil servants was reformed and re-introduced. Now the Confucian civil servants were finally in a position to stand up to members of the regional and local nobility.

Certain symptoms of decay had already appeared during the rule of Emperor Taizong. After his death, the palace was riddled with intrigues. This was much to the advantage of Wu Zetian, the first and only enthroned empress of China. She ruled this enormous country for 20 years, until her son Xuanzong took over. He is alleged to have neglected his duties because of his infatuation with the beautiful concubine Yang Guifei. This led to the revolt of An Lushan, which was put down, but left the country in ruins economically and militarily. Local governors and army officials exploited this power vacuum. The eunuchs ruled in the Emperor's palace, and the country was shaken by peasants' revolts and nomadic tribes in the North gained strength. The Tang

China, the centre of the Song rule, the town merchants attained a significantly higher status. Confucianism became the political and ethical philosophy as it is still known today (Neoconfucianism). Repeated clashes with nomadic tribes continued throughout the Song era. In 1126, the Nuzhen conquered Kaifeng and founded the Jin Dynasty. Song fled to the South and founded the Southern Song Dynasty.

Towards the end of the 12th century, a new threat to the Song loomed in the North,

Dynasty finally toppled in the year 907.

The Song Dynasty followed after the short interlude of the Five Dynasties and Ten States. There was a division into the Northern and Southern Song Dynasties. This was the time when Chinese civilisation reached an absolute peak. Under the rule of the Song, there were impressive developments in agriculture, trade and commerce. The monetary system grew, and paper money came into circulation. Movable print types were invented 400 years before Gutenberg. There was gold, silver, copper and iron ore mining. Iron was being melted down and gun powder had already been invented. In Southern

namely the Mongols. Genghis Khan had united the Mongol tribes, and between 1218 and 1253 had succeeded in conquering all of Central Asia, Russia and some Eastern European peoples. In 1234 they overthrew the Jin Dynasty and in 1276 the Southern Song. Once the province of Guangdong had been conquered in the year 1279, the whole of China belonged to the enormous Mongol empire. For the first time, parts of Europe and Asia were united under one rule. Traffic along the Silk Road flourished. In 1275, the Venetian merchant Marco Polo took this route to Khanbalik (the Beijing of today), which was then the capital of the Yuan

Dynasty. For 17 years he served Genghis Khan and upon his return he wrote the first comprehensive report on that legendary country in the East.

During the Mongol Yuan Dynasty, the Han Chinese were socially and politically discriminated against. At the same time, though, the Mongols were dependent on the Chinese civil service for the administration of the Chinese part of their empire. With other nomadic groups, attempts at assimilation with the Chinese had been made, yet this poverished. Increasing poverty and national discrimination were reasons enough to lead to insurrection. Often gangs of robbers would have entire areas under their control.

After a long period of insurrections and disturbances, the Mongols were overthrown by Chinese troops under the leadership of Zhu Yuanzhang. He was enthroned as Emperor Taizu of the Ming Dynasty in 1386. Nanjing became the capital; he banished the Yuan Emperor Shundi and the Mongol nobility from Beijing. Now there was once

was not the case with the Mongols. They were tolerant in religious matters, and encouraged Lamaism, in particular. During their rule, Tibet became part of China, which explains why China still claims the right to Tibet today. The peasants and the Chinese nobility were dispossessed of their land which was distributed amongst the Mongol nobility and Lamaist monasteries. Taxes were increased, and the peasants were im-

Left, bronze dating from the Western Han Dynasty (206 B.C.-A.D. 24); wine container with silver inlay. **Above**, funeral garment sewn with gold thread.

again a "Chinese" Dynasty in China. The third Ming emperor chose Beijing as the capital, and it retained this status until 1911.

The Ming were able to consolidate the economy again, agriculture was subsidised, irrigation was improved and for the first time cotton was planted. Taxes were lowered, and in some cases, land taxes were dropped altogether. As a result, the central government's position was strengthened. Chinese ships sailed all over the world. Under the command of the Muslim eunuch Zheng He, the fleet sailed to the Indian Ocean and the South Seas. Trade links were established, and the first Chinese colonies abroad were set up.

Trade and manufacture in particular experienced a significant upswing. In the 14th and 15th century, China was far superior to Europe, both economically and technically. Yet in the 16th century, this relationship was reversed – the reasons for this are still being debated amongst historians.

During the rule of the Ming, the first missionaries came to China. In 1516, Portuguese ships arrived in Canton. The danger to the Ming emperors, however, continued to come from the North and Central Asia. The

was the last of the Chinese dynasties. The Manchus originated from the Nuzhen, a nomadic people who settled on the Songhua River. Towards the end of the 16th century, their ruler Nurhachi had already been successful in uniting the various nomadic tribes. In 1616, he established his own dynasty in the north-east of China. In the following years he conquered vast areas of the northeast until finally – with the help of the Ming General Fu Lin – he succeeded in surmounting the Great Wall at Shanhaiguan and oc-

Great Wall was reinforced to protect them from the belligerent nomads. The wars against the Mongols had lasted until well into the 15th century. Towards the end of the Ming Dynasty, the peasants rapidly became impoverished, while land ownership was concentrated considerably. The intrigues of the eunuchs paralyzed the court and the empire; the secret police were attempting to suppress even the slightest signs of opposition. At the beginning of the 17th century, there was another major peasant uprising.

The Manchus exploited this situation. In 1644 they toppled the Ming Dynasty and established their own Qing Dynasty, which

cupied Beijing. By the end of the 17th century, the Qing had occupied the entire Chinese heartland. In several big campaigns into Central Asia and to the south, the Qing managed to consolidate their power. They were also able to lay the groundworks for the greatest expansion the Chinese empire was to undergo. Taiwan was taken in 1683, Tibet and East Turkestan (Xinjiang) were securely integrated. The Qing reached the height of their power in the middle of the 18th century, at which time their territory covered more than 4.3 million sq miles (11 million sq km).

In the north-east, the Qing empire reached beyond the river Heilongjiang. The neighbouring states in the south – Myanmar (formerly Burma), Nepal and Vietnam – were forced to acknowledge Chinese supremacy. At the time of the Qing, the population had already grown to 400 million. The first 150 years of Manchu rule – with important emperors like Kangxi (1662-1722) and Qianlong (1736-1796) – marked a period of expansion, yet there were also signs of stabilization. The economy was reflated with the help of lenient tax and agricultural policies. The areas for cultivation were increased,

orthodox Confucians. At the same time, almost all the Qing emperors continued to pay homage to their Shamanist views and were also mostly religious Lamaists.

The Manchu clans, headed by the emperor, governed the Qing empire along strictly patriarchal lines. The Chinese were again discriminated against. One obvious sign of this was the plait which the Manchu forced them to wear. Towards the end of the 18th and the beginning of the 19th century, there were more and more revolts. They

trade was boosted, industries were built (mining, salt extraction, etc.), foreign trade was strengthened and, lastly, the waterways and dams were improved. After all, the Qing were a minority, foreigners ruling over this vast empire, hence they needed to exercise prudence. From the onset, the Qing emperors had relied on the Confucian administration. Some of the Qing emperors, such as Qianlong in particular, were regarded as

Far Left, the Qing Emperor Kangxi. **Left**, Qing Emperor Qianlong. **Above left**, the emperor's widow Cixi; **above right**, the last emperor of China, Puyi.

were usually caused by the unbearable exploitation of the peasants by local officials and the rise in taxation. One factor which contributed to the decay of the empire was a growing contradiction between the enormous population of China (in 1850 there were already 430 million people, as opposed to 266 million in Europe) and the technological stagnation it had experienced since the late Ming and early Qing Dynasties. The increasing population density soon exhausted the technical potential and the amount of land which could be cultivated. The Manchu had one solution to this problem – namely to allow Chinese peasants to settle in Northern China, in Manchuria.

The Qing Empire had traditionally focused its foreign policies on areas of Central Asia and thus was not able to withstand the increased threat from European forces. In the Opium War (1840-1842), the empire was weakened by its first defeat. The compensation payments which China was obliged to pay to foreign powers were simply passed on to the peasants and tradesmen in the form of higher taxes. More and more of them began to band together secretly. Finally Hong

The disturbances of the civil war caused severe famine and forced many Chinese to emigrate to the United States or to other Asiatic countries. Corruption and extravagance at court increased, especially during the rule of the emperor's widow Cixi. The court was unable to introduce any reforms. The "Boxer" movement in the year 1900, which opposed the persistent humiliation of China, was brutally put down by foreign powers. Thereafter, the imperial court was even more seriously weakened. One more

Xiuquan, a village school teacher from the province of Guangdong, led the Taiping revolt. This shook the Chinese empire in the years between 1850 and 1864. With references to Christianity, the rebels demanded political and social equality and justice. The Qing were able to suppress the Taiping rebellion, though only by taking advantage of internal wrangling at the Qing court and receiving military aid from abroad and from local military troops. In the second Opium War (1858-1860), the Qing had to grant the foreigners further concessions.

The Taiping unrests are alleged to have claimed between 20 and 30 million lives.

desperate attempt to fight back was made with campaigns into Central Asia. Yet the Qing Dynasty was doomed, and it was overthrown in 1911 by the Republican Revolutionary League led by Dr. Sun Yatsen. In February 1912, Puyi, who had taken the emperor's throne after the death of Cixi in 1908, was forced to sign a declaration of abdication. Puyi continued to live in the palace in Beijing until 1924, but the rule of the sons of Heaven on the dragon throne, which had begun around 2000 B.C., had already come to an end.

Above, ancestor worship.

CHRONOLOGICAL TABLE OF CHINESE DYNASTIES

Xia approx. 21st - 16th cent. B.C.
Shang approx. 16th - 11th cent. B.C.
Zhou approx. 11th cent. - 221 B.C.
Western Zhou approx. 11th cent. - 770 B.C.
Eastern Zhou 770 - 221 B.C.
Spring and Autumn Period 770 - 476 B.C.
Warring States Period 475 - 221 B.C.
Qin 221 - 206 B.C.
Han 206 B.C. - A.D. 220
Western Han 206 B.C. - A.D. 8
Wang Mang Period 8 - A.D. 23
Eastern Han 25 - A.D. 220
Three Kingdoms 220 - A.D. 280
Wei 220 - 265
Shu 221 - 263
Wu 222 - 280
Jin 265 - 420 A.D.
Western Jin 265 - 316
Eastern Jin 317 - A.D. 420
Southern and Northern Dynasties 420 - 589 A.D.
Southern Dynasties 420 - 589

Song 420 - 479
Qi 479 - 502
Liang 502 - 557
Chen 557 - 589
Northern Dynasties 386 - 581
Northern Wei 386 - 534
Eastern Wei 534 - 550
Western Wei 535 - 557
Northern Qi 550 - 577
Northern Zhou 557 - 581
Sui 581 - A.D. 618
Tang 618 - A.D. 907
Five Dynasties and Ten Kingdoms 907 - A.D. 960
Song 960 - A.D. 1279
Northern Song 960 - 1127
Southern Song 1127 - 1279
Liao 907 - 1125
Jin 1115 - 1234
Yuan 1279 - 1368
Ming 1368 - 1644
Qing 1644 - 1911

The Emperors of the Ming and Qing Dynasties

Ming

Emperor's Title	Emperor's Name	Period of Rule	Date of Rule
Taizu	Zhu Yuanzhang	Hongwu	1368-1398
Huidi	Zhu Yunwen	Jianwen	1399-1402
Chengzu	Zhu Di	Yongle	1403-1424
Renzong	Zhu Gaochi	Hongxi	1425
Xuanzong	Zhu Zhanji	Xuande	1426-1435
Yingzong	Zhu Qizhen	Zhengtong	1436-1449
Daizong	Zhu Qiyu	Jingtai	1450-1456
Yingzong	Zhu Qizhen	Tianshun	1457-1464
Xianzong	Zhu Jianshen	Chenghua	1465-1487
Xiaozong	Zhu Youtang	Hongzhi	1488-1505
Wuzong	Zhu Houzhao	Chengde	1506-1521
Shizong	Zhu Houcong	Jiajiang	1522-1566
Muzong	Zhu Zaihou	Longqing	1567-1572
Shenzong	Zhu Yijun	Wangli	1573-1620
Guangzong	Zhu Changluo	Taichang	1620
Xizong	Zhu Youxiao	Tianqi	1621-1627
Sizong	Zhu Youjian	Chongzhen	1628-1644

Qing

Emperor's Title	Emperor's Name	Period of Rule	Date of Rule
Shizu	Aisin-Gioro Fulin	Shunzhi	1644-1661
Shengzu	Aisin-Gioro Xuanyue	Kangxi	1662-1722
Shizong	Aisin-Gioro Yizhen	Yongzheng	1723-1735
Gaozong	Aisin-Gioro Hongli	Qianlong	1736-1796
Renzong	Aisin-Gioro Yongyan	Jiaqing	1796-1820
Xuanzong	Aisin-Gioro Minning	Daoguang	1821-1850
Wenzong	Aisin-Gioro Yizhu	Xianfeng	1851-1861
Muzong	Aisin-Gioro Zaichun	Tongzhi	1862-1874
Dezong	Aisin-Gioro Zaitian	Guangxu	1875-1908
—	Aisin-Gioro Puyi	Xuantong	1909-1911

Marco Polo's reports about a legendary country in the East and the Mongol Emperor's magnificent capital left many of his contemporaries amazed and in a state of disbelief. They even called him "il milione", the braggart. During the rule of the Mongols in the 13th and 14th century, there were for the first time in world history, extended and organised contacts between East Asia and Europe. This was a historical feat which many Chinese historians today continue to rate as a positive achievement. Some of the knowledge which the Europeans gained about China fell into oblivion later on, but nevertheless a basis for better understanding and closer contacts had been created.

At the height of its power, the Ming Dynasty had sent its ships on expeditions as far afield as the Pacific and the coasts of Arabia. But the Ming Emperor Yongle ordered the fleet to be destroyed, the reason being that he considered it unnecessary for the Chinese to travel to other parts of the earth. This insularity was no doubt one of the main reasons why China did not recognise the significance of the slow but steady advance of the Europeans into Asia and China. Until the Portuguese arrived in Guangzhou (Canton) in the 16th century, the Chinese had regarded their empire as "the Middle Kingdom", the centre of culture and civilisation. According to Chinese ideas, the emperor ruled because of his superior moral qualities; and he could bestow these qualities upon all, Chinese as well as non-Chinese barbarians. When envoys from nomadic tribes or South-East Asian regions came to China, the Chinese believed that they were doing so in order to ensure the Emperor's goodwill and to learn from the Chinese culture. The delegations from these border areas usually arrived at the emperor's court with many gifts. They were lavishly entertained and often returned home with presents which were far superior to the ones they had brought with them. This may have

indicated condescending generosity or diplomatic considerations, but certainly not the meeting of equals. The first foreigners who arrived in the "Middle Kingdom" during the second half of the Ming Dynasty were approached with the same attitude.

The arrival of Europeans in South China

The first Portuguese landed in Guangzhou on the South coast in 1517. They were

described as bearers of gifts from a foreign country. The Chinese found their long noses and deep-set eyes very conspicuous. Even today, foreigners are called "long noses" in colloquial Chinese. When they arrived, the Portuguese fired a salute and created great excitement among the Chinese, as weapons were prohibited in Guangzhou at the time and this custom was unknown. From the very first encounter, relations were marred by misunderstandings, mutual disrespect and distrust. The damage was done, the effects of which are still felt today.

After the Portuguese, the Spanish, Dutch and English arrived. In the 16th century, the

Preceding pages: invading German troops in combat with Chinese soldiers. **Left**, the Jesuit priest Matteo Ricci. **Right**, the British importing tea from China.

first European missionaries came to China, notably Matteo Ricci, the founder of the Catholic mission in China and Adam Schall von Bell. They were not very successful in their missionary work, but thanks to their excellent knowledge of science, they were able to gain a foothold at court and became advisors to the emperor. They were captivated by Chinese culture, and fascinated with Confucianism so much so that the Pope in Rome finally decreed incompatibility. The perceptions which Europeans had of

regarded it as the large empire of despotism and stagnation, a country which was not progressing, which remained trapped in an endless cycle, like the Buddhist wheel of life.

First colonisation of China

After a promising start, Christian missionary work was once more prohibited by the Chinese emperors at the end of the 18th century. Even in 1793, the time of the industrial revolution in Great Britain, Emperor

China were strongly influenced by the Jesuit missionaries; it was an image of fascination on the one hand and disparaging rejection on the other. In the 17th and 18th century, *chinoiseries* were very fashionable at royal palaces in Europe and in elegant homes, there was often a Chinese room. Many European scholars were fascinated by Chinese theories and concepts. Influenced by the system set out in the "Book of Changes", Leibnitz developed a binary number theory which was to become the basis of computer technology. Other scholars, notably Hegel and Marx, completely rejected China. They simply

Qianlong informed a British envoy that China was economically well off and able to support itself, and that it had no need for goods from abroad. Foreign merchant ships were only allowed to use the port of Guangzhou and business relations were subject to stringent regulations. Gradually, things began to change. The Qing Dynasty, which surpassed the prime of its power around 1800, did not acknowledge this new and increasing threat which came from across the sea. They were preoccupied with the Central Asian regions and the belligerent nomads and underestimated the modern weapons of the "barbarians" from overseas:

goods, capital and canons. In the end, it was these weapons which opened China to foreign traders and companies.

The British did not hesitate to use opium as a means of forcing the Chinese Empire to its knees. For years, the Chinese had enjoyed the monopoly in the trading of tea, which was very popular in Great Britain. As a consequence, more and more silver had been paid to China. Between 1800 and 1820 alone, the "Middle Kingdom" earned ten million *liang* in silver through foreign trade.

This provided a welcome opportunity for the British to demonstrate their "superiority" and finally to open China's gates to British industry, opium dealers and missionaries. During the First Opium War which lasted from 1839-1842, the British advanced as far as Nanjing. According to the Treaty of Nanjing, the first of numerous "unequal treaties" (as they are still referred to in China today), the "Middle Kingdom" was forced to pay 21 million silver dollars in compensation. It was also obliged to open several ports

Yet – for the reasons mentioned earlier – they refused to import any goods. Around 1816, the British East India Company decided to smuggle more opium into China, and demanded to be paid for it in silver. In this unscrupulous way, they ruined the national budget of the Qing empire. As a reaction, the smuggling of opium was stopped in 1839. The Chinese government intercepted 20,000 crates of opium in Guangzhou and made a public showing of their burning.

Left, in 1841, the British negotiated and enforced the opening of Chinese ports to trade. **Above**, the Qing Emperor receives a foreign envoy.

– among them Shanghai and Guangzhou – and to agree to the import of opium and to granting foreigners extraterritoriality (which meant that foreigners were no longer subject to Chinese jurisdiction).

It is doubtful whether the Qing court realised what far-reaching consequences these concessions would have. They were incapable of understanding the signs of the times and even tried to pass the costs of the war onto the population. One of the consequences of this was the Taiping uprising. In the Second Opium War (1857-1860), British and French troops advanced as far as Beijing; the emperor was expelled and his summer palace was burnt to the ground. The "unequal treaties" which followed this war led to the final opening of China to foreigners. Now 43 ports were accessible to Western merchants. Adventurers, explorers, merchants and missionaries were allowed to move freely throughout China. The foreign enclaves in the ports from which "Chinese and dogs" were banned developed into extraterritorial zones.

Other colonial powers followed the British example. Russia was intent on haggling position to the activities of the missionaries. These opposition groups, the so-called "Boxer Movement", were – sometimes secretly, sometimes openly – supported by the Court. In a concerted effort, the troops of the colonial powers defeated the "Boxers" in 1900, destroyed Beijing and then demanded high reparation payments from the government, which were to be paid over the next 40 years. (The payments were discontinued in the 1930s.)

The Boxer Movement heralded a growing

for a part of China. Japan began to make its claims in 1895, having won the war against China and gained control over Korea and Taiwan. The Germans made the Province of Shandong theirs. The Qing Empire seemed unable to counter these challenges. Around 1900, China was threatened by the same fate as Africa, namely to be split up between a number of colonial powers. In the second half of the 19th century, xenophobia among the Chinese population increased. These feelings were especially strong in the Province of Shandong, where the Germans had taken the Bay of Jiaozhou on a lease and where there was increasing protests and op-

national consciousness. Under Sun Yatsen, a new political force grew which favoured the unification of China as a republican nation-state. Sun Yatsen was influenced by Western and Christian ideas, and later, also by Marxism. He and many of his followers, who had studied abroad, had been forced to seek asylum there and had often retreated to foreign regions for fear of repressions and persecutions. The republicans did not play an important role after the fall of the imperial Dynasty, yet their influence grew. They felt increasingly betrayed by the Western powers who, contrary to their promises, did not want to let go of their privileges in China.

Instead, they used the war to make further territorial demands. At the Versailles Peace Conference, the former German territories were handed to Japan, which was a further humiliation for China. The demands for unrestricted national sovereignty increased. The British sailed their gunboats up the Yangzi River one last time in 1927, but in the meantime new political forces had emerged.

In the 1920s, the newly-formed Soviet Union for the first time approached Sun Yatsen's Republic as equal to itself. The

intellectuals who demanded a final end to imperialism had a lasting influence on opinions which were formed at the time. In 1928 Chiang Kaishek took over as president of China. Customs and the postal system were once again put under Chinese control, the abolition of extraterritory was declared in 1930, and foreigners were to be subject to Chinese jurisdiction. These measures were finally put into force after the end of World War II in 1945. Having fought the war on the side of the allies and suffered under Japanese occupation, China was now accepted as a power with equal rights. After the successful revolution in 1949, all foreign privileges and ownership of foreign capital in China were abolished.

In the first years of the People's Republic, the attitude towards foreigners was still relatively lenient. Then general suspicions took hold and foreigners were, for instance, accused of being "imperialist agents". After 1960, the year in which China and the Soviet Union broke off relations, a new phase of isolation began and peaked during the Cultural Revolution (1966-1976). In contrast to the time from 1840 to 1949, when China had so often been humiliated, everything that was Chinese was now considered superior. Any contact with foreigners was watched by the police and, if necessary, punished. Numerous Chinese who had lived abroad and returned to China for patriotic reasons after 1949, were suspected of espionage and put under surveillance or sent to labour camps. Only towards the end of the 1970s did the attitude to foreigners become more open again. One can, however, clearly sense a greater national consciousness among the Chinese, which is sometimes combined with the traditional arrogance towards the "barbarians".

By now, *waiguoren*, the foreigners, hardly attract special attention. The Chinese are receiving an increasing amount of information from abroad, and in the West radio and television, newspapers and books report on China. Knowledge about the "Middle Kingdom" has grown considerably. This is also reflected in the growing number of people who learn the Chinese language. Foreign languages have again become fashionable in China. Relations between the *Zhongguoren*, citizens of the "Middle Kingdom" and the *Laowais*, the "old foreigners", as they are politely referred to, seem to be normalising and are no longer burdened by the past which was so humiliating to the Chinese. The easing of the situation remains limited though, as foreign countries are still regularly and sweepingly blamed for all that is bad or threatening.

Left, the murderer of Baron von Ketteler, a member of the Boxer Movement, is executed before foreign officers. **Above**, the grave of Baron von Ketteler in Beijing.

The ancestor cult of the Chinese is based on the assumption that a person has two souls. One of them is created at the time of conception, and when the person has died the soul stays in the grave with the corpse and lives on the sacrificial offerings. As the corpse decomposes, the strength of the soul dwindles, until it eventually leads a shadow existence by the Yellow Springs in the underworld. However, it will return to earth as an ill-willed spirit and create damage if no more sacrifices are offered. The second spiritual soul only emerges at birth. On its heavenly voyage it is threatened by evil forces, and is also dependent on the sacrifices and prayers of the living descendants. If the sacrifices cease, then this soul, too, turns into an evil spirit. But if the descendants continue to make sacrificial offerings and look into the maintenance of graves, the soul of the deceased ancestor may offer them help and protection.

Inscriptions on oracle bones from the Shang Dynasty (approx. 1600-1100 B.C.) and inscriptions on bronze, dating from the Zhou period (approx. 1100-476 B.C.) prove that an ancestor cult of high nobility, a cult of the high God *Di* and one of nature gods, had existed in early Chinese history. Originally, the ancestor cult had been exclusive to the king. Only a few centuries before Christ did peasants begin to honour their ancestors. At first, people believed that the soul of the ancestor would search for a human substitute and create an abode for the soul during the sacrificial ritual. It was usually the grandson of the honoured ancestor who took on the role of substitute. It was only 2,000 years ago that genealogical tables were introduced as homes for the soul during sacrificial acts. Up until that time, the king and noblemen had still used human sacrifices for ancestral worship. Even today, the Chinese worship their ancestors and offer the deities sacrifices of food. This is widely practised during the Qingming Festival.

The original religion of the people focused on the worship of natural forces. Later, the people began to worship the Jade Emperor, a figure from Daoism, who became the highest god in the popular religion after the 14th century. Guanyin, the goddess of mercy, originated in *Mahayana* (Great Wheel) Buddhism. Among the many gods in popular Chinese religion, there were also earth deities. Every town worshipped its own town god. Demons of illness, house spirits, the god of the hearth, and even the god of latrines had to be remembered. The deities of streams and rivers were considered to be particularly dangerous and unpredictable. Apart from Confucianism, Daoism and Buddhism, there was also a popular religion so-called Daoist Buddhism.

China had been divided into numerous small states. Only after the Qin Empire had won over its rivals in 221 B.C. did the first emperor over a united China came to power. At that time, there were a great number of philosophical schools of thought. Only Confucianism and Daoism gained acceptance in the Han period (206 B.C.-A.D. 220). Central concepts of Daoism are the *Dao*, which basically means "way" or "path", but it also has a second meaning of "method" and "principle"; the other concept is *Wuwei*, which is sometimes simply defined as passivity, or "swimming with the stream". The concept of *De* (meaning virtue) is closely linked to this, not in the sense of moral honesty, but as a virtue which manifests itself in daily life when *Dao* is put into practice.

One with nature

The course of events in the world is determined by the forces *Yang* and *Yin*. The masculine, brightness, activity and heaven are considered to be *yang* forces; while the feminine, weak, dark and passive elements of life are seen as *yin* forces. Laozi (which means "old master" in English) was the founder of Daoism. He lived at a time of crises and upheavals. The Daoists were opposed to feudal society, yet they did not fight actively for a new social structure. They preferred living in a primitive pre-feudalistic tribal society.

Laozi, it is said, was born in a village in the province of Henan in 604 B.C., the son of a distinguished family. For a time he held the office of archivist in Luoyang, which was then the capital. But he later retreated into solitude and died in his village in 517. According to a famous legend, he wanted to leave China on a black ox when he foresaw the decline of the empire. Experts today are still arguing about Laozi's historical existence. Since the second century A.D., many legends have been told about the figure of Laozi. One of them, for instance, says that he was conceived by a beam of light, his

the relativity of experiences and he strived to comprehend the *Dao* with the help of meditation. Zhuangzi (4th century B.C.) is especially famous for his poetic allegories. The ordinary people were not particularly attracted by the abstract concepts and metaphysical reflections of Daoism. Even at the beginning of the Han period (206 B.C.-A.D. 220), there were signs of a popular, religious Daoism. As Buddhism also became more and more popular, it borrowed

mother was pregnant with him for 72 years and then gave birth to him through her left armpit. His hair was white when he was born, but he prolonged his life with magic powers.

The "classic" work of Daoism is the *Daodejing*. It now seems certain that this work was not written by a single author. The earliest, and also most significant followers of Laozi were Liezi and Zhuangzi. Liezi (5th century B.C.) is particularly concerned with

Preceding pages: Buddhist sculptures in the Guiyuansi Temple in Wuhan; guardian deities in the Buddhist Temple Huayansi in Datong. **Above**, statue of the Jade Emperor.

ideas from Daoism, and vice-versa, to the point where one might speak of a fusion between the two. The Daoists and Buddhists both believed that the great paradise was in the Kunlun Mountains, in the far West of China, hence the name "Western Paradise". It was believed to be governed by the Queen mother of the West (Xiwangmu) and her husband, the royal count of the East (Dongwanggong). Without making any changes to it, the Daoists also took over the idea of hell from Buddhism.

Religious Daoism developed in various directions and schools. The ascetics retreated to the mountains and devoted all their time to meditation, or they lived in monasteries. In the Daoist world, priests had an important function as exorcists, medicine men and interpreters of oracles. They carried out exorcism and funeral rites, and read mass for the dead or for sacrificial offerings. Historical and legendary figures were added to the Daoist pantheon. At the head were the "Three Commendables"; this "trinity" was probably influenced by early Christian ideas. The highest of the three deities, the heavenly god, is identical to the Jade

other miraculous deeds.

While Laozi was active in the South of China, Confucius lived in the North of the country. For him, too, *Dao* and *De* are central concepts. For more than 2,000 years, the ideas of Confucius (551-479 B.C.) have influenced Chinese culture. It is debatable whether Confucianism is a religion in the strictest sense. But Confucius was worshipped as a deity, though he was only officially made equal to the heavenly god by an imperial edict in 1906. Up until the year

Emperor who was worshipped by the people. There is hardly a temple without Shouxinggong (the god of longevity), a friendly-looking old man with a long white beard and an extremely elongated, bald head. There are also the god of wealth (Caishen), the god of fire (Huoshen), the kitchen god (Zaoshen), the god of literature (Wendi), the god of medicine (Huatou) and others. Only the "Eight Immortals" are truly popular and well-known. Some of them are derived from historical personalities, some are fanciful figures. They are believed to have the ability to make themselves invisible, bring the dead back to life and do

1927, the Chinese public were offering him sacrifices. Mencius, a Confucian scholar, describes the poverty at the time Confucius was born as follows: "There are no wise rulers, the lords of the states are driven by their desires. In their farms are fat animals, in their royal stables fat horses, but the people look hungry and on their fields there are people who are dying of starvation."

Confucius came from an impoverished family of the nobility who lived in the state of Lu (near the village of Qufu in the West of Shandong Province). He lived from 551 to 479 B.C. *Kong Fuzi* (which means Master Kong in English) tried for years to gain office with one of the feudal lords, but he was dismissed again and again. So he travelled around with his disciples and instructed them in his ideas. All in all, he is said to have had 3,000 disciples, 72 of them highly gifted ones who are still worshipped today. Confucius taught mainly traditional literature, rites and music, and is thus regarded as the founder of scholarly life in China. The Chinese word *ru*, which as a rule is translated as "Confucian" actually means "someone of a gentle nature" – a trait which was attributed

to a cultured person. Confucius did not publish his philosophical thoughts in a book. They have therefore to be reconstructed from fragments of the comments he made on various occasions.

The thoughts of Confucius were collected in the *Lunyu* (Conversations) by his loyal disciples. Some of the classic works on Confucianism are: the book of songs (*Shijing*), the book of charters (*Shujing*), the book of

Left, worshippers light candles in their temple.
Above, the statue of Laozi, one of the many stone carvings near Dazu.

rites (*Liji*), the spring and autumn annals (*Chunqiu*) and the book of changes (*Yijing*). Confucianism is, in a sense, a religion of law and order. Just as the universe is dictated by the world order, and the sun, moon and stars move according to the laws of nature, so a person, too, should live within the framework of world order. This idea, in turn, is based on the assumption that man can be educated. Ethical principles were turned into central issues. Confucius was a very conservative reformer, yet he significantly reinterpreted the idea of the *Junzi*, a nobleman, to that of a noble man, whose life is morally sound and who is, therefore, legitimately entitled to reign.

Confucius believed that he would create an ideal social order if he reinstated the culture and rites of the early Zhou period (approx. 1100-700 B.C.). Humanity (*ren*) was a central concept at the time, its basis being the love of children and brotherly love. Accordingly, the rulers will only be successful in their efforts if they can govern the whole of society according to these principles. Confucius defined the social positions and hierarchies very clearly and precisely. Only if and when every member of society takes full responsibility for his or her position will society as a whole function smoothly. The following family ties were considered to be of fundamental importance: father/son (the son has to obey the father without reservations); man/woman (the woman does not have any individual rights); older brother/younger brother; friend/ friend; ruler/subordinate (identical to the father/son relationship).

In the 12th century, Zhu Xi (1130-1200 B.C.) succeeded in combining the metaphysical tendencies of Buddhism and Daoism with Confucianism, which is more concerned with political ethics and practical situations. His systematic work includes the teachings about the creation of the micro and macrocosm as well as the metaphysical basis of Chinese ethics. This system, known as Neo-Confucianism, reached canonical status in China; it was the basis of all state examinations and remained a determining factor for Chinese officialdom until the present century.

The Chinese initially encountered Buddhism at the beginning of the 1st century, when merchants and monks came to China on the Silk Road. The type of Buddhism which is prevalent in China is the *Mahayana* ("Great Wheel") which – as opposed to *Hinayana* ("Small Wheel") – promises all creatures redemption through the so-called *Bodhisattvas* (redemption deities). There were two aspects of this new religion which were particularly attractive to the Chinese: the teachings of *Karma* provided a better explanation for individual misfortune and also a hopeful promise for life after death. Nevertheless, there was considerable opposition to Buddhism which contrasted sharply with Confucian ethics and ancestor worship.

At the time of the Three Kingdoms (A.D. 220-280), the religion spread in each of the three states. The trading towns along the Silk Road as far as Luoyang became centres of the new religion. After tribes of foreign origin had founded states in the north and the gentry from the North had sought refuge in the Eastern Jin Dynasty (317-420), Buddhism developed along very different lines in the North and South of China for about two centuries. During the rule of Emperor Wudi (502-549), rejection and hostility towards Buddhism spread among Confucians. And during the relatively short-lived Northern Zhou Dynasty (557-581), Buddhism was officially banned (from 574 to 577).

Buddhism was most influential in Chinese history during the Tang Dynasty (618-907). Several emperors officially supported the religion; The Tang Empress Wu Zetian, in particular surrounded herself with Buddhist advisers. During the years 842 to 845, however, Chinese Buddhists also experienced the most severe persecutions in their entire history: 40,000 temples and monasteries were destroyed, and Buddhism was blamed for the economic decline and moral decay of the dynasty.

In the course of time, ten Chinese schools of Buddhism emerged, eight of which were essentially philosophical ones which did not influence popular religion. Only two schools have remained influential until today: the *Chan School* (school of meditation or Zen Buddhism) and the *Pure Land School* (Amitabha-Buddhism). The masters of Chan considered meditation to be the only path to knowledge. In Mahayana Buddhism, worship focused on the *Bodhisattva Avalokiteshvara*. Since the 7th century, the

ascetic *Bodhisattva* has been a popular female figure in China. She is called Guanyin, a motherly goddess of mercy who represents a central deity for the ordinary people. Guanyin means "the one who listens to complaints".

In Chinese Buddhism, the centre of religious attention is Sakyamuni, the founder of Buddhism who was forced into the background in the 6th century by the Maitreya Buddha (who was called Milefo in China or redeemer of the world). In Chinese monasteries he greets the faithful as a laughing Buddha in the entrance hall. The worship of *Amitabha* was closely linked to

Left, golden statue of Buddha Sakyamuni in the Lingyinsi monastery near Hangzhou. **Right**, demonic tutelary gods in the entrance hall guard the monasteries.

the *Pure Land School*. Since the 14th century, the Amitabha cult had dominated the life and culture of the Chinese people.

The most influential Buddhist school was the so-called *School of Meditation* (Chan in China, Zen in Japan), which had developed under the Tang Dynasty. It preached redemption through buddhahood, which anyone is able to reach. It despised knowledge gained from books or dogmas, as well as rites. They used liberating shocks or guided meditation in order to lead their disciples

intent on completely eradicating Buddhism. The autonomous Tibet was hard-hit by these excesses. Only a few important monasteries and cultural objects could be protected and were completely or only partly preserved. The new constitution of 1982 guarantees religious freedom to the people of China. Today, there are Buddhists among the Han Chinese, the Mongols, Tibetans, Manchus, Tu, Qiang and Dai (Hinayana Buddhists).

In the 7th century A.D., another type of Buddhism called *Tantric Buddhism* or

towards the experience of enlightenment. Other techniques used to achieve final insights were long hikes and physical work. The most important method was a dialogue with the master who asked subtle and paradoxical questions, to which he expected equally paradoxical answers.

In 1949, the year the People's Republic of China was founded, there were approximately 500,000 Buddhist monks and nuns and 50,000 temples and monasteries. A number of well-known Buddhist temples were classified as historical monuments.

At the beginning of the Cultural Revolution in 1966, it seemed as if the Red Guards were

Lamaism was introduced into Tibet from India. With the influence of the monk, Padmasambhava, it replaced the indigenous *Bon* religion, while at the same time taking over some of the elements of this naturalist religion. The monasteries in Tibet developed into centres of intellectual and worldly power, yet there were recurring arguments. Only the reformer Tsongkhapa (1357-1419) succeeded in rectifying conditions which had become chaotic.

He founded the sect of virtue (*Gelugpa*) which declared absolute celibacy to be a condition and re-introduced strict rules of order. Because the followers of this sect wear yellow caps, this order came to be known as Yellow Hat Buddhism.

Tsongkhapa had predicted to two of his disciples that they would be re-born as heads of the church. He had therewith anticipated the continuous transfer of powerful positions within the church, for instance the position of the Dalai Lama and the Panchen Lama. The Dalai Lama represents the incarnation of the *Bodhisattva* of mercy (*Avalokiteshvara*) who is also worshipped as the patron god of Tibet. The Panchen Lama

In Lamaism, there is a complex pantheon; apart from the Buddhist deities, there are figures from the Brahminical and Hindu world of gods and the old Bon religion. Magic, repetitive prayers, movements, formulae, symbols and sacrificial rituals are all means for achieving redemption.

Islam probably became established in China in the 7th century, and its influence has been very long-lasting. Ten of the 56 recognised nationalities in China profess themselves to Islam. They are the Hui, Uz-

is higher in the hierarchy of the gods and is the embodiment of Buddha Amitabha. The present 14th Dalai Lama, who was enthroned in 1940, fled to India after an uprising in 1959 and has been living in exile since then. The Panchen Lama died in Beijing in January 1989 at the age of 50 after he came to an understanding with the Chinese authorities following the uprising.

Left, women on a pilgrimage visit the Lengyin monastery near Hangzhou during the Qingming festival (day to commemorate the dead). **Above**, hand of a praying Tibetan, the "rosary" has 108 beads.

beks, Uighurs, Karachs, Kirgiz, Tatars, Shi'ite Tadshiks, Donxiang, Sala and Bao'an – a total of 14 million people. The Hui are, as a rule, Han Chinese. They are the only group who enjoy the special status of a recognised minority solely on the basis of their religion.

Mohammed was born in Mecca around the year 570 (the exact date is unknown). From the age of 40 onwards, he preached the Koran. Islam came to China on two different routes: one was the famous Silk Road, the other from across the sea to the south-eastern coast of China. During the Yuan Dynasty (1271-1368), Islam finally became permanently established in China. The imperial observatory was built in Beijing and the Arab astronomer Jamal-al-Din took charge of it.

The policies of the Qing Dynasty were – though it may be oversimplified to say so – hostile to Muslims. In the 18th century, slaughtering according to Islamic rites was forbidden, the building of new mosques and pilgrimages to Mecca were not allowed. Marriages between Chinese and Muslims were illegal, and relations between the two groups were made difficult.

Some of the Muslim sects were declared illegal during the Qing Dynasty. Over the last years, the People's Republic of China has been attempting to bring socialism and religion closer together and achieve a harmony between them. Believers (irrespective of their religion) are expected to be patriotic and law-abiding, but not to give up their faith. The Cultural Revolution led to many restrictions for religious people. Today, there are around 21,000 mosques in China. The Muslims celebrate their festivals and Chinese-Muslim societies organise pilgrimages to Mecca.

Christianity was first brought to China by the Nestorians in the year 635. The founder of this Christian sect was Nestorius, who was born in Antioch in 381 and later became patriarch of Constantinople (428-431). Because he developed his own theories, which contradicted the dogma of the Roman-Catholic church, his teachings were condemned and he himself banned. The followers of Nestorian Christianity disseminated their teachings with the help of a Persian called Alopen, who was the first missionary. The symbol of Nestorianism was a cross with two spheres at the end of all four beams. A stele dating from the Tang Dynasty is decorated with such a cross and is on display in the museum of the Xi'an Province.

For a period, in spite of religious persecutions, this religion had spread to all the regions of the empire, and in some parts of the country was practised until the end of the Mongol Dynasty. At the same time, initial contacts were made between China and the Roman-Catholic church. The first Catholic church in China was probably built when John of Montecorvino, a Franciscan monk from Italy, arrived in Beijing in 1295.

During the Ming period, Catholic missionaries began to be very active in China. A leading figure among the Jesuit missionaries who began to play an important role was the Italian, Matteo Ricci. At the time of his death, there were about 2,000 to 3,000 Christians in China. Ricci's successor was the German Jesuit, Adam Schall von Bell (1591-1666), who was appointed by the Qing Dynasty to improve the calendar. In 1650, he was given permission to build a Christian church in Beijing.

The fanatical anti-Christian Yang Guangxian, a Chinese who had converted to Islam, tried to portray the Christians as members of secret societies and accused them of plotting against the emperor. As a consequence, all churches were closed and all the missionaries, except the four living in Beijing, were sent back to Macau. In 1668 the Jesuit fathers were reinstated and the Flemish, Ferdinand Verbiest, was appointed to the imperial observatory where he took the place of Schall von Bell, who had in the meantime passed away.

Finally, not only the Jesuits, but the

Franciscans, Dominicans and Augustinians were granted the right to carry out missionary work in China as well. Around 1700, nearly half of the 130 missionaries, were Jesuits. There were an estimated 300,000 Chinese Christians at the time, and the number might have increased had it not been for disagreements within the Christian communities which led to a dispute about rites. The Jesuits on the one hand, the Dominicans and Franciscans on the other, could not agree on how the Christian concept of God should be described in Chinese, nor to what extent the worship of Confucius and of the ancestors could be tolerated from Chinese Christians. The Pope in Rome and the imperial court in Beijing were drawn into this dispute. The Pope eventually decided against the Jesuits and the imperial court against all missionaries.

The Jesuits had used their excellent knowledge of western sciences in order to forge links with Chinese scholars. They were primarily interested in spreading the Christian faith, and not Western customs. In 1633 Spanish monks from the Dominican, Franciscan and Augustinian orders had come to China from the Philippines. Some of them were fanatics who thought that death as a martyr was the same as saving heathen souls. They fought against any religious ceremony the Chinese practised, such as ancestor worship. As a consequence, the Chinese authorities introduced counter measures and the Christians were once again persecuted.

The Qing Emperor Kangxi respected the Jesuits as astronomers, mathematicians and cartographers. But Kangxi's immediate successor declared Christianity as heresy, and under the Manchu emperors, Qianlong (1736-1796) and Daoguang (1821-1851), the Christians were repeatedly persecuted.

At the onset of the 19th century, the Protestants – with men like R. Morrison and W.H. Medhurst – began their missionary activities. Initially they were only concerned with converting people and studying languages. They distributed religious pamphlets and ran hospitals. The methods used to convert people were not always scrupulous. People who were starving or were suffering because they had been the victims of a natural disaster would give in to anything which offered a chance of survival. Nevertheless, the number of people converted remained an almost negligible minority. In 1864 there were 89 Protestant missionaries in China, in 1893, there were about 55,000 Protestant Christians. In 1948 (the year before the People's Republic was founded)

there were already 3 million Catholics and 1 million Protestants.

The Vatican had taken an extremely anti-communist stance during the 1940s and 50s and as a result of this, the Chinese government ordered that the Catholic church in China should become separate from and no longer be accountable to the Vatican. Moreover, the Vatican to this day recognises the Guomindang government in Taiwan as the only legitimate government for the whole of China. However, since the beginning of the 1980s, the Vatican has been making attempts to reach an agreement with the People's Republic of China.

Left, mosques characterise the towns in the north-west of China (Ürümqi). **Right**, Christian church in the north-eastern seaport of Dalian.

79

Since the middle of the last century, the dominant themes in China have been: How can the Western challenge be met, how can the weakened China become strong enough again to have equal rights and take its place among the states and peoples of the world? The decline of the old Confucian China was inevitable and all too obvious, but what would take its place? Were reforms possible, or was a revolutionary coup the only way towards modernising the country?

In the declaration of abdication by the last emperor Puyi, it says: "Yuan Shikai, who was recently elected president of the National Assembly in Beijing will now be able to unify the North and South. He should therefore be given the power to do this and form a provisional government. This was done with the consent of the representatives of the People's Army in order to safeguard the peace and to allow the Chinese, Manchu, Mongols, Mohammedans and Tibetans to form one large state which would be named Republic of China."

The dynasty had been overthrown, but no other stable political order replaced it, so the wish for peace was not fulfilled. The North was ravaged by so-called warlords (feudal military rulers), who instigated wars and brutally exploited the power vacuum to their own advantage. After the death of Yuan Shikai in 1916, Sun Yatsen founded a republic in Canton (Guangzhou), which he used as a base from which to fight the warlords.

During World War I, a new left-wing intellectual movement emerged in China. This young political force manifested itself in a big student movement on 4 May 1919. The immediate cause for what came to be known as the "May Fourth Movement" was the Versailles Peace Treaty which granted the former German territories in Shandong to Japan and not to the Chinese as they had demanded. The patriotically-minded intellectuals were furious about this humiliation.

Preceding pages: the personality cult surrounding Mao marked the demonstrations during the Cultural Revolution; a march with the slogan "the whole country is red". Left, selling peanuts in the old part of Beijing.

They called for and carried out boycotts of Japanese goods and trading houses and staged strikes in many cities. The immediate successes of the movement were minimal: the warlords in the North could not be overthrown; the Western powers remained unimpressed. Nevertheless, the "May Fourth Movement" is still regarded as the first big national movement in China and is considered to have been a decisive turning point in modern Chinese history.

A new political force – the Communists

In July 1921 only 13 delegates, representing only 50 members, met in Shanghai to found the Communist Party of China. The young Mao Zedong was one of these bold founder members. In the first half of the 1920s, the Chinese Communist Party established itself surprisingly fast. Following the European example, attempts were made to instigate strikes among workers in the cities, but they were usually unsuccessful. The Guomindang (National People's Party), which was led by Dr. Sun Yatsen, also increasingly turned to the Soviet Union. They were disappointed by the lack of support from the West and were impressed by the Russian revolution. There was an official coalition between the Guomindang and the Communist Party of China. They jointly set up a military academy in Whampoa near Canton. Chiang Kaishek was in charge of the academy, while the Communist party leader Zhou Enlai was his deputy. In a joint venture, the Southern Republic fought against the local military commanders in the North. Chiang Kaishek, the commander-in-chief of the Nationalist forces, had, by February 1928, succeeded in controlling the whole of China.

His main enemies were the Communists, with whom he had broken off relations towards the end of the "northern expedition". The fight against them consumed huge sums from the state budget.

The Communists were able to avoid the Guomindang and their numerous campaigns to eradicate them and they retreated to the Jinggang Mountains in the South-East. This was where Mao Zedong developed a new strategy for the revolution in the late 1920s. Until then, influenced by Soviet advisers from the Communist International (Comintern), the main focus of attention was on the cities and the industrial proletariat. Mao realised that in China, it was the peasants who would be the most important force for a revolution. At the same time, he developed guerilla strategy and tactics. The most important item in the political programme was land reform which, of course, the impov-

Chinese Communists and remained in this position until his death in 1976.

As early as 1931, Japan had annexed parts of North-Eastern China and founded a puppet state (Manzchuguo), headed by the last, abdicated Manchu emperor Puyi. But the Japanese were planning further conquests in China. Faced by this threat, Chiang Kaishek was unable to use his troops against the Communists. Furthermore, some criticisms were being voiced within his own party. The critics wished to end the civil war and join

erished peasants agreed to and supported.

Between 1931 and 1935 Chiang Kaishek started five campaigns to annihilate the Communists. In order to escape the constant attacks, the Communists left Southern China, where they were based, and began their legendary Long March. It led through 11 provinces of this enormous country and covered a distance of 7,460 miles (12,000 km). Only one tenth of the 130,000 people who set out at the very beginning of this gruelling survived, but nevertheless the march had considerably improved the Communist Party's standing. In 1935 Mao was able to establish himself as leader of the

forces with the Communists against the Japanese. They even "persuaded" Chiang Kaishek to agree to an alliance with the Communists: two Guomindang generals had detained Chiang in Xi'an in 1937 and forced him to negotiate with the Communists. This alliance agreed to unite both armies under one Supreme Command. The Communists agreed to abandon parts of their programme, because anything other than the task of national resistance should be put aside.

The Japanese provoked an incident at the Marco Polo Bridge in Beijing on 7 July 1937 which was to lead to the Japanese-Chinese War. In the same year, Shanghai was bombarded and captured by the Japanese. Chiang Kaishek retreated to Chongqing in the province of Sichuan. The Communists fought a guerilla war from their bases in the North, while Chiang's troups resisted the Japanese invaders in the South. The Guomindang and Chinese Communists eventually stopped the Japanese advance. As a result, the Americans gained military superiority over the Japanese after 1942, and this was a turning point in the events of World War II.

After Japan had capitulated in September

campaigns into Southern China, there was a decisive battle on the Yangzi River, after which the Guomindang were weakened to such an extent that they retreated to the island of Taiwan with the rest of their troops and nearly 2 million refugees.

The founding of a Republic

With the words "China has risen again!" Mao Zedong proclaimed the People's Republic of China from the Gate of Heavenly

1945, the positions were clarified: on the one side was Chiang Kaishek supported by the Americans, on the other side the Red Army and the peasant guerillas. Soviet support during the civil war was minimal. Looking back on the four-year civil war, it was an easy victory for the Communist party, as the Guomindang had lost support from all sections of the Chinese population.

In a number of major offensives, Beijing and the other towns in the North were occupied by the Red Army. After several

Left and above, poverty and underdevelopment in rural areas drove the peasants to revolt.

Peace (Tiananmen) on 1 October 1949. The Communists had succeeded in uniting China and forming a central government. At the time, China was considered the sick man of Asia. The population had suffered incredibly, as is illustrated by the following statistics: only about one out of ten school-age children was able to read and write; before 1949 the yearly death rate was 3 percent of the population; the average life expectancy was 36 years; out of 1,000 children born, 160 to 170 died in infancy; only 84,000 hospital beds were available to 500 million people.

In addition, war and civil unrest had weakened the economy and the infrastructure. There was no modern industry worth mentioning. China had a gross national product of US$50 and ranked as one of the poorest countries in the world. There was hardly any help coming from abroad; the Soviet Union was preoccupied with its own problems after World War II, and the Americans were very suspicious of this new socialist state. The Communists had taken on a difficult task. They had won the revolution, but how were they to rebuild the country?

In the early years of the People's Republic

from the big landowners. Hundreds of thousands of wealthy landowners were put before the so-called people's tribunals and were mostly sentenced to death.

One of the most important successes in internal politics during these early years was that areas which, since the fall of the Qing Dynasty in 1911, had only marginal or were no longer linked to the Chinese Empire, were now firmly established as part of the country again. This included Tibet, Xinjiang, Inner Mongolia and the southern Chinese prov-

of China, the war damage was settled and this created a conducive environment for industrialising and modernising the country. Mao Zedong developed the idea of a New Democracy, which meant working together with the patriotically-minded national entrepreneurs who had not collaborated with foreign "imperialists" before 1949. Initially they were allowed to retain possession of their factories, but all enterprises which were controlled by foreign capital or the bourgeoisie were nationalized. The most important event of this time was the land reform in 1952. Hundreds of millions of peasants were allocated land which had been expropriated

ince of Yunnan. The Soviet Union withdrew its troops from Manchuria and relinquished its right over this area.

With support from the Soviet Union and East European states, the People's Republic set up its first five-year plan (1953-1957) which concentrated on developing heavy industry. By the end of this period, nearly all the enterprises had been nationalised. After a short period of independence, the peasants were grouped together in cooperatives. In 1954, the People's Republic declared that the transitional period of the New Democracy had ended. In its first constitution, it was defined as a socialist state, ruled by the proletariat, led by the Communist Party. A rigid centralist government was set up and any opposition from within was increasingly suppressed. Intellectuals tended to be the victims. In 1956, there was heavy criticism both from within and outside the party of its politics modelled on Stalinist Soviet Union. This phase of liberalisation was very short-lived and ended in 1957, when any critics were declared as right-wing radical bourgeois and hundreds of thousands of them were interned in prisons or labour camps.

1958, virtually all the peasants had been concentrated in large collectives where they often took on several jobs. They resembled military organisations and labour was often not paid for. The peasants who had supported the communists until 1949 because they had been promised land allocations, now felt deceived by the party. Opposition against the policies which robbed them of their last patches of private land grew. The "Great Leap Forward" ended in disaster; none of the aims they had strived for were achieved. As

The economic situation at the end of the first five-year plan was much improved. Mao Zedong, encouraged by this and supported by virtually all members of the party leadership, propagated the "Great Leap Forward" in 1958. In a period of just a few years, China wanted to be on an equal footing with economically advanced countries, such as Great Britain, and match their production rate. The communes were to be the main means for achieving this aim. By the end of

a result of the massive deployment of labour, there was a shortage of workers in agriculture. Workers and peasants reached the limits of their physical capabilities. Many large projects, for example the construction of dams, were carried out inadequately. Crop failures and natural disasters led to a dramatic aggravation of the situation, and around 30 million people died in a famine.

In the settlement areas of the national minorities, the "great leap into communism" meant that attempts were made to do away with customs and traditions. The latent national conflicts soon developed into armed insurrection. In 1959, the Tibetans started an

Left, coming from the country, Mao Zedong wins the Civil War, here at Yan'an. **Above**, in the towns, workers take up arms.

unsuccessful revolt against the Chinese. Their leader, the Dalai Lama, fled to India and has lived there in exile ever since.

In 1960 an open conflict broke out between China and the Soviet Union. Both states accused each other of betraying Marxism-Leninism. Furthermore, the Soviet Union had refused to make the atom bomb available to the Chinese, in spite of their demands. In the year 1960, the Soviet Union ceased all forms of economic aid and recalled its advisers and all their technical documentation.

the following years he made an attempt to re-establish his political credibility. He was of the opinion that a pragmatic approach would lead back to capitalism and undermine the power of the Communist party of China. He opposed pragmatism, and was strongly supported by the defence minister Lin Biao, who was designated to become his successor.

Between 1958 and 1961, the urban population had increased by 20 million; agriculture was quite incapable of producing sufficient food for such a vast population. In order

Between 1961 and 1965 which followed the disastrous "Great Leap Forward", internal politics were characterised by a pragmatic attitude for which politicians like Liu Shaoqi and Deng Xiaoping were responsible. The institution of the communes was retained, but attempts to gain alliance from several countries were partly withdrawn and private enterprise was again permitted to a limited extent. The economy began a slow recovery after the severe set-backs it had suffered during the years of the "Great Leap" and by 1965, it had reached the level of 1957 again. Mao Zedong's image had suffered because of the failure of the "Great Leap"; in

to ease the situation, young people were sent to work the land in underdeveloped regions.

In 1966, the discontent of the young people culminated in massive protests at the universities. Mao Zedong exploited these protests in order to eliminate his opponents within the party. He initiated the "Great Proletarian Cultural Revolution"; compliant cadres provoked a mass movement of the Red Guards so that the country was once again in chaos and close to a civil war. Politicians, intellectuals and artists fell victim to the terror of the Red Guards. One of these victims was Mao's main opponent Liu Shaoqi, who had succeeded him as president in 1959. Hundreds of thousands of people lost their lives during the "revolutionary excesses". Schools were closed for years, artistic life came to a stand-still. While many of his opponents were being deprived of their positions and persecuted, Mao enjoyed being worshipped almost like a god in a personality cult which was unprecedented anywhere in the world.

Lin Biao, who had been instrumental in creating the personality cult around Mao and had been designated as his successor in

between the two sides in any party political clashes. In 1973 he recalled Deng Xiaoping as his deputy, and developed a more pragmatic approach in order to rebuild the economy and education system of the country.

Zhou Enlai also made great efforts to overcome the isolation from foreign countries. After China had become a member of the United Nations in 1971, President Nixon visited the country in 1972 (ping-pong diplomacy). The Federal Republic of Germany also established diplomatic ties with China

1969, also began to disagree with Mao's politics. After one failed attempt on his life, he died in 1971 while attempting an escape. According to official sources, he was involved in a plane crash over the Mongolian Republic.

In the following years, the debates between the moderate and radical political factions increased in intensity. One key figure was prime minister Zhou Enlai, who had always taken on the role of mediator

Left, on 31 January 1949, the Red Army marched into Beijing. **Above**, on 1 October 1949, the People's Republic is declared in the Square of Heavenly Peace.

in 1972. Relations with the Soviet Union, however, had reached an absolute low: in 1969 there had even been several border disputes on the Ussuri at which weapons had been deployed.

The group around Mao's widow Jiang Qing, who were called "the Gang of Four", showed increasing determination in their attempts to put an end to the pragmatic politics of Zhou and Deng and to take over the leadership of the party. Zhou Enlai died in January 1976; on commemoration day for the dead in April of the same year, there were spontaneous mass demonstrations against the Gang of Four and in favour of Zhou Enlai and Deng Xiaoping. Mao Zedong died on 9 September 1976. A month later, the leaders of the radical groups were arrested.

Once the radicals had been deprived of power, the conditions were set for a change. Changes only became concrete after 1978/79 when Deng Xiaoping came to power again. The Cultural Revolution had disastrous results: in the mid-1970s China had her own industry which was not dependent on other countries, but the country was in a deep economic crisis as a result of the numerous which were being propagated officially, this movement demanded a fifth modernisation, namely democracy. Although the movement was prohibited by the Communist Party of China and some of its leaders were imprisoned, it nevertheless made basic changes in internal as well as foreign politics. In the same year, collectivism of agriculture ceased and the peasants were again allowed to use their land privately. Free markets were once more permitted, the establishment of light industry and the service industries were

political clashes. The reputation of the Communist Party reached its lowest point. In the mid-1970s peasants had the same standard of living as they had 20 years before, and the same was true of the workforce in the cities. The Communist Party of China estimated that between 150 and 200 million people were threatened by starvation at the end of the 1970s. There was a rapid increase in the number of beggars, and also more and more complaints about the bureaucracy and the despotic rule of the party cadres. In 1978 the "Democratic Movement" began to form itself in Beijing and other major cities. In addition to the "Four Modernisations" strongly encouraged. The economic measures were accompanied by a cautious liberalisation; religious freedom was granted again, and there were opportunities for literature and the arts to unfold. People who had been unjustly persecuted during the Cultural Revolution were re-instated to their former positions.

Since then, the ideology of the Communist Party of China has been to overcome the Cultural Revolution and its effects by introducing a system of economic and political reforms which take into account the real situation of the country; the long-term aim is to create a mixture of both state and market economy. In the last few years, private enterprises have again been permitted in China. It was also their aim to build up a socialist legal system. In 1982 a new constitution came into being. Although it still defines the Communist Party as the leading force in the Chinese nation, it too shall be subject to constitutional laws in the long term. An open door policy to foreign countries is one important step in the modernisation programme which is designed to quadruple China's economic power by the year 2000.

and artists, as well as against fashions like long hair and Western music which were being imported from Hong Kong. The debates on internal politics essentially centred around the extent of the reforms and the timetable for their implementation.

At the end of 1986, students demanded more democracy; this led to the conservative party leadership pressuring Hu Yaobang to retire as the party's general secretary because he felt sympathetic towards the students and their grievances.

This programme of modernisation and reform is not without controversies. When Deng Xiaoping's protege Hu Yaobang became general secretary of the party in 1981 and Zhao Ziyang became prime minister, opposition grew in conservative circles, especially in the army. At the end of 1983, a campaign was set in motion against the "mental pollution"; many serious criminals were being publicly executed as a deterrent, but the fight was mainly against intellectuals

Left, Red Guards waving Mao's Red Book of quotations. Above, Mao's successor Hua Guofeng is celebrated in Changsha in 1979.

Zhao Ziyang, who was regarded as a relative liberal, succeeded Hu, and in 1988 Li Peng took over from him as prime minister. After the suppression of the democracy movement in 1989, Zhao – who, like Hu before him, appeared sympathetic to the protesters – was sacked. Jiang Zemin became general secretary.

By 1993, Deng Xiaoping had officially retired from politics, but remained de facto ruler of China. The Chinese media carried reports that Deng, who turned 89 in August of that year, was in good health. But these reports did not stop many people asking the question: what will happen after Deng dies?

POLITICS IN THE 20TH CENTURY

Almost without exception, it was the men who made history in China. This was the case in Confucian times and is still true today.

After the fall of the Qing Dynasty, **Yuan Shikai** (*above left*) who was born in 1859, made a futile attempt to establish himself as emperor. He came from a family of civil servants in Xiangcheng in the province of Henan. He had a brilliant military career and was a favourite of the emperor's widow Cixi; but she dropped him because he held too many powerful offices. China's last reigning monarch, Puyi, reinstated him in 1911 to save the throne. But Yuan Shikai had understood the signs of the times and joined the republicans, only to betray them shortly afterwards because he did wish to become emperor of China. He died on 6 June 1916, shortly before the planned enthronement.

His direct opponent was **Dr. Sun Yatsen** (*above right*). Born in 1866 as Sun Wen, he lived near Macao in Cuiheng in the district of Guangdong. Influenced by Christian and Western ideas, he plotted the overthrow of the Qing Dynasty and founded the republican Guomindang (National People's party). Initially he was dismissed by Yuan Shikai; undaunted, he founded a government in Guangzhou (Canton) in 1920 which was to rival the military powers in the North; after 1923 he reorganised the Guomindang with the help of the Soviet Union. He died in Beijing on 18 March 1925, while preparations for the Northern campaign were still in progress. Nowadays he is honoured as "the father of the Republic" in the People's Republic and in Taiwan.

Chiang Kaishek (*centre left*) became his successor. He was born in 1887, went through his military training, then joined the Guomindang and became Sun Yatsen's intimate friend at the beginning of the 1920s. After the defeat in the civil war, he fled to Taiwan where his dictatorial government was able to boost the economy with the help of the United States. He died in 1975, without achieving his aim, namely to overthrow the Communist government and capture the mainland again.

The great opponent to Chiang Kaishek, as well as all other Chinese politicians, was **Mao Zedong** (*centre right*); no one else had such a lasting influence on the country in this century. He was born in 1893, the son of a peasant family near Changsha, province of Hunan. At a very early age, Mao joined the revolutionary movement in China and in 1921 became co-founder of the Communist Party of China.

During the Long March he established himself as leader of the Communist Party of China and he retained this position until his death in 1976. He led the country out of its economic misery, only to let it sink into chaos twice: the first time during the Great Leap Forward (1958-1969), then during the Cultural Revolution (1966-1976). The unique personality cult around Mao emerged during the Cultural Revolution, and he became a living monument. Mao had unlimited power and governed the country like a dictatorial emperor.

The second most important person after Mao Zedong was **Zhou Enlai** (*below left*). He had been Mao's closest ally since the Long March in 1925. He was the son of a wealthy family of the gentry, born in Huai'an, province of Jiangsu, in 1898. After studying in Germany and France during the 1920s, Zhou Enlai joined the Communist movement and played a leading role soon after his return to China. His special skill, namely diplomacy, became apparent very soon. He was promoted to foreign minister in 1949, and then to prime minister. Some well-thought out maneuvres and operations during the Cultural Revolution put him in a position where he was able to avoid too much damage being done. His successes in foreign politics are particularly significant; China emerged from isolation after becoming a member of the UN in 1971. He died in Beijing in 1976; as opposed to Mao Zedong, he was loved and honoured by the Chinese population.

Deng Xiaoping (*bottom right*), born 22 August 1904, was Zhou Enlai's right-hand man and close friend. Hailing from a peasant family in Sichuan, Deng had an eventful past. In 1920, he first went to France as a student and worked his way through university. After his return six years later, his career in the army and the party advanced rapidly; he took part in the Long March and was one of the most prominent politicians after 1949. In 1973, he was appointed by Zhou Enlai as deputy prime minister. Now the absolute leading figure of political life in China, he was responsible for opening China's door to the world and was the driving force behind the country's modernisation programme. Despite some setback to his chosen course – most notably the events leading to the supression of the democracy movement in June, 1989 – Deng has shown amazing tenacity by steering China back into the enclaves of the international community through a series of astute political maneuvers.

Early morning; a park in a Chinese city. In one corner, where there are trees and benches, the park is alive with birdsong. Not the song of wild birds – even in most rural areas, China's wildlife is impoverished – but of caged birds. There are laughing thrushes with "beautiful eyebrows" – *hwameis* – and Mongolian larks, each in bamboo cages that are either hung from a tree branch, or placed on the ground. Nearby are the birds' proud owners; most are elderly, all are men. They gossip together or sit quietly, enjoying the flutings and whistlings of their birds.

Elsewhere in the park, men and women seem locked in solemn, slow motion combat with invisible adversaries, swaying and turning and pushing into the air as they work through *taijiquan* routines. Some thrust swords into the air while others inhale deep breaths and tauten muscles as they practice *kung fu*. Yet others who are not pursuing a serious exercise may be engaged in some sport such as playing badminton across nets suspended between trees.

Old folks may jog by in a soft shoe shuffle that barely beats a walking pace. Or they join a group exercise session, gathering in front of an instructor who commands them to bend, twist and stretch in unison.

Such group activities start young for the Chinese. Before their lessons begin, schoolchildren may "exercise" together. Taped music and a male voice blare out from speakers: "yi er san" – "one two three" – says the voice, and the children massage their eyes, in a routine to counteract eyestrain resulting from too much swotting.

Morning streets are crowded with commuters. Armadas of cyclists pour through cycle lanes and scatter across junctions. Until early last decade, the cycles were mostly black, chunky, unstylish and ungainly, yet even so were prized possessions – a Flying Pigeon brand cycle was something of a status symbol. Now, however, there are also colourful, trendy models made by wholly Chinese firms and by joint ventures between China and foreign companies such as Raleigh.

The riders, too, are a diverse lot. Once obligatory blue "Mao" suits and dowdy hairstyles are now for the unfashionable and the poor. Today's city Chinese prefer more westernised attire. Men are mostly in sober greys and browns with white shirts. Young women may be in cheerful colours; perhaps sporting short skirts and tights, along with make-up including foreign lipstick or eyeshadow, and their hair is permed in the latest style – all unthinkable in the China they were born in.

Buses lurch along the streets, sometimes slowing to a snail's pace as they meet traffic jams. They are always packed: people trying to get on would push their way into the throng, standing crushed against their neighbours, watching in case a seat becomes free, then pushing their way out when they reach their destinations.

Around 80 percent of the commuters are bound for state-run companies, where they are members of work units, or *danwei*. The rest work for the private sector, which has grown rapidly since being permitted again in 1979, and now accounts for at least a tenth of the national economy.

Chances are that, whether they are headed for state-run or private companies, the women will have only jobs in the bottom rung of the company's hierarchy. "Women hold up half the sky" proclaimed Mao, but even under his rule, women rarely achieved high positions. The years since have seen further official affirmations of sexual equality, which is, if anything, even further from being realised in practice. A survey based on the real status of women in various countries ranked China 132nd in the world.

Age-old beliefs are largely to blame – according to Confucius, "A woman without talent is virtuous". Besides regarding women as problematic and less innovative, employers are also concerned that if a woman becomes pregnant, she will be legally entitled to nine months' maternity leave. Adding to the woes of working women is the fact that they are also suffering from increasing sexual harassment. (They may, however, be the bosses at home.)

Left, serious-looking Chinese girls assembled under a coat of arms at a sports festival in Shanghai.

Income and consumption

At noon or soon afterwards, it is time for lunch. Even where the lunch break officially lasts an hour, workers will often halt work for a couple of hours – time to eat, then take a nap. This lengthy break is typical of state-run companies, which in many cases are pervaded by a day-long, relaxed atmosphere. The "iron rice bowl" – as the system of permanent jobs and guaranteed wages is

called – has proved a disincentive to hard work and few people are willing to put in more effort for no extra reward. There are even "workers" who are simply content to receive food and money in return for doing no work at all. Not surprisingly, many state-run firms are uneconomical; some even make huge losses.

China has moved to stem the losses, cutting 762,000 jobs in state-run companies during the first half of 1993. But the job cuts have met with resistance: sacked workers have assaulted managers.

By contrast, the flourishing private sector is characterised by vitality and vigour; lunch

breaks are more likely to be restricted to an hour or less. Time is, after all, money.

Money is also driving changes in rural areas. Thanks both to farmers being able to profit from their crops, and to the rural enterprises that have proliferated in recent years, incomes in the countryside have risen dramatically since the late 1970s. Even so, they are lower than, and have lately failed to keep pace with, urban incomes. And there are wide imbalances between differing parts of China. Farmers living near cities can reap the benefits of crops such as water melons that fetch high prices in free markets. Away from cities, and especially in the inland provinces, rural areas are typically poor.

Each year, tens – or hundreds – of thousands of people from these impoverished areas swarm into the cities, especially booming, alluring Guangzhou. Many find their dreams are quickly soured. If they find jobs, they are probably menial, the sort that city dwellers eschew. If not, they may return home disappointed. Or they may run out of the little money they brought with them, and perhaps turn to begging, or crime, or, far from friends and family, die on the streets. A very few might succeed, gaining the permits they need to become permanent city residents and leading lives that, back in their villages, seemed like remote fantasies.

"To get rich is glorious" Deng Xiaoping announced in 1978. The people responded with gusto. Urban incomes, which had averaged 445 yuan per year in 1953, 624 yuan five years later, and had dipped to 615 yuan in the year Deng took charge, soon rose, almost doubling by 1985, and reaching 2,140 yuan by 1990.

Despite the increases, China's current income levels are still very low compared to the West – nationwide, averaging around US$350 in 1993. The figures are, however, deceptive. This is partly because rents for most workers are still heavily subsidised, with apartments perhaps costing the equivalent of US$2 or US$3 per month, and other prices are invariably low by comparison with the West. Then, there are salary supplements, such as for haircuts, buying newspapers and seniority ranking. Moreover, many Chinese have second jobs or run their own businesses, but declare little or none of the the extra income.

Certainly, the rise in purchasing power seems out of all proportion with the rise in incomes. In 1978, only 7.8 percent of Chinese owned a bicycle; by 1990, the figure had risen to 34.2 percent. The numbers of television sets per 100 persons also leaped from 0.3 in 1978 to 16.2 in 1990. In urban areas, possession of once out of reach consumer goods has become even more commonplace: by 1992, for every city household, there were 73.7 colour televisions, 72.2 video recorders, 52.6 refrigerators, 82.9 washing machines, 23.7 cameras and 2.6 motorcycles.

Coupled with this rise in purchasing power has been a shift in the goods a well-to-do family desires – the "three hot buys". During the 1960s and 1970s, the three hot buys were bicycles, watches and radios. Then, as these items became the norm in the 1980s, households wanting to keep up with the Wongs saved to buy colour televisions, refrigerators and washing machines. In March 1993, when these in turn had become passé, the *China Daily* speculated on the three hot buys for the 1990s – some people said cars, houses and telephones but, the paper reported, the Chinese were yet to reach consensus on the matter.

Not that Chinese consumers restrict themselves to the hot buys. Foreign goods are popular: the three record opening days for McDonald's outlets were at the company's three restaurants in China; the country is Coca-Cola's second largest market in Asia; and Pepsi is injecting millions of dollars into its Chinese operations. Designer goods are snapped up by cash-rich Chinese who may be businessmen, officials, offspring of officials, and girlfriends, wives and even mistresses of the wealthy.

Upmarket Japanese department store chain, Yaohan, has opened a branch in Beijing, and in autumn 1992 broke the ground for what will be Asia's largest department store in Shanghai. Stores owned by other companies

have also opened, and more are planned. Yaohan's experience, however, suggests that they will not find doing business in China plain sailing. Within a year of opening, Yaohan's Beijing store was reportedly suffering from a combination of inexperienced local management and problems arising from China having two currencies, one convertible, one not.

Similarly, the Chinese wannabes have not found that getting rich is always gloriously straightforward. By autumn 1993, the larg-

est mental hospital in Guangzhou was overflowing, with all wards full, cots in hallways, and hundreds of new patients arriving each day. Most of the new arrivals were in their 20s and 30s, and suffering chiefly from work pressures, anxiety over relationships, and business failures.

However – in Beijing at least – some young Chinese are rejecting the get rich quick culture. They opt instead to become beatniks, espousing freedom of expression.

The male beatniks are unlikely to be viewed as eligible bachelors by most single Chinese women. While there are still arranged marriages in China, single people are

Left, on the catwalk at a beauty contest in Guangzhou. **Right**, a game of badminton during a lunch break, park scene in Nanjing.

increasingly free to marry as they please. And, in China as elsewhere, there are plenty of material girls for whom Mr Right means someone who can supply the clothing, make-up, jewellery and so forth that will impress their friends and family. The men, in turn, are invariably looking for a pretty face.

Population growth

In China, family lines are passed on through the male child. Partly because of this, and

male ratio is different from the norm for other races. However, while the ratio may have resulted partly from the fact that many female children are not registered, the evidence is compelling that the main reason there are so many boys is that female foetuses are aborted.

In the 1953 and 1964 censensuses, the sex ratios at birth were a little under 105 to 100. Ultrasound scanners, allowing determination of the sex of foetuses, were first introduced in 1979, and as they became increas-

because – especially in rural areas – male offsprings are more likely to support ageing parents, sons are preferred to daughters. In the past, this preference led to female infanticide. Some reports suggest this remains a problem in rural areas, especially since the government finds it difficult to control as cases are not easily detected. Far more common nowadays is the abortion of female foetuses. This has resulted in a skewing of the male to female ratio of newborn children, which by 1993 had risen to around 120 boys to 100 girls.

At least one official has claimed this ratio is natural, and that the Chinese male to fe-

ingly widespread, the ratio climbed: it was 107.5 in 1982, 113.8 in 1990, and roughly 118.5 in 1992.

Doctors are officially banned from disclosing the results of ultrasound scans. But gifts of money or cigarettes can often persuade them to tell. Also, private businessmen now offer the service, which can turn in handsome profits.

The pressure to ensure a baby is male is high in part because of the one child policy. Sometimes, even when a female baby is born, she is sold or given away, so the parents can try again.

With so many hopes riding on them, the

single children are usually spoiled by doting parents and especially, grandparents. These kids have been dubbed "little emperors", for their every wish is granted. One result is that unlike in earlier decades, Chinese children are often overweight, sometimes obese. "More than 90 big-fat kids aged from 8 to 16 took part in the Beijing Summer Slimming Camp '90," runs a caption in the *People's Republic of China Yearbook 1991/1992*. "Photo shows these big-fats doing slimming exercises" proclaims another caption.

if trends continued, there would be a 50- to 70-million strong "army" of bachelors by 2000. According to the Women's Federation of Shanghai, this could exacerbate the recent resurgence of gangs that kidnap women and sell them as wives.

But in at least one city, by 1993 there were some parents who said they wanted to have daughters. Their reason: they foresaw healthy "dowries" which might be boosted in a marriage market in which young women are at a premium.

More disturbingly, the children who called a Beijing radio phone-in show during early 1993 showed themselves to be rude and spoiled, threatening to beat their parents if they refused their demands. The show's presenter, Pamela Pak, predicted that China will have major problems as the "little emperors" grow to adulthood.

Given the sex ratio, many of the male "emperors" will find they cannot fulfill all their desires. In 1993, Beijing predicted that,

Left, mannequin on display in the Friendship Store in Beijing. **Above**, street cobbler having a nap, in Chongqing.

Chinese dinners

Early evening is time for dinner. As their rich and varied cuisine demonstrates, the Chinese love to eat. The rise in living standards is well reflected at meal times – city folk, to whom even pork was once special, are now buying more and more beef, fish, and shrimps.

While meals in the home may be relatively simple, with a small selection of dishes to choose from, restaurant meals can be veritable banquets. This is especially the case if the meal is accounted to entertainment expenses, or is being paid for by a businessman who wants to impress – the Chinese do not usually go "Dutch" on meals. To many officials, grand dinners are like perks; their salaries may be meagre, but their bellies are richly rewarded.

For a banquet to really impress, it should include rare delicacies, such as exotic fungi or, sadly – and illegally – endangered wildlife, such as tiger. One restaurant in Guangzhou even has a banquet which could include a substance most of us do not even think of as food: gold. "Fat cats" could, according to a 1993 report in the *South China Morning Post*, dine on delicacies such as abalone, sharks' fin, crocodile and clam sprinkled with gold leaf.

Whether or not the meal includes delicacies, there should be more food than the diners can eat. Sometimes, banquets end with tables still piled with food. By one estimate, the Chinese waste enough food each year to feed 100 million people.

Evening pursuits

Until recently, dinner was the chief evening event. It may remain so for many people, who may do little more after eating then leave crowded, claustrophobic homes for the street outside, to meet neighbours or read under street lights. With little or no privacy at home, young couples may head for parks in search of romance (despite privacy being hard to come by, one survey found that between 20 and 30 percent of men and 15 and 20 percent of women claimed to have had sex before marriage).

Others may stay at home and watch television. China's national and regional television stations are improving but, even though they feature imported as well as domestic programmes, their efforts rarely grip viewers. "There is too much garbage on television," said propaganda supremo Li Ruihuan in 1992. "The task of television stations is to liven things up (but) in every respect, television programmes are far too dull and serious; there is not enough action." Nevertheless, some series, including soap operas, have attracted large audiences. However, because programmes that have proved winners with the masses have often

drawn flak from ideologues, the stations remain cautious, and are unlikely to rush to follow Li's exhortations to be more "open" and "courageous".

However, increasing numbers of people are no longer limited to watching domestic stations. The masses may be officially banned from receiving foreign satellite television – with its Western "bourgeoise" influences – but state-run factories have been enthusiastic in producing satellite dishes, which now dot city rooftops and often serve many house-

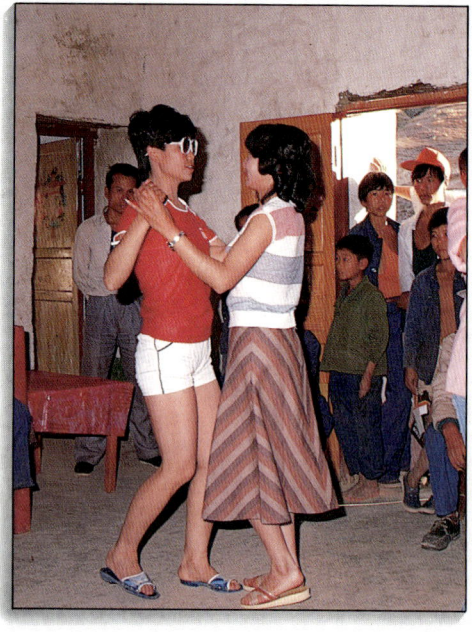

holds. Hongkong-based Star TV can be received throughout China, and includes a Mandarin channel together with its English-language offerings.

When neither domestic nor satellite channels offer anything worthwhile watching, many households can watch videos instead. Nowadays, the choice of video fare include an action movie or comedy from Hongkong or Taiwan.

Cinema audiences can also enjoy these commercial productions. Domestically produced box office successes are rare as, like television, the movie industry is stymied by ideologues. Even so, there have been successes, such as *Yellow Earth* by Chen Kaige, and *Red Sorghum* and *Judou* by Zhang Yimou. The latter was only approved for release in China after achieving critical acclaim in the West.

Until the economic boom got underway, China was no place for nightlife. Now, however, there are discos – some basic, some swanky – as well as dance halls where men can hire dancing partners; a few pub-like bars, and venues holding occasional rock concerts. Then there is karaoke as well.

Worried that such decadent music may be a bad influence, China's officialdom has struck back with home-grown products. In 1991, Chongqing city government opened Bayu tea house, China's first establishment to provide a Sichuan opera karaoke service. The same year, the country's Communist propaganda department produced a series of karaoke videos with songs including *Our Leader Mao Zedong* and *On the Golden Mount of Beijing*, which compares Mao to the golden sun. Guangdong cultural cadres

Karaoke, the Japanese-invented singalong craze, has swept China. Karaoke bars range from the modestly priced to those which are costly even by Western standards. A few are fronts for prostitution and risk the ire of the authorities, which may seek them out and close them down in order to "eliminate the social evils and purify the air of society". Overwhelmingly, the songs patrons prefer are from Hongkong and Taiwan; there is also middle of the road material from the West – including songs by the Carpenters.

Left, modernisation has reached the rural areas too. Above, karaoke fever hits China.

and businessmen, meanwhile, joined forces to market a disc to help the masses spend their evenings singing revolutionary songs. Titles include *Sing a Folk Song for the Chinese Communist Party*, and *Chairman Mao is my Dearest*, and *Blood-stained Honourable Image*. According to cultural officials, the disc, called "Golden Path", had "positive significance in reinforcing the national revolutionary spirit of self-entertaining activities like karaoke".

During a visit to China, you may gauge for yourself whether karaoke patrons are singing such material, or songs from Hongkong, Taiwan, and the West.

增产节约 实现四化

人人为祖国多作贡献

BEHIND THE FACADE

"Seeing is easy, learning is hard" goes an old Chinese proverb. The traveller is always in danger of seeing a great deal yet understanding little. This is by no means an individual shortcoming – even the tourist who is intent on gaining understanding will soon find out that we perceive things quite differently from those who are themselves affected.

In many respects, China is strange, incomprehensible, even exotic, so it has – over the centuries – become a kind of "Counter-Occident", a symbol of hope, sometimes even a promised land. Curiosity about Eastern philosophy did not always lead to a fruitful outcome, while nevertheless it is not in vain – any attempts to analyse another way of thinking must surely be the precondition for mutual understanding.

The spirit, the consciousness of a people is expressed in its culture; art can tell a great deal about sensitivities, about thoughts and yearnings. The following contributions, though little more than a glimpse, touch on painting, literature and theatre. Much of the Daoist way of thinking becomes perceptible in traditional painting – the relationship of man to nature, the principle of a harmonious integration into the stream of existence. In arts and crafts we come upon characters from mythology, actual history and the world of fairy tales. Traditional architecture provides insights into cosmic ideas as well as the social hierarchies of antiquity.

Chinese medicine is based on totally different principles than orthodox Western medicine. It is an empirical medicine which uses the experiences of numerous generations and embraces a holistic approach to the nature of man. The philosophy of Chinese medicine is also apparent in the various techniques of fighting and concentration, such as *taiji* and *qigong*.

Food must rate as one of the most beautiful and pleasant sensual experiences one can have in China. Nowhere else in the world has cooking developed into such a sophisticated skill, nor eating into such a unique ceremony.

So *please* look behind the facades of the country, try and meet the people; then you will come to understand and recognise what seemed so strange and exotic. "No one is as blind as he who does not wish to see" goes another Chinese proverb.

Preceding pages: a futuristic poster in Beijing, heralding the modernisation of the country; avenue of birch trees leading to the Heavenly Mountains; evening scene in a Luoyang street; street trader in Chongqing. **Left**, section of the palace roof, a dragon's head with a fishtail.

What would an English village be without its church spire? Just as inconceivable would be China without its countless pagodas. In keeping with their original religious significance, they are mostly found in the centre of places of worship and monastic institutions or near them, and are used for the safekeeping of relics. These tall and slender towers are also found on hilltops rising high out of the landscape, catching the eye of the traveller. Pagodas assume an aesthetic vivid-

1651 for the reception of the fifth Dalai Lama at the court of the Emperor of China. Who would have guessed that there was a connection, a common origin, between this building and the **Pagoda of the Six Harmonies** (*Liuheta*) on the Qiantang river near Hangzhou? These two pagodas cover the entire development span of Chinese pagoda design as well as the religious and cultural function and significance of these buildings. We find pagodas of boundless diversity throughout

ness as a result of their location and unique form, and become one of the enduring impressions of every traveller to China. Nevertheless, the variety of architectural styles, materials and forms are at first confusing for the uninitiated.

China's capital city, Beijing, is known above all for its imperial palace complex, but the visitor's eye is irresistibly drawn to another building: the **White Dagoba** (*Baita*) in the **Beihai Park**, which rises majestically to the west of the palace, above the entire imperial city. The white massive structure in the shape of a bell is set on a square base in the style of a Tibetan Chörten; it was built in

Asia – wherever the Buddhist religion is present. In the beginning, these buildings were nothing other than burial places. Indian rulers at the time of the Gautama Siddharta, the authentic Buddha, were buried in tombs which consisted of a semi-spherical solid core structure rising from a cylindrical plinth.

The first Buddhist missionaries spread the teaching of Buddha across northern India to China. Many Chinese monks later travelled the same route back to North India to study ancient writings and visit the places directly influenced by Buddha. In this way, in addition to Buddhist teachings, reports of burial rites, religious art and the impressive monastic and temple architecture filtered into remote China.

By way of etymology, too, it can be concluded that the pagoda is representative of the enrichment of Chinese architectural forms derived from Buddhism. The word pagoda is not Chinese but was probably adapted from the Sanskrit word *Bhagavan* which has a similar meaning to the word "Lord", commonly used to address divinity. In Chinese, a pagoda is called *ta* which earlier was

manifest itself in the finished building. The largest building of this kind is the **Chörten of Jiangzi**, a monumental structure which fulfills the function of a temple at the same time. A square four-storey base structure rises from a polygonal plinth with a surrounding gallery at each level – giving access to one small chapel after another – surmounted by a cylindrical core with a conical shape and large "umbrella" sitting at its top. Above those are the symbols from Buddhist teaching such as

tappna, a Chinese rendering of the Indian word "stupa".The style of Buddhist tombs resembling the Indian *stupa* can be found in Tibet. The Tibetan chörten were used for the burial of Lama high priests including the Dalai and Panchen Lamas; however, in the imaginative world of Tantrist Buddhism, which is dominant in Tibet, the building of a chörten is more meaningful than simply a mere tomb. It is a symbolic ceremonial act as a result of which the presence of Buddha will

Left, the Tibetan Kumbun Chörten at Jiangzi.
Above, the top of the twin pagoda at Suzhou is very reminiscent of the Indo-Tibetan prototype.

the sun, recumbent half-moon and flames. The White Dagoba (*Baita*) in Beijing belongs firmly to this Tibetan chörten tradition.

The pagoda as an architectural work of art

The diversity in the artistic development and stylistic form of these cult buildings throughout Asia evolved within China to the characteristic elongation of the structure while dispensing with the plinth. The Chinese pagoda is, to some extent, an over-scaled representation of the umbrella-like superstructure built along the central shaft which in the case of Tantric Buddhist buildings carried as many as thirteen "umbrellas". These symbolise the number of ways of attaining salvation. With Chinese pagodas, the shaft becomes a tower and the "umbrellas" become accessible storeys.

The first pagoda structures found in China go back to the 3rd and 5th centuries A.D. and were presumably constructed in timber; none of these survive. Later, in the north of China, solid construction using bricks and tiles was adopted whereas in the south – in the absence of alternative building materials – timber construction was developed further. The oldest surviving pagoda is found in the district of Dengfeng near the old imperial city of Luoyang and close to the famous Shaolin monastery. This 131-ft (40-metre) high, twelve-sided **Songyue Pagoda** was built in A.D. 523; for 1,400 years it has withstood the ravages of weather, natural disasters and revolutions from the Mongol invasion to the Cultural Revolution.

At the nearby Shaolin monastery, there is another rare sight: the **Forest of Pagodas** (*Talin*), a cemetery with more than 200 stone funerary pagodas – the last resting place of monks and abbots. These pagodas are only a few metres high and have, at chest height, a square core to which are attached memorial tablets or small recesses for offerings. Their function and symbolism corresponds to the original Indian stupas, but not their architectural style. Some other ancient structures include the possibly best-known pagodas in China – the two Wild Goose pagodas in Xi'an. The **Great Wild Goose Pagoda** (*Dayanta*) was built at the instigation and to the design of the monk Xuanzang who, in the 7th century A.D., undertook an adventurous journey to North India which took years. It is still known to today's Chinese as a legend from the novel trilogy *Journey to the West*. The Great Wild Goose Pagoda is used to store his writings and was the religious focal point of a large monastic institution.

The curious name of the pagoda goes back to a legend supposedly brought back from North India by the monk Xuanzang. According to his account, it was here that Buddha – whose religious sect forbades the partaking of meat – successfully resisted the

temptation of a wild goose. As a warning and reminder of this threatening occurrence, a pagoda was erected on the very same spot where he had been tempted.

The smaller 13-storey 141-ft (43-metre) high **Little Wild Goose Pagoda** (*Xiaoyanta*) originally had another name but was simply re-christened, in the course of time, because of its striking similarity to its larger companion, the Great Wild Goose Pagoda. It is of approximately similar age but appears – because of its greater number of storeys, its

slender form and gently curved topmost point – much more graceful than the monumental and somewhat clumsy Great Wild Goose Pagoda. As solid brick stepped pagodas, both are typical examples of the Tang period style.

The tradition of Chinese architecture

The Chinese are well-known as highly skilled assimilators of all foreign influences. Just as they adapted Buddhism by rapidly mixing the original teachings of Buddha with traditional superstitions and ancestor worship, likewise they invested the genuine style of the Buddhist pagoda with their own forms and building traditions.

China has been known for its massive tower structures since the Han dynasty. This form of construction was used mainly for city walls as well as court and palace gates. Chinese craftsmen developed timber frame construction to its ultimate form which can still be admired in the old palaces and temples. Posts and beams satisfy structural requirements and are often built without the aid of glue or nails. Corbels and brackets, art-

expression of Daoist philosophy.

The German poet Goethe, who was not unaffected by Chinese philosophy and culture, describes in a poem the unfamiliar turn of his creative style. He describes a Chinese on a visit to Rome; all the buildings, both ancient and new, seem heavy and clumsy to him. He wishes that the poor Romans could understand how fine columns of wood can carry an entire roof, that carved and gilded beams are a joy to the eye of a sensitive and educated beholder.

fully combined into incredibly complex structures, support the roofs. Walls resolve into openings or, at least, skilfully pierced surfaces which blend with the natural setting outside. Intricately designed curved roof shapes with finely carved figures encapsulate this style of building which, without a doubt, strongly reflects Daoist philosophy in its aim at complete harmony between man and nature. This style of building so typical of China represents the architectural

Left, the Great Wild Goose Pagoda at Xi'an, dating back to the Tang dynasty. **Above**, detail of a brick-built stepped pagoda.

Chinese palace architecture

Early antecedents of Chinese palace architecture were found by archaeologists at Erlitou near Luoyang. Excavation at the Shang dynasty site revealed a terrace which must have been the floor of some large hall. Architecture made great strides in the Qin and Han dynasties. The basic plan configuration of later palaces was already fully developed. Timber frame construction had been considerably refined. The infill panels between the posts and columns which carried the roof became subtle decorative screens. These can readily be examined because during the Han dynasty clay models of these were placed in graves as a parting gift.

Today, the main features and peculiarities of Chinese palace architecture are, of course, best observed at the **Imperial Palace** or some of the other palaces and temples in Beijing – mostly dating from the Ming dynasty. The Imperial Palace best exemplifies the element of palace architecture. Large buildings like the three great Halls of Harmony in the front part of the Palace rise from a terrace. It acts as a base but also serves a

whole of the palace grounds; in three raised levels, the whole terrace is framed by a finely decorated marble balustrade.

From the earliest days, the Chinese favoured timber as a building material because it was not only easily transported but was also very practical. Heavy posts are capable of carrying the roof while the wood could be carved for decoration and embellishment. For the columns of the Imperial Palace, the particularly hard and precious, nanmu wood (brought from the south-west-

practical purpose – namely to protect the hall from any ingress of water. Old texts, however, point clearly to a symbolic cosmological meaning when they state: "The Heavens cover and the Earth carries." The terrace, in these terms, represents the Earth, and the roof Heaven.

The size of a terrace is determined by the ranking of the building in the total context; buildings along the central axis generally count for more than subsidiary ones. This architectural principle can again be studied readily at the Imperial Palace. The **Hall of the Highest Harmony** (*Taihedian*) has the largest and most splendid terrace in the

ern provinces of the country) was used. In summer, the infill panels between the load-bearing columns of simple houses were easily removed and in winter, the open timber grilles were covered with rice paper to keep the cold at bay.

Corbel construction, between the tops of columns and the roof of palacial halls, reached the peak of fine craftsmanship. A visually confusing impression of longitudinal and cross beams, and involved timber components originally intended just to carry the gutters, becomes decorative embellishment in palace architecture – without diminishing their function as load dispersing elements of the structure. These corbel systems also give a clue to the social status of the owner of a house because ordinary people were not permitted to have them – being the prerogative of people of rank.

The roofs of Chinese palaces lend these generally large and massive buildings an air of weightlessness; the slightly up-turned eaves gutters seem to let the entire roof float above the building – as if carried on invisible columns. Another way of achieving this illusion of floating is the double roof; here

the roof is constructed in two stages and the low wall separating the two suggests a small additional storey.

The roofs of palaces are covered with glazed tiles – in the case of the Imperial Palace the emperor's colour was yellow; while the Temple of Heaven is appropriately covered in blue tiles. The tiles at the end are round or half-round decorated finials – in the case of the Imperial Palace, carrying the dragon symbol.

Left, detail of the Temple of Heaven – beams, corbels and decorated roof tiles. **Above**, the dome of the Temple of Heaven.

Architecture and superstition

Very conspicuous on palace roofs is the ridge decoration: two dragon-like animals with their fish-like tails pointing heavenwards, facing each other, while their gaping mouths seem to carry the ridge. Chinese mythology ascribes to the dragon the ability of being able to make rain. He thus protects the vulnerable timber building against fire. Usually the hilt of a sword projects from the body of the dragon, for legend has it that once upon a time, men nailed the protective fabulous beast to the roof with a sword.

The mythological beasts at the ends of the ridge of palace roofs have a similar significance: to protect the building from evil spirits. At the same time, the importance of the building can be derived from their number. Ten animals and one immortal decorate the ridge ends of the two-tier roof of the Hall of the Highest Harmony in the Imperial Palace. The animals include a lion, dragon and phoenix, a flying horse, unicorn, and other fabulous creatures.

Lower down, on most of these roofs, you will find a man riding a hen – another common figure intended to protect the building and occupants against disaster. Legend has it that this represents a tyrannical prince from the state of Qi (3rd century B.C.). After his defeat and death, the inhabitants of Qi are said to have fixed replicas of him riding on a hen to their roofs in order to keep away disaster and stigmatize the tyrant. Superstition has it that the evil tyrant on the hen cannot leave the roof because the hen cannot carry him in flight.

Such superstitious imaginings are often reflected in Chinese architecture, as for instance in the so-called *ghost's wall*. This was usually put up behind the entrance of all apartments and palaces to bar the entry of all evil spirits because they were believed to be able to move in a straight path only and not around corners. In the large palaces, the splendid Nine Dragon Wall (*Jiulongbi*) fulfilled this function. Even at the entrance to the government and party offices (*Zhongnanhai*), you will find such a *ghost wall* directly behind the gate, complete with quotations from Mao Zedong.

Painting in China, like most other cultural pursuits, has a long history; cult murals in tombs, temples and palaces are known to have existed already in the 3rd to 1st century B.C. as well as scroll paintings. Interest in paintings is a matter of very early historical record – earlier than that of the Europeans. This is explained by the extraordinary importance the Chinese had placed on the art of brush painting. This is clearly evident, both in the past and present, in poetry, callig-

Rabbit and pine marten fur

The close connection between writing and Chinese painting is also evident from the customary incorporation of written words in most Chinese pictures, such as a poem or simply the name of the painting, the painter's name and date of completion, as well as the painter's name stamp, generally red, and sometimes also the collector's name stamp. These written additions consisting of skilful

raphy and only secondarily, in painting.

The important place given to the art of brush painting is also due to the intimate association between writing and painting, resulting from the original pictographic character of Chinese script. As Chinese writing is not phonetic, anybody who is literate in whatever region and independent of a local dialect will be able to understand a written text. This nationwide unifying and historically continuous script was therefore always more important than the spoken language; the art of rhetoric – as practised for instance in ancient Greece – never developed in China.

calligraphy are deemed to be part and parcel of the painting. Conversely, there are examples of calligraphy where the ideograms stray so far from the characters as to virtually become paintings.

In China, painting comprises monochromatic and coloured work in ink on fabric or paper, mural reproductions such as wood block prints, calligraphy as well as some related techniques such as embroideries or woven pictures and decorative paintings.

Writing and painting utensils are referred to in China as the Four Treasures of the Study. They consist of the brush, ink, rubbing stone and paper – tools held in high esteem by poets, scholars and painters. There are reliable records of brush and ink already used in the 1st century B.C. Today, a paintbrush consists of a bundle of rabbit fur set in a slim bamboo tube; finer brushes are made of pine marten fur. These brushes differ from the European watercolour brushes by their softness and, above all, by coming to a very fine point at the end which allows a brushstroke to be gradually broadened by a movement of the hand – from a

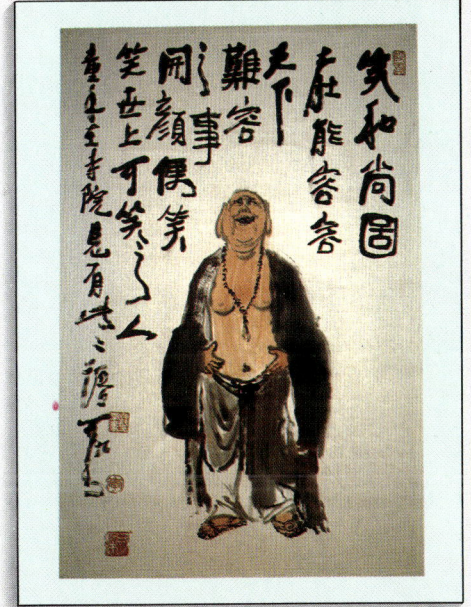

hairline to the full breadth of the brush.

In monochromatic painting, several brushes are generally used. The same brush is used for painting thick and thin lines only within a single formal segment; when colours are introduced, a separate brush is used for each one.

As its French name *encre de Chine* suggests, Chinese ink was only taken up in Europe as a distinct kind of paint in the 17th century. There is no doubt, however, that this

Left, woodblock print, ladies-in-waiting (Tang dynasty). **Above**, painting of the famous contemporary painter Li Keran with calligraphy.

ink was already widely used in China during the Han period. It is made from the soot of coniferous resin with the addition of glue; ink of good quality even has perfume added, such as musk in former days, but nowadays cloves are commonly used. The substance is pressed into various wooden moulds giving it the shape of slabs, bars or prisms. Solid ink became an aesthetically meaningful article of use and roused the collector's passion of letters. It gained cult significance early on because it was esteemed as the most important calligraphic material.

Ink in solid form is used both for writing and painting although liquid ink is now also available. However, this deprives the painting process and calligraphy of some of its comtemplative attraction because the rubbing is not just a practical procedure but, at the same time, attunes one to the artistic activity and aids concentration. The process involves dripping water onto a stone pestle, rubbing solid ink on it and then diluting the solution with water if necessary.

Paper is the usual medium for painting on. In former days, silk and fine linen were often used, but are now rarely used because they do not allow as much technical refinement as paper – itself another ancient Chinese invention, developed by Cai Lun and used from A.D. 106 onwards. Paper is produced in different qualities, each offering the painter alternative possibilities depending on absorption and texture.

Painting is learned in much the same way as writing: individual subjects are not usually absorbed or practised by nature study, but rather through copying old masters or proper textbooks of which *Flowers from a Mustard Seed Garden* is one of the most famous. A painter is considered a master of his art only when the necessary brushstrokes for a bird, a chrysanthemum or a waterfall flow effortlessly from his hand. This method is one of the unique features of Chinese painting. The technique does not lack strong fascination, but is also responsible for a degree of stagnation in Chinese ink painting. The strong emphasis placed on perfection of the craft aspects quickly leads to specialization by painters on specific subjects. In this way, for instance, Xu Beihong (1895-1953) became known as the painter of horses as Qi Bai-Shi (1862-1957) is famous for his shrimps. Routine and spontaneity, constant copying and the attempt at catching the finest nuance of individual expression, artistic mastery of the material and meditative preoccupation with the subject are each closely related and ideally, fully amalgamated. Such is the attitude to painting – which also applies to other spheres of art in China – the roots of which undoubtedly lie in

developed; painting in China remained above all a devout pursuit strongly inspired by the Buddhist religion.

Unfolding a masterpiece

More favoured and popular, however, was landscape painting – clearly influenced by Daoist philosophy. Notable characteristics of this form of painting are perspectives which draw the viewer into the picture, plain surfaces (unpainted empty spaces) which

Chinese philosophy and ideology. Already in the 4th century A.D., painters began to take the view that what mattered in painting was not so much the reproduction of reality but the evocation of a feeling.

Some of the most famous and magnificent Chinese works of art like those of the Zen painter Mu Qi (about 1220-1290), or the Qing period painter Badashanren (about 1626-1705), were the result of meditative ecstasy – or simply a state of total inebriation – created in seconds but with an almost dreamlike assurance of composition and grasp of the subject. In contrast to European painting, the figurative approach hardly

give the picture a feeling of depth, and the harmonious relationship between man and nature with man depicted as a small, almost disappearing, figure in nature. An original Chinese ink painting does not acquire anything like the prestige of a western original because perfect copying in the form of woodblock prints is considered high art. It is difficult indeed for the uninitiated to distinguish an original from a good copy, and even Chinese connoisseurs rely on reports and experts for the provenance of a picture when judging its originality. A peculiar feature is the presentation of the picture as a hanging or horizontally-positioned scroll. It is first painted on silk or on extremely thin paper, backed with stronger paper and mounted in a complicated way on a long roll of silk or brocade. Then a wooden stick is attached at the lower end (left end in the case of the horizontal scroll) which projects on each side with a knob extending beyond the fabric. Typically, the picture was stored away rolled up and brought out only on special occasions to be slowly unfurled, revealing only parts of a scene that is pieced together in the mind of an observer, subtly pages turned. The underlying thought was to create a bond between picture and observer – an intimate merger – whereas Western painting on panel or canvas impose a rational distance. In keeping with this, a landscape painting often has a path or bridge in the foreground to bring the viewer into the picture. The painting demands a transposition into the framework of the picture; the viewer is to identify with the little persons placed in the landscape and to absorb the painting as it were from within by

drawing him into the picture, making him a participant and not just a mere observer. After it has been displayed, the scroll was carefully put away again.

Thus the picture was handled in order to be looked at, i.e. touched by hand while being scrutinized. With horizontal scrolls, always unrolled little by little, the hands were in constant movement. Something similar applies to the other two forms of presenting classical painting – the fan which needed unfolding and the album leaf which needed

strolling about it. The legend of the 8th-century painter, Wu Daozi, is an example of how far such identification can go:

Wu Daozi did not die.
Once, already an old man,
he painted at the palace.
The landscape he painted on the wall
was so wonderful
that even the Emperor admired it.
Wu Daozi decided
to enter the picture:
He walked upwards along the path
and vanished in the mountain mists.
Nobody ever saw him again.

Left, calligrapher at work. **Above**, young painters trying out Western style of painting.

It is not surprising that the written word is more important in Chinese than the spoken one. Its characters developed from a pictographic writing system and not only represent sounds, but also meaning.

The earliest evidence of the Chinese script was found on the so-called oracle bones, on tortoise shells or shoulder blades of animals, onto which questions regarding the weather, the yield of crops or the outcome of battles were carved. They were then thrown into a fire, and the oracle was interpreted according to the cracks which were formed by the heat. These forms of writing are more than 4,000 years old, and can, of course, not be described as literature, though they provide information on the development of the Chinese script.

The oldest Chinese books were written on strips of bamboo which were fixed together almost like a roller blind. This explains why the old way of writing in Chinese runs from top to bottom and from right to left. Apart from the classic philosophical works of Confucianism and Daoism, there also exists to this day the "monument to the bound language" called *Shijing* (book of odes or book of songs). Legend has it that these songs were collected amongst the peoples of the different states by a civil servant called Cai Shiguan. The government wished to gain insight into the life of the people with the help of these songs in order to be able to administer the country more effectively. It is said that more than 3,000 songs were collected. Confucius selected 300 of them and compiled them in the *Shijing*. The contents of the odes are wide-ranging; there are love songs, songs about the land, songs glorifying outstanding personalities or outstanding personal qualities.

Most of the songs in the *Shijing* originate in the area of the Yellow River (Huanghe). The *Chuzi*, another collection of songs, comes from the south of China. Its creation is attributed to the poet Qu Yuan (approx. 322-295 B.C.). Poems in the lyrical or epic style play an extremely important part in Chinese literature. To be able to read and write poetry was part of the elementary education of the higher social classes. Students and civil servants of any rank or age were expected to be able to write a poem for any possible occasion. Girls and women who knew how to recite poems graciously were ensured the admiration of the opposite sex.

The Tang dynasty (618-907) was the beginning of the golden age for Chinese poetry. No other period in history has enjoyed such a great number of poets and works of poetry on such a scale and of such quality. The large and complete collection of Tang poetry (*Quan Tangshi*) contains 48,900 poems by 2,200 poets.

One of the most famous poets of the time was Li Bai or Li Bo (699-762), who is said to have written his best-known poems in a state of total inebriation. The story goes that he was also drunk when he was appointed as an official at the palace. Nevertheless, he immediately wrote a poem at the emperor's request which earned him much praise from the public.

Du Fu (712-770) must be mentioned together with Li Bai, though his style of poetry is very different. He held office at court for a short time, but was forced to flee due to political upheavals and led an unsettled, wandering life for a long time. He finally settled in Chengdu, where one can still visit the straw hut (*Du Fu Caotang*) which served as his home. From today's point of view it is hard to say which of the two poets is more significant. Li Bai is a natural talent, free, open and humorous, devoted to nature and close to the Daoists. Du Fu became a poet through diligence and practise, he is bold and serious, greatly concerned about the political and social situation. His lamentations are closely linked to Confucian ideas.

Prose or fiction, which almost always had an educational aspect, were usually considered trivial and not serious in ancient China. A status-conscious intellectual would regard it as undignified to concern himself with prose or fiction. This attitude was to change in the 20th century. Nevertheless there are a number of novels from different epochs which have survived as testaments of time and are still read and appreciated by many Chinese today.

Classical fiction

Every child in China knows the novel *The Journey to the West* and its famous heroes: the king of the apes Sun Wukong, the pig Zhu Bajie, the monk Sha and the Buddhist pilgrim and monk Xuanzang. The novel describes the adventure of the king of the apes, who, together with the other figures, accompanies the monk Xuanzang from China to the West – by which India is meant

about the robber Song Jiang and his companions, who wandered through what is now the province of Shandong around the end of the Northern Song Dynasty (960-1127). Just like Robin Hood, they fought injustices according to their own code of honour. They finally submitted to the imperial doctrine and fought against the rebels who were threatening the state system. This novel, too, became extremely popular. It is said to have been Mao Zedong's favourite book, yet

– in order to collect the holy scriptures from there. The novel mixes Indian folk stories and legends with Chinese, Buddhist and Daoist elements. Though the story no doubt existed much earlier, the version which is known today is attributed to Wu Cheng'en who lived in the 16th century.

The *Shuihuzhuan*, which is known as *The Bandits of Liangshan Moor* in English, is a novel about robbers dating from the Ming period; its origins are not clear either. The story is partly based on historical documents

during the time of the Cultural Revolution it was considered a negative illustration of capitulation.

The Chinese genre novels

The epitome of the genre novel is the *Jinpingmei* (which means *The Plum Blossom In A Golden Vase*) dating from the Ming Dynasty. In contrast to the novels which are heavily influenced by religion and sometimes have almost fanatical tendencies, the *Jinpingmei* portrays people as individual characters and describes the many amorous adventures of its hero Ximen in a rather

Above left, writer Qu Yuan. **Above right**, an old Illustration from the novel *Journey to the West*.

realistic way. Furthermore, this novel conveys a very precise portrayal of social conditions in the 16th century. It describes how upstarts and scroungers who gave themselves up to a totally unrestrained life became rampant. It tells of greedy civil servants, of old women who acted as matchmakers; it describes how idlers and layabouts were curious to find out about the private lives of others behind the scenes, of Buddhist and Daoist priests who took to womanizing. All in all, it provides a unique

Its main character is Jia Baoyu, the amorous and sentimental son of a high-ranking official. There are also Lin Daiyu, Xue Baochai and others, twelve girls in total, who are living at the house of the Jia family. The novel describes the prime and decline of the house of Jia. In an imaginative and humorous style, the author has given the male and female members of staff – more than 400 people in total – individual and distinctive traits. Cao Zhan portrays the domestic life of a distinguished Manchu

portrayal of life as it was lived by the so-called higher echelons of society.

It is not clear who the author of *Jinpingmei* was, but in 1617 a second edition was published of which a few copies have survived. In the year 1687, the Emperor Kangxi banned the book; yet it continued to be read, and in the year 1708 it was even translated into Manchurian. Emperor Qianlong again banned the book in 1789. Even today, this book is on the banned list of the People's Republic.

The *Hongloumeng* by Cao Xueqin (English: *Dream of the Red Chamber*) is rated as the best novel of the Qing Dynasty.

family in all its detail. Because the novel is so popular, it has given rise to specific research into *Hongloumeng*.

Since the May Fourth Movement of 1919, which amongst other things was aimed at reforming language, prose literature has increasingly been regarded as a means for social change. One of the most outstanding figures in new literature was Lu Xun; in his novel *Ah Q,* he uses biting irony to describe the self-destructive and insolent attitude of the underlings who are steeped in tradition and superstition. It was also Lu Xun who, in a brilliant way, introduced the essay form into Chinese literature.

In *The Diary of Sophia*, the author Ding Ling describes the lifestyle of her like-minded contemporaries with sceptical distance. Ba Jin wrote critical novels like *The Family* which, following in the tradition of *Hongloumeng*, describes the decline of a civil servant's family at the beginning of this century. Also well-known for his critical attitude to society was the author Mao Dun; his novel *Midnight*, for example, mainly exposes the contradictions between foreign businesses and nationalistically minded en-

trepreneurs in Shanghai of the 1930s. Lao She's best-known play *The Teahouse* has been performed in the West after the author was rehabilitated in the 1980s. The author who wrote *Rikshaw Coolie* had committed suicide at the time of the Cultural Revolution.

Many writers of this time were sympathetic to the communist movement, and as this grew stronger, the direction and content of the literature were defined more clearly.

Far left, the Tang poet Du Fu. **Left**, his contemporary Li Bai, who was very fond of drinking. **Above**, photo of the most important writer of modern times, Lu Xun.

After Mao Zedong's speech on art and literature, held in Yan'an in 1942, socialist realism was established as the only legitimate form. But other writers were busy singing the praises of workers, peasants and soldiers, and glorifying their struggles against wicked people such as feudal landlords. In 1956 – the period of the Hundred Flowers – some writers expressed dissatisfaction with certain policies. At the end of this period, they were branded "rightists"; their works were "poisonous weeds".

The Cultural Revolution, from 1966 to 1976, virtually halted literary endeavours. Once it was over, there was a resurgence of literature. With his story "Scar", Lu Xinghua gave the name to wound literature, analysing the traumas caused by the Cultural Revolution. This wound literature was itself part of the so-called New Realism, which typically looked at society's imperfections. But in 1980, the overriding political goals of China's literature were reasserted. Deng Xiaoping wrote, "It is impossible for literature to be independent of politics. Any progressive and revolutionary worker cannot but think of his works' social influence and must consider, therefore, the interests (of) the nation and the party... The party wishes, without compulsion, that literary workers first consider the public interests."

The 1980s saw a burst of literary creativity where new literary techniques were tried; most of the 2,000 novels produced from 1979 to mid-1993 appeared during this decade. By comparison, only 320 novels were published between 1949 to 1966, and few or none during the Cultural Revolution. Since 1989, some writers have published little, as they have not wanted to risk criticism for expressing views that might be regarded as supporting bourgeoise liberalism. Some writers, meanwhile, have found commercial success by writing "pop literature" such as sentimental love stories and martial arts sagas.

At a 1993 meeting of 30 eminent Chinese writers, party general secretary Jiang Zemin in a speech urging the creation of works that would both satisfy the people, and rally the country around the Communist Party, said, "To make socialist literature prosper is the glorious task of literature and art workers."

As early as the third century B.C. a profession came into being, which was to take charge of the cultural entertainment of court society. Chinese theatre art was perfected in the Southern Song Dynasty in the 12th century and reached its peak during the Mongolian Yuan Dynasty (1271-1368). A group of dramatists came together and 150 plays had already existed, amongst them the *Chalk Circle*, which was translated into European languages in the 18th century and was the inspiration for Brecht's *Caucasian Chalk Circle*. In the following six centuries up to 260 "local operas" emerged.

Local operas are recited and sung in the dialect of their place of origin and are typical of repertory plays. Although the influence of local operas was originally limited to a region, they began to compete for the best artistic forms of expression. In the development and formation of the Chinese theatre, music and singing played an important part and together with the spoken dialect they would often become the decisive attributes of a style of opera.

During the Ming period (1368-1644), the regional differences in theatre music became increasingly distinct. The Kunqu opera was created in the 16th century and remained the most important form of opera in China until the early 19th century. The name is derived from its place of origin, the Kunshan area in Jiangsu province, near Suzhou. The *Kunshanqian*, or *Shuimoqiang* (music polished by water), as it is sometimes called, was played by string and wind instruments. The cool, lamenting sounds of the bamboo flute are typical of this form of opera. Initially, the Kunqu seemed to appeal to a broad section of society, but eventually developed into a distinguished, aesthetic style of music.

During the Ming period, 330 well-known dramatists wrote around 990 Kunqu operas. People of high rank employed their private Kunqu theatre groups. Kunqu was per-

formed at banquets and on boat rides, when scholars and poets went on outings, in tea houses and inns. Under the emperors Kangxi (1662-1723) and Qianlong (1736-1796) this form of opera experienced a further artistic rise thanks to the patronage of the court.

At the beginning of the 19th century the Beijing opera began to establish itself and was eventually favoured by the court. Kunqu actors from the imperial palace joined other groups. So at that time, the Kunqu opera was

influencing the Beijing, Sichuan, Canton, Anhui and other local operas, until it disintegrated as an opera form in its own right. Inspite of occasional performances, Kunqu was as good as dead on the eve of the founding of the People's Republic of China.

The Beijing opera has existed for the last 200 years. Many of the stylistic elements in the songs, dance and music date back to the Kunqu opera. It developed from merging the styles of two local opera groups from Anhui and Hubei at the end of the 18th century.

Local operas are determined by their dialect and songs from that particular region and they are often limited to offering either dance

Preceding pages: performance of a classical court dance. **Left**, Beijing opera – the figure of Sun Wukong, King of the Apes. **Above**, a musician in traditional court dress from the Tang period playing the pipa.

or acrobatics. The Beijing opera, on the other hand, merged all the different elements of its predecessors – songs, dialogue, mime, dance and acrobatics – and adapted its language and singing according to the taste of its Beijing audiences.

The four main features of the Beijing opera are songs, dialogue, mime and acrobatics. The prime distinction is made between *Wenxi* (civilian plays) and *Wuxi* (military dramas); in addition there are also comedies and farces. Many of the themes are derived from folk tales, legends or classical literature.

Colourful stage settings

The Beijing opera distinguishes between leading parts for men, women's parts, parts for actors with painted faces and male and female jesters. All of these are again divided into sub-groups, and there are also extras (guards, soldiers, ladies-in-waiting, etc.). The female characters, which incidentally used to be played by men, are made up in white with different shades of carmine red, and light pink around the eyes. They are required to walk with soft sliding steps.

Their half-sung manner of speaking, and their whining singing are very typical. The actors with painted faces represent warriors, heroes, state officials, adventurers and supernatural beings. Each mask is like a small work of art, painted according to very precise rules. You can easily recognise a jester, as the area around his eyes and nose is painted white. They often act as farmers, servants or labourers and their remarks in every-day language greatly amuse the audience.

The costumes for all the parts are inspired by the clothes which used to be worn at court during the Tang, Han, Song and mainly the Ming dynasties. They are by no means realistic. The beggars' costumes in particular illustrate this: the beggars on stage wear costumes made of silk with patches in many different colours, artistically arranged. The colours and symbols of the painted masks reveal details about the character being played. Red stands for a loyal, upright, brave character. Black symbolizes a kind but

forceful, sometimes rather rough nature. The colour blue symbolizes wildness and intrepidity, as well as arrogance. Yellow stands for the same, albeit somewhat weakened traits. Green is used for unsteady characters. Orange and grey symbolize old age. Gods and goddesses wear golden masks. Good characters are painted in fairly simple colours, while hostile army commanders and multi-faceted types like bandits, robbers, rebels, etc. have very complex designs on their masks. Characters

who are mysterious and difficult to fathom have the most diverse colour and pattern combinations.

The form and presentation of the Beijing opera are unique. The initiated spectator primarily enjoys the music and the singing. A well-known player once noted in his diary: "When someone told me he was going to watch the Beijing opera, it sounded quite ridiculous, for it showed quite clearly that he was not a connoisseur. The connoisseurs would go and hear an opera and when there was a long singing part, they would not look at the stage but sit with their eyes closed and listen, clapping to the rhythm and thinking about every word of the song."

The audience at the Beijing opera tends to be rather noisy; even nowadays people talk to each other or to the children who are often present too. Unless the performance on stage is quite outstanding, there is very rarely any applause. During song recitals or if the spoken words are difficult to understand, the text is projected onto the walls on either side of the stage, as even the Chinese cannot always understand the contents without help. The orchestra is usually placed on the

right-hand side of the stage. The orchestra of the Beijing opera includes the following instruments: *Erhu* and *huqin*, the fiddles with two strings (whereby the *erhu* usually accompanies the *huqin*, which is tuned lower and has a softer sound); the mouth organ *sheng*; the moon guitar with four strings; *pipa*, the Chinese lute; the *suona*; drums and different kinds of bells, bowls and last but not least the *ban*, castanets made of hardwood and a wooden percussion instrument called "time rattle".

Left and above, conspicuous painted masks are a distinguishing feature of Chinese opera.

In Beijing opera, anything superfluous is omitted and attention is focused on the essential: props are only rarely made use of. An oar in the hand of a boatman is sufficient to indicate that a boat trip is in progress. Every soldier with a flag in his hand stands for a larger troop. Beijing opera becomes particularly enjoyable to the spectators if they are able to understand the hidden messages. The smallest movement of the eyes, the mouth or of a single finger can be significant. Nothing is left to chance; the movements of the feet, indeed of the entire body, are exactly predetermined and are quite different for each individual part. Older people love the opera, but you only rarely come across younger spectators. It appears that in recent years opera has not been able to compete with cinema, television and pop music. Those working in the theatre have been forced to face up to this problem. They organised a festival in Beijing with the aim of promoting Beijing and Kunqu opera. On this occasion, 20 traditional plays were revived which had not been performed on stage for a long time. In recent years, some high schools and universities have founded societies for the promotion of Beijing and Kunqu opera.

Timeless dramatic art

After the founding of the People's Republic, all plays had been scrutinized; "the wheat was to be separated from the chaff," which meant that any play influenced by feudalistic ideas were to be singled out. Such ideas were thought to include superstition, fatalism, suppression of women, blind devotion and respect towards those in power, glossing over the deeds of feudalistic dictators. On the one hand, traditional plays were especially selected and adapted, on the other hand there were attempts to create modern and contemporary plays. The new plays include the "newly adapted historical plays" and "modern plays" are concerned with themes of contemporary life. During the ten years of the Cultural Revolution (1966-1976) it was even prohibited to perform the traditional Beijing opera. Only model plays like *Conquering the Tiger Mountain with Tactical*

133

Skill or *The Red Signal Lantern*, which were set at the time of the Revolution or after the founding of the People's Republic were performed. The costumes were modern, and the music contained elements of well-known pieces of classical western music.

Today China has 3,300 professional theatre groups employing more than 220,000 people. More than 370 types of opera exist, though the majority of them are only regionally significant. The Sichuan opera, for example, is common in the provinces of

the Tibetan opera date back to the 8th century. From the 17th century onwards, a distinction was made between opera and religious ceremonies; episodes from folk tales were added and opera established itself as an art form in its own right. The performances took place in the open air, the musical accompaniment was closely related to Tibetan drinking songs and folk dances. Tibetan operas consist of three parts: the prologue, in which the gods were thanked and implored to provide protection; the main

Sichuan, Guizhou and Yunnan. The Hai opera is a relatively young form of opera, which is particularly popular in the region north of the Changjiang (Yangzi river). The Puxian opera was developed in Puxian and Xianyou, and the plays, which are sometimes 700 years old, are still performed in these regions on special occasions like weddings, moving house, welcoming Chinese returning from abroad or birthdays.

Opera is also widespread amongst the minority groups in China. The Tibetan opera is particularly well-known. During the Cultural Revolution it was considered feudalistic and reactionary. The origins of

part and the ending (also called blessing or epilogue). During the epilogue, a dance of joy was performed and the spectators were handed ceremonial silk scarves.

Plays, which include acrobatics, are the most accessible to foreigners and often the most pleasing visually. Acrobatics is, after all, self-explanatory. Only specialised actors are given the parts in which the emphasis is on acrobatics and extraordinary virtuosity is a precondition. Daring jumps, somersaults, sabre duels and combat scenes require enormous suppleness, precision and coordination, all of which are achieved by thorough and strict training. In the sabre duels the weapons only miss the opponent by a hair's breadth, and in the combat scenes all the old weapons are used and the spectator gets the impression of a huge battle in progress, although none of the actors touch each other. Acrobatics is very common and popular in China and is often performed as an art in its own right. Every large town has its own acrobatics troupe.

Outstanding skills have made Chinese acrobatics famous throughout the world. Acrobatics is one of the oldest forms of

tables. Some artists can balance between seven and ten tables stacked upon each other. Particular artistic skills used to be passed on within a family, and to some extent this is still the case today. Even at the time of Confucius, during the Spring and Autumn period (770-476 B.C.), acrobatics had developed into a fully recognised art form. Paintings dating back to the Tang Dynasty illustrate impressive acrobatics displays, dances and singing, as well as circus performances. In a state of decline before

theatre in the world; in China its history dates back 2,000 years. It was, and still is, an art of the people, closely linked to their experience of work and every-day life. In their performances, the artists not only use weapons, but many every-day objects like chairs, vases, tables, pots, plates and bowls. The Chinese have always been great masters at juggling with such objects. The *piece de resistance* might be a pyramid of chairs and

Left, heroic figures from the opera, colourfully dressed and made-up. **Above**, a woman general, with banners on her back symbolizing the strength of her troups.

1949 and considered to be an offensive street spectacle, acrobatics regained the status of a recognised performance art in the following years. Chinese acrobatics includes juggling, balancing, cycling, dance performances, voice imitations, clowning, magic and animal training.

The standard programme of the Shanghai acrobatics ensemble includes an act in which a panda blowing a trumpet is taken for a ride in a small wagon drawn by a monkey on a bicycle. A visit to China is not complete without spending an evening at the Beijing opera and attending an exhilirating acrobatics performance.

Calligraphy, painting, poetry and music are regarded in China as the noble arts, whereas the applied arts are considered merely as an honourable craft. All the same, in the West, these skilled crafts always held a special fascination: when thinking of China, one thinks of silk, jade and porcelain.

The cultivation of the silkworm is said to go back to the 3rd century B.C. Legend has it that planting of mulberry trees and keeping silkworms was started by the wife of the mythical Yellow Emperor (Huangdi). For centuries, **silk** held the place of currency: civil servants and officers as well as foreign envoys were frequently paid or presented with bales of silk. The precious material was transported to the Middle East and the Roman empire via the Silk Road. The Chinese maintained a monopoly on silk until about 200 B.C. when the secret of manufacture became known in Korea and Japan. In the West – in this case the Byzantine empire – such knowledge was acquired only in the 6th century A.D. The Chinese had prohibited the export of silkworm eggs and the dissemination of knowledge of their cultivation, but a monk is said to have succeeded in smuggling some silkworm eggs to the West. Today's centres of silk production are areas in the South of China around Hangzhou, Suzhou and Wuxi; in this region, silk can be bought at a lower price. Hangzhou has the largest silk industry in the People's Republic. In Suzhou, there are workshops where silk embroidery has been brought to the highest artistic level.

The Chinese invented **porcelain** sometime in the 7th century, which means a thousand years before the Europeans. The history of the development of Chinese ceramic artifacts goes back, however, to neolithic times. Along the Yellow River (Huanghe) and the Yangzi (Changjiang), 7,000 to 8,000-year-old ceramic vessels, red and even black clayware with comb and rope patterns have been found. The Yangshao and Longshan cultures of the 5th to 2nd millennium B.C. developed new types of vessels and a diver-

sity of patterns in red, black or brown; quasi-human masks and stylised fish were produced. Hard dense thin-walled stoneware, with kaolin and lime feldspar glazes, was created. Light grey stoneware with light grey-green to dark green glazes known as *Yue* ware – named after the kilns of the town of Yuezhou – were typical designs of the Han period. Even during the Tang dynasty, China was known in Europe and the Middle East as the "Home of Porcelain".

The most widespread form of ancient Chinese porcelain was known as *celadon*, a product of a mixture of iron oxide with the glaze which resulted, during firing, in the characteristic green tone of the porcelain. *Sancai* ceramics, i.e. ceramics with three-colour glazes from the Tang dynasty, became world famous. The colours were mostly strong green, yellow and brown. *Sancai* ceramics were also found among the tomb figurines of the Tang period in the shape of horses, camels, guardians in animal or human form, ladies of the court, and officials. The Song period *celadons* – ranging in colour from pale to moss green, pale

Left, camel in three-colour glaze from the Tang Dynasty. **Right**, carving ivory.

blue or pale grey and brown tones, were also technically perfect. A technique from Persia was used for underglaze painting in cobalt blue (commonly known as Ming porcelain) as early as the Yuan period. Some common themes seen throughout the subsequent Ming period were figures, landscapes and theatrical scenes. At the beginning of the Qing dynasty, blue and white porcelain attained its highest level of quality. Since the 14th century, Jingdezhen had been the centre of porcelain manufacture. Today, relatively

clear emerald green is valued most highly. According to ancient legend, *Yu*, as the jewel is known, came from the holy mountains and was thought to be crystallized moonlight. In fact, jade came from Khotan which lies along the southern Silk Road.

Nephrite is quite similar to jadeite but not quite as hard and more common. During the 18th century, nephrite was quarried in enormous quantities in the Kunlun mountains. It comes in various shades of green (not the luminous saturated green of jadeite), rarely

inexpensive porcelain can be bought throughout China. However, antique pieces are still hard to come by because the sale of articles pre-dating the Opium Wars is prohibited.

Jade, with its soft sheen and rich nuances of colour, is China's most precious stone. Jade is not a precise mineralogical concept but comprises two minerals: jadeite and nephrite. The former is more valuable because of its translucence, greater density and hardness, as well as its rarity. The Chinese have known jade since antiquity but it became popular only in the 18th century. Colours vary from white to green, but there are also red, yellow and lavender jade. In China, a

in pure white, faint to strong yellow (both greatly valued) and black. The oldest jades so far discovered come from the neolithic Hemadu culture (about 5000 B.C.). The finds were presumably ritual objects. Circular disks called *Bi*, given to the dead to take with them, are frequently found. Later, the corpses of high ranking officials were clothed in suits made of more than 2,000 thin slivers of jade sewn together with gold wire. The ring disk, symbol of heaven, is still worn today as a talisman; and jade bracelets are believed to protect against rheumatism.

From about the 5th century, jade has been used to make ornaments and decorations. It has always been the noblest mineral substance for the Chinese. Since the 11th century, the Jade Emperor has been revered as the superior godhead in Daoist popular religion. In the jade carving workshops in present-day China, there are thought to be as many as 30 kinds of jade in use; this includes stones like white jade (nephrite), jadeite, agate and many others. Famous among the jade workshops are those in Qingtian (Zhejiang province), Shoushan (Fujian province), and Luoyang (Hunan province).

Lacquerware is attractive not only to the eye but also to the hand because no other material is as appealing to the touch. The bark of the lacquer tree (*rhus verniciflua*), which grows in Central and South China, exudes a milky sap when cut, which solidifies in moist air, dries and turns brown. This dry layer of lacquer is impervious to moisture, acid, knocks and scratches and is therefore ideal protection for materials like wood or bamboo.

The oldest finds of lacquered objects date

Masters of jade work include Zhou Shouhai from the jade carving establishment in Shanghai, and Wang Shusen in Beijing. The latter specializes in Buddhist figurines. In government shops, jade can be relied on as being genuine. On the open market and in private shops, however, caution is advised. Genuine jade always feels cool and cannot be scratched with a knife. Quality depends on the stone, its colour, transparency, pattern and other factors. If in doubt, an expert should be consulted.

Left, hand painting on porcelain in a factory. **Above**, precious ivory carving.

back to the 5th millennium B.C. To produce lacquerware, bowls, tins, boxes, vases, and furniture made of various materials (wood, bamboo, wickerwork, leather, metal, pottery, textiles, paper, etc.) are coated with a skin of lacquer. A base coat is applied to the core material followed by extremely thin layers of the finest lacquer which, after drying in dust-free moist air, are smoothened and polished. In the dry lacquer method, the lacquer itself dictates the form: fabric or paper is saturated with lacquer and pressed into a wood or clay mould. After drying the mould is removed and the piece coated with further layers of lacquer. Vessels, boxes and plates were already made in this way in the Han period.

During the Tang dynasty, large Buddhist sculptures were produced by the lacquerware process. If soot or vinegar-soaked iron filings are added to the lacquer, it will dry into a black colour; cinnabar turns it red. The colour combination of red and black, first thought to have been applied in the 2nd century B.C., is still considered a classic. In the Song and Yuan periods, simply shaped monochromatic lacquerware was most

highly valued. During the Ming period, the manufacture of lacquered objects was further refined. The cities of Beijing, Fuzhou, Guangzhou, Chengdu, Yangzhou and Suzhou were renowned for exquisite lacquerware which was enriched and decorated with carving, fillings, gold paint and inlay.

The carved lacquer technique, which began at the time of the Tang dynasty reached its highest peak during the Ming and Qing periods. The core, often of wood or tin, is coated with mostly red layers of lacquer. When the outermost coat has dried, decorative carving is applied with the knife pen-

etrating generally to the lowest layer so that the design stands out from the background in relief. Today, lacquerware is mainly produced in Beijing, Fuzhou and Yangzhou. The most well-known lacquerware is the Beijing work which goes back to the imperial courts of the Ming and Qing dynasties. Emperor Qianlong (1734-1795) had a special liking for carved lacquerware; he was even buried in a coffin magnificently carved using this technique.

The **cloisonné technique** – used to create metal objects with enamel decor – reached China from Persia in the 8th century A.D., was then lost and rediscovered in the 13th century. In the cloisonné technique, metal bars are soldered to the body of the metal object and these form the outlines of the ornamentation. The spaces between the bars are filled with enamel paste and fired in the kiln. Finally, metal surfaces not covered with enamel are gilded. During the Yuan dynasty, Yunnan was the centre of cloisonné production. However, the golden age of this technique was the Ming period. It was during this period that the techniques of melting enamel on porcelain was developed.

Ivory as a craft material is as old as jade and early peices can be traced to as far back as 5000 B.C. During the Bronze Age, wild elephants were not a rarity in North China. Some of them were tamed during the Shang dynasty. The old artist carvers regarded elephant tusks as a most desirable material from which to make jewellery, implements and containers. The once large herds of elephants in the South of China thus shrank to a small remnant, and eventually ivory had to be imported. Ming dynasty carvings exemplify the best craft skills and superior taste. During Qing times ivory carving was further refined. Beijing and Guangdong province were famous for such work. Today's centres for ivory carving are the cities of Beijing, Guangzhou and Shanghai. All the ivory are imported from Thailand and several African countries. When buying ivory in the People's Republic of China, keep in mind that its import is prohibited in many countries.

<u>Left</u>, golden globe of heaven, from the Qianlong period. <u>Right</u>, carving in nephrite.

"Fodder comes first, then morality" – this quote from Brecht illustrates an attitude that is still prevalent today in China, a country which, until quite recently, was repeatedly ravaged by famines. Even the phrase used by people greeting each other reflects the fact that food is of great importance in China – "*chiguolema?*" means "have you eaten yet?" and you will hear people saying it everywhere around the usual mealtimes.

Only around 10 percent of the entire area of China is arable land. This is very little compared to the size of the population, and it explains why – in densely populated areas like Sichuan and the provinces in the South-East – even the tiniest plot of land, which is not used for a building or a street, is used agriculturally. Every square centimetre needs to be cultivated, even if there is only enough space to grow one cabbage. This is also one of the reasons why there is very little dairy farming in China. On the one hand, it is very expensive to buy cows, and on the other hand, there are no pastures. The few cows there are, are usually kept in barns and fed on the little grass which is cut along train tracks and the sides of roads.

In cities like Beijing, it is now possible to buy milk, yoghurt and sour milk at certain shops. Beijing has adjusted to the demands of the resident foreigners, and many a Chinese has by now acquired a taste for yoghurt and considers it fashionable to be eating it. On the whole, however, it is still the rule that the animal proteins are largely replaced by products which have been derived from the soya bean.

No doubt most foreigners can, under normal circumstances, adjust to Chinese food very easily, for it is very varied and tasty. The Chinese, on the other hand, suffer if they cannot get their usual dishes and it is quite common for them to develop serious health problems if they eat European foods. Young people in the cities find it enjoyable to eat out in Western restaurants which are rare, not particularly authentic, yet terribly expen-

sive. Instead of sitting in tea houses, as they used to, the young prefer going to a cafe nowadays. We may find it somewhat surprising that the coffee is sometimes served in water glasses and the cake is eaten with chopsticks. Similarly the Chinese may find it amusing to see that their food is eaten on plates with knives and forks in Chinese restaurants in the West.

Finely shredded and cooked quickly

Lack of land and shortage of fuel are the reasons for the way in which the Chinese process and cook their food. The ingredients are usually chopped up very finely in order to reduce the time required for cooking. Cutting the food correctly is very important in Chinese cuisine. The names of everyday dishes are derived from the way in which the meat or vegetables are cut – usually in strips, slices or cubes.

For cutting up the food, the kitchen hatchet, which looks positively lethal, as well as a chopping board, are essential. The wok, the Chinese frying pan with the rounded base, has a particularly good shape for reducing cooking time, especially for the widely used stir-frying method. The wok also uses less oil for deep-frying and is also useful for steaming and boiling food. The basic Chinese kitchen is not complete without a ladle and spoon for stirring and steaming baskets, several layers of which are placed in the wok, useful for the preparation of several dishes at the same time.

The title of the chapter points to a prejudice which is still believed by many in the West, namely that the Chinese eat obscure things like snakes, so-called "thousand year-old eggs", dogs, cats and other similar odd things. The tourist travelling in the North, North-East, West or Central China will soon realise that this is not the case when he visits one of the restaurants to eat typically Chinese food away from the hotel.

The South of China, especially Guangzhou, is one exception. Even in other parts of China there is a well-known saying about the Cantonese: "The Cantonese eat everything with four legs, unless it happens to be a table;

Preceding pages: an enjoyable banquet around the fire pot. **Left**, packaged mooncakes on sale for the festival.

everything which flies, unless it happens to be an aeroplane; and everything which swims, unless it is a boat."

Snakes are a specialty in Canton and many restaurants display the delicacies alive in the window. The snake is not only considered a delicacy, but also a fortifying food, which like so many dishes is not only eaten for enjoyment or to relieve hunger, but for its positive effect on certain organs of the body, and on the entire well-being of a person; it even has healing properties. This effect of meat, vegetables or crabs, the sweet ones with puree from lotus kernels, bean or nut paste. In Guangzhou and in Hongkong they are often served for breakfast. As opposed to other areas of China, breakfast in these parts of the country is often taken in a restaurant. In large restaurants, small steaming baskets of *dim sum* are wheeled through the room on a trolley and a dish is chosen according to what appeals the most and payment is made according to the number of empty steaming baskets left on the table.

Spicy Sichuan food

food on the body, the mind and the soul must always be taken into consideration, and people have very definite ideas on when a certain food should be eaten and how much of it is beneficial.

Cantonese food

The Cantonese cuisine is one of the three most famous ones in China. It has a great variety of dishes, which are well-known throughout the country. The small delicacies made of pastry, called *dim sum*, are particularly appetising and come in all sorts of shapes; the savoury ones are filled with

Because the province is rather isolated, Sichuan has retained its typical and traditional gastronomic culture. The food in Sichuan is "*la*", which means spicy, as chillies are used in many ways, but it is also "*ma*" which is difficult to translate, but roughly means "numbing" – the feeling you have in your mouth after eating the Sichuan or flower chilli. This spice is used liberally. The most famous Sichuan dish, written of by the Tang poet Du Fu, is *mapo doufu*, which means "soya bean curd of the pock-marked old woman".

The proverbial spiciness of Sichuan food may also stem from the fact that the humidity in the area is very high throughout the year. This is particularly unpleasant in winter, when temperatures drop as far as below freezing point; as most of the houses do not have any heating, spicy food helps to keep the body warm for a few hours and avoid the danger of rheumatism.

One very enjoyable and unusual way to eat Sichuan food is from the fire pot (*huoguo*), which is particularly popular in Chongqing.

A wide selection of vegetables, meat, fish, soya bean curd or offal is displayed. Whatever is ordered is brought to the table washed and cut into small pieces. The pieces are then immersed in broiling broth using either chopsticks or a small strainer. The food is cooked very quickly, and in order to cool it off, each piece is dipped into a small bowl of sesame oil or a beaten egg.

This used to be considered a poor person's meal because it was a way of making cheap vegetables, low-quality meat and innards

There are entire streets with small restaurants, each with just two or three tables, specialising in *huoguo*. The *huoguo* pot rests in the centre of the table and is heated by a small gas burner which stands under the table. In the pot, there is a reddish brown broth, consisting mainly of chillies and Sichuan pepper. The pot is usually divided into individual sections, so that there is one for each person and even people who do not know each other can enjoy a meal together.

Left, a colourful shop selling spices in Chengdu. **Above**, making noodles is a particularly interesting skill.

like duck's intestine, cow's stomach, thickened pig's blood and so on more palatable. Nowadays, it is an enjoyable social occasion to eat around the fire pot. This Sichuan speciality is relatively expensive but certainly worthwhile.

The tea houses, which used to be very common in Sichuan, are once again popular and new ones have been sprouting everywhere. They provide a pleasant setting for observing and participating in the leisure time of the Chinese. It is mainly men who frequent the tea houses, where nothing but tea is served. Sometimes there are musicians who play, or story-tellers entertaining with

147

old or new stories. Pay a few fen for the tea leaves which is then placed in the tea cup; the person serving then pours on boiling water. Green tea, flavoured with jasmine leaves, is the most popular.

If more tea is required, simply overturn the lid of your bowl and this gesture will be understood as a request for more. Green tea can be used more than once, and it is said that the second brew is much better than the first. However, if you are a guest and your host has poured hot water onto the same tea leaves

Food in the North

The assumption that the Chinese eat mainly rice is proven wrong throughout the north of China. In this region, people generally prefer wheat products such as noodles, steamed dumplings (*mantou* or *baozi*) or *jiaozi* which are small pockets of dough filled with meat or vegetables, similar to the Italian ravioli; they are eaten boiled, steamed or fried. When times were bad, *jiaozi* were eaten on special occasions, especially during

more than three times, consider this as a delicate hint to leave.

Shanghai's cuisine

The cuisine of Shanghai and the provinces around it is certainly considered to be just as excellent as the two areas mentioned above. There are not as many unusual dishes, but there is a great variety of seafood. A slightly sweet taste is typical of the food found here. Not only the sea, but also the numerous rivers and lakes provide the ingredients for the delicious fish dishes, such as sweet and sour or crunchy deep-fried fish.

Chinese New Year, when the entire family help with the lavish preparations. Even today, this dish is prepared in a traditional manner, each piece of dough is still rolled out with a special rolling pin and filled by hand. Nowadays, almost any occasion is used as an excuse to prepare a meal of *jiaozi*.

The style of cooking in Northern China is rather plain compared to the sophisticated cuisine in other parts of the country. A large amount of onions and garlic is used, but it lacks the variety of vegetables which are available in the southern provinces. The reason for this is the climatic differences; even the capital Beijing experiences shortages in the supply of vegetables during the winter, and for weeks there may be nothing else but cabbages piled up along the streets and on market stalls.

As far as the variety of dishes is concerned, Beijing is exceptional, for groups of people from all over China have come to settle here over the centuries. The Emperor employed only the best cooks of the land, and a top cook was able to reach the rank of a minister. In the kitchens of the palace, dishes of exceptional quality were created, and they

dients which required the highest of skills from the cook and which only the emperor could afford. Nowadays, even an ordinary citizen can sample the so-called palace cuisine in special restaurants.

Enjoying a convivial Chinese meal

A Chinese meal is served in a slightly different order to a European one. It begins with cold starters made from vegetables, eggs and pickled meat; depending on the

soon became part of the culinary tradition throughout the Empire. They were varied and refined, yet the basic recipes have remained unchanged. It was in those kitchens that original recipes were invented and they now belong to the repertoire of a sophisticated cuisine: Peking duck, phoenix in the nest, mandarin fish, lotus crabs, terrine of puréed peas, rice crust soup, mu-shu pork, thousand layer cake – all delicious dishes. There were dishes made of unusual ingre-

Left, deciding who is to buy the next round of drinks. **Above**, even the most simple of meals is a social occasion.

occasion, they are often beautifully arranged on platters. Each guest has a bowl and chopsticks and can help himself to whatever he likes. In general, the food is brought to the table on serving dishes and guests are not served with individual portions.

The starters are not really regarded as part of the meal, but are meant to stimulate the appetite and are served with alcoholic beverages such as strong spirits or sweet wines (nowadays beer and Western soft drinks are quite common). There is no social drinking in China. There are no bars where people might go to meet and talk to friends over a drink. Privately, too, friends are never in-

149

vited just for a drink, except perhaps for tea.

"*Ganbei*" is the Chinese toast, an invitation to empty your glass in one go and then to turn it over as proof that you have done so. "*Manman chi*" (eat slowly) is what you would say instead of "enjoy your meal" and it is most appropriate at a banquet or if one is invited for a special occasion. After the starters, warm food is brought to the table. The host would never consider serving just one dish for everyone. There is always a selection of dishes, their number usually corresponds

roughly to the number of guests at the table.

The dishes are more or less the same size because of the quantity of food that can be prepared in a wok at one time. Try as they may, the guests at a party will often be unable to finish the food and at least a third of it will be left over. If all the food was eaten, the host would be considered mean and lose face.

When planning a meal, care is taken to serve as many meat dishes with vegetables as possible, at least one vegetable dish and also a fish dish, to have contrasting tastes and colours, and for the meal to appear harmoniously balanced. Thus a spicy dish may be followed by a less spicy one, a sour one by a slightly sweet one, etc. The Chinese like to serve fish because the word for fish (*yu*) sounds the same as the word for abundance, which the host either wishes to demonstrate or conjure up. The warm dishes are prepared and brought to the table throughout the meal, so that the person doing the cooking – even at a private house – is forced to spend all his or her time in the kitchen.

Everyone eats in a slow and measured manner, sampling a little of everything on the table. At the same time, there is drinking, chatting and even smoking. Rice is only served when faces begin to look flushed and glasses are finally emptied. The actual meal can now begin, the word for eating is "*chi-fan*", which literally means "to eat rice". The rule is to put plenty of rice into the eating bowl, and eat a good portion of the dishes on the table. Only at the end of the meal is the soup served, which is very light and helps to calm the stomach. The only exception is Guangzhou, where the soup is drunk at the beginning of the meal. Desserts as we know them do not exist, sweet dishes are served as one of the courses of the main meal.

Table Manners

There are few rules about table manners, and initially, Europeans may find it somewhat disturbing that people eat rather noisily. It must be remembered that a meal is a social occasion: helping a neighbour with dishes they have trouble reaching is common practice. It is advisable not to pick out the best pieces, but to help yourself from the side of a serving dish which is nearest to you. Apart from this, anything which adds to a feeling of well-being is allowed. There is no need to search helplessly for a plate to put aside bones or other debris. If there is none on the table, just put the debris on the table next to your bowl; in simple restaurants, the debris are simply spat out under the table. It is no wonder that sweeping the floor after clearing the tables is a well-established habit. Many a Chinese dining table looks like a battlefield after a meal.

Left, ducks waiting to be consumed. **Right**, *jiaozi*, the filled dumplings.

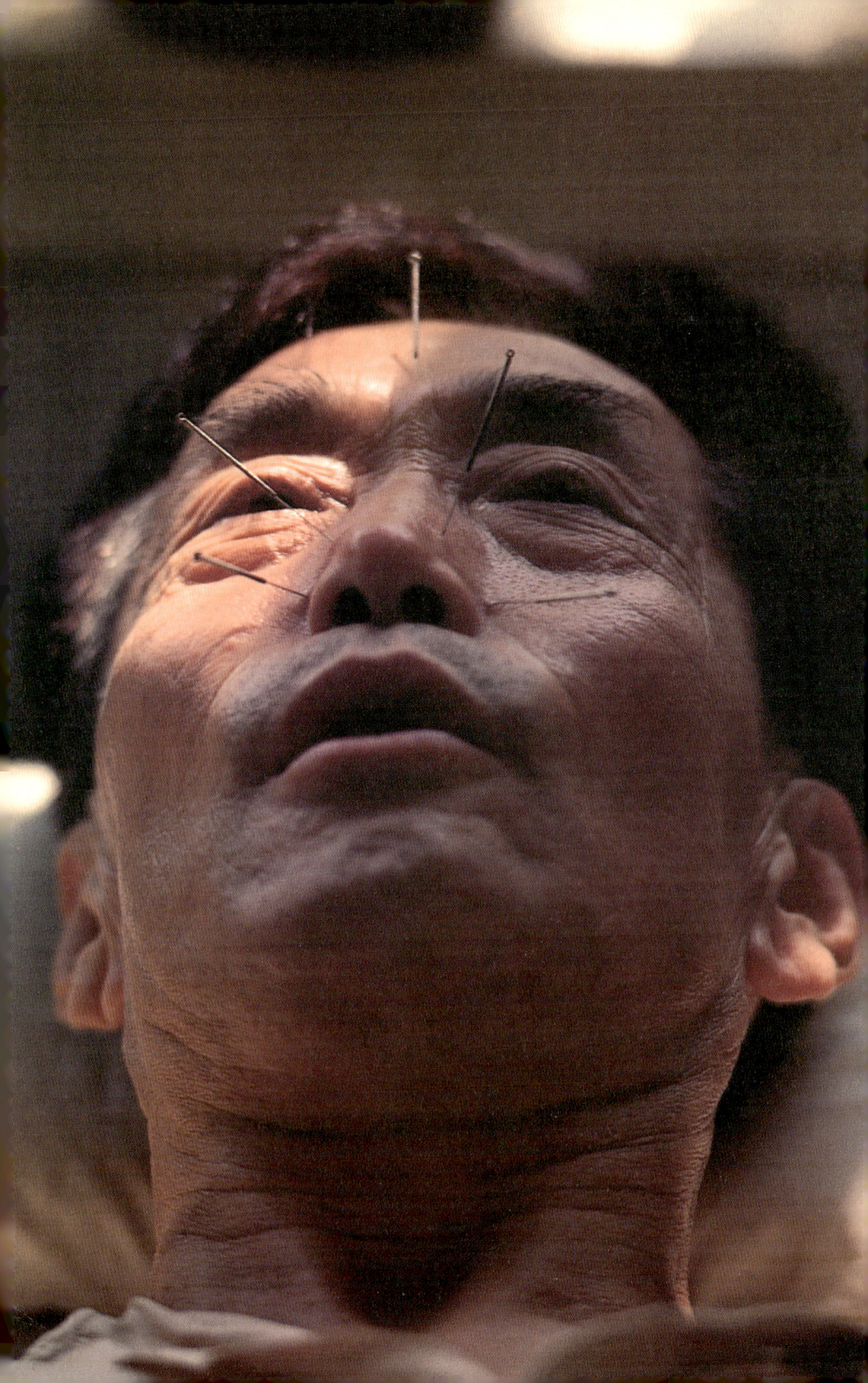

ENCOUNTER WITH CHINESE MEDICINE

Whenever "traditional Chinese medicine" is mentioned nowadays, we immediately think of acupuncture. We imagine that small needle, which has become increasingly popular all over the world in the last twenty years. Orthodox Western medicine is still somewhat reluctant to accept acupuncture as part of an alternative approach to medicine. However, there is hardly a "pain centre" anywhere in the Western world, which does not offer acupuncture as a therapy.

Yet medicine in China is not just traditional medicine. The tourist will be astonished to learn that Western medicine has taken first place in China, too. The large public hospitals in all the cities – called *Renmin Yiyuan* – use the Western approach to treatment (*Xiyi*) almost exclusively. The hospitals for Chinese medicine (*Zhonggi*) are smaller, less well equipped and harder to find.

The second surprising fact is that traditional Chinese medicine entails more than just acupuncture. The knowledge of remedies (*zhongyao*) is a very important factor. Patients are treated with different kinds of massage and chiropractics (*tuina*), as well as breathing and movement therapies, such as *tajiquan* (shadow boxing) and *qigong* (breathing therapy).

Thirdly, it is interesting to note that traditional medicine does not only take place within the walls of a hospital. When you are travelling through China, you will have many opportunities to observe – even in public places like the street or a park – the efforts the Chinese make to keep healthy.

When you wander through the streets of a Chinese town, you will again and again see farmers in the street selling a certain natural produce. Often you will not realize that this is a remedy, but think of it as food, for instance the *giou qize*, a small, oval-shaped fruit, which is carmine red and tastes rather bitter. You may be told that this "relieves congestion of the liver and gets rid of anger." If the look on your face remains blank, he

might add that it "is also beneficial against high blood pressure." Initially, the terminology used in Chinese medicine is incomprehensible to us, because we still differentiate very strictly between the body and the mind.

In the pharmacy

At some time during your stroll you will pass a traditional Chinese pharmacy, and you will be fascinated by its colourful

display. You will see the well-known ginseng root, dried or immersed in alcohol, and you will notice that it really does look like a human figure. The character for ginseng contains the sign *ren* which means person. You will also recognise the acupuncture needles and the cupping glasses made of glass or bamboo. Pluck up your courage and go into the pharmacy and you will be met by a unique smell, or rather a mixture of 1,001 scents. No, you have never been in a pharmacy like this! And let us assume that you are in the famous Tongrentang pharmacy which was founded in 1850 and lies in the old City of Beijing, South of Tiananmen. First of

Left, needles for relieving pain and healing. **Right**, with the help of special charts, this young doctor explains the position of the acupuncture points.

all, you will have to get accustomed to the enormous size of this pharmacy and the overwhelming selection of remedies. What are the small and large eggs, the snakes wound up in spiral shapes, the dried monkeys, the toads, tortoises, centipedes, grasshoppers, the small fish, the octopuses, the stags' antlers, the horns of rhinoceroses, the testicles and penises of animals doing in a pharmacy? And the thousand kinds of herbs, blossoms, leaves, berries, mushrooms and fruits, all dried, roasted or conserved and

So it is hardly surprising that people began to search for a solution to the endless strife. Innumerable thinkers, philosophers and social reformers with as many diverse ideas emerged, this is often referred to as "hundred schools". It was the time when ideas were born which were to influence all aspects of life in China for the next 2,000 years – and this included medicine. The two most important schools of thought at the time were those of Confucianism and Daoism. They shared the wish for peace and harmony, but their

stored by another method? Are these supposed to be medicines? In fact, there is hardly a plant, mineral or an animal substance in China, which is not used as a remedy. The *Encyclopaedia of the Traditional Chinese Pharmacopoeia* published in 1977 has 2,700 pages listing 5,767 substances with medical properties. The foundations of traditional Chinese medicine were laid during the last two hundred years before Christ, in the era of the Warring Empires, a time in which China was split up into many quarreling princedoms.

This stage in Chinese history, marked by fighting and misery, lasted a few centuries.

views on how this was to be achieved differed. Harmony was interpreted as the interaction of opposite forces, for example the adjustment of human behaviour to ecological and social conditions. If this harmony was interfered with, the disturbance would result in social or physical illness. The theory of the opposite forces of *yin* and *yang*, the theory of the "five phases of change" and the concept of *qi* were the most influential within the far-reaching theoretical background to traditional Chinese medicine. They formed the framework within which medical thinking took place.

At a time when one could only rely on very

little knowledge of anatomy and biology, these theories provided points of reference. They enabled people to observe not only the relationship of the human microcosm to the macrocosm of the environment, but also the effect which physical and emotional changes have on each other. Thus the feeling of fury was related to the wind which can come up very suddenly and with elemental force; fury was also brought into connection with a sour type of taste, with muscles and sinews which become cramped due to

ideas on anatomy, as anatomical research was never carried out. Nowadays, the Chinese will usually visit a doctor trained in Western medicine if they feel that they are seriously ill and wish to be diagnosed. If no organic failure is found, the patient will go and see a traditional doctor who is far more likely to be able to restore the lost harmony.

Acupuncture is certainly not a cure for everything and seldom performs the miracles which were often attributed to it in the past. In one aspect, however, its effect is un-

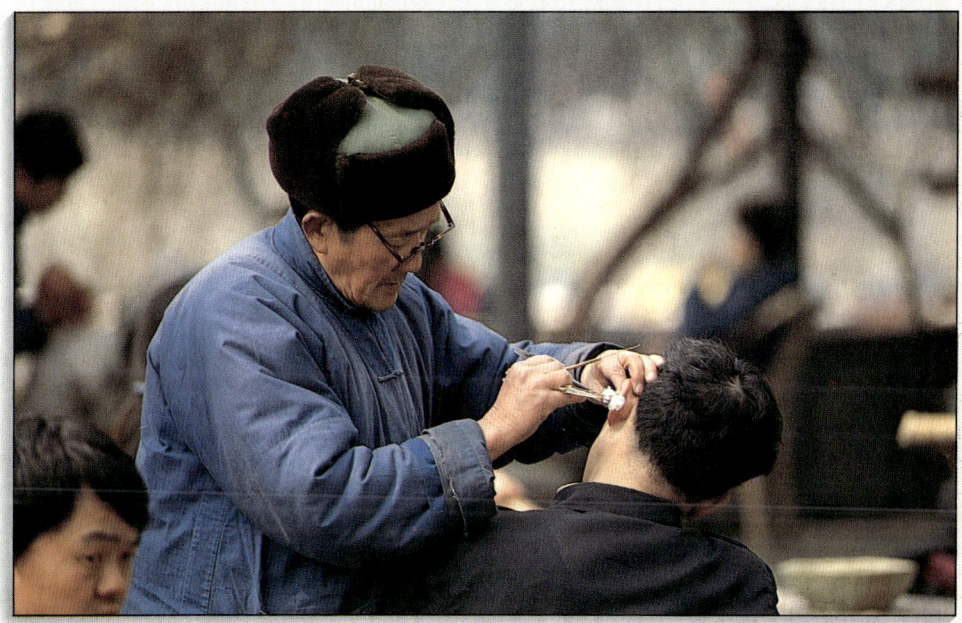

aggression. The *Inner Classic of the Yellow Emperor,* which is around 2,000 years old, also mentions that people with gall bladder problems must have fallen ill due to unsatisfied ambition and pent-up anger. A special form of medicine developed in China, which concentrated particularly on the functional expressions of our bodies.

Chinese medicine had some weaknesses, it never developed any surgery which can be taken seriously, and there are many incorrect

Left, Chinese pharmacies often look more like herb shops. **Above**, self-employed helpers care for personal hygiene.

disputed and valued by a billion Chinese, namely in the relief of pain. While our patients rely on drugs with various side effects, the Chinese go to the acupuncturist. Many cases of acute pain in the back can be cured by sticking just one needle in the *renzhong* point between the top lip and nose! Chronic problems, however, require a longer healing process inspite of acupuncture.

A new form of painless acupuncture is that of ear acupuncture done without needles. Small round seed kernels are stuck onto certain points of the ear and massaged by the patient himself every so often. This method is not only very successful in the treatment of pain, but also relieves allergic complaints such as hay fever.

When you enter an acupuncture clinic, you will notice the similar 1,001 scents of a Chinese pharmacy, this is the typical smell of the *moxa* herb which is the same as Artemisia (mugwort). It is considered especially helpful in the treatment of illnesses which, in Chinese medical terminology, are classified as "cold", for example stomach and digestive complaints without fever, certain rheumatic illnesses, chronic pains in

the back, cramped shoulder and necks, etc. The mugwort is formed into small cones and placed on slices of fresh ginger; then it is made to grow slowly, the plant, with its beneficial effect, is placed on to the acupuncture point. Alternatively, it is placed on the end of an acupuncture needle (the so-called "hot needle"), or it is made into the shape of a cigar and rolled back and forth over the skin of the patient.

At some stage during your trip you should definitely make a point of visiting a park at six o'clock in the morning. There you will come across groups of people doing certain exercises together. The most common type

of exercise is *taijiquan*, the so-called shadow boxing. You will probably not be familiar with the *qigong* exercise, which is often translated as breathing therapy in the West. With certain exercises, which may or may not involve conscious breathing, the patient learns to control his *qi* and thus to influence the course of a particular illness. The *qi* is a person's vital energy. Guiding one's *qi* means becoming aware of any part of the body, understanding it and being able to influence it. So there is also a psychological aspect to the *qi*.

During the Cultural Revolution *qigong* was actually forbidden because it resembled "superstitious" practices too closely. Yet in 1980, new *qigong* groups sprang up everywhere. It was a lay movement which soon gained a large following. Some forms of *qigong* involve hardly any movement, breathing and "sinking into oneself" are of prime importance. Other forms, like the "wild goose *qigong*", entail a lot of movement and are very aesthetic. The changes of the mental and emotional state follow a certain pattern of movement. The most extreme of these forms is the "crane *qigong*" which causes violent, sometimes even cathartic emotional outbursts with many patients. They scream, cry or laugh, dance and jump around. They experience what the Chinese call *fagong*: to abandon oneself to spontaneous movements. At the sight of the crane *qigong*, our pre-conceived ideas about the quiet and introverted Chinese become somewhat shaken up. The popularity of *qigong* is a clear indication that medicine in China is very much alive and open to further developments. It also proves that many types of traditional practice were suppressed for the last forty years, because they were not in keeping with the high school of traditional Chinese medicine.

Some methods, which Daoist temple healers and *shamans* had practised for centuries are nowadays only kept alive amongst Chinese groups living outside the People's Republic of China.

Left, teams of doctors give free check-ups on the street. Right, exercising with heavy balls is supposed to keep one young and mentally fit.

Since the beginning of the 1980s, *wushu* mania has swept through China; all over the parks and in the streets you will encounter youngsters handling swords and sticks and making strange movements. Night after night, Chinese television shows one of the many *wushu* films with titles like *The Shaolin Monastery*, *The Sons of Shaolin* or *The Wudang Mountains*. Whole series, which usually combine classical martial arts with patriotic themes, attract viewers of all ages – even in far-off Tibet. Early in the morning, there will be older people practising *taijiquan* in the parks; others may be doing *qigong* exercises. Even before going to work or school, young people do their training with swords and lances, trying to emulate the acrobatic movements of their screen heroes.

The **Shaolin Monastery** in the Songshan Mountains near Luoyang is the home of all Asian martial arts. Today, even followers of kung fu from abroad make their pilgrimages to the monastery. The bald-headed Shaolin monks, well-known for their inimitable shaolin boxing, have recognised the signs of the times and opened a training centre for foreigners in the vicinity of the monastery. For a hefty fee, they will be taught *shaolin* fighting techniques. In the traditional *wushu* centres – for instance in the district of Gong'an in Hunan province, in the Cangzhou district in the Heibei province and the Jinan region in Shandong province – around 40 percent of the population, and 70 percent of young people, practise one of the numerous Chinese martial arts. In the meantime, karate, shadow boxing, *qigong*, etc. have become leisure activities on offer in many European and American cities. In shadow boxing classes, and in kung fu courses, the stressed city dweller in the Western city is introduced to the secrets of Asian combat and meditation techniques.

Be it kung fu or karate, taekwando or judo, they all originated in ancient China. They were originally used as techniques in the fight of one man against another, yet nowadays they are used primarily for physical

Left, shadow boxing to loosen weary limbs.

training and strengthening of willpower. Many a Chinese youngster dreams of becoming as perfect as that monk and abbot from the Baoguangsi monastery near Chengdu, who is still able to do a handstand on two fingers even at an advanced age.

A variety of self-defence techniques

Wushu – simply "the art of fighting" in English – is the overall term for all these self-defence sports, some of which may be carried out with the fists or the legs, or with the help of swords or lances. The mastery of the various techniques used to entail very esoteric knowledge, which would only be passed on within a family, or a monastery, or from master to pupil. Nowadays, *wushu* is a national sport in the People's Republic of China, with competitions taking place every year. In the first half of this century, all types of *wushu* – just like traditional Chinese medicine – were less widely known; during the time of the Cultural Revolution, they were considered relics of feudalism and therefore despised. Since the 1950s, the martial arts have enjoyed increasing popularity.

For an outsider, the variety of *wushu* styles is very confusing and they are best grouped into four categories: fighting with hands or fists, fighting with swords and other weapons, training in pairs, and training in a group. The various fighting patterns use clever combinations of attack and defence, advance and retreat, movement and silence, acceleration and slowing down, hardness and elegance, pretence and reality.

One *wushu* technique is "long boxing" or *changquan* which depends very much on dexterity and speed and is particularly popular with children and youngsters. Another technique is imitation boxing *xingyiquan*, which favours forceful and balanced movements and is therefore popular with middle-aged people. *Nanquan*, the Southern style of boxing, combines all schools South of the River Yangzi and is characterised by small jumps and strong arm movements, often accompanied by loud screaming. *Nanquan* boxing is based on the movements of tigers, leopards, snakes and cranes. This is to some extent also true of *shaolin* boxing, which is more common in the North and originated in the Zen Buddhist Shaolin monastery.

Of drunks, monkeys and cranes

The monk Bodhidarma, who founded the Shaolin monastery, came to the Songshan mountains in the year 527. He realised that many Buddhist monks were unable to keep up demanding meditation exercises in which *wushu* still has to offer today.

The monks of Shaolin have made history several times. They served as bodyguards to the Tang Emperor Li Shimin (626-649) and helped him defeat his rivals. During the Ming Dynasty, *shaolin* boxing was introduced in Japan; there it merged with existing martial arts, *jiujitsu* for instance, and became the famous martial art judo ("the soft path" in English). Other martial arts which were also influenced by or developed from *wushu* are the Japanese *karate* and

complete quiet and concentration. Based on observations of the movements of animals, Bodhidarma is said to have developed an exercise which he described as "method of physical training", and this in turn became the origin of *shaolin* boxing. This type of boxing must surely be one of the most sophisticated Asian martial arts. *Shaolin* karate, as opposed to many other approaches, applies very hard blows geared primarily to attacking the opponent. Exercises like the "drunks boxing", in which the *shaolin* fighter feigns drunkenness, or the "monkey boxing" and the "crane boxing" are amongst the most meaningful exercises

aikido, *taekwando* in Korea, *siamqu* in Thailand and the *art of stick fighting* in the Philippines. Even today, there is a sport called *tangshoudo* in Korea, which means "the Tang way of boxing" and clearly refers to its origin in the Chinese Tang Dynasty.

Wushu can also be grouped into an "inner direction" and an "external direction". The latter includes the martial arts mentioned above and the *shaolin* boxing, which is also known as kung fu abroad. Kung fu simply means a fighting competition. If someone is a good fighter, one says that he has real kung fu technique. The films from Hong Kong with Bruce Lee made *shaolin* kung fu popular in the West.

In stark contrast to this is *taijiquan*, shadow boxing, which takes an "inner" approach. *Taijiquan* is a gentle method which aims to dispel the opponent without the use of force and with minimal efforts. It is based on the Daoist idea that the principle of softness will ultimately overcome hardness. According to legend, it is also – just like *shaolin* boxing – derived from observing the movements of animals. A monk who lived in the remote mountains

attack and to let it disappear into thin air. *Taijiquan*, with its quiet, flowing movements, has begun to conquer the world. In China it is mainly older people who use it for meditating and strengthening the body, it was originally a method of self-defence.

It has been proven that shadow boxing dates back around 300 years. It developed from the self-defence techniques which were inspired by Daoism. In the 17th century, when China was ravaged by battles and civil wars, *wushu* was widely used as a

some 600 years ago is said to have observed the fight between a snake and a crane. While the crane put all his energy into fast, hard blows, the snake adroitly avoided the crane until he was so exhausted that the snake won the fight. The monk interpreted this as a confirmation of his Daoist beliefs that soft, round and flexible is superior to the hard. Based on this he developed a method with slowly circling movements which are geared to breaking the momentum of the opponent's

Left, shadow boxers like the early hours of the morning best (Hangzhou, Western Lake). Above, synchronised exercises in a group.

method of self-defence. New techniques were emerging, and at the end of the 18th century, Wang Zongye developed the *taijiquan* style.

Initially, *taijiquan* was only known in the villages of the Henan province; the village of Chenjiagou in the Wen district of the province is said to be the place where *taijiquan* originated. It was here that Chen Wanting developed the earliest forms of *taijiquan* which were then passed on from generation to generation within the Chen family. Chen's contribution to further developing the *wushu* towards shadow boxing was in adding new techniques of

161

fighting to the existing ones. On the one hand he introduced the *daoyin* technique (which concentrated on training the inner forces), on the other hand the *tuna* (breathing exercise). These methods for perpetuating life stem from Daoism and can be traced back to the 6th century A.D. By merging external techniques with inner concentration the basis was created for shadow boxing which still exists today: the unity of body and mind in motion, meditation in the movement, and the simultaneous development of inner and

slowly and breathing must be controlled and allowed to circulate freely. Through consistent practise of *taijiquan* one eventually comes very close to the ideal of Daoism, namely the *wuwei* (doing without a purpose).

The art of peaceful fighting

Taijiquan may be relaxing, but it requires heavy concentration. The name *taiji* is a concept in classical Chinese philosophy

outer forces. Lastly, shadow boxing depends on the application and mastery of the life energy *qi*, which can be directed to all parts of the body with the help of mental training. *Qi* must flow and circulate freely in the body. The round movements of *taijiquan* is derived from this – they can be firm or loose, hard or soft, be directed forwards or backwards, but the movement must always be smooth and flowing. The circulation of the *qi* around the body is achieved by standing in a particular position, the centre of which is below the navel. The trunk remains upright, and all the movements stem from the central point. The movements are carried out very

which is used to describe the highest point in the sky (the pole) or the upper side of a cube. *Taiji* is therefore the principle around which everything revolves, like the centre of a circle which always remains in the same position even if the circle itself turns. The most important aspect of *taijiquan* is the central point below the navel.

In the middle of the 19th century, *taijiquan* became known in Beijing and thereafter all over the country. The four most important schools of *taijiquan* are the *yang* style with its quiet relaxed movements, the *wu* style with compact, gentle movements, the quick and nimble *sun* style and the traditional *chen* style. From the *yang* style, the most popular of these, a form with 24 different movements was developed and this is commonly seen all over the People's Republic. Like with many other *wushu* techniques, the individual movements have been given names which point to their origin: "the white crane spreads his feathers", "beautiful woman at the loom", "parting the mane of a wild horse", "catching the bird by the tail", etc.

Taijiquan can also be practised with swords and other weapons, or indeed with a

partner. For fighting with weapons, one of the four categories of *wushu*, there are several sub-categories: long cutting or stabbing weapons like spears, sticks and wide swords; short weapons like daggers, short swords and hooks; and flexible weapons like the whip with nine sections, the stick in three parts and the hammer chain, a chain at either end of which a piece of iron in the shape of a hammer is attached.

In a wider sense, *qigong* (i.e. breathing

Left, a master of *qigong* throttling himself with an iron wire. **Above**, *qigong* artists can swallow swords as far up as the handle.

technique) is also part of *wushu*. Records show that it dates back 3,000 years. In *qigong*, certain techniques for regulating the breathing in prescribed positions can bring about concentrated thinking and a state of inner calm; if applied to specific cases, it can improve health and prolong life. There is also a more difficult version of *qigong*, called *liangong*, with which artists can perform amazing feats: lorries roll over the rib cage, stones are broken on their heads, iron bars broken off with a foot or the head, etc. All *wushu* methods, especially the gentle ones, rely on regulating the breathing and letting energy circulate freely.

For psychosomatic illnesses in particular – but not exclusively for these – *wushu* techniques are being used therapeutically. There are, for instance, experiments being carried out in the People's Republic of China using various *qigong* breathing exercises to treat cancer patients. Studies carried out by Chinese doctors show that *taijiquan* is successful in treating many illnesses. Regular practise ensures that the spine retains its natural posture and inner structure. *Taijiquan* has a positive effect on the metabolism; amongst other things, it lowers the cholesterol level. High blood pressure is far less common amongst people practising *taijiquan*, and it is beneficial for the prevention of arteriosclerosis. Depending on age, anyone of these methods can be practised, provided training is done on a regular basis. For the methods using the "external approach", the body needs to be moderately supple, while exercises from the "internal" method can be learnt even at an advanced age. One can take it up for health or therapeutic reasons, but also in order to gain a new attitude to life.

Those who learn *taijiquan* as a martial art must never forget one thing: the highest honour is not to beat one's opponent, but to avoid a fight altogether. Students are accepted based on their attitudes and way of thinking. It is said that *taijiquan* can make one supple like a child, healthy like a woodcutter, and calm like a wise man. So why not try it yourself sometime? Just go and join a group of people in the park and copy the *taijiquan* movements.

Barnaul
Abakan
Čeremcho
Karaganda
Rubcovsk
Bijsk
Semipalatinsk
RUSSIA
Irk
KAZAKHSTAN
Ust'-
Kamenogorsk
Balchaš
Lake
Zaysan
MONGO
Lake
Balkhash
Cimkent
Džambul
Taškent
Namangan
Alma-Ata
Ürümqi
G
O
KYRGYZSTAN
TIAN
SHAN
TAJIKISTAN
Kashi
(Kashgar)
Shache
PAKISTAN
Yumen
KUNLUN
SHAN
Islāmābād
Golmud
Xining
Amritsar
Lahore
Ludhiāna
Ludhiāna
H
I
M
XIZANG ZIZHIQU
CHINA
Delhi
Morādābād
(TIBET AUT. REGION)
Chen
Bareilly
A
Jaipur
Aligarh
L
Lhasa
Agra
Ganga
A
NEPAL
Y
Jhānsi
Kañpur
Allahābād
Kathmandu
A
Dibrugarh
Bhopāl
Vārānasi
Patna
BHUTAN
Indore
Jabalpur
Brahmaputra
INDIA
BANGLADESH
Gauhati
Nāgpur
Dacca
Kunming
Amrāvati
Howrah
Raipur
Calcutta
Chittagong
Geji
Mandalay
Cuttack
Hyderābād
BURMA
LAO
Rājahmundry
Vishākhapatnam
Bay of Bengal
Chiang Mai
Guntūr
THAILAND
Viangcha

RUSSIA

Lake Baikal
Ulan-Ude
Čita
Blagoveščensk
Chabarovsk
Amur
Manzhouli
Bei'an
MANCHURIA
Songhua
Shuangyashan
Ulaanbaatar
Qiqihar
Harbin
Baicheng
Changchun
Vladivostok
Nachodka
Ch'ŏngjin
Sea of Japan
Shenyang
Fushun
Jinzhou
Kimch'aek
Baotou
Hohhot
Zhangjiakou
Dandong
NORTH
KOREA
Huang He
(The Yellow River)
Datong
Beijing
(Peking)
KOREA
BAY
P'yongyang
Yinchuan
Taiyuan
Tianjin
Dalian
BO HAI
Kyoto
Seoul
SOUTH
KOREA
Ōsaka
zhou
Jiaozuo
Shijiazhuang
Jinan
Qingdao
Pusan
Hiroshima
Kitakyūshū
Baoji
Zhengzhou
Xuzhou
Huang He
(The Yellow River)
Kwangju
Fukuoka
Nagasaki
Miyazaki
Xi'an
Yellow Sea
JAPAN
Hefei
Nanjing
East China Sea
Nanchong
Chang Jiang
(Yangzi River)
Yichang
Wuhan
Chang Jiang
(Yangzi River)
Shanghai
Hangzhou
Chongqing
Jingdezhen
Ningbo
Zigong
Nanchang
Zunyi
Changsha
Shaoyang
Hengyang
Fuzhou
Pacific Ocean
Guiyang
T'aipei
Chilung
TAIWAN
Shaoguan
Xiamen
T'ainan
Liuzhou
Guangzhou
(Canton)
Shantou
Kaohsiung
Xun Xi
Nanning
Macau
Hongkong
(Xianggang)
-noi
Hai-phong
Gulf of
Tonkin
Zhanjiang
Haikou
South China Sea
Philippine Sea
PHILIPPINES
China
TNAM
Hainan
500 km

ONE LOOK IS WORTH
A THOUSAND WORDS

For more than a millennium there was only one link between Europe and China: the land route via the ancient Silk Road. The ancient Greeks provided the first reports of a people that lived even further east than the Scythians and who produced silk. Silk may have been the first product to establish the trade between East and West. Exchanges of culture followed those of goods: Islam and Buddhism arrived in the Middle Kingdom via the Silk Road.

In the early 16th century, new worlds opened up to the Europeans, as Portuguese ships sailed as far as the South China coast and began to trade with the Chinese from the Portuguese base in Macau. The missionaries who followed them and travelled into China left records of the first maps. Only the scale of the coastline is correct on these maps – the further they go into the interior, the more distorted the cartography becomes.

There are no blank spaces left in China today. We have countless books which describe China to us, and yet all those words can never replace our own experiences. One look is indeed worth a thousand words. Nearly all areas are open to tourists. Travelling in China is no longer an undertaking that puts your life in danger, even if faults in the infrastructure do not make journeys equally comfortable in all regions. As a rule, you will have more problems to deal with the farther you travel into the interior.

When describing the travel routes in this book, we have decided on self-contained descriptions of geographical areas, making use of our experience creating and supervising travel routes. China is in no way a monolithic culture. The influence of Han Chinese civilisation may seem overwhelming, but the colourful, lively culture of the south west, the deep religious feeling of Tibet, or the eastern Turkic culture of Xinjiang, are just as much a part of China. If you travel to China often, you will get to know the differences in outlook between the north and the south, with the Yangzi river, in a sense, acting as a boundary. However, this variety cannot be seen at first glance. China is worth more than just one trip.

BEIJING – THE NORTHERN CAPITAL

In traditional Chinese thought, the world was not imagined as the flat, round disk of the Ptolomaean vision in the West, but was conceived as a square. A city, too – and especially a capital city – was supposed to be square, a reflection of the cosmic order and following its geometrical norms. In no other city in China has this basic idea been realised as completely as in ancient Beijing.

The country around Beijing was already settled in prehistoric times, proven by the discovery in the little town of **Zhoukoudian** of the skull of *Sinanothropus pekinenes* (Peking Man). Since A.D. 1000, the city has served as a main or subsidiary residence for a series of dynasties. Under the rule of the Mongol emperor Kublai Khan in the 13th century, it was known as Khanbaliq (the city of the Khan) and flourished as an especially splendid and magnificent winter residence of the emperors.

The city did not receive its typical form, which still survives today, until the rule of the Ming dynasty. The Emperor Yongle is considered its actual planner and architect. In 1421 he moved his seat of government from Nanjing to the city of Beiping (Northern Peace), renaming it Beijing (Northern Capital), which, in a rather unfortunate attempt at Romanisation, became known as Peking in the West.

The plans of the third Ming emperor, Yongle, followed the principles of geomancy, the traditional "doctrine of winds and water", which strive to attain a harmonious relationship between human life and nature. Screened from the north by a semi-circle of hills, Beijing lies on a plain that opens to the south. In an analogue to this position, all important buildings in the city are built to face the south, protected from harmful *yin* influences from the north such as the

Siberian winter winds or the enemies from the steppes, for it was in the south that the generosity and warmth of the *yang* sphere was thought to reside. As a result, it was not by chance that Qianmen, the Outer or Southern Gate to the city, was the largest, most beautiful, and most sacred of its kind. The Coal Hill (Jingshan) to the north of the Imperial Palace, which when the air is clear has a beautiful view of the rooftops of Beijing, was probably created according to geomantic considerations.

A line from north to south divides the city into an eastern and western half, with a series of buildings and city features laid out as mirror images to their equivalents on the opposite side of the city. For instance, the **Altar of the Sun** (Ritan) has its equivalent in the **Altar of the Moon** (Yuetan). Planned in an equally complementary way were Xidan and Dongdan, the eastern and western business quarters, which today still serve as shopping streets.

Some of the most notable buildings of old and new Beijing are to be found on the gigantic symmetrical axis itself. Going from the north, the **Bell and Drum Towers** (Zhonglou, Gulou), the two huge clocks of the city, and the Coal Hill, from the south the **Outer Gate** (Qianmen), and more recently the **Mao Mausoleum** together with, on the **Square of Heavenly Peace** (Tiananmen), the "Monument to the Heroes of the Nation" are lined up one after the other like pearls on a string. In the middle of this chain of historically significant buildings lies the heart of ancient Beijing, the **Dragon Throne**, from which the Son of Heaven, holding the reins of political power and ritual mediator between Heaven and Earth – with his face turned to the south – attempted to steer the fate of his enormous empire. The seat of the emperor was considered the centre of the physical world, the Earth, which was imagined as a gigantic chessboard, its square and mostly walled elements are clearly given a defined place in a hierarchy de-

Left, entrance, at the Gate of Heavenly Peace, to the Imperial Palace beyond.

pending on how far they are removed from the centre. The imperial throne is embedded in a majestic palace, which is also square and surrounded by high purple walls on all sides – the **Forbidden City**. Around it lies the **Imperial City**, which in earlier times also formed a square surrounded by walls.

Part of the Imperial City was the huge chain of lakes, its northern part today forming the centre of the **Beihai Park**, while on the shores of the central and southern waters lies, since 1949, the **Government Quarter** (Zhongnanhai), the Party's Holy of Holies, which foreign observers like to call the "new Forbidden City", as only highly placed officials and important state guests are ever allowed in. Crowded around the Imperial City was a sea of mainly single-storeyed houses: the **Inner City**. Its roofs, curved like the crests of waves, were not allowed to rise above the height of the Imperial Palace. Here the

tasteful homes of the wealthy and influential officials were to be found, the houses of important Manchus, the elegant private residences of princes. Even nowadays, this part of Beijing is still considered to be the actual Inner City or old city. However, only a few monumental gates of the mighty defensive walls that once surrounded it have survived, gates such as the Qianmen mentioned above or, in the north, the Deshengmen. They tower up into the sky like impregnable fortresses, remains of a system of fortifications which had to make way for a fast-lane highway.

Adjoining the Inner City to the South was the **Outer City**. In Qing times, these two residential areas were known as the Tatar City and the Chinese City. In the Chinese City, the doors of the houses were lower, the *hutongs*, as the alleys of Beijing were known, were narrower, and the rice bowls were less well filled. Hot water was drunk instead of tea; people wore straw sandals on their feet instead of satin boots. However, bored officials and wealthy merchants, from time to time, liked to flee their respectable surroundings and come here. There were tea and opera houses, bathing houses and brothels, specialty restaurants and bazaars, all competing for the favours and money of tipsy literati, mahjong-playing monks, lusting mandarins, and from time to time, the occasional prince in disguise.

Even today, things are livelier to the south of the Outer Gate (Qianmen) than they are in other parts of the city. However, the little theatres are no longer reserved for the brilliantly painted and costumed performers of Beijing opera nor for supple acrobats. Kung fu films and trite romances bring in more money. The famous gourmet restaurants are usually hopelessly crowded. Dazhalan, a small street running at right angles to Qianmendajie, has old established shops and businesses of excellent reputation, is still an attraction for the people from the Beijing suburbs as well as the provinces. Not far away is **Liu-**

Left, gilded lions guard the entrances to the palace.

lichang, a shopping street restored to its original style for tourists, which offers almost everything that China can show by way of art and kitsch. The number one shopping district today is still Wanfujing, a street which runs in a northerly direction from the Beijing Hotel.

Outside these historic city districts, huge faceless concrete tower blocks have sprouted. In the north west lies the scientific and intellectual quarter with the most famous universities – the Beijing and Qinghua universities. The Chaoyang District to the east is the largest industrial area of the city. Traffic on the city streets is still dominated by the never-ending flow of bicycles. The local public transport system is insufficiently developed and hopelessly overcrowded. Up till now, the metro has not been of much help.

The rhythm of the seasons is similar to that in Central Europe. The summers, are hot and long, winters are cold and dry. When sandstorms whirl through the city in spring, Beijing hardly dares to breathe. The fine dust forces its way through all the cracks and crevices in the homes, which are badly insulated.

A morning walk through the park offers undreamed-of impressions and acoustic delights: the sound of a moon fiddle, accompanied by an aria from a Beijing opera, the chirping of birds, their cages hung in the trees, the sight of graceful sword dancers and noiseless *taiji* practitioners, and more recently gymnastics for the elderly, accompanied by disco music.

The Forbidden City

In the past, in the early morning when the fourth watch of the night was proclaimed by powerful strokes from the **Drum Tower** (Gulou), the mandarins in the Imperial City would push their silken bed curtains aside and step into

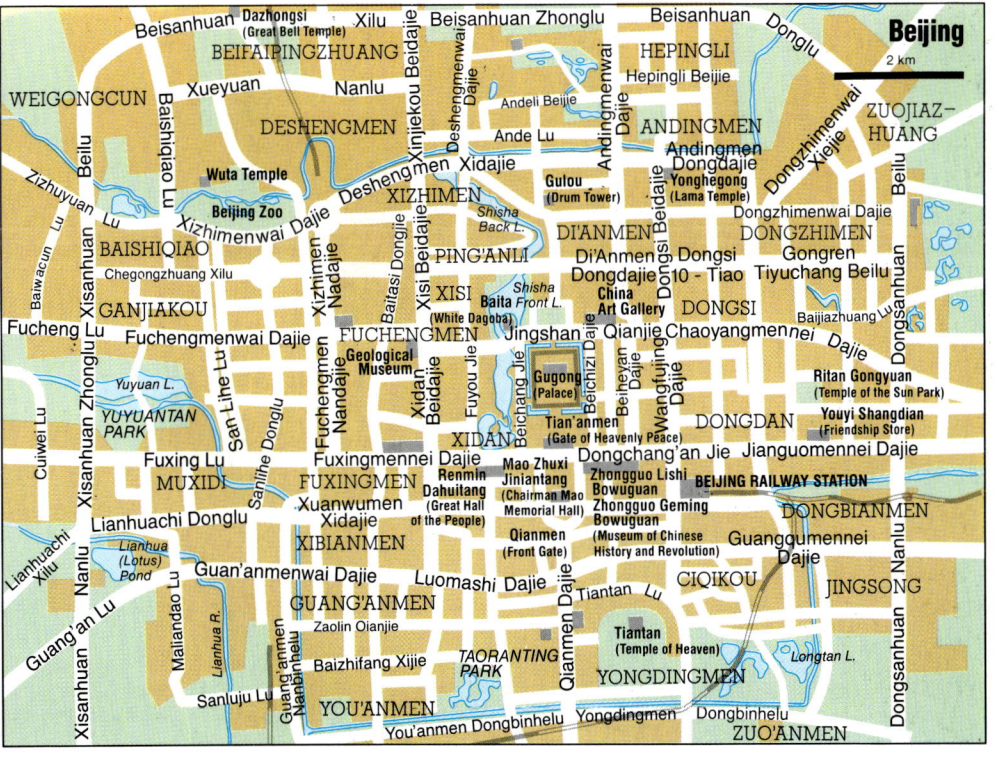

their swaying litters, which bore them to the imperial morning audience in the Forbidden City. A eunuch would show them their place arranged according to rank, and there, kneeling in silence, they would receive instructions from the Son of Heaven on the Dragon throne. This was Beijing in the 19th century.

Behind the walls, more than 30 ft (10 metres) high, and within the 164-ft (50-metre) broad moat, life in the Forbidden City (entrance was denied to ordinary mortals) was determined by a multitude of rules and taboos. Today, the gateway serves as a gigantic entrance for Chinese and foreign visitors; it leads to one of the most fascinating displays of Chinese cultural history, and to what is probably the best preserved site of classical Chinese architecture. In 1421, after 17 years of building works, the Ming Emperor Yongle moved into the palace, and up until the founding of the republic in 1911, the palace served as seat of government and residence for 24 emperors from the Ming and Qing dynasties, right up until the "Last Emperor" Puyi. It has 9,000 rooms in which an estimated eight to ten thousand inhabitants lived (among them some 3,000 eunuchs as well as maids and concubines), all within an area of 180 acres (72 hectares); it was a city within a city.

The whole site can be divided into two large areas: in the front (southern), the **Outer Court** (Waichao) and the rear **Inner Apartments** (Neiting). Approaching from the **Meridian Gate**, you will come first to the three great halls and courtyards of the outer area. The **Hall of Supreme Harmony** (Taihedian) is the first and most impressive of these, and at the same time it is the largest building in the Forbidden City. In its centre is the skilfully carved, gold-coloured Dragon Throne, from which the emperor would rule over the Middle Kingdom. This was where the most

The snow-covered square in front of the Hall of Supreme Harmony.

solemn ceremonies – such as the New Year's Festival or the enthronement of a new emperor – were held; the courtyard belonging to the building is supposed to hold 90,000 spectators. On the other side of the imposing architecture of the Outer Court, to the north and separated from it by the **Gate of Heavenly Purity** (Qianqingmen), lies a labyrinth of gates, doors, pavilions, gardens and palaces: the living accommodation of the imperial family. The emperor was the only potent male who could enter.

The centre of this private section is formed by the three rear halls (Sanhougong). However, the emperors did not live there after the Qinq period, but carried on state business primarily in front of the **Palace of Heavenly Purity** (Qianqinggong). However, the actual political decisions were taken in the interlinked rooms to the left and right of this palace, the **Six Eastern** and **Six Western Palaces**. Here the more influential eunuchs and concubines were rivals for power and influence within the nation, this was the scene of plots and intrigues and also of natural and unnatural deaths. The well right in the north east of the site, just behind the **Palace of Peace and Longevity** (Ningshougong), is closely connected with the tragic fate of the Pearl Concubine of the Emperor Guanxu, who, on 15 August 1900, dared to oppose the ambitious Empress Dowager Cixi and thereupon, rolled in a carpet, was thrown by eunuchs into the narrow shaft of a well.

Since 1925 the Eastern Palaces have served as exhibition rooms for the **Palace Museum** and has on display, bronzes, porcelain, scroll paintings and calligraphy. Nestling closely against the southern walls of the Forbidden City, the **People's Cultural Park** and the **Sun Yatsen Park** continue to display the impressive imperial architecture and landscaping. Today, both these sites serve as places for recreation and recuperation for the people of Beijing, plagued by stress and dust. In the Sun Yatsen Park there used to be a temple

honouring the gods of the earth and of fertility. The triumphal arch near the southern entrance was originally set up in a different place in honour of the German ambassador, Baron von Ketteler, who was murdered at the beginning of the Boxer Rebellion.

The former shrine of the imperial ancestors, now known as the **People's Cultural Park** and functioning as a kind of further education college, also dates from the Ming dynasty. Here the ancestral tablets of the imperial forebears, which the emperor was required to honour, were kept.

To the north west of the Forbidden City, in the grounds of today's **Behai Park** (Northern Lake Park), lay the winter residence of the Mongol emperor Kublai Khan. Only legends remain of his former palace on **Jade Island** (Qinghuadao). Nowadays this is the site of the **White Dagoba** (Baita), 115 ft (35 metres) tall, a Buddhist shrine in the Tibetan style dating from 1651. At the foot of the shrine, on the shores of the wide lake which dominates the park and gives it its atmosphere, you can enjoy the imperial cuisine in appropriate style in the Beijing gourmet restaurant Fangshan. The **Round Town** (Tuancheng) in the southern part of the grounds was once the administrative centre of the Mongol Yuan dynasty. From the Round Town you can get a good view of the **Southern and Central Lake** (Zhongnanhai), the seat of the Politbureau and the State Council.

The Square of Heavenly Peace

On 1 October 1949, Mao Zedong, Chairman of the Communist Party, proclaimed the founding of the People's Republic of China from the **Gate of Heavenly Peace** (Tiananmen). Today, his portrait gazes south from this spot to the Square of Heavenly Peace, which was quadrupled in size during the 1950s so that up to a million people can gather in the square. Innumerable rallies of the Red Guards took place here during the

Cultural Revolution. Incidents after the death of Zhou Enlai (1976) also became well known, presaging the fall of the "Gang of Four." In the centre of the square is an obelisk, unveiled in 1958, the **Monument to the Heroes of the Nation**, a perfect example of the Socialist Realism style, which symbolises the resistance of ordinary people to "feudal powers" and foreign colonialism. In 1959 the **Great Hall of the People** (Renmin Dahiutang), on the west side of the square, was officially opened. This is an impressive building in the Soviet Neo-Classical monumental style. The People's Congress meets here.

The massive facades of the **Museum of Chinese History** and the **Museum of the History of the Chinese Revolution** border the huge square to the east. Between 1949 and 1959, the heart of new China was built on and along the important north-south line, only a few yards to the south of the old imperial centre of power, the Forbidden City. After the death of the Great Chairman, the present consummation of this restructuring, the **Mao Mausoleum**, was added. Even today, when the teachings of the Little Red Book have long gone out of fashion and badges with Mao's portrait are sold off to tourists in fleamarkets like antiques, the youth of the nation, from all over the country, still file respectfully past the yellowing embalmed body in its glass coffin.

The great aesthete and Qing emperor Qianlong, who ruled from 1736 to 1795, had a huge masterpiece of landscaping and architecture created in the north west of Beijing. This is the **Old Summer Palace**, or as the Chinese call it, the **Garden of Perfect Purity** (Yuanmingyuan). One of the glories of these magnificent grounds were the palaces in the Western style, built according to plans by the Italian Jesuit Castiglione and based on European models such as, for example, the palace of Versailles. Only a few ruins remain today, for during the Second Opium War (1856-1860) British and French troops reduced the site to rubble and ashes.

The dynasty looked for a replacement, and found it in the grounds which had also been laid out by Qianlong, as a place of retirement for his mother. The new summer residence received its definitive form from the famous (and infamous) Empress Dowager Cixi, who realised a wonderful, if rather expensive, dream in 1888. With money that had actually been intended for the building of a naval fleet, she constructed the **Garden of Cultivated Harmony** (Yiheyuan), or **Summer Palace** as it is known in Chinese. It was a far cry from the sternness of the Forbidden City. Originally a concubine of the third rank, Cixi placed herself on the Dragon Throne after the death of the emperor and ruled in an unscrupulous and self-centred way for 50 years, in the name of her young child and one other child emperor.

As in every other classical Chinese garden, water and mountains (or rocks)

Below, the Hall of Prayer for Good Harvests in the Temple of Heaven. **Right**, the Tower of the Incense of Buddha in the Summer Palace.

180

determine the landscape: the **Kunming Lake** covers three quarters of the total area of more than 12 sq miles (30 sq km), and there is the **Hill of Longevity** (Wanshoushan). In order to make it more difficult for strangers to see into the grounds, the **Hall of Benevolence and Longevity** (Renshoudian) was built right next to the eastern gate (Dongmen), now the main gate. Behind it lay the private apartments of the Empress Dowager; today these rooms also house a theatrical museum. Here Cixi used to enjoy operatic performances by her 384-strong ensemble of eunuchs.

A small, light wooden construction, decorated with countless painted scenes from Chinese mythology, the **Long Corridor** (Changlang) runs parallel to the northern shore of the lake linking all the scattered buildings into one harmonious whole. It ends in the vicinity of the famous **Marble Boat** (Qiuyangfang), in which Cixi, looking out

over the lake, had tea. Over bridges and up stairs, through gates and halls, you come to the massive **Pagoda of the Incense of Buddha** (Foxiangge), which crowns the peak of the **Hill of Longevity**. Only a few visitors stray into this part of the Summer Palace, behind the Hill of Longevity. However, here, right in the eastern corner, is a special jewel of the classical Chinese art of garden design, the **Garden of Joy and Harmony** (Xiequyuan), a complete and picturesque copy of a lotus pool garden from the Wuxi district.

Twice a year, a splendid and magnificent procession of about 1,000 eunuchs, courtiers and ministers would leave the Forbidden City in a southerly direction for the **Temple of Heaven** (Tiantan). Only twice a year, then, would the western gate be opened for the emperor, and each time the Son of Heaven would spend a night fasting and remaining celibate in the **Palace of Abstinence**

The Bridge of Seventeen Arches over Lake Kunming in the Summer Palace.

(Zhaigong), before carrying out the ritual ceremonies of sacrifice the next morning. At the winter solstice he expressed thanks for the previous harvest, and on the 15th day of the first month – at the time of the Lantern Festival – he begged the spirits and gods of sun and moon, clouds and rain, thunder and lightning to bless the coming harvest.

Set in the middle of a park of 666 acres (270 hectares), the **Temple of Heaven**, an outstanding example of religious architecture in the Middle Kingdom, dates from the Ming period, but was destroyed several times after being struck by lightning and was last rebuilt in 1890. The temple complex has only been open to the public since 1949. The entire site is square, although the northern edge follows a semi-circle, a symbolic expression of the fact that the emperor, in offering his sacrifices, had to leave the square-shaped earth for the round-roofed heaven.

An exquisite example of Chinese wooden buildings, constructed without the use of a single nail, is the round, 128-ft (39-metre) high **Hall of Prayer for Good Harvests** (Qiniandian). The roof with its three levels, covered with deep blue tiles symbolising the colour of heaven, is supported by 28 pillars. The four most massive ones in the centre symbolise the four seasons; the double ring consisting of two twelve pillars represents the 12 months plus the traditional divisions of the Chinese day, each comprising of two hours. In the south of the park lies a white, circular marble terrace, the **Altar of Heaven** (Hianqiutan), and also the **Echo Wall**, famous for its acoustics, against which the tourists press their ears in order to hear the messages whispered at the other end.

As an imperial city, the Beijing of Ming and Qing times was not just a favoured place for magnificent palaces and broad parks. Here, also, the great religions of China, this country of many peoples, had their most impressive sacred buildings. Many of the Buddhist, Daoist, and Tibetan shrines, many mosques and churches, and the majority of the small temples, mostly dedicated to local gods, have been destroyed since 1949 or have been turned into factories, barracks or schools. Since the socialist revolution the religious element of everyday life in Beijing has been pushed into the background. However, the most historically important religious sites are being restored and have been reopened to the public.

The **Temple of the Source of Buddhist Doctrine** (Fayuansi), a Buddhist shrine dating from the 7th century, is probably the oldest surviving temple in the city, situated in the south western Xuanwumen district. Today it serves as a training centre for Buddhist novices. Just around the corner, in the appropriately named Cattle Street (Niujie) – after all, Muslims don't eat pork – is the oldest **mosque** in Beijing. The architectural style of the building, which is almost a thousand years old, is an interesting combination of traditional Chinese architecture with elements in an Arabic-influenced style.

The most magnificent and most elaborately-restored sacred building in Beijing must be the **Lama Temple** (Yonghegong) in the north east of the old city. Originally the private residence of a prince, it was turned into a monastery when its owner was promoted to emperor in 1723, for according to ancient Chinese custom the former residence of a Son of Heaven had to be dedicated to religious purposes once he had left. From the mid-18th century on this was a centre of Tibetan art and religion, which at the same time offered the central imperial power most welcome opportunities for influencing and controlling the ethnic minorities in Tibet and Mongolia. In the three-storeyed central section of the **Pavilion of Ten Thousand Happiness** (Wanfuge) is a statue, 75 ft (23 metres) tall, of the Maitreya Buddha, which is supposed to have been carved from a single piece of sandalwood.

Only a few steps away, unnoticed by

noisy visitors, is the **Confucius Temple**, inviting you to take a quiet look round. Dating from the Yuan dynasty, it now houses part of the City Museum of Beijing. The **White Cloud Temple** (Baiyunguan) was once the greatest Daoist centre of north China. Today a small group of old and young monks live here. Because of the political climate between 1960 and 1976 a "middle" generation could not be recruited.

The temples which lie at a distance from the dusty asphalt of the inner city and the suburbs have their own special charm. The **Temple of the Azure Clouds** (Biyunsi) with its impressive **Pavilion of 500 Luohan** and its 115-ft (35-metre) high stupa lies at the feet of the Western Mountains, right next to the **Fragrant Hills Park** (Xiangshan), among some of the most delightful scenery to be found in Beijing and in the surrounding countryside. Not far away is the extensive complex of the **Temple of the Reclining Buddha** (Wofosi). Its main attraction is a reclining bronze figure depicting Buddha shortly before his entry into nirvana.

The only work built by human hands which is visible to the naked eye from the moon, the **Great Wall** (Wanli Changcheng) winds its way like an endless slender dragon from the Yellow Sea through five provinces and two autonomous regions right up into the Gobi Desert. The very earliest stages of the building of the Wall date from the 5th century B.C., but the present course was basically determined around 220 B.C. by Qin Shi Huangdi, the first Chinese emperor and the founder of the empire. He had the old sections linked and extended northwards to ward off the horse-riding, very mobile nomad peoples. Soldiers and peasants from all parts of the country were conscripted to spend several years of their lives building this "Wall of ten thousand li" (1 li = 547 yards or 500 metres). Blocks of rock weighing several hundredweight had to be heaved up the steep slopes, and many people paid with their lives for this project.

From ten in the morning to three in the afternoon, the **pass of Badaling**, the section of the wall which is most easy to get to from Beijing, turns into a tourist carnival. The avalanche of visitors streams past countless stalls selling souvenirs towards the great symbol of Chinese civilisation. Then it moves in two different directions, attempting to conquer the steep climb with sensible shoes. From the high points you can get a view of the breathtaking scenery, where the mighty wall climbs up and down in the midst of a fascinating mountain landscape.

The scenery at **Mutianyu** is almost as imposing. This part of the wall, some 75 miles (120 km) to the north of Beijing, was restored a few years ago and is less busy than Badaling.

A visit to the Ming tombs

A visit to Badaling is normally combined with a trip to the **Ming tombs** (Shisanling). Protected by a range of hills to the north, east and west, the tombs of 13 of the 16 Ming emperors lie in this geomantically favourable spot. Coming from the south, you enter the extensive site on the valley floor through numerous gates of honour along the **Soul Path** (Shendao), which is flanked by stone guardians of the tombs. The guard of honour of twelve human figures is composed of civil and military dignitaries and officials; lions, horses, camels, elephants and mythical creatures – in total, 24 stone figures form the guard of honour of animals.

Two of the 13 tombs are open to the public. The **Changling Tomb** is the final resting place of the Emperor Yongle. The mound of the tomb has not been excavated, and you can only admire the magnificent hall of sacrifice. In Yongle's day, in the 15th century, human sacrifice was by no means unusual; 16 imperial concubines accompanied him on his journey to the underworld. In Emperor Wanli's reign (1573-1620) this terrible custom was no longer practiced, and innocent tourists, when entering the 89-ft (27-metre) deep, dank vault, do not have to fear being haunted by the ghosts of women who were buried alive. The entrance to Wanli's tomb, the **Dingling**, was long sought for in vain and was not found until 1957. His main wife and one concubine are buried with the emperor.

Tianjin, Chengde and Beidaihe attract many visitors from Beijing out for the day – usually on a day trip by train.

Tianjin, which used to be Romanised as Tientsin, has a population of 7 million and is one of China's major cities. Situated some 87 miles (140 km) to the south east of Beijing, it is famous for its port and its carpets and, because of its architecture, has more of a city atmosphere than the old cityscape of Beijing with its *hutongs*.

Chengde, formerly Jehol, was the summer residence of the Qing emperors and, at the same time, a politically important meeting place for the leaders of ethnic minorities. The **Eight Outer Temples** were built for the latter, in the style of the minority peoples (for instance those of Tibet). The "Palace for escaping from the heat" – the Chinese name of Chengde – is surrounded by a magnificent park.

Beidaihe, some five hours away from Beijing on the Bohai Bay of the Yellow Sea, is the most favoured seaside resort for people from Beijing, because of its wonderful sandy beaches. In the hot summer months, it is visited by thousands upon thousands of Chinese workers, all in need of a well-earned rest. Seafront hotels overlook beaches reserved for their guests. In out-of-the-way villas, the old guard of party bosses meet for their traditional annual summer conference. At nearby Shanhaiguan, sections of the Great Wall have been restored and are open to visitors.

View of houses in the old city in the western part of Beijing.

DONGBEI –
THE COLD NORTH

To the north of Beijing lies the fruitful North China Plain, with the three Chinese provinces of Liaoning, Jilin and Heilongjiang. The latter is named after the river that forms the border between China and the Soviet Union, known as *Amur* in Russian. The Chinese call this area Dongbei, which literally means East-North. To the west, the north eastern provinces border the Mongol steppes, to the east the Korean peninsula. The old name Manchuria, still in use outside China, goes back to the fact that this was once the territory of the Manchu. During World War II, the Japanese attempted to separate this region from China once more by setting up the puppet state of Manchuguo under the rule of the last Chinese emperor Puyi. The Manchu Qing dynasty had prohibited the settlement of Chinese in this region. Not until the middle of the last century was a major settlement of Han Chinese permitted, under the pressure of the expanding population and the confusions of the Taiping Rebellion (1850-1864). Today about 100 million people live in this north eastern region.

From Beijing you can cross north eastern China by the Trans-Siberian Railway; the train travels via Changchun, Jilin, and Harbin, via Qiqihar, Hailar and the border town of Manzhouli to the Soviet Union. **Shenyang**, the capital of Liaoning Province, is 523 miles (841 km) from Beijing. It takes 12 hours to get there by express train; by plane you can cover the distance in an hour and a half. The rail journey travels for long stretches along the coast of the Bohai Sea. Apart from the seaside resort of **Beidaihe,** it also passes the town of **Xingcheng**, which dates from Ming times, has many interesting sights to offer and is a favourite resort. A good time to travel to Shenyang – and north east China in general – is in summer, as the long winters are bitterly cold. This town, with a population of 4½ million today, is also known by its Manchurian name of Mukden.

Shenyang, an important meeting point of several transport routes in the north east, is also one of the most important industrial cities in China. Although Shenyang's history – and that of the entire province of Liaoning – can be traced a long way back into history, the city did not gain any importance until the Song dynasty, when it became a centre of trade for nomadic livestock breeders. Its rise to fame came under the Qing dynasty, for Liaoning was and still is the home of the Manchu. Today, more than half of the Manchu ethnic minority live in this province. Up until the end of the 1970s, the Manchus were considered to have been completely assimilated; but in recent years, the special customs and traditions of the Manchu ethnic group are once more being emphasised. In Liaoning Province itself there are several autonomous regions mainly inhabited by Manchu, where displays of traditional Manchu folk culture are put on specially for foreigners nowadays. In the autonomous Xiuyuan district a **Museum of Manchu Art and Culture** has recently been opened.

The greatest building dating from the time of the Manchu Qing dynasty in Liaoning is the **Imperial Palace in Shenyang**, the most complete and best preserved palace complex after the Imperial Palace in Beijing. It was built in 1625, after the Manchu had declared Shenyang to be their capital, and contains more than 300 buildings in an area covering more than 666,666 sq ft (60,000 sq metres). This imperial palace, which was maintained after the Qing emperors had moved to the capital of Beijing, was the residence of Nurhachi, the founder of the Qing dynasty, and his successor Abahai (*Hong Taiji* in Chinese). The main buildings – an amalgamation of Chinese, Manchu and Mongol architecture – are the Chongzheng Hall, the Qingning Palace, the

Left, ice bathing, an exclusive sport in the cold northeast of China.

Dazheng Hall and the Wensu Pavilion.

Of the three **imperial Qing tombs** in Liaoning Province, two are in Shenyang: the **Northern Imperial Tomb, Beiling** – it was built in 1643 for Nurhachi's son Abahai in the middle of a park in the north of Shenyang – and the **Eastern Imperial Tomb, Dongling**, the final resting place of Nurhachi, five miles (eight km) outside the actual city. The third tomb, **Yongling**, built by Nurhachi for his ancestors, is in the Xinbin district. Also worth seeing in Shenyang is the **Lama Temple** (Shishensi) dating from the 17th century, situated in the western part of the city. The **Liaoning Province Museum** is also worth a visit.

From Shenyang, the train leaves the main line and goes southwards towards **Anshan**. Anshan – some 50 miles (80 km) from Shenyang – is a city of millions, and here one of the largest iron and steel works in China is to be found. Anshan is a base for a pleasant visit to the scenically attractive **Qianshan Mountain**, with its ancient pines, pavilions, temples and monasteries dating from the Ming and Qing periods. Even nowadays temple markets are still held here every year in April.

From Anshan the journey continues through broad fields of millet and soya bean to the tip of the Liaoning peninsula, where the port of **Dalian** lies. Dalian can also be reached by plane – directly from Tokyo, among other routes. The ice-free harbour is one of the most important in the People's Republic of China. The city, surrounded by greenery in the summer, is also a favourite place for holidays and excursions, not least because of the miles of beaches and the mild maritime climate. Particularly charming and well worth a visit is the **Nature Park of Laohutan**, right by the sea. The main impression of the city, which lies in a bay and was once known as Dairen, is of a busy harbour, broad streets and big squares planted with greenery. You should not miss the opportunity to visit one of the

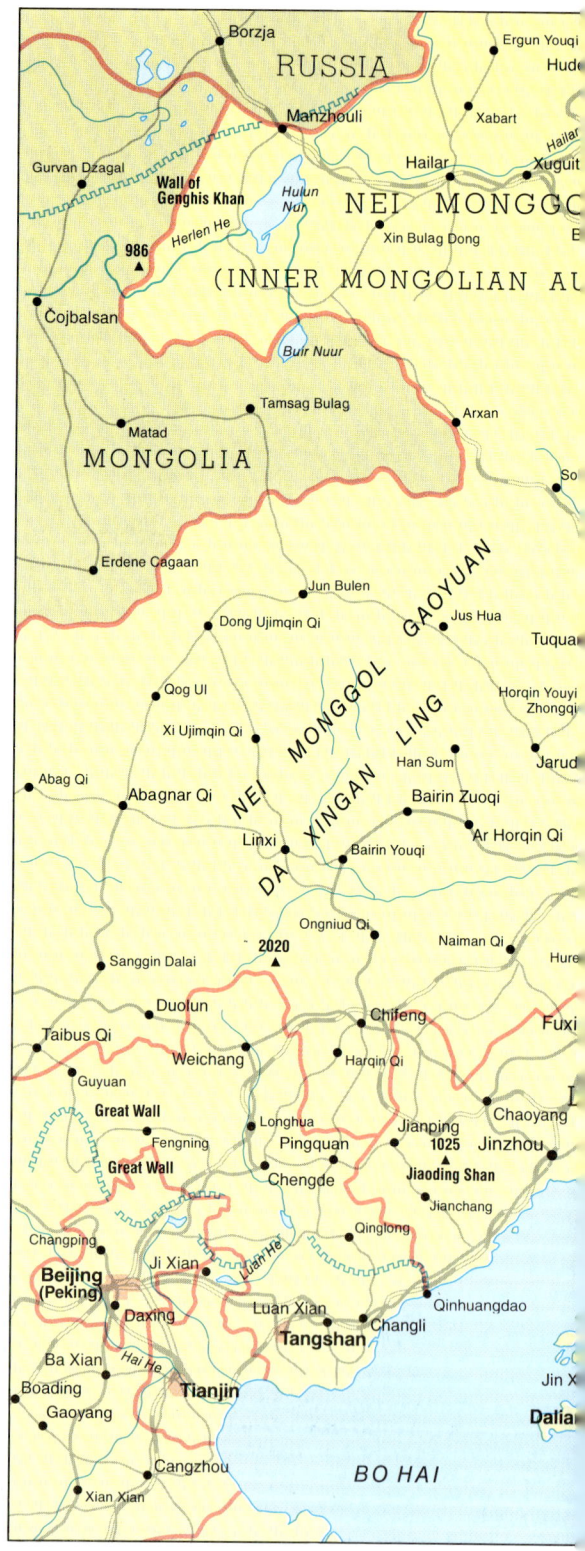

Handaqi
Huolongmen
Zavitinsk
Arhara
Birobidžan

RUSSIA

Sunwu
Xunke
Xinmin
Xueshuiwen

Nenjiang
Xinqing

ZHIQU
Nehe
Jusheng
Daheiding Shan
1047
Luobei
Hegang
Fujin

GION)
Bei'an
Yichun

Butha Qi
Laha
Yi'an
Kedong
HEILONGJIANG
Shuangyashan

Fuyu

Qiqihar
Lindian
Zhenxiang
Qing'an
Jiamusi
Baoqing
Dal'nerečensk
Bikin

Jalaid Qi
Daqing
DONGBEI
Yilan
Qitaihe
Muling He
Hulin

Tailai
Anda
Mulan
Fangzheng
Mishan

Hot
Zhaodong
Bin Xian
944
Yanshou
Jixi
Ozero
Chanka

Baicheng
Harbin
Shangzhi
964
Arsen'ev

Da'an
Fuyu
Suiyang

Tao'an
Yushu
Mudanjiang
Lazo

282
Songhua Jiang
Ning'an
Dongning

Changling
Nong'an
Tianqiaoling
Vladivostok

Jilin
Jiaohe
Chunhua
Nahodka

Changchun
Dunhua
Yanji

JILIN
Huaide
Songhua Hu

Shuangliao
Huadian
Hongshi

Siping
Liaoyuan
Helong

Tiefa
Kaiyuan
Hailong
Fusong
Baihe
Najin

Zhangwu
Tieling
Hunjiang
Baitoushan
Ch'ŏngjin

henyang
Fushun
Qingyuan
Linjiang
2744
Sea of Japan

ING
Chengxiangtun
Tonghua
Hyesan

Huanren
Kilchu

Anshan
Kuandian
Kanggye
2522

ngkou
1110
Fengcheng
1823
Pukch'ŏng
Kimch'aek

Maokui Shan
Paegamsan

Weizi
Dandong
Hŭich'ŏn
Hamhŭng
NORTH

Zhuanghe
Sinŭiju
Hŭngnam
KOREA

Chengzitan
Chŏngju
Anju
Kowŏn

Wŏnsan
Pacific Ocean

P'yongyang
T'ongch'ŏn

KOREA BAY
Namp'o
Songnim
1638
Kumgangsan

Haeju
Kaesŏng
Ch'unch'ŏn

Uijŏngbu
SOUTH KOREA

numerous fish restaurants here. From Dalian you can get to the town of **Ganjizi**, to the north of the bay, by bus or by taxi. Here, you can visit a **brick tomb dating from the Han dynasty** with interesting wall paintings. Some 37 miles (60 km) away from Dalian lies Lüshun, once known as Port Arthur, where the harbour has, however, lost much of its former importance.

Travelling south east from Shenyang via Benxi you arrive at **Dandong** near the Korean border, where you will find the scenically attractive **Dagushan Mountains**. From Dandong the railway carries on into North Korea as far as its capital of **Pyongyang**. The main route from Shenyang runs east at first, to the nearby industrial town of **Fushun**. Here you can visit the prison for war criminals in which the last emperor of China was imprisoned until 1950.

From Fushun onwards the railway turns north until it reaches the capital of Jilin Province, **Changchun**. On its way, the train runs through huge fields of grain, for here in the north east, there are still enormous farms owned by the state. From the train, however, you can also still see old villages with their mud huts. The town of Changchun (Eternal Spring) on the Yitong river did not become important until the end of the last century, when it became the terminus of the Manchurian railway, built by skilled Russian labour. In 1932 the town, then known as **Xinjing**, became the seat of the government of the Japanese puppet state of Manchuguo. Today the town still shows signs of Japanese urban planning in its ruler-straight boulevards. The **palace of the Emperor Puyi** has once more been restored to its old form. **Changchun**, an industrial and university town, is also well-known for its car manufacturing works. Because of its large parks (the **South Sea** is well worth seeing), Changchun is often also known as the "town of woodland". A great many films are produced here in one of the biggest **film studios** of the People's Republic of China.

To the south east of Changchun, an overnight journey by train, lies **Tonghua**, a wine-producing town in the south east of Jilin Province. Apart from sights such as the **Monastery of Heaven** and the **Mausoleum of Yangjingchu**, there is a wine cellar to be visited. From Tonghua you can get to **Ji'an**, on the Chinese-Korean border, by train or by bus. Ji'an lies on the upper course of the Yalu river and was once the capital of the Korean kingdom of Koguryo. There are numerous **tombs** in the vicinity, but only some of them can be visited. Ji'an lies in the middle of an autonomous region of the Korean minority. There are about 2 million Koreans living in China, and more than 60 percent live in the Jilin Province. The capital of this autonomous region – there are two in Jilin – is **Yanji**, where the Koreans also have their own university. At Ji'an, the border river Yalu is only some 98 ft (30 metres) wide, and the life here is quite

Women in traditional clothing at a festival in Shenyang.

190

idyllic. In the summertime, women chat across the border while doing their laundry, and children bathe in the river together, although it is not officially permitted to swim to the opposite bank. The Korean element, by the way, is not noticeable here alone. In some parts of Shenyang, Changchun, Jilin and Mudanjiang, too, visitors could feel that they have been transported to Korea. People wear Korean costumes, signs are written in Korean, and Korean is the main language spoken in the market places. In Shenyang, there is a cemetery dedicated to the memory of the Chinese who died in the Korean War.

The most famous peak along the Chinese-Korean border is the **White Head Mountain** (Baitoushan) with its crater lake, the beautiful **Lake of Heaven**. In its clear waters, monsters like the ones believed to dwell in Loch Ness have reportedly been seen several times (the last sighting was in 1981). How-

ever, these sightings are believed to be reflections from the sky. Nearby is a waterfall, one of the sources of the Sungari river. This mountain is considered sacred by Koreans and Manchus. It lies in the centre of the **Changbai Nature Reserve**, which covers 772 sq miles (2,000 sq km). In the Changbai mountains, which lie along the Chinese-Korean border, many animals survive which have become extinct elsewhere, such as sables, snow leopards, tigers, bears and blackcocks, and excellent ginseng grows here, too.

From Changchun the journey continues via the Trans-Siberian Railway to **Harbin**, the capital of Heilongjiang Province, with its population of 3 million. The distance from Beijing to this point is almost 870 miles (1,400 km), and the train covers it in 18 hours. Harbin (Place for Drying Fish) can also be reached by plane from Changchun and Beijing. The city lies along the

Palaces and castles of carved blocks of ice are built for the Ice Lantern Festival in Harbin.

Songhua river, which joins the Amur (Heilongjiang in Chinese) river to the north. The impression of this industrial city is one of industrial sites and newly-built apartment houses which all look alike, and are a familiar sight all over China. A marked contrast is formed by the older, sometimes almost European-looking residential areas. Many White Russians fled here after the October Revolution of 1917, and formed the majority of the inhabitants together with those Russians already living here. After World War II, most of them went back to the Soviet Union.

Some districts of Harbin are still reminiscent of Russian cities today. Russian influences can be detected in the architectural style of many of the buildings, not least in the old churches with their unmistakable onion domes. There are 17 Christian churches in Harbin, many of them built in Neo-Gothic style. Another of the few interesting

sights is the **Jile Temple** (Jilesi), built in 1924, in the Nangang district.

The winters are very cold, and temperatures can fall as low as minus 38 degrees Celsius. For this reason, ice sailing is one of the most popular sports in Harbin. Every year during the winter, there are big exhibitions of ice sculpture in the city. Human figures, pavilions and whole palaces are hacked out of huge blocks of ice.

China takes on a Siberian aspect in the Heilongjiang Province. In the north, the densely-forested **Lesser Xingan Range** runs right across the province. Even today, Manchurian tigers and other rare animals can be found here. Near Yichun, about 285 miles (60 km) to the north of Harbin, there is an ancient forest along the Tangwang river composed mainly of Korean pines, this has now been declared a nature reserve and is a perfect place for long hikes. About 60 miles (100 km) south east of Harbin, surrounded by beautiful scenery, lies the town of **Mudanjiang**. The train from Harbin runs on to the north west towards the Soviet border. After three hours of travelling, you come to **Daqing**, China's biggest oilfield.

About 162 miles (260 km) from Harbin to the north west is the big city of **Qiqihar**. Qiqihar has only a few sights of cultural interest – among them a Buddhist temple and a mosque. In the winter, ice sculptors exhibit their works in some of the big parks. Some 13 miles (20 km) from Qiqihar, in the swamps around the **Zhalong Lake**, is a nature reserve where the rare red-crowned and white-naped cranes live. Not far to the west of Qiqihar, the train route towards the Russian border crosses into Inner Mongolia, where you pass through the **Greater Xingan Range**. The first town in Inner Mongolia is **Hailar**, in the middle of the Mongolian steppe, which has a Siberian atmosphere. On the Chinese side, the journey ends in **Manzhouli**, where you can begin the journey to Moscow and eventually to Berlin, which lasts several days.

Left, there is no room for geese in the streets. Right, the harsh north leaves its traces in the faces of its people.

Shandong – The Home Of Confucius

The bridge over the Yellow River at Jinan, the provincial capital, is definitely not an architectural sensation. But, it is still pointed out with pride to visitors – possibly as a symbol of the apparent taming of the Yellow River (Huanghe), one of the two fateful rivers of China. It changed its course countless times over the years, and caused disastrous floods in the western part of Shandong; not until 1933 did its lower course find its present outflow into the Bohai Sea. And yet half the province of Shandong (Mountainous East) lives off the fruitful flood plain of the river.

Culturally and historically, Shandong – today, with 75 million inhabitants, one of the most populous provinces of the country – is a region with a wealth of traditions. This was the home of the important states of Qi and Luo; and the heartland of the Confucius cult – the "Great Teacher" came from Qufu. A mere 50 miles (80 km) away, in a sort of religious counterpoint, is the mountain of Taishan, a Daoist national shrine. Shandong was the home of the famous, noble-spirited "bandits of Liangshan Moor". In the very same spirit as Robin Hood, they distributed the spoils they had gained from the wealthy, among the poor. Here, too, the Society for Peace and Justice had its beginnings, which was to enter history under the name of "Boxers" around the turn of the century.

Malicious tongues claim, not without justification, that there's nothing worth seeing in the provincial capital of Jinan. All the same, there are many fountains in the parks, and pleasure boat rides on the Daming Lake, the "Lake of Great Purity". Weifang, situated in the middle

Preceding pages: the Bixiagong Temple on the holy mountain of Taishan. Below, it is a long climb up to the south gate, which leads to Heaven.

of the peninsula, is famous for its New Year pictures and kites. In the north is Yantai with its inviting beaches and scenery. Not far away, on a high rock projecting into the sea, is Penglai, the legendary home of the "Eight Immortals" of Daoist mythology.

In popular Chinese religion, mountains are seen as living beings. Their stabilising power perpetuates the cosmic order; they create clouds and rain. Taishan, the "Exalted Mountain", is the most easterly of the five sacred mountains of Daoism, and, as life comes from the east, it is the holiest of them all. It is supposed to have risen from the head of *Pangu*, the creator of the world according to Chinese mythology.

Tai'an is the name of the town at the foot of the mountain. In its centre lies the Daimiao, the **Temple of the God of Taishan**, a magnificent temple complex of more than 600 buildings which contains the **Hall of Heavenly Gifts** (Tiankuangdian), one of the most massive classic temple halls in China. It contains a monumental fresco which is more than 197 ft (60 metres) long. Less than half a mile to the north of the temple, at the **Gate of the God of Taishan** (Daizong Fang), lies the starting point of the seemingly endless ascent to the 5,070-ft (1,545-metre) high summit. In earlier years, emperors and mandarins were carried up the 6,293 steps in litters. Pilgrims and travellers would need a whole day for the journey, or they can cheat a bit and ride to a halfway point by minibus, then go by cable car almost as far as the summit. But those who take the quick way miss the splendid variety of this open-air museum: temples, pavilions, shrines, stone steles, inscriptions and waterfalls. A little way off the main path, in the **Stone Sutra Valley**, the text of the *Diamond Sutra* has been engraved in a huge block of stone. The 1,050 characters, each some 20 inches

Taishan – waiting for the sunrise on a rock facing the sea.

(50 cm) high, are considered a masterpiece of the calligrapher's art. Once past the **Middle Gate of Heaven** (Zhongtianmen), the "Gate in the middle of the Way to Heaven," the ascent becomes steeper. Passing the "Pines of the Fifth Order of Officials" (Wudaifu Song), which, according to legend, were given this title by emperor Qin Shi Huangdi after sheltering him from a thunderstorm, the path to the Heavenly Way leads to the **Southern Gate of Heaven** (Nantianmen), which is the entrance to the realm of the immortals on the summit of the mountain.

Up here – it is pleasantly cool in summer and uncomfortably cold in winter – the **Path of Paradise** leads to the main shrine of the mountain, the **Temple of the Princess of the Azure Clouds** (Bixiasi). As the daughter of the god of Taishan, the princess is an attraction for the country people, particularly for the women, who come to pray for the well-being of their children and those yet to come. The Jade Emperor is the supreme Daoist god, and a small temple dedicated to him is accordingly placed on the actual summit of the mountain. If the air is clear, the view is overwhelming. However, all too often there are clouds just below the ridge of the mountain, and even the main attraction of Taishan, the much-praised natural spectacle of the sunrise, can only be seen in all its colourful splendour on less than 100 days in a year.

On 8 November 1919, during a visit to Beijing, Duke Kong Linyu died, at the age of 76. He was a descendant of the philosopher and moral teacher Confucius. He had fathered two girls before his death, and according to tradition they could not continue his line. But his concubine Wang was in the fifth month of her pregnancy. The rival factions of the Kong clan waited for her confinement. As a precaution, guards were

Tomb of a descendant of Confucius in Qufu.

posted outside the chamber of the the pregnant woman. All the doors of the house were opened, in order to make it easy for the "wise ancestor" to find his way back for rebirth. On 23 February 1920 Kong Decheng was born, representing the 77th generation after Confucius. This decided the question of the succession, and the "first family under Heaven" heaved a sigh of relief.

However, 17 days later the ambitious Madam Tao, Kong Linyu's childless main wife, poisoned her rival, the mother of the heir, for fear of losing her position of unlimited power in the household. The murder went – almost – unpunished. A distant relative who provided the poison took opium, at the time a favoured method of committing suicide. The scene of this aristocratic thriller and family drama was the **Kong family residence in Qufu.**

Ever since the Han period, the increasing reverence accorded to Confucius has gone hand in hand with the continuous and unstoppable growth of the prestige and power of his successors. The importance of Confucian thought in upholding the state was acknowledged by the imperial house insofar as they awarded the Kong family more and more titles, privileges and land. Towards the end of the last century, the Yangsheng Duke, the duke "as the successor of the Wise One", was one of the wealthiest property owners in the country, presiding over his own judicial system and a private army.

The outside of the residence, which dates from the 16th century, looks rather plain, but with its 600 rooms it is a small city within a city. Several hundred servants were once employed here in the front part of the building, the *Yamen*, which consists of administrative buildings and audience halls. In the rear part, which could only be entered by a few selected servants and ladies'

Ceremony in front of the main hall of the Confucius Temple.

maids, were the living quarters of the ducal Kong family. The contents of the residence consist of valuable works of art, calligraphy, articles of clothing and extensive archive material. Nowadays there is a hotel in the western wing.

Qufu was the home of Master Kong, Kong Fuzi in Chinese, which was then Latinised to Confucius. He was born in this neighbourhood and taught for many years trying to influence every-day practical politics with his moral doctrine. This is where Kong Fuzi died. He is buried in the forest belonging to the Kong family (Konglin), a few miles to the north of the town, under a simple grass-grown mound. However, the way to the mound is lined with human and animal figures in stone, a custom other-wise reserved for emperors.

In imperial times, Qufu was *the* sacred town of China, almost on the same level as Jerusalem or Mecca. Still bearing witness to this former status is the size and splendour of the Confucius Temple in the centre of the small town. A temple is supposed to have been built on this site as early as 478 B.C., one year after Confucius' death.

Coming from the south, you first see the three-storey, 75-ft (23-metre) high Kuiwen Pavilion, whose origins date back to the 11th century. Passing the 13 pavilions in which steles with imperial inscriptions are kept, the road leads to the main hall of the temple (Dacheng-dian), in which the sacrificial rites in honour of the "master" used to be carried out. Unique from an artistic and his-torical point of view are the 28 stone pillars, which are reported to have 1,296 dragons carved on them. The yellow colour of the roof, otherwise reserved exclusively for the Imperial Palace, once again emphasises the unique po-sition of the great philosopher Kong Fuzi in Chinese tradition.

Ferdinand von Richthofen, baron,

Seaside promenade in Qingdao, the former German colony.

geographer and adventurer, had been keeping a lookout for a place in which the German Reich could realise its colonial ambitions on Chinese soil. The eastern part of the Shandong peninsula seemed to have been created specially for his purpose. When, in 1897, two fathers of the Catholic Steyler Mission were killed by Boxers, this provided an excuse for the German emperor Wilhelm II to establish himself as a colonial ruler of the Far East.

Before the first German frigates and gunboats moored in the harbour, Qingdao, the "Green Island", was still a little fishing village. The military superiority of the "foreign devils" forced the Chinese to agree to lease the Bay of Kiaochow (now known as Jiaozhou) to them. This was the smallest of German concessions (220 sq miles/550 sq km) and the foreign devils rapidly settled in a thoroughly German fashion. Soon German officers, sailors and businessmen

Below, a Catholic church in Qingdao. Following pages, the terracotta army of Emperor Qin Shi Huangdi near Xi'an.

were promenading up and down the Kaiser Wilhelm Ufer, reading the home-made East Asian version of *Lloyd's* and dining in the seafront Prinz Heinrich hotel. They drank beer from the Germania brewery, which is still exported all over the world today under the name of Tsingtao (the old transcription of Qingdao). This beer, however, owes its excellent flavour not only to the brewing expertise of the former colonial rulers, but to the excellent water of the Laoshan, a nearby range of mountains popular with visitors because of its wild and beautiful scenery and its many Daoist temples.

There is still evidence of colonial past hovering over the rooftops of Qingdao, where 19th-century Neo-Gothic style of the buildings is reminiscent of small German towns. There are bright red tiled roofs, half-timbered façades, sloping gables, triangular windows in the attics, the tall towers of the Catholic and Protestant churches and, a special little jewel, the former governor's palace, which has the flair of a Prussian hunting lodge. It is left to the Chinese pagoda on top of what was once known as "Bismarck Hill," around which the houses of the town are grouped, to restore the picture of the actual geographical surroundings. The German presence in the Far East did not last long. In 1914, at the beginning of the World War I, Japan conquered the German colony.

Even though the suburbs of Qingdao have now become unattractive, the town has preserved its character as a holiday and seaside resort. By September, the busloads of trippers from the works outing have gone, as have the cadre limousines (Shanghai or, more popular these days, Mercedes) with their little lace curtains. In the picturesque district of Badaguan you will now be able to find a hotel room easily. You may even find one in one of those ostentatious villas which are reserved for the aging leadership of the party, and are equipped with wheelchair ramps and hand grips in the marble baths.

XI'AN – CRADLE OF CIVILISATION

The region at the bend of the Yellow River (Huanghe) in central China, in the provinces of Shaanxi and Henan, is the cradle of Chinese civilisation. Here, in the fertile valleys of the loess-covered landscape, the ancestors of the Chinese settled in the 3rd century B.C. The fertile loess soil attracted the first human settlements, while irrigation difficulties forced people to work in close cooperation. As a result, the first and strongest states developed in this region.

The capital of Shaanxi Province, Xi'an, lies in the protected valley of the Wei river, a few dozen miles to the west of the confluence of the river Wei and the Yellow River. In recent years, important excavations have been carried out in the Wei valley. It was here that the first emperor, Qin Shi Huangdi, unified China for the first time. During the Tang Dynasty (618-907) Xi'an, which was called Chang'an (Heavenly Peace), was the largest city in the world. It was linked to many central Asian regions and Europe via the Silk Road, and thousands of foreign traders lived in the city.

For more than 1,000 years Xi'an served as the capital for 11 imperial dynasties. Following the demise of the Tang Dynasty, Xi'an lost its importance and began a gradual decline. In 1936, however, a historic incident took place in Xi'an: two generals of the Guomindang kidnapped their leader Chiang Kaishek to compel him to cooperate with the Communists against the Japanese. The "Xi'an Incident" is considered a turning point in modern Chinese history in favour of the Communists.

Today, Xi'an is a modern industrial town, known amongst other things for its aviation and textile industries. Xi'an also has several universities and research institutes. Present-day Xi'an has about 3 million inhabitants and is an important centre for travel to the interior. The old imperial capital can easily be reached from all the important cities and towns in China. A direct flight from Beijing takes about two hours, while the train journey of around 724 miles (1,165 km) takes almost 24 hours.

The climate in Xi'an is relatively harsh, with considerable seasonal variations. The winters are not too cold, while in summer the temperature can rise to 30 degrees centigrade. At the beginning of spring and autumn, the days are pleasantly cool; the rainy season lasts from mid-July to October. There can be considerable flight delays during the rainy season in Xi'an. A new international airport is being built which should ease these problems and cope with the constantly increasing volume of flights.

Despite its modern buildings and the many new roads and districts, the centre of Xi'an still retains the old layout from the Tang Dynasty. At that time, the

Left, each of the more than 6,000 clay soldiers has individual facial features. **Below**, the Great Wild Goose Pagoda in Xi'an.

metropolis was surrounded by a large city wall; the town itself stretched over five and a half miles (nine km) from east to west, and over four and a half miles (seven and a half km) from north to south. All the roads were built in a grid pattern running straight north-south or east-west, and met at right angles. This can still be noticed in the city centre.

The old imperial city of Xi'an

The layout of the ancient city is not quite identical with the modern one; the **Great Wild Goose Pagoda** (Dayanta) was then situated in the centre of the town. Although the walls built during the Tang Dynasty are no longer there, the eight and a half mile (14 km) long city wall from the Ming Dynasty still surrounds the centre. In recent years, a start has been made in rebuilding the 39-ft (12-metre) high and 39-ft (12-metre) thick city walls, and the moat outside the wall has been reconstructed and integrated with a park which almost completely surrounds the walls. One can walk along the city wall or occasionally take a horse drawn carriage.

Today, Xi'an has wide treelined avenues which give shade in the summer and give it the look of a "green city". Right in the city centre, where Xi'an's two main roads cross, is the **Bell Tower** (Zhonglou). The 75-ft (23-metre) high tower, which dates from 1384, has in recent years been renovated. Around the Bell Tower is the shopping and commercial centre; from the Bell Tower to the east runs Dongdajie with many shops and restaurants. From Dongdajie to the north is Jiefanglu, leading to the railway station. One of the biggest free markets in Xi'an is not far from the Bell Tower towards the south of the town. It has many snack bars run by Hui Muslims, which sell delicious food (mutton-filled sesame rolls).

Further south, directly by the city wall, in a former Confucian temple, is the **Shaanxi Provincial Museum** (Shaanxi Bowuguan). It holds more than 4,000 exhibits in three buildings. The first building has a chronologically arranged exhibition about Chinese history from earliest times to the end of the Tang Dynasty with very well preserved artefacts (including unusual bronze objects). The museum's centrepiece is the Forest of Steles with a collection of around 1,100 stone tablets on which ancient Chinese texts, including those of the Confucian classics, are engraved. The third section of the museum houses animal sculptures in stone, Tang Dynasty stone friezes, bronzes and jewels as well as Buddhist sculptures and ceramic tiles from the Han Dynasty. The Shaanxi Provincial Museum, one of the best and most important in the whole of China, regularly holds special exhibitions.

A few minutes' walk from the Bell Tower in a north-westerly direction is the **Drum Tower** (Gulou), which resembles the Bell Tower, dates from the 18th century and was rebuilt after 1949. From the Drum Tower, in a westerly direction through alleys crossing the Hui Muslim quarter you reach the **Great Mosque** (Qingzhensi). Some 60,000 Hui Muslims live in Xi'an. The alleys from the Drum Tower to the Mosque are lined with numerous souvenir shops. The Mosque, which dates back to the Ming period and has been renovated several times, bears more resemblance to a Chinese temple, with its inner courtyards. The main prayer hall has in recent years been renovated. Farther along the road in the direction of Xidajie is the **Western City Gate** (Ximen), which you can climb and visit. In the hall above the gate are interesting historic exhibitions.

In a southerly direction from the Bell Tower, in the grounds of the former Jianfusi temple complex, about a mile (one and a half km) outside the South Gate (Nanmen), is the 131-ft (43-metre) high **Small Wild Goose Pagoda** (Xiaoyanta) which was built in the 8th century. It was severely damaged during an earthquake in the 16th century, but was repaired in the late 1970s.

More significant than the Small Wild Goose Pagoda is the 240-ft (73-metre) high, seven-storey **Great Wild Goose Pagoda** (Dayanta), situated in the south west at the end of Yanta Street. It was built at the beginning of the Tang Dynasty, in the 7th century. The famous monk Xuanzang went on a pilgrimage to India in 629 and returned with many Buddhist scriptures which were stored in the Pagoda and translated into Chinese. Though only a few buildings remain of the original temple structure which had 13 courtyards and over 300 rooms, over the years some monks have returned to the monastery. There is a lovely view of the city from the top floor of the Great Wild Goose Pagoda.

The most important sight in Xi'an is undoubtedly the underground **Army of Terracotta Warriors** of the first Chinese emperor, Qin Shi Huangdi. It lies 22 miles (35 km) south of Xi'an at the foot of Mount Lishan, in the county of Lintong which is famous for its pomegranates. In 1974, peasants digging a well uncovered these life-size horse and warrior figures. Some of the approximately 7,000 figures from the tomb have been restored by archaeologists and are exhibited in a hall built above the excavation site. The figures are arranged in battle formation in 11 corridors – soldiers holding spears and swords, others steering horse drawn chariots, and officers, all about 5 ft 6 inches (between 1.8 metres and 1.86 metres) tall. Each head has been specially modelled with individual facial expressions, each face is different. Several hundred thousand workers spent 36 years building the tomb which the emperor ordered to be built at the age of 13, shortly after he ascended the throne. The tomb was constructed underground, and fortified with columns, walls and a wooden roof to hold up the

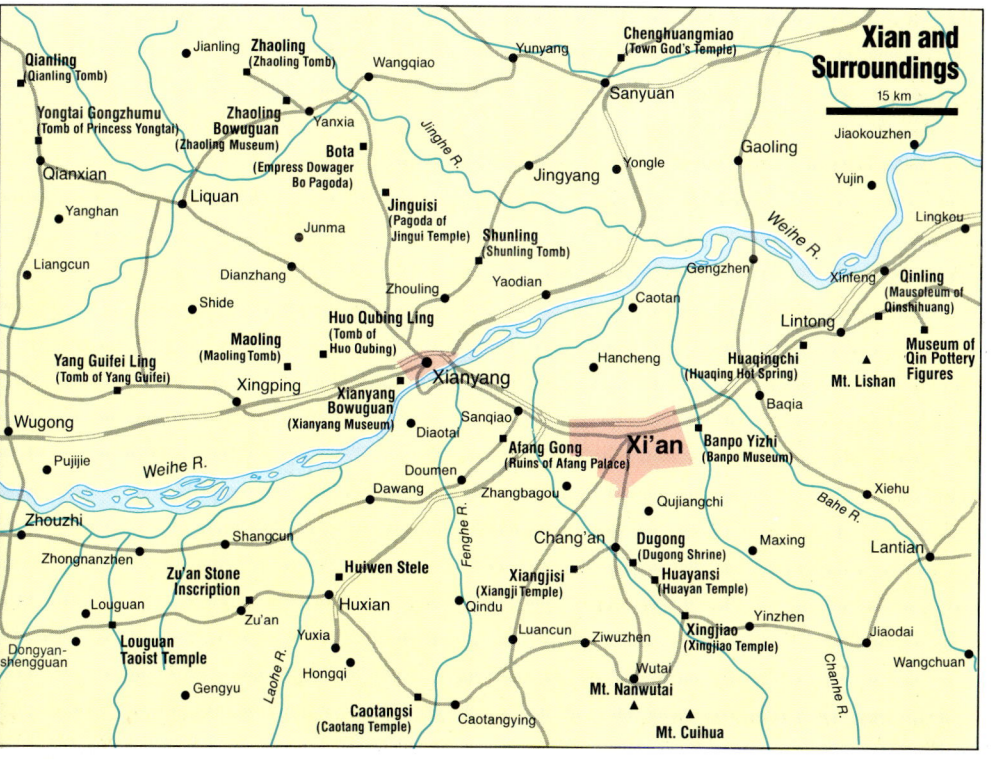

mound of earth above. In 206 B.C., shortly after the death of the emperor, the tomb was destroyed and plundered by rebelling peasants.

In the main hall is a model of the entire necropolis (main tomb and other tombs) and video films are shown about the excavation work. In one of the two side buildings you can see the terracotta figures and weapons. The production process – similar to large, assembly line production – is also documented. The other building contains a sensational exhibit: the miniature model of a bronze chariot with horses and coachman from the Qin Dynasty. The carriage was discovered in 1980 about 22 yards (20 metres) to the west of the tomb and is similar to the carriages used by Qin Shi Huangdi during his inspection tours.

The main tomb of the emperor is less than a mile (one and a half km) away to the west; but to date it has not been possible to open it. According to his-toric surveys, a splendid necropolis is hidden under the 154-ft (47-metre) high mound, which apparently depicts the whole of China in miniature. According to old historical records, the ceiling is said to be studded with jewels depicting the sky, and mercury was pumped in mechanically to create images of flow-ing rivers. Trial digs have revealed high contents of mercury, and it is hoped that excavations can begin soon .

In order to open up the entire necro-polis, 12 villages and seven factories in the area would have to be relocated because excavations would have to be made over an area of 19 sq miles (50 sq km). The entrance to the tomb has not been found. It is said that all the workers and supervisors were sealed in the tomb. Rumour has it that the first Qin emperor was so superstitious and fear-ful that he only had the necropolis built to deceive people and is in fact buried somewhere else.

Peasants in the countryside around Xi'an sell traditional embroideries.

On the way back from Lintong County you can visit the **Hot Springs of Huaqing** (Huaqingchi). They have been known for over 3,000 years. There are baths and pavilions in the beautiful park area. This is where, during the Tang Dynasty, the most famous concubine in China, Yang Guifei, bathed. A reproduction of the bath she is supposed to have used can be seen. Farther up in the mountain is the place where Chiang Kaishek was recaptured by two of his own generals during an escape attempt after he had been taken prisoner in 1936.

A visit to the **neolithic settlement of Banpo** on the way back to the town is worthwhile. It lies six miles (10 km) to the east of Xi'an. Some relics, including ceramics from the Yangshao culture are exhibited. The excavated village shows the outlines of houses and cooking areas and is part of the museum. There is still a debate about whether the people who lived here 6,000 years ago were a matriarchal community.

The country around Xi'an

About 37 miles (60 km) from Xi'an is the county town of Xianyang, which was the capital during the reign of Qin Shi Huangdi. Few traces are left of the numerous legendary palaces from that time. In Xianyang, there is a **museum** in a former Confucian temple which contains over 3,000 artefacts from the time of the Warring Kingdoms and the Han and Qin Dynasties. The collection of miniature terracotta horses and soldiers from the Han Dynasty, each about 20-inches (50-cm) high, is particularly impressive. It was discovered in a tomb in Yangjiawan.

Forty-three miles (70 km) to the north west of Xi'an is the burial place of the emperor Taizong of the Tang Dynasty. The **Zhaoling Tomb** also contains, in addition to the tomb of Taizong, 167

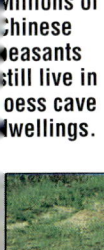

Millions of Chinese peasants still live in loess cave dwellings.

burial sites for the members of the imperial family. The site, near the town of Lingquan, covers over 50,000 acres (20,000 hectares). Some tombstones and smaller relics from the tombs can be seen in the Zhaoling Museum.

About 53 miles (85 km) to the north west of Xi'an is the **Qianling Tomb**, the joint burial place of the Tang emperor Gao Zong and his wife, the empress Wu Zetian. The tomb itself has not been opened. The approach to the tomb is worth seeing because of its "ghost avenue" of large stone sculptures of animals and dignitaries. There is a group of 61 stone sculptures said to represent foreign dignitaries, with their heads missing. The peasants of the region are said to have knocked them off when there was a famine which they believed was caused by the presence of these "foreigners".

Six of the 17 smaller tombs nearby have been excavated since 1960. A few

minutes by car from the main tomb are the **tombs of Princess Yongtai and Prince Zhanghuai**. They contain exquisite frescoes from the Tang Dynasty. The trip to the Tang Tombs can be combined with a visit to one of the villages. Wheat and cotton is grown in the region around Xi'an. In some villages you can still find the traditional loess cave dwellings which, however, are increasingly being replaced with more modern brick buildings.

Yan'an, Symbol of the Revolution

The market town of Yan'an is 168 miles (270 km) to the north of Xi'an, where the Yan river cuts a path through the dry loess mountains. It can be reached from Xi'an by overland bus (24 hours) or by plane (flight time one hour; flights are twice a week). Yan'an can also be reached by plane from Beijing, Shenyang and Taiyuan. If you take the

The Buddhist Longmen Caves near Luoyang.

overland bus from Xi'an, you pass the county town of Huangling after 75 miles (120 km), where you can visit the **Tomb of the Yellow Emperor** (Huangdiling), the father of the Chinese people, in a park. It continues to be a place of pilgrimage for the Chinese.

In the area around Yan'an you can still see the caves which are typical of this central Chinese loess landscape, and which were used during the second world war by the leaders of the Communist Party and the Red Army as habitations and meeting places. Yan'an was then the symbol of the Chinese Revolution. The **Pagoda Baota**, which dominates the city, originates from the Song Dynasty and was restored in 1950. Until the 1970s, when Yan'an was the national centre of pilgrimage of the Chinese Revolution, it was at least as well known as the Emperor's Palace or the Temple of Heavenly Peace in Beijing. The headquarters of the military commission of the Chinese Communist Party and the houses of the communist leaders Mao Zedong and Zhu De are still preserved in the Fenghuang Mountain north of Yan'an. The **Museum of the Revolution** in the Town contains over 2,000 documents and objects from the Yan'an period which is still praised by many older functionaries of the Chinese Communist Party as the "golden revolutionary era". There are also some interesting Buddhist and Daoist Temples in the area surrounding Yan'an.

The sacred mountain Huashan

Seventy-five miles (120 km) by train from Xi'an in an easterly direction, near the railway station (stop at Huayin), is **Huashan**, one of the sacred mountains of China. Its name means "flowering mountain", and its cultural significance, which goes far back into history, is Daoist. There are numerous temples along the mountain up to the top; the ascent via the north peak to the 6,890-ft (2,100-metre) high south peak starts at the **Garden of the Jade Spring** (Yu-

quanyuan), four and a half miles (seven and a half km) east of Huayin. The ascent takes at least half a day. Behind the **Cloud Gate** (Yunmen), where you have a lovely view of the landscape, the path climbs up and you must be free of vertigo to climb to the north peak and from there to the south peak. Many visitors and Daoist pilgrims enjoy the sunrise from the east peak.

Luoyang, the Eastern Imperial City

While Xi'an was the capital of the western Han Dynasty (206 B.C.-A.D. 9), the residence of the emperors of the subsequent eastern Han Dynasty (A.D. 25-220) was in Luoyang; for this reason, Luoyang is sometimes called the "eastern imperial city". The train from Xi'an to the historic rival metropolis of Luoyang, east of Xi'an, takes about seven hours. The train goes past the town of Sanmenxia. One of the largest hydro-electric power plants in China, with an estimated potential of 25 million kilowatt, was built at the **Three Gate Gorge** (Sanmenxia).

Luoyang, like Xi'an, served as the capital for several dynasties. It flourished during the Tang and Song Dynasties, but then gradually lost its importance in comparison to the increasingly prosperous coastal towns. It had barely 100,000 inhabitants before 1949, and the town appeared desolate. This changed after 1949. Luoyang became an industrial city, many factories were built, including the first tractor factory in China. Numerous monotonous-looking working class districts were added, so that today Luoyang is a modern industrial town with all the unpleasant features accompanying such a development. An attempt has been made to make it more pleasant by creating green spaces, and there are many herbaceous areas in the town; when the peonies are in bloom, Luoyang looks like one big flower garden.

Almost all visitors stay at the Friendship Hotel, which is located in the western part of the town on Yan'anlu, at the corner of Dongfanghonglu. Yan'anlu and its continuation, Zhongzhoulu, are the main axis of Luoyang. The **Provincial Museum** is fairly central; it gives a good overview of the historic development of the town and its environs from the Neolithic period to the Tang period. Not far from there, in Wangcheng Park, are **two underground tombs from the Han Dynasty**, which had been excavated at a different location in the 1950s. One can still see some houses in the style of the Song, Ming and Qing dynasties in the old town which lies to the east. It is worth strolling through its alleys with their shops and stalls.

To the south of the town, about five miles (eight km) from the centre, is the **Tomb of General Guanyu** who is worshipped in China as the god of war and is a popular subject for the New Year pictures which are widely produced. A stele erected at the mound of Guanyu's

tomb has been engraved with the biography of the General, who came from the state of Shu in the period of the Three Realms (220-265).

To the east, eight miles (13 km) outside the town, is the **White Horse Temple** (Baimasi). The monastery, founded in A.D. 68, is said to be the oldest monastery in China. The name of the temple relates to a legend. Two monks on a white horse delivered Buddhist scriptures to Luoyang. You can still see the statues of the two monks and their burial places. Only a few ruins remain of the old monastery at the back of the building. Today the monastery, which has recently been restored, houses more than 60 monks of Zen Buddhist order, and is again a centre for followers of Zen Buddhism. To the east of the temple is a pagoda from the Song Dynasty, the **Skyscraper Pagoda** (Qiyunta).

The most spectacular cultural and historic sights are the Buddhist **Longmen Caves**, eight miles (13 km) south of the town along both sides of the Yi river. They were created between the 5th and 7th century. Most of the figures and grottoes were sponsored by noblemen. There are over 1,300 grottoes and 700 niches containing 40 pagodas, 2,780 inscriptions and more than 100,000 statues and images. Many of the most beautiful sculptures were stolen (at the turn of the century) and can today be seen in museums in the West or are in private collections. Despite this, the Longmen Grottoes are still, together with the grottoes at Datong and at Dunhuang, a unique document of Buddhist creative art. In the Longmen Grottoes you can study the different styles, from the northern Wei Dynasty to the Tang Dynasty. The biggest statue is more than 55 ft (17 metres) tall, the smallest one less than an inch (two cm). The structures on the western river bank are well preserved, containing the sculptured stone figures and grottoes.

The most striking part of the site is the **Fengxian Temple**, which contains the 56-ft (17.4-metre) tall central statue, sur-

A demon deity representing a guard in the Longmen caves.

212

rounded by bodhisattvas and heavenly guards. Just the ears of the Buddha are 79 inches (1.9 metres) long. The statue was completed in 676 during the reign of the Tang emperor Gaozong and is said to have been inspired by the empress Wu Zetian. In Luoyang itself, it is worth visiting the Hui (Chinese Muslim) quarter. An excursion from Luoyang to one of the longest bridges across the Yellow River is available. It will take about half a day to get there and back.

Shaolin Boxers in the Songshan mountains

Some 50 miles (80 km) south east of Luoyang, in the county of Dengfeng, is the **Shaolin monastery**. This "Temple of the Small Forest" at the western edge of the Songshan mountains can be reached in about three hours by car on a reasonable country road. The journey takes you through the countryside, passing villages with their mud houses. The Shaolin monastery is known beyond China's frontiers for the special form of unarmed combat developed by its monks. It is considered as the cradle of Chinese forms of martial arts.

In recent years it has become something of a place of pilgrimage, as a result of the 1982 film *The Monastery of Shaolin*, a true story of how Shaolin monks helped a Tang emperor, which was very popular among the young people. In recent years a new training hall has been built next to the monastery – mainly for wealthy foreigners – which unfortunately has destroyed the beautiful harmonious landscape. The founder of the monastery, the monk Bodhidharma – who is seen as the founder of Chinese Zen Buddhism which had arrived from India in 527 – would certainly not find peace here now for his meditation. He is said to have sat in front of a rock face and meditated for 10 years. As a result, his silhouette is said to have been imprinted on the rock.

The Shaolin monastery was badly ruined but has been restored in recent years and now houses monks again. You can still see dents in the stone floor of the main hall of the temple, the **Thousand Buddha Hall** (Qianfodian), reminders of the tough combat exercises carried out by the monks. South west of the monastery is the **Pagoda Forest** (Talin) with 220 tombs, the oldest of which probably go back to the Tang Dynasty. You can spend the night in the county town of Dengfeng. The county is known throughout the world for its *wushu* arts. The hotel will arrange a demonstration of these martial arts.

Several other sights can be reached from Dengfeng in the Songshan Mountains, for instance the Daoist **Temple of the First Patriarch** (Chuzu'an) and the Daoist **Zhongyue Temple** (Zhongyuemiao), in which sacrifices to Songshan used to be made. Four big iron figures in combat position guard the Heavenly Pavilion where the emperors used to make their sacrifices. Also worth a visit

Iron guard in Zhongyue Temple in the Songshan mountains.

is the **Observatory** (Guanxingtai), built in 1279 and situated nine miles (15 km) south east of Dengfeng in the small town of Gaocheng. From Dengfeng you can take a bus to Zhengzhou.

Meeting point: the town of Zhengzhou

Located some 50 miles (80 km) north east of Dengfeng, on the south bank of the Yellow River on the edge of the North China Plain, lies the town of **Zhengzhou** (Kingdom of the Zheng). Today it is the capital of the Henan Province. Zhengzhou can be reached by plane from several airports in China; the town is also an important railway junction for lines from Shanghai to Xi'an and Beijing to Guangzhou. The 435-mile (700-km) journey to Beijing takes nine hours by train. Although it was already populated during the Shang period, the town did not attain great historic significance then. It developed with the construction of the railway lines at the end of the last century; during World War II it was attacked several times by the Japanese because of its importance as a railway junction. The Guomindang troops blew up the dykes of the Yellow River as a defence against the Japanese. Thousands of Chinese people tragically lost their lives as a result of the subsequent flooding. The breaches in the dykes were only repaired in 1947 with American assistance. In the 1950s Zhengzhou, which had been badly destroyed during the civil war of 1948-1949, became an industrial development area.

Today Zhengzhou is an industrial town with 1½ million inhabitants. The town, which has few historic sights, has many parks and green areas. The Old Town with its maze of narrow alleys and remnants of the city wall is worth a visit. The monument for the victims of a general strike of railway workers in

The Pagoda Forest (Talin) near Shaolin monastery.

1923, which was brutally suppressed, stands right in the commercial centre. It represents one of the most important milestones in the history of the Chinese workers movement. There is a permanent exhibition about the Yellow River in Zhengzhou, and the **Henan Provincial Museum** contains exhibits which have been found in the region since 1949, especially in Dahecun, about six miles (10 km) north of Zhengzhou. In the 15th century B.C. it was named Ao, the capital of the Shang Dynasty. In the north of the town, by the Yellow River, rises Mount Mang (Mangshan). Water pipes have been laid from the bank of the river up the mountain. A modern pumping station supplies irrigation for the surrounding area. You can get a wonderful view of the river landscape from Mangshan.

The town of Kaifeng

Further east from Zhengzhou along the railway line to Shanghai, south of the Yellow River, is Kaifeng. The town has around 300,000 inhabitants. From the time of the Warring Kingdoms (476-221 B.C.), the town served as the capital for seven dynasties and flourished under the Song Dynasty. The 39-ft (12-metre) long scroll painting, *Upriver to the Qingming Festival*, which is stored in the Imperial Palace in Beijing and describes life in the flourishing commercial town, dates from that time. After that, the town experienced continuous decline; in 1644 the dykes of the Yellow River were opened to stop the Manchu soldiers, and over 300,000 people lost their lives. Kaifeng did not become an industrial centre, and it still looks like a really old Chinese town. It traditionally produced silk and embroidery work.

There are not many sights left in Kaifeng. In the north western part of the town is the **Iron Pagoda** (Tieta), which originates from the Song Dynasty. It has 13 storeys and is over 164 ft (50 metres) high. Its name comes from the rust colour of the bricks which from a distance look like cast iron. The most ancient, still preserved building in the town is the **Fan Pagoda** (also called Pota) which is three storeys high. It contains numerous Buddha figures in various niches. Other sights in Kaifeng are the **Old Music Terrace** (Yuwangtai), the **Dragon Pavilion** (Longting) and the **Xiangguo Monastery** in the town centre. The monastery, built in A.D. 555, was for many centuries the centre of the Buddhist religion in China. It was destroyed in a catastrophic flood in 1644 but was later rebuilt. An octagonal pavilion which has a remarkable ceiling made of wood is worth noting, as is a gold-plated Guanyin statue made of gingko wood. Kaifeng is also known for having had a sizeable settlement of Jews, as already noted by Marco Polo. The synagogue ceased to exist in 1850, though a stele at a supermarket commemorates the former site of the building.

The oldest brick pagoda in China: Songyueta in the Songshan mountains.

The Yellow River

250 km

MONGOLIA

Wall of
Genghis Khan

Suj

Bayan Obo

Qog Qi

Darhan
Muminggan Lianheqi

NEI MONGGOL GAOYUAN

Tamsag Bulag

Bayan Mod

Wujia He

Wuyuan

Dashetai

Guyang

Ulansuhai Nur

Urad Qianqi

Baotou

Tumo
Youq

Huang He
(The Yellow River)

NEI   MONGGOL   ZIZHIQU
(INNER MONGOLIAN   AUT. REGION)

Dengkou   Wuhai

Juntuliang

Dongsheng

Yabrai Yanchang

Ejin Horo Qi

Dongzhen

Shizuishan

Otog Qi

Kuye He

▲
1481

Pingluo

MU US SHAMO

Sher

Minqin

Yinchuan

Xing

Wuwei

Wuzhong

Uxin Qi

Yulin

Great Wall

Great Wall

Huang He
(The Yellow River)

Gulang

Zhongwei

Yanchi

Jingbian

Suide

Dingbian

HUANGRU
GAOYUAN

Maomao Shan
▲
4070

NINGXIA HUIZU

Zichang

Yongdeng

Tongxin

Wuqi

(The Yellow River)

Jingyuan

ZIZHIQU

Huan Xian

Luo He

Yan'an

Huang He

Lanzhou

Xiji

Guyuan

Huan Jiang

Qingyang

Ji Xia

Linxia

Huining

Zhenyuan

Pingliang

Huangling

Yichuan

Jisha

Dingxi

Jinghing

Changwu

Hancheng

Lintao

5020
▲

Tongwei

Long Xian

Xunyi

Tongchuan

Chengcheng

Weiyuan

Yao Xian

Joné

Gangu

Qianyang

SHAANXI

Wei He

Weinan

Tanghao

Tèwo

Tianshui

Wei He

Baoji

Xianyang

Linghao

Min Xian

Xi'an

1997
▲
Hua Shan

Lu

Feng Xian

Hot Springs

Zhouzhi

Shang Xian

Zhugqu

2370
▲
Taiyang Shan

Liuba

Fuping

Shanyang

Kang Xian

Wudu

Lüeyang

Dan

ALONG THE YELLOW RIVER

An eight-hour train journey from Beijing towards the west takes you to the large town of **Datong** in the Shanxi Province. From there, the train continues, through **Hohhot**, the provincial capital of Inner Mongolia, towards the Mongolian People's Republic and then into Russia and finally to Europe. Alternatively, from Hohhot you can head west via **Baotou**, **Yinchuan** to **Lanzhou** and further to Ürümqi; the Ürümqi Express takes about four days from Beijing. While the northern railway line leads directly into the steppe and desert areas of the vast Gobi, the other line takes us to the **Yellow River** (Huanghe) whose scenic valley stretches via Baotou in a south westerly direction to Lanzhou.

On the journey from Beijing to Datong you can, time and again, see parts of the **Great Wall**, which in the past marked the frontier of Chinese civilisation. The journey goes through the hilly loess landscape of the north, and passes past numerous villages surrounded by clay walls, with their mud houses and cave dwellings.

Life here is not pleasant because of the cold north winds and the constant dust in the air. The average annual temperature is only six degrees centigrade; during the height of summer, the thermometer rises to 38 degrees centigrade, while in winter it can fall to minus 30 degrees centigrade.

Datong, which lies 3,993 ft (1,217 metres) high in the north of the coal province of Shanxi, gained its historic importance from the central Asian peoples who, in A.D. 386, founded the Northern Wei Dynasty (386-534). The Wei rulers, who were sympathetic to

Preceding pages: the Hanging Monastery (Hengshansi) in the region near Datong.

Buddhism, undertook the construction of a great cultural site, the **Yungang Caves**. Work on this site was only completed during the Tang Dynasty.

Historical caves

The Yungang Caves are the greatest sight in Datong. They lie in a westerly direction about 10 miles (16 km) from the town, at the base of the sandstone are the Wuzhou Hills. In 53 caves there are more than 51,000 statues; the biggest is 56 ft (17 metres) tall and the smallest less than an inch (two cm); there are also numerous reliefs in the caves.

The caves are spread along the hillside over a height of more than 3,280 ft (1,000 metres). The Yungang caves suffered both natural erosion and plunder: about 1,400 figures were broken during the first decades of this century or taken abroad; they can today be seen in American or European museums. On the way to the Yungang Caves you pass the **Guanyin Hall**, dating from the Liao period, it was restored in 1651 after it was completely destroyed during the Cultural Revolution.

In Datong itself there is the Lower Huayan Monastery and the Upper Huayan Monastery as well as the Shanhua Monastery. Some buildings and figures can still be seen in the two **Huayan Monasteries**, which are 1,000 years old. Several of the clay figures in the main hall of the Lower Huayan Monastery date back to the Liao period. The frescoes with themes from Buddhist legends are also worth seeing. What is interesting and unique is that all the entrances to the temple buildings face the east. This is because the Liao were sun worshippers who prayed towards the east. The main hall dates back to the Jin Dynasty; it houses five gold plated Buddha statues. The Shanhua Monastery was founded as early as the Tang Dynasty.

After the demise of the Liao and Jin dynasties (1115-1234), Datong gradually declined in importance and only

served as a fortification for the Ming emperors. The **Nine Dragon Wall** (Jiulongbi) in the old city dates from the Ming period. It has coloured glazed bricks and used to be at the entrance to a palace in which the thirteenth son of the first Ming emperor lived.

From Datong, you can take a lovely excursion through the loess landscape to Hengshan, 37 miles (60 km) to the south east, one of the five sacred mountains in China. Here, three miles (five km) outside the county town of Hunyuan, the **Hanging Monastery** (Xuankongsi) nestles against an enormous rock, supported by extra rafters. From there you can travel on by bus to the mountain range **Wutaishan** which includes one of the four sacred mountains of Buddhism. The Buddhist god of wisdom, Manjusri, is still worshipped in the numerous monasteries along Wutaishan. During the Ming period, there were more than 300 monasteries,

The Diamond Throne Pagoda (Wutasi) in the Mongolian capital Hohhot.

of which only a few remain. **The Temple of the Light of Buddha** (Foguangsi) and the **Nanchan Temple** are worth mentioning.

A bus journey of 109 miles (175 km), which takes a day, takes you from Wutaishan to **Taiyuan**, the capital of Shanxi Province with more than 2 million inhabitants. The climate is moderate here; in January, temperatures fall to minus 12 degrees centigrade; in July, the average temperature is 25 degrees centigrade.

Fascinating Taiyun

In Taiyuan, it is worth sampling some of the dishes of Shanxi cuisine, for instance *tounao*, a thick soup made of mutton, lotus roots, yam, herbs and rice wine, or *shaomai*, which consists of steamed stuffed dumplings made of wheatmeal. Taiyuan's history goes back to the Spring and Autumn period (770 - 476 B.C.). The town was opened to trade at the beginning of this century with the construction of a railway line, and has been constantly expanding into an industrial town since 1949.

The surrounding area of Taiyuan is rich in important historic relics of great beauty. Just 16 miles (25 km) outside the town, on the slopes of Mount Xuanweng, is the **Jinci Temple** with its **Mother Goddess Hall** (Shengmudian) where numerous painted clay figures are stored. They are considered amongst the most important artefacts of the Song period. In the south eastern suburbs of Taiyuan is the **Two Pagoda Temple** (Shuangtasi) from the Ming period which has become the symbol of the town, and the **Chongshan Temple,** whose construction goes back to the Tang Dynasty. Not far from Taiyuan, there are also the Daoist **Longshan Caves** and the **Dayun Temple** in the county town of Lingfen. The **Provin-**

Camel herds in the Mongolian grasslands.

221

cial **Museum** in the town centre contains a collection of Buddhist stone statues from the 5th to 10th centuries and a collection of sutras from the 3rd and 4th centuries.

We return to Datong to continue the journey along the Yellow River. The next stop is **Hohhot**, which is the capital of the province of Inner Mongolia. Be prepared for the journey as it takes about 13 hours by train from Beijing. The large city of Hohhot lies at the southern outskirts of the Gobi Desert on a high plateau on the edge of the Mongolian grassland. The Mongols form a minority in Inner Mongolia; they only make up around 10 percent of the total population. It is thus not surprising that, today, Hohhot looks more like a Chinese town than a Mongolian one and that it reminds one of the fact that in the 16th century it had been founded by the Mongol sovereign Altan Khan as a Mongolian settlement.

There are some buildings of religious interest in Hohhot, for instance the more than 400-year-old **Dazhao Monastery** which was renovated in 1985 (it houses a well stocked library with splendid scriptures); the **Lamaist Temple Xilitu Zhao**, a great **Mosque** dating from the 17th and 18th century; and the **Five Pagoda Temple** (Wutasi), a building from the 18th century.

The Mongolian way of life

To see real Mongolian life, it is better to travel to the grass steppe, for instance to Baiyunhesha (about 106 miles/170 km), Wulantuge (some 50 miles/80 km), or Huitengxile (79 miles/127 km). Here – although tourism has already intruded – you can gain an insight into the life of Mongolian nomads living in tents known as *yurts*, and enjoy the beautiful sunsets. A visit to the grasslands in summer is particularly interesting because of the traditional *Naidam* festival, when riding games, wrestling and archery are on offer. Mongolian specialities such as mutton and lamb are served,

roasted or grilled over an open fire.

Three hours' train journey from Hohhot is Baotou, the "steel city of the grasslands". Baotou used to be an important trading centre; from the 17th century onwards, the Qing emperors systematically populated the town with Han Chinese.

The Mongols once called this area "Land of Red Deer"; in socialist China, it became an important centre for the iron and steel industry. Baotou stretches along the banks of the Yellow river, which crosses Inner Mongolia as far as 497 miles (800 km). There are few interesting tourist sights in Baotou to lure the traveller. You can go by landrover to the Lamaist **Willow Monastery** (Wudangzhao) in the Daqing mountains 47 miles (75 km) away.

You can also take an excursion to the **tomb of Genghis Khan**, 75 miles (120 km) south in the Banner of Yijinhoroqi. (A Banner is an administrative area that

Mongol nomads in front of their *yurt*, with which they travel from one pasture to another.

is comparable to a county). There is a small, village-style museum at the burial site; it shows Mongolian customs and traditions.

From Baotou, the train carries on in the direction of **Yinchuan**, the capital of the autonomous region of Ningxia. It has 700,000 inhabitants, and is the city of the Hui (Chinese Muslims). The landscape along the Yellow River alternates between fertile plains and arid regions. To the north and west of the Yellow River, the desert-like landscape stretches to the river bank, steppes and semi-steppes alternate with fertile areas which have been artificially irrigated from the waters of the Yellow River. The closer you come to Yinchuan, the greener and more fertile the landscape becomes. The Chinese used the Yellow River 2,000 years ago to irrigate the agricultural land in this area by building canals. The irrigation systems were extended over the centuries and the canals continue to form the basis of Yinchuan's wealth.

The **Yellow River** (Huanghe) has, however, played a devastating role in Chinese history. It is 3,395 miles (5,464 km) long; its middle part crosses the provinces of Gansu, Ninxia and Inner Mongolia and further on forms the border between Shanxi and Shaanxi provinces before reaching the northern Chinese plain. It contains a lot of loess and other deposits, hence its name.

This was not always the case; it used to just be called the "River"; only in the Han Dynasty did it begin to be called "yellow". This may be an indication that the constantly increasing deposits in the river resulted from the vast deforestation which took place in central China from the 6th century A.D. onwards. Ships can only use part of the Yellow River, as its estuary on the Shandong peninsula is so shallow that no boat connection to the sea is possible. Over the last 2,000 years, it has changed course twelve times and flooding has caused great devastation. Only where people succeeded in utilising the fertile flooded areas and the water, was the river beneficiary to humans.

The area around Yinchuan is still the most fertile, wealthiest part of the autonomous region of Ningxia of the Hui people. The bare, mountainous southern parts of the autonomous region are the poorest part of the country. Afforestation projects supported by the UN aim to provide financial aid to the peasants. Around 4 million people live in the autonomous region; some 32 percent are Hui Muslim. The Hui here are visibly different from the Han Chinese. All the men wear white caps, and some of the women in the villages still wear the veil.

Exploring Yinchuan

The town of **Yinchuan** has a history going back more than 1,500 years and has become a rapidly growing industrial town. The division between the old and new town is clearly recognisable. The old town can easily be explored, on foot or bicycle, from the only hotel for foreigners which is located there. The 177-ft (54-metre) high **North Pagoda** (Beita or Haibaota), dating from the 17th century, to the north of the old town is worth a visit. You can get a good view of the town, its surroundings and the Yellow River from here. In the south west of the old town is the 212-ft (64½-metre) tall **West Pagoda** (Xita) whose roof is made of green ceramic tiles.

The most interesting sight on offer in Yinchuan is its old town with the many small shops and snack bars around the **city gate**, which resembles the Gate of Heavenly Peace in Beijing. The Muslims predominate here: the white caps of the Hui are everywhere, and you can recognise many of the Muslim restaurants by their blue signs.

A trip through the environs of Yinchuan takes you through many Hui Muslim villages. Located just 19 miles (30 km) away is the ancient burial site of the **Western Xia Dynasty** (Xixia Lingmu) which contains the tombs of eight kings and 70 other graves.

A lovely bus-ride from Yinchuan southwards via Wuzhong takes you to the hydroelectric power plant in the **Qingtong Gorge**. From here you can take a boat trip on the very muddy Yellow River to the 108 pagodas on the other bank. In the very south of the autonomous region of Ningxia, in the **caves near Guyuan** in the Xiumishan mountains, you find a 62-ft (19-metre) statue of Buddha.

From Qingtong Gorge, you can continue your journey in the direction of **Zhongwei**. Near Zhongwei, the Tenggeli desert comes right up to the river. Unfortunately, the only interesting sight in Zhongwei is the **Gao Temple**. You can spend the night in Zhongwei and take the train the next day for Lanzhou.

History, food and temples

Lanzhou is the capital of Gansu province, one of the poorest regions in China. Ethnic minorities, including Tibetans, are settled here. Lanzhou, which has 2 million inhabitants and stretches along the banks of the Yellow River, is a modern industrial town and the centre of Chinese atomic research. Unfortunately the town does not live up to its name – Orchid City. Only in the old town can one still sense a certain atmosphere which gives a hint of the town's 2,000 year history. You can get the best view of the town and the Yellow River from **White Pagoda Hill** (Baitashan) on the northern bank of the River. Near the bridge is a small Muslim market. In the various markets in Lanzhou, you will find spicy noodles, lamb kebab and oriental bread on offer in the small snack bars.

A 600-year-old temple site is located on a slope in the **Park of Five Springs** (Wuquan Gongyuan) in the north of the town. **Chongqing Temple** (Chongqingsi) contains a 16-ft (five-metre) tall bronze statue of the Buddha from 1370, and a five-ton iron bell from 1202. **Lan-**zhou Zoo is in the Park of Five Springs. The neolithic pottery and bronze artefacts from the Zhou period in **Gansu Provincial Museum** are worth seeing. Do not miss the the the most splendid exhibit in the museum – the *Flying Horse of Gansu* from the time of the Eastern Han Dynasty.

In summer there are boat trips on the Yellow River (if the water isn't too shallow) to the **Binglingsi Caves** which jut out of the water. The trip takes about three hours and one highlight is the large number of Buddha figures carved into the sandstone by several artists in the 5th century.

From Lanzhou, you can visit **Labrang Monastery**. The journey of 161 miles (260 km) takes about eight hours and is fairly strenuous. The monastery was founded in 1710 and it is one of the most important monasteries of the Yellow Hat sect. If you have sufficient time, it is worth making the trip, but you should allow three days for the journey. An excursion to the **Liujia Gorges** by the Yellow River is an equally worthwhile trip.

The journey along the Yellow river ends in Lanzhou. From here, **Xining**, the capital of Qinghai Province, can be reached in three to four hours by train. Not far from Xining is the **Kumbum Monastery** (Ta'ersi) which is important to Tibetan culture. The present Dalai Lama was born near it. From Xining, the railway carries on to Golmud; from here, **Lhasa** is within reach via bus or car.

You could also continue the journey towards the north west, passing **Jiayuguan**, the end of the Great Wall, and crossing **Dunhuang** with its famous cave grottoes, **Hami** and the oasis **Turfan**, and finally reaching **Ürümqi**. In a south westerly direction, the railway goes from Lanzhou through the hilly, furrowed landscape to Gansu in the Wei River valley. The Wei is one of the numerous tributaries of the Yellow River which accompanies us on our journey to Xi'an.

224

THE SILK ROAD

China's vast "Wild West" is accessible to foreign visitors along the classic Silk Road. This ancient trade route starts in the old capitals of **Luoyang** and **Chang'an** (now Xi'an), reaches the Yellow River (Huanghe) at **Lanzhou**, follows along the "Gansu Corridor" and stretches along the edge of deserts and mountains. It divides into two routes in the oasis of **Dunhuang**. The northern route goes to the oasis of **Hami**, winds along Bogdashan mountain to the oasis of Turfan, comes close to Ürümqi (Urumchi), goes across several mountain passes through the Tianshan range to **Karashahr** and **Korla** and, via **Kuqa** (Kucha), **Kysyl**, **Kumtura**, **Aksu**, **Tumtchuk** and **Lailik**, finally arriving at **Kashgar**.

The southern route goes from Dunhuang between the river oases on the northern slopes of Kunlunshanmai mountains (Kunlun mountains, also called Altyndagh) and the sand desert of Taklamakan (Taklimakan). The best known oases along this route are **Charklik**, **Cherchen**, **Endere**, **Niya**, **Kerija**, **Chotan** and **Yarkand**. In Kashgar, the two routes rejoin.

In the year 200 of our time scale this transcontinental route linked the Roman Empire at the time of Caesar in the West and the Han Dynasty of China. Trade was carried on by traders who belonged to neither of the two old empires, but were mostly Parthian.

Before the discovery of the sea route to India, the Silk Road was the most important connection between the Orient and the West. It experienced its last great era during the time of the Mongols, when the entire route from China to the Mediterranean was part of one empire. At that time, Nicolo and Marco Polo (1254-1323) travelled from Kashgar to the Far East along the southern route, as has now been ascertained.

The overland link quickly lost its importance as trade across the seas developed. In recent times, it has been replaced; in China, with the railway line Lanzhou-Hami-Ürümqi. The last part, to Alma-Ata in Kazatchstan, was completed around 1992. The trade route was never known as the Silk Road historically. The German geographer Ferdinand Freiherr von Richthofen (1833-1905) gave it that name.

You can reach **Jiuquan** from Lanzhou by train in 16 hours, or by plane. The overland journey is very attractive because of the varied loess landscape and the many contrasts offered by the desert regions. In the south, the snow-covered peaks of the **Qilianshan** mountains flank the railway line at a distance. You reach the flat, more than 497-mile (800-km) long **Gansu Corridor** when you arrive at the old administrative and garrison town of **Wuwei**. Wuwei became a district capital in 115 B.C. The *Flying Horse*, a bronze statue from the

Eastern Han period (206-208 B.C.) which was excavated in 1968, comes from near Wuwei. The original is now located in a museum in Beijing; a beautiful replica can be found in Lanzhou Provincial Museum.

The train passes **Shandan** where in l943 New Zealander Rewi Alley (1897-1988), built a famous technical and vocational school. The city wall was extended and renovated in the Ming period. A pagoda, on the site where a hair of the Indian Buddhist emperor Ashoka (264-227 B.C.) was found, originates from that period.

Zhangye, the capital of the prefecture of the same name, is 37 miles (60 km) to the west. Zhangye, which was founded in 121 B.C. as a garrison town, has a bell tower (originally drum tower, Jinyuanlou or Gulou) in the town centre. It dates from 1509 with a bell from the Tang period. The Wooden Pagoda found here also dates from the Tang period though its first six floors, out of a total of eight, are actually made of brick. It is generally not possible for travellers to stay in these places. Some of them are militarily restricted areas, though bus trips along the entire route are allowed.

Jiuquan, which is a growing industrial town, was founded in 111 B.C. as a garrison town. Between 127 and 102 B.C., the Han emperors relocated 980,000 peasant families as paramilitary peasants, including at least 700,000 victims of the flood in Shandong. The old town quarter around the drum and bell towers is currently under renovation; the small alleys are being torn down and skyscrapers built.

The charming **Springs Park** (People's Park, Renmin Gongyuan) at the edge of the town was built as a memorial to General Huo Qubing, who is once said to have been given a barrel of wine by the Han emperor Wudi (140-87 B.C.) as a reward for having gained a decisive victory over the Xiongnu, thought to be related to the Huns who, in the 5th century A.D., overran Eastern Europe. To let his soldiers enjoy the wine too, he watered it down with water from a spring. The spring is in front of a newly landscaped garden in a modest, rectangular basin.

About nine miles (15 km) south west is the Buddhist **temple site of Wenshushan**. At the time of the Qing emperor Qianlong (1736-1795), 300 monk's cells are said to have existed here, but they were demolished by rebellious Chinese Muslims after 1865. The small **Thousand Buddha Caves** (Qianfodong or Mogaoku) with its poorly-preserved paintings date from the Northern Wei period (386-535).

A good 17 miles (30 km) further to the west is Jiayuguan, which since 1372, was part of the western end of the Great Wall. The fortification, 5,817 ft (1,773 metres) above sea level, was completed four years after the victory of the Ming Dynasty. A square inner courtyard is enclosed by walls and two gates. On top

The Ürümqi express takes more than three days to travel from Beijing to Ürümqi.

of the 33-ft (10-metre) high and 2,100-ft (640-metre) long wall, on which you can walk, are 56-ft (17-metre) high watch towers from the late Ming and the early Qing period (mid-17th century). The wall was first restored around 1507, again during the Qing period and in recent years. At the southern entrance (towards the town of Jiayuguan) rises an elevated, pavilion-like stage. Dignitaries used to watch plays from the pavilion located opposite to the right-hand side. The wall, from the Ming period, which is still intact, stretches south-westwards to the foothills of the Qilianshan and approximately northwards to the Beishan. The construction, which dominates the landscape, is particularly impressive when approached from the west. A monument with the inscription "Strongest Fort of the World" has stood outside the West Gate since 1809 (Year 14 of the emperor Jiaqing).

Eight tombs from the Wei Dynasty

(220-265) and the **Jin Dynasty** (265-420), called Weijin Bihua Mu, are situated around 12½ miles (20 km) to the north east. They contain wall murals depicting scenes from everyday life.

The old town of **Yumen**, which can only be reached by funicular railway (a new part of the town named Yumen Dongshan is in the middle), lies around 37 miles (60 km) to the west. The town has little charm, but the **Changma Caves** (Changmadong) 37 miles (60 km) farther to the south east have been built in similar style to certain grottoes of Mogao near Dunhuang. At Qiaowan, the road to Dunhuang turns off to the west away from the railway line. It follows the river Shulehe to **Anxi**. About 25 miles (40 km) before Dunhuang, you pass a well-preserved watchtower (1730), which is an example of the type of communications used at that time: by daylight, flag signals were given from the top platform; at night, fire signals.

Sand dunes in Taklamakan desert.

To reach Dunhuang by rail, you have to travel to **Liuyuan** and from there go on for several hours by bus. After crossing the drained plain of the Shulehe, you can see, near the **village of Zhangjiaquan** in the flat desert to the west, remnants of the Great Wall from the eastern Han period. The structure of the clay and fascine construction is surprisingly easy to see.

Dunhuang

The oasis town of Dunhuang lies in an irrigated cotton-producing oasis. The local museum (Dunhuang Bowuguan) near the hotel has some local finds, graphic representations and models of the oasis, and gives an impression of the historic significance of this settlement. Between cotton fields and threshing areas, at the edge of the town, is the **White Horse Dagoba** (Baimata), which is reminiscent in its shape of the

White Dagoba in Beijing. This is where the white horse of the Indian travelling monk Kumarajiva (344-431) is said to have died.

There are 492 grottoes at the **Mogao Caves** some 15 miles (25 km) south east of the town. Of these, around 70 can be visited. The first caves are said to have been built by the monk Lezun in 366, the last ones were carved out at the time of the Mongolian conquest (1277). After that, Mogao sunk into oblivion, until the monk Wang Yuanlu settled there around 1898. The first cave he opened is the one now numbered [16]. In the next cave [17], he found more than 40,000 manuscripts. The Hungarian-British explorer Sir Aurel Stein bought 6,500 manuscripts from Wang between 1907 and 1914; the Frenchman Paul Pelliot bought a further 6,000 scripts. The grottoes show an uninterrupted history of Chinese painting, particularly landscape painting, over a

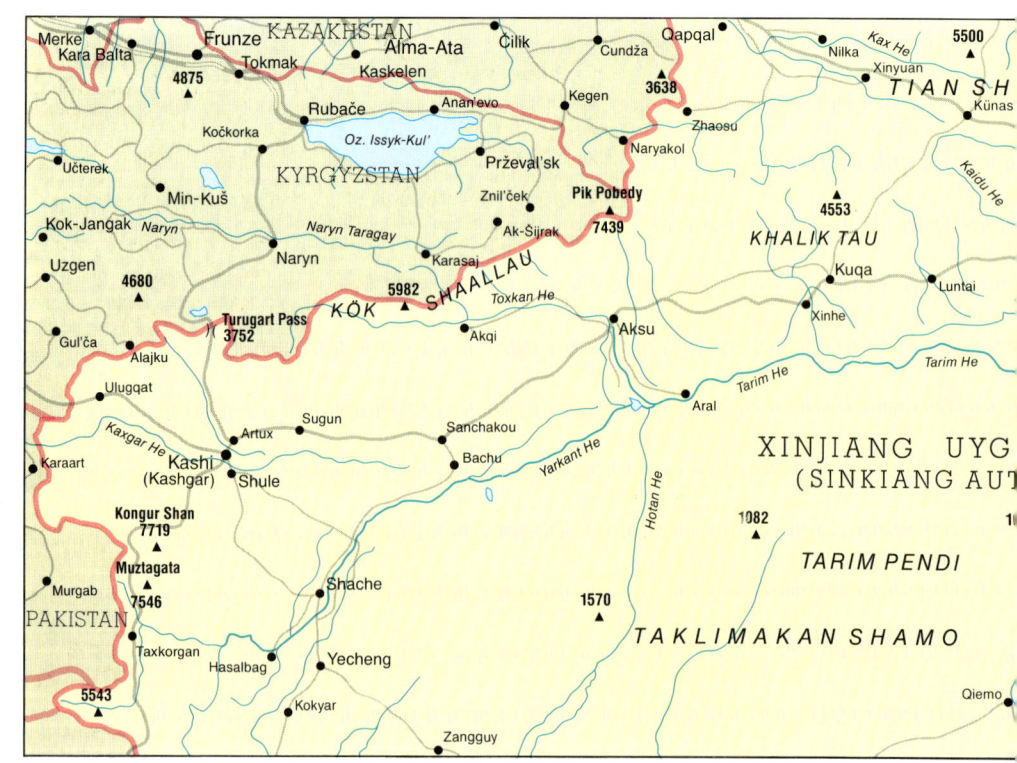

period of nearly a thousand years. Visiting them is the high point of any journey along the Silk Road, but, because of the inadequate information, you need to be very well prepared. The following hints give the numbers of the individual caves in square brackets.

The paintings of the time of the Northern Wei (386-535) are mainly concerned with Buddhist legends (Jataka) and saints such as Kumarajiva [272]. The Jataka of King Sivi [275] depicts the self-sacrifice of a monarch for a dove. The four excursions of Buddha Sakyamuni [27] confront him with the real world. The Jataka of the Deer King [257] shows the rescue of a deer and the punishment of a hunter. The victory of Buddha over the Temptor Mara [254] and the Jataka of the Sacrifice of Prince Sudana for a hungry tiger [254] are other examples. Many paintings [263 and 249] depict the preaching Buddha.

The form and contents of painting developed further under the Western Wei and the Northern Zhou (535-589); now scenes from daily life, such as hunting scenes, appear [240]. One Jataka describes how 500 reformed bandits recover their eyesight [285]. The representation [285] then turns towards bodhisattvas and guardians of the world. Flying elves, male Gandharva [290] and particularly female Apsara [404] became important subjects.

In the Sui period (589-618) further Jatakas [419] and legends from the Lotus Sutra [419] or from Buddha's entry into Nirvana [295] appear. The blackening by time of the often-used white lead gives the outlines of the figures a particular charm. The depiction of people becomes more realistic [303], and there is a first depiction of Paradise [420]. The paintings from the Tang period (618-909) exudes beauty and perfection. There are representa-

tions of the Western Paradise [329], [217], [172], which is of significance for the "Pure Country" Sect (Jingtu), but also of worldly sponsors [329] and scenes of meditation [172], a picture of the historic monk Xuanzang [217], pictures of orchestras [220] and weddings [445], pictures of ploughs in the rain [23], of dancers and musicians [320], and again paintings of Buddha's entry into nirvana [158], monks studying [201], battle scenes [12], servants [17], and finally landscapes such as the Wutaishan [61]. One of the most beautiful caves [323] shows an Indian Buddha statue made from sandalwood being presented to the emperor.

In the following Five Dynasties (to 960), the formal mastery of the painters is preserved; sponsors such as the King of Khotan [98] are painted more realistically. Under the Northern Song (960-1126), interesting pictures of temples [61] and Arhats (Luohan, disciples of the Buddha) [97] are painted. After that, the artistic creativity declines. However, there is one masterpiece from the first Yuan period which shows the bodhisattva Avalokiteshvara [3] with a thousand arms and a thousand eyes.

Purely touristic attractions in Dunhuang are the **Lunar Lake** (Yueyaquan) and the **Singing Sand Mountain** (Mingshashan). A day trip to the **Jade Pass** (Yumenguan) 43 miles (70 km) away, the ruins of a border town from the Han period, gives a good view of the landscape, but if possible, you might pass them over in favour of another excursion to the Mogao Grottoes.

The population of Xinjiang is predominantly Islamic. The Uighur people of the autonomous republic speak Turkish and are Muslims; they constitute approximately 45 percent of the total population. The Han Chinese population has increased from 7.9 percent (1940) to 40.4 percent (1982 census).

Lake of Heaven in the Tianshan mountains near Ürümqi.

Han people live mostly in the larger cities and in new settlements; that is where the youth from the huge towns of the east, who were "sent to the countryside" after 1958, have settled. The smaller oases and nomad areas – partly also the agricultural areas in the north of Xinjiang – are still predominantly populated by Uighur people and (as far as the nomads are concerned) Kazakhs.

The capital of the Autonomous Region, Ürümqi (Urumchi), which lies 2,953 ft (900 metres) above sea level, is a huge town. About 75 percent of its population are Han Chinese and only 10 percent each are Uighur and Hui peoples; it is the departure or destination point for all journeys to Xinjiang. The development of industry has resulted in considerable environmental pollution in recent years.

The **Museum of the Autonomous Region** is worth a visit. Apart from significant archaeological finds it also exhibits life-size models of the houses and tools of the most important nationalities in the region. In the old town, there are (again) numerous small **mosques** and bazaars full of activity. A pavilion in the style of a Chinese garden lodge and a small pagoda, both symbols of the town, are located on the **Red Mountain** (Hongshan), which also offers a good view of the town. The town itself has modern skyscrapers. Some buildings date from the time of the Russian, evidence of Soviet presence, amongst them the main post office and the state guest house. The walls and gates described in l936 by Sven Hedin were demolished some time ago.

It is worth taking an excursion to the **Lake of Heaven** (Tianchi), some 62 miles (100 km) away. It lies 62,336 ft (1,900 metres) high in the Tianshan mountains at the foot of the 17,864-ft (5,445-metre) high Bogdashan; and the journey passes some scenic landscapes.

Even in the desert, traffic rules should be heeded.

Just 93 miles (150 km) east of Ürümqi is the Chinese settlement of **Shihezi** whose structure and outline goes back to its colonisation under the Qing emperor Qianlong (1736-1795). The town, with 100,000 inhabitants, is typical of the Han Chinese pioneering towns in areas with artificial irrigation. Turfan (also called: Turpan, Tulupan) can be reached from Ürümqi in a half-day bus journey or by rail; the station is 37 miles (60 km) from the town. The road leads westwards through the desolate industrial belt of Ürümqi, then through pastures along the northern slope of Tianshan to **Dabancheng**, a market town near a pass which leads to the valley of the Baiyanghe (White Poplar river), which is richly forested. At the end of the Baiyanghe, the road reaches a stony desert which stretches to the edge of the Turfan oasis. The Turfan oasis, which stretches 93 miles (150 km) from east to west, is 93 miles (150 km) below sea level; **Moonlight Lake** (Aydingkol), a salt lake which is drying up, is 505 ft (154 metres) below sea level. In summer, the temperature in the oasis, which is bordered in the north by the Tianshan and in the south by Kuruktag, rises to 47 degrees centigrade.

Only a few old buildings have been preserved in Turfan. The **Emin Minaret** (Sugongta), built with clay bricks in 1776, and the sparsely furnished mosque next to it are the symbols of the town. The underground irrigation system (Karez) is worth visiting. In the Karez, the melting water from the mountains is channelled underground to the oasis over long distances, to prevent the water from evaporating. The local museum shows relics from the Silk Road, mummies from the Astana Graves, silks from the early period of transcontinental trade and funerary objects. Towards the east, the **Flaming Mountains** (Huoshan), a range of bare

The Imin Minaret at Suleiman Mosque in Turfan.

sandstone mountains rising up to 6,073 ft (1,851 metres) stretch for 56 miles (90 km). In direct sunlight, the temperature rises up to 75 degrees centigrade. The mountain range achieved fame in the novel *The Journey to the West,* which describes the travels of Xuanzang. Born in Luoyang around 602, Xuanzang entered a Buddhist monastery at the age of 13, and quickly became a thorough expert in the religious scriptures. He departed for India in 629, with the support of the Tang emperor Taizong (627-649), studied and debated at the Buddhist academy Nalanda near present-day Patna, returned after 17 years with 657 scrolls to China, taught in Chang'an (present-day Xi'an) and died there in 664.

Just 31 miles (50 km) from Turfan is the ruined city of **Gaochang**, the ancient Karachotcha or Khocho. The town was founded as a garrison under the Han emperor Wudi (140-86 B.C.) and be-

came a prefecture around 400 B.C. In 460, it declared its independence from the partly Turkish rulers. In 640, the Tang emperor Taizong (629-649) took it back from from Qu Wentai, the last independent ruler. During its heyday it had 30,000 inhabitants and more than 30 Buddhist monasteries; remnants of some of these, where Xuanzang preached in A.D. 639, can still be seen. Around 1300 the town capitulated after 40 years of fighting during which the irrigation system was destroyed. Today, you can see the division of the town into a centre with sacred buildings and into the suburbs with trade centres, bazaars and housing estates.

Next door, to the north west, is **Astana** (Asitana or Sanbao, "Three Citadels"), a burial ground with well over a thousand tombs. Three tombs dating from the 5th and 6th centuries are open to visitors; their wall murals show characteristics of the elements: earth,

Uighur children at a spice stand.

gold, jade and stone, six types of geese which are also assigned characteristics, and three mummified bodies. At present, it is not possible to visit tombs from the Han period which contain wall murals with everyday scenes. Similar murals are in the tomb of General Zhang Huaiji, from the Tang period.

To the north of Gaochang, in the **Flaming Mountains**, is the ancient **cave monastery of Bezeklik** (Qianfo-dong, "Thousand-Buddha-Caves"). The trip there through the Murtuq canyon begins at a watchtower dating from the Qing period (around 1770) opposite the cave monastery site **Samgin** (Murtuq), which is not open to visitors. It was used from around 450 to the 13th century. The **Caves of Bezeklik** – around 70, of which only a dozen can be visited – have been carved into the cliff face some 295 ft (80 metres) above the western bank of the river. The plunder of valuable paintings by German and British archaeologists (Albert von Le Coq, Albert Grünwedel, and Aurel Stein) damaged the pictorial representation of the Buddha and bodhisattvas in caves 29 and 39. After 1860, Islamic fanatics destroyed most of the facial depictions. Nevertheless, the remains are still worth a visit. Work on the caves began around 430; and the monastery was abandoned in the 13th century.

Six miles (10 km) to the west of Turfan is the **ruined city of Jiaohe Gucheng** ("Old City by Two Rivers"), which in the past was called Yariko or Yarkhoto, and was founded in the Han period. It was the centre of a kingdom until the 5th century. Jiaohe lies on a plateau between two rivers, a natural fortification. Civil wars and lack of water at the time of Mongol rule (ca 1230) brought the town to ruins. The central sacred site and the remnants of Buddhist monasteries and stupas in the north west, which are most prominent among the ruins, are still well preserved. You can clearly distinguish between the bazaar and artisan quarters near the eastern gate and the ancient settlements. The remnants of underground dwellings, which offered protection from the summer heat and the freezing winter, are of special interest.

The city of **Kashgar** (or Kashi, Kaxgar) lies 4,265 ft (1,300 metres) high on the bank of the Tuman river in the middle of an irrigation oasis with cotton and agricultural cultivation. The population of 240,000 (1988 census) is predominantly Uighur. Kashgar only became Chinese around 200 B.C., again during the Tang period, and finally during the period of the Qing emperors Kangxi (1662-1722) and Qian-long (1736-1795).

Kashgar is the furthest away from the sea of all the big towns; it is closer to Moscow, Islamabad, Delhi, Kabul and Teheran than to Beijing. The borders to Kyrgyzstan (75 miles/120 km), Tajikistan (100 miles/160 km), Afghanistan (186 miles/300 km) and Pakistan (248 miles/400 km) are close. The climate is extreme: in winter the temperature can fall to below 24 degrees centigrade and in the summer months it regularly reaches above 40 degrees centigrade; the frost-free period lasts 220 days annually.

The **Id Kah Mosque** (Aitika) in the town centre was renovated in 1981 and is China's biggest mosque, with a central dome and two flanking minarets. Behind the gate are open, tree-lined squares for prayer and 109 yds (100 metres) behind is the Great Prayer Hall, open only for Friday prayer. The side halls are covered in precious carpets. A stylised picture of the *Kaaba of Mecca* adorns the entrance to the Great Prayer Hall. The building, dating from 1445, dominates the town. The steps in front of the side walls are a popular meeting place, particularly for old people. On religious feast days, up to 50,000 worshippers come for Friday prayer.

To the north runs an extremely lively bazaar street with barber shops, book and fur traders, smithies, bakers and, directly by the Mosque, dentists. The covered bazaar, where mostly cloth, haberdashery and food are sold, goes as far as the Great Square. By strolling through the bazaar you reach the modern shopping avenue, with the striking "Department Store of the Minorities" (Minzudian) and craft shops and workshops. Opposite the entrance to the covered bazaar along the Great Square are snack bars, tea houses and numerous small shops. No donkey or horse drawn carriages, the traditional means of transport, are allowed here. They stop at the northern edge near the street leading to the Id Kah Mosque.

Directly where the horse carriages stop is **Qini Bagh** (Chinese Garden), which was the British Consulate from 1895 to 1947 and is now a hotel where mostly Pakistani traders and individual travellers and backpackers stop. In a building in front, the state travel agency Lüxingshe has a local office and offers cars for rent. The main buildings are in danger of crumbling, though the site retains its historic charm for the mo-

The faithful gather for prayer in front of Id Kah Mosque in Kashgar.

ment. The formerly famous wine gardens have had to make way for a bus parking area. One can still sense the atmosphere of the time of the Consul Sir George MacCartney who resided here for 28 years. Explorers such as Sven Hedin, Sir Aurel Stein and many others frequented the house.

The former Russian (subsequently Soviet) Consulate at the other end of the town, which was opened from 1865 to 1961, is now also a hotel (Seman). At the time of Consul Nikolaj Petrowski, the rival of MacCartney, the great explorers also called here. The newly added buildings are from the time of the Soviet advisers.

The **Apak Hoja Mausoleum** dating back to 1583 and 1640, and renovated in 1980, is worth seeing. It is a memorial to the Hoja family. Apak Hoja (*Aba Hezhuo*), who died in 1583, was an outstanding politico-religious leader of Kashgar. His sarcophagus, one of 57,

which together house 72 corpses of the family, lies on an elevated pedestal in the centre of the main hall of the central building, which is reminiscent of a mosque (but not turned towards Mecca), and is flanked by slightly leaning minarets. In the near left corner is the sarcophagus of Xiangfei (Fragrant Concubine), the daughter of the last Hodja. According to legend, Xiangfei is said to have refused to sleep with the emperor Qianlong, who took her to Beijing after the repression of a rebellion in 1758, and was killed as a result. Her body was taken back to Kashgar in a carriage whose remnants are exhibited in the Small Mosque. Jakub Beg, the leader of the rebellion of 1877 which was repressed by the Qing, is buried in the nearby cemetery. The exact place of his grave is no longer known. The memorial built in 1887 by the Imperial Russian Geographic Society for the German traveller Adolf Schlagintweit, who

was murdered here on 8 August 1857, can also no longer be found.

The most important weekly event is the **Sunday market** (*basha*, a Chinese version of bazaar), is still held by the banks of the Tuman, which has several bridges and steps leading to town. Some 40,000, sometimes even 60,000 visitors, buyers and sellers come to this market, reputedly the biggest in Asia. The market area, which is divided into sections selling similar goods, offers, in a clockwise direction from the main entrance: grain and flour, camels, sheep, cows, yaks and horses, furriery and leather products, wood, doors and furniture, spices and salt, bread, vegetables, and cloth. The numerous market alleys are lined with tea shops, snack bars, hairdressers, workshops and bakers. The cattle market is particularly lively in the mornings and it carries on till lunchtime. Nearly all the central Asian minorities visit the market – Pakistani traders are there in great numbers – giving it an international atmosphere.

The great **Mausoleum of Mahmud al Kashgarli** (1008-1105) was built here. The building, which is about 37 miles (60 km) away near the road to Pakistan, towers over a mosque destroyed in an earthquake. A portrait of Mahmud hangs in the entrance hall, and on his sarcophagus lies a copy of his main work, *Divan Lugat Atturk*, written between 1072 and 1074 while in exile in Baghdad. It is one of the oldest Arabic-Turkish dictionaries with 7,500 entries. Mahmud, who came from the house of the ruling Karachanids and was one of the most important scholars of his time, was exiled after their overthrow in 1058 and only returned to Kashgar shortly before his death. The Mausoleum was visited in 1983 by the then prime minister Zhao Ziyang and is visited mainly by Turkish travellers.

Farther to the south west, 118 miles (190 km) from Kashgar, at the beginning of the Pamir high mountain region, is **Lake Karakul**. The ice-covered peaks, Muztagata (24,700 ft/7,546

Islamic architecture is predominant in the north west of China.

240

metres) and Kongur (25,300 ft/7,719 metres) rise up here. On a clear day they can apparently be seen from Kashgar. They are the second and third highest peaks in the Pamir Mountains.

The Buddhist **Caves of the Three Immortals** (Sanxiandong), on a sheer rockface by Qiakmak river, are less interesting than those of Bezeklik or Dunhuang. The ancient residence of the Karachanides, **Hanoi** (Halvoi), which flourished during the Tang and Song periods and was abandoned in the 11th century, is today a ruin with few remnants (amongst them the Mor Pagoda and the Karez irrigation systems). It lies 19 miles (30 km) to the east of Kashgar.

Taxkorgan

About 155 miles (250 km) from Kashgar is Taxkorgan (Taschkurgan, or Sariköl, Stone Tower) at 11,800 ft (3,600 metres) high. It is the "last outpost" in China before Pakistan, and the capital of the Autonomous District of the same name with a majority of Tadzhik peoples. According to accounts by Ptolemy (around A.D. 140), traders from east and west used to trade their goods here, though people did not cross the borders.

From Kashgar you can cross to Pakistan through the Karakorum Mountains (Black Wall). There are always Pakistanis in Kashgar offering hotel accommodation in the Pakistan Hunza valley. The 468-mile (753-km) long track across the Khunjerab Pass (Blood Valley), whose peak reaches 15,069 ft (4,593 metres), was reopened after prolonged disburbances in May 1986 but is not very safe because of uncertain weather. About 168 miles (270 km) south of the peak is the first Pakistani airport **Gilgit**. Along the mountain road, you can see many wall murals, engravings and sculptures from the period of the Silk Road.

Below, a high mountain pass leads across the Khara Korum mountains to Pakistan. **Following pages**: avenue lined with stone figures leading to the tomb of the first Ming emperor in Nanjing.

NANJING – CHINA'S SOUTHERN CAPITAL

Nanjing, the former capital of the rich southern Chinese province Jiangsu, is considered one of the most beautiful cities in China. It has 4½ million inhabitants. Its wide tree-lined avenues, dotted with old two- or three-storey wooden houses, invite you for a leisurely stroll. The forested **Purple Mountains** (Zijinshan) frame the city in the east with their fresh green foliage, and give it an atmosphere which only few other Chinese towns still have to offer.

Together with Wuhan and Chongqing, Nanjing is one of the "three furnaces of China"; in summer, the temperatures rise to above 40 degrees centigrade. There may be snow in winter, but the winter season is very short, as it is in the whole of southern China.

Nanjing can easily be reached by train, boat or plane. If you come by train from the north, you have to cross China's longest river, the Yangzi, via the great **Yangzi Bridge** which was opened in 1968. Before it was built, trains crossed on a ferry, which took several hours. The bridge, which is to the north west of the city, has become a symbol of Chinese independence and national pride. When relations between the Soviet Union and China were severed in 1960, the Chinese built the bridge with their own resources in the space of eight years. It took 9,000 workers more than eight years to construct the bridge, struggling against the strong currents of the Yangzi.

The two-tier bridge measures 5,108 ft (1,577 metres) between the two towers on either side, car traffic travels across the upper bridge, while the railway line crosses the lower bridge. The bridge acted as a catalyst and was responsible for speeding up the economic development of Nanjing. Today Nanjing is a centre for shipbuilding and engineering industries, as well as chemical and petrochemical industry in China.

Nanjing is also a city of higher learning; it houses the famous Nanjing University amongst other institutes.

The history of Nanjing goes back a long way, right to the 5th century B.C. This region has been populated for more than 5,000 years. Between the 3rd and 6th centuries A.D., Nanjing was several times the capital of southern dynasties at a time when foreign peoples were ruling in the north of China. Not much has been preserved from that time, with the exception of some animal sculptures and steles in the surroundings of Nanjing and the Buddhist cave grottoes in Qixia.

In the city itself, the Shitoucheng, a partly preserved wall north of Lake Mochou, is a reminder of that turbulent historical period. Only the seven storey, rust-coloured pagoda on Niutou Mountain seven miles (12 km) south of Nanjing, has been preserved from the

Left, marble statue of Dr. Sun Yatsen in his mausoleum. **Right**, the Lingguta Pagoda was built in 1929 in memory of the victims of the revolution.

Tang period.

Under the Song Dynasty, whose capital was Kaifeng, Nanjing developed into a centre of the textile industry and coin minting. Each year, about 70 million coins are minted. The park on **Lake Xuanwu** in the north of Nanjing originates from that time. Today, this large park, with its pavilions and small islands linked to the shore by dams and curved bridges, its attractive lotus covered ponds and its willow trees provides an ideal atmosphere for a quiet time. A nine-mile (15-km) long promenade follows the shores of the lake. There is also a small zoo in the park, an open air theatre and an aquarium.

Nanjing reached national importance under the Ming, whose first emperors had their seat of government here in the Southern Capital – which was a literal translation of the name Nanjing – until they transferred it to Beijing at the beginning of the 15th century. The well-preserved **city wall** in Nanjing dates from the Ming period. It is best viewed from the **Zhonghua Gate** in the south of the city.

Memorials and Mausoleums

The first Ming emperor, Zhu Yuanzhang, had a wall erected on the foundations of an old wall, built of reddish sandstone, in the 3rd century. It is still preserved today. To the south of Zhonghua Gate is the **Rain of Flowers Terrace** (Yuhutai), where in the 4th century, according to legend, the Buddha made flowers rain from the sky. Today, there is a **Memorial** in the park for the victims of Chiang Kaishek from the time of persecution of the communists in 1927.

At the end of the 14th century, some 500,000 people lived in Nanjing, because of its big manufacturing sector. Unfortunately, none of the palace struc-

Staircase decorated with flowers, leading to the Sun Yatsen mausoleum.

tures from that time have been preserved. Only the ruins in the north east, near the Purple Mountains, remind one of the **Palace of the Ming Emperors**; here, in the foothills of the **Purple Mountains** was the **Mausoleum Mingxiaoling** of the First Ming Emperor Hongwu (Zhu Yuanzhang). It was plundered during the Taiping uprising. The tumulus has up to now not been opened; the **Sacred Path**, which has been preserved, is worth seeing. Similar to the Ming Tombs in Beijing, it leads directly to the tomb, though it is narrower and more crooked. It is lined with stone animals and figures of people.

A bit farther to the east of the Ming mausoleum is another mausoleum of more recent times, though also of imperial proportions: the **Sun Yatsen Mausoleum** (Zhongshanling), which was built here after the death of the founder of the Republic in 1925 in Beijing. The complex covers an area of 20 acres (eight hectares).

The body of Sun Yatsen was moved here in 1929. The Cantonese, Sun Yatsen, wanted to find his last resting place here amidst the lovely Purple Mountains. An avenue, lined with beautiful plane trees, has 392 granite steps that lead to the white memorial hall, its roof covered with blue ceramic tiles. The vault is slightly below the memorial hall: various inscriptions on the walls, reflect the political heritage of Sun Yatsen. An inscription in Chinese says: "The world belongs to all."

To the east of the mausoleum in the Valley of the Souls (Linggu) is the **Linggusi Temple**, which was built at the end of the 14th century. Only the temple site Wuliangdian, which has been restored several times and has been built entirely from stone, without any wooden rafters, remains of the former large structure. The area is popular with Nanjing residents for excur-

The three-mile long bridge across the Yangzi river.

sions because of its shady pine forests. Behind Wuliangdian Hall is the 200-ft (61-metre) high **Pagoda Lingguta** which was built in the 1920s in memory of the victims of the Northern Campaign (1926-1927). There is a magnificent view of the surrounding landscape from the top floor. Atop the Purple Mountain, widely visible, stands the **Observatory**, built in 1934 and extended in 1949. It has a museum with old and new astronomical instruments. Also in the eastern part of the city, in Dongzhongshanlu 312, is the **Nanjing Museum**. Its display of ceramics, bronzes and porcelain from Nanjing and the province of Jiangsu covers 5,000 years of history. The most important exhibit is a 2,000-year old shroud from the Eastern Han Dynasty, made from 2,600 green jade rectangles sewn together with silver wire.

From the Nanjing Museum you can reach the city centre along Dongzhong-

shanlu. The fourth main turning to the right (north) is Changjianlu, where the **Residence of the Heavenly Kings** (Tianwangfu) is located. Hong Xiuquan, the leader of the Taiping movement (1850-1864), which had made Nanjing its seat of government, resided here for 11 years. Only a few halls and a marble boat have been preserved in the park adjacent to it. The **Museum of the Taiping Kingdom** was built in memory of the historically important Taiping peasant revolutionaries, known as the "ancestors" of the Chinese communists. It is in the southern part of the city, near Zhonghuamen Gate.

Towers with a view

Xinjiekou Square is in the centre of the city where several main roads converge, amongst them Dongzhongshanlu. The largest and most modern hotel in Nanjing, the 36-storey **Jingling Hotel**, is on Xinjiekou Square. You can enjoy a panoramic view of Nanjing from its revolving restaurant on the top floor, at night there is music and dance.

To the south west of Jingling Hotel is **Lake Mochou**, named after the Lady Without Sorrows (*Mochou*) who is said to have lived here in the 5th century. Various Qin pavilions are in the area. Near Lake Mochou is the **Chaotian Palace**, which dates back to the Ming Dynasty and is considered the best-preserved Confucian temple (it has been used for this purpose since the last century). From Jingling Hotel to the north, along Zhongshanlu, you reach the centrally situated **Drum Tower and Bell Tower**. You can get a beautiful view of Nanjing from the Drum Tower, which is used as an exhibition hall and has a cafe. There is a permanent open market nearby; it is also worth walking from here to Shanxi Square, a busy local market area.

Some seven miles (12 km) north of the city rises **Swallow's Rock** (Yanziji), which when viewed towards the Yangzi river resembles a flying swal-

The tomb of the first Ming Emperor is a good place to have a rest.

low, hence its name. In the north east of Nanjing are **tombs** of rulers and noblemen from the time of the Three Kingdoms and the Southern dynasties. The more than 10-ft (three-metre) high, beautifully hewn stone sculptures of animals and mythical figures which line the paths between the tombs are particularly impressive.

There are several ways of travelling from Nanjing to the other towns and areas, one is through lovely picturesque fertile areas with fields planted with rice, wheat and vegetables. The railway stops first in **Zhenjiang**, already made popular in reports by Marco Polo. Zhenjiang is situated on the southern shore of the Yangzi in a colourful countryside with green hills, old trees and bamboo groves. The three mountains, **Jinshan, Jiaoshan** and **Beigushan** with several preserved temples and pagodas, are worth visiting.

Forty-three miles (70 km) north west

of Nanjing, north of the Yangzi, lies **Yangzhou**, which flourished between the 10th and 14th centuries. It can be reached by bus from Nanjing or Zhenjiang. Marco Polo spent several years here. At that time, the town Yangzhou attracted many poets and artists. The Academy of Art of the "Eight Eccentrics" whose paintings can be seen in the Yangzhou Museum is important and famous. Yangzhou played an important role for Japanese Buddhists; this is where the monk Jian Zhen began several expeditions to Japan in the 8th century. In recent years, Japanese Buddhists have given donations and erected a memorial hall for the monk.

In Yangzhou there are several very beautiful parks and pavilions, as well as Islamic tombs from the Song period at the eastern canal bank. Yangzhou is famous today for its excellent craft works, including lacquer objects, jade carvings, papercuts and embroidery.

Guard at a bicycle parking area.

SHANGHAI – THE MODERN METROPOLIS

This city, which in its glamorous days was called the "Paris of the East", is at least in one way different from the model imposed on it: it wakes up even earlier. From 4 a.m. the first typical noises start, leaving no doubt which country you are in. Chamber pots are emptied, lungs, throat and teeth are thoroughly cleansed, and all this necessity often happens in the street, since many of the houses in this colonial-style metropolis have neither toilets nor running water.

The metropolis, or monster, lies by the river Huangpu, the 49-mile (80-km) long artery of Shanghai of which 19 miles (30 km) of its upriver flows into the Yangzi and thus guarantees access to the sea. (The name Shanghai means "upriver to the sea"). Locals and outsiders agree on one thing: *Ren tai duo* – there are too many people in the biggest city in China. And they are very individualistic: they speak a Shanghai dialect which nobody else can understand, and consider themselves to be the cream of the avant-garde and miles ahead of their rival city Beijing.

Administratively, Shanghai is a city without a province; it is made up of 10 surrounding rural districts and 12 city districts. The entire city state has over 13 million inhabitants; the city area itself covers 145 sq miles (375 sq km) and has 8 million inhabitants. Almost 19,000 people are crowded into half a square mile (one sq km).

The place was already known as a trading centre in A.D. 960 and flourished in the following centuries, becoming an important port with wine houses, temples, shops, schools and storehouses. The Japanese pirates were attracted by this, and after many attacks, a protective wall was built in the mid-16th century which surrounded the old city centre until 1912.

While the wall kept the pirates out, it failed to prevent the attack of colonial greed aroused by the good infrastructural possibilities of the city. As a result of the Opium Wars (1840-1842), the British imposed the Treaty of Nanjing in 1842 which also envisaged the opening of Shanghai. As a result, a cosmopolitan centre developed whose foreign residents reflected world political maneuvering.

Political interference

Political radicalism has a tradition here: the Communist Party was founded in Shanghai in 1921, and the Cultural Revolution began here and had its headquarters here. Nevertheless, many buildings from colonial times have survived the Revolution and the wars.

You can get a first impression of this at the famous **Bund** (adapted from the

Preceding pages: sailors at the Bund in Shanghai, the largest port in China. Left, Shanghai harbour, with Hotel Shanghai Mansions in the background. Right, reminders of the past.

Sanskrit word for river dam), the Waitan, which is officially called **Zhongshan Donglu**. Here too, directly opposite the Peace Hotel (Heping Binguan), the day starts between 5 and 6 a.m., as in all Chinese parks, with shadow boxing. It is definitely worth getting up early to see this spectacle, and it gives you the opportunity to fortify yourself with breakfast in Breakfast Alley, Shashi Lu, and/or at the Peace Hotel. Breakfast Alley runs parallel to Nanjing Donglu, the best known shopping street, and can easily be reached by walking a short way westward along Nanjing Street, leaving the Bund behind, and turning off south into Sichuan Street by the Donghai cafe which is famous for its iced coffee. You can get all sorts of local dishes such as *baozi* (steamed buns) and *youtiao* (dough pockets fried in lard) and, of course, strongly sweetened Shanghai coffee.

The former Cathay Hotel (today the Peace Hotel) offers a 1930s atmosphere; you can see the Bund and the Shanghai skyline from its eighth floor, look at the river and watch the boats, and have breakfast on old silver plates. You will get an impression of the former colonial splendour.

Today, Shanghai harbour is the third biggest in the world and an important factor in the city's industrial prowess. You can get the best impression of it by taking a tour of the harbour, starting at Huangpu Park and carrying on to the confluence with the Yangzi. The tour will show you the international character of the harbour.

Faded colonial splendour can also be found on the other side of the Suzhou river: Waibaidu Bridge leads directly from Huangpu Park, which used to be famous and notorious for its signs warning "prohibited to dogs and Chinese", to the Seamans Club and the Shanghai Dasha Hotel. The bridge is usually in-

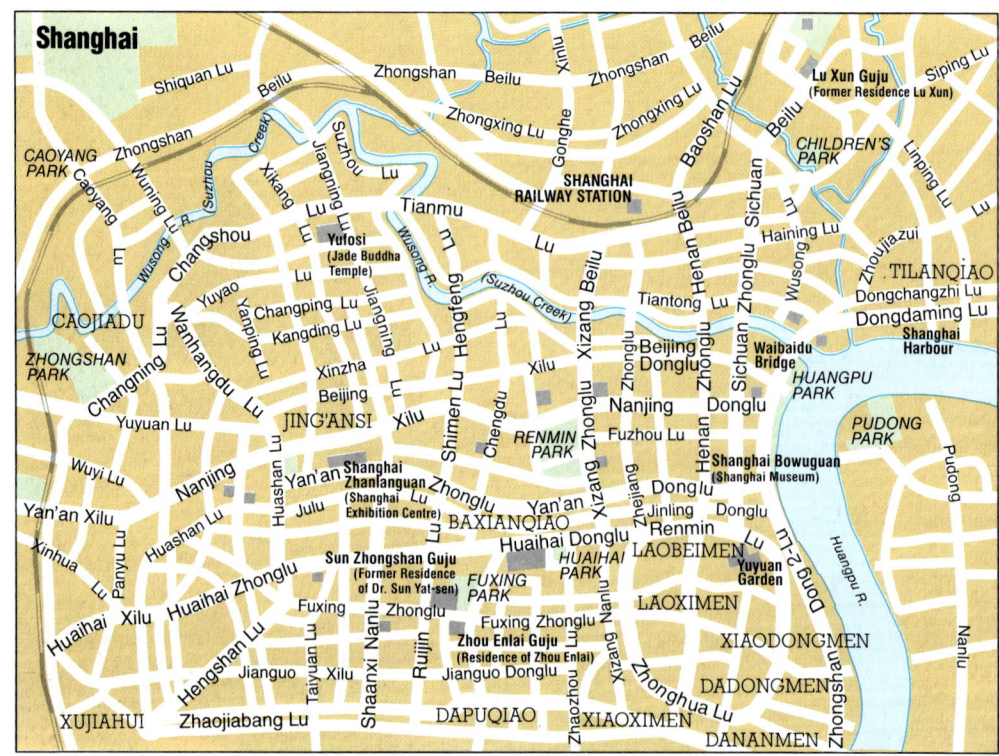

credibly crowded with pushing pedestrians and cyclists. Waibaidu Bridge, formerly called Garden Bridge, used to connect the American with the British district until, in 1863, both merged into the International Settlement. From 1937 it formed the border with the Japanese-occupied territory north of the Suzhou River. The Seamans Club, which used to house the Russian Consulate, is still a meeting place for seamen and students from around the world.

Sights and scents of Sichuan Street

Sichuan Street leads towards the north into Hongkou district, which has its own, southern charm. Washing is hung everywhere from balconies on bamboo canes, and in the side streets elderly people sit outside on stools, chatting, chopping vegetables, playing cards or just guarding the bedding which has been spread out in the street

Shadow boxing early in the morning at the Bund.

to give it an airing.

West of Sichuan Street is the new railway station which was opened in 1988. Here the day begins really early, and on every corner, stalls offer breakfast dishes which are too complicated to cook at home. It is worth taking a walk through the streets of Hongkou in the evening, even though the canals are terribly smelly in summer. There are several cafes which are meeting places for mostly young men; it's an alternative to the evening's tourist programme with hotel disco. It is worth watching the jazz band at the Peace Hotel at least once, though.

At the edge of the northern part of Sichuan Street is Hongkou Park, one of the loveliest green areas in Shanghai. The park is famous because of the grave of Lu Xun, which was moved here, and the Lu Xun Museum. He is the most famous Chinese writer of this century, and lived in Shanghai from 1933 to his

255

death in 1936. His former home in Dalu Xincun No. 9, a side alley of Shangyin Street, is just a few minutes (eastwards) from the park.

Hongkou was already in Japanese hands before the occupation of 1937, and had the nickname "Little Tokyo"; a large part of the 30,000 Japanese lived here, and Japanese shops and printing works were located here.

Within "Little Tokyo", "Little Vienna" was created when most of the Jewish refugees, who succeeded in escaping from the German fascists, settled here. Until 1941, China was one of the last countries to emigrate to, since it required neither an entry visa nor proof of financial means. Although these conditions were tightened after 1939, the Jewish community – considered a valuable asset in Shanghai – used to give assistance with money and job opportunities. By 1939, 14,000 refugees had reached Shanghai; some 15,000 Jewish refugees lived in the ghetto in Hongkou (built by the Japanese in 1943 in response to demands from the Nazis) in 1944.

But back to the **Bund** and to Nanjing Lu, which is famous in the whole of China for its many shops, and has given Shanghai its reputation as a shopper's paradise. Chinese consumerism is not limited to just numerous clothes shops or special silk shops, which at times offer the same products more cheaply than they are sold in the Friendship Shop, but also shops which sell things such as theatre props, Chinese musical instruments (Nanjing Street 114), and a stamp shop on the first floor selling stamps from the 1950s, reserved for foreigners (opposite the Xinhua Bookshop). Art and antique shops confirm the picture of Shanghai as a capital of consumerism. The most interesting bookshops, mostly selling antiquarian books, are concentrated in Fuzhou

Restaurant in the Jinjiang hotel: European-colonial atmosphere.

256

Street, south of Nanjing Street. It can be reached via Henan Street. On the corner of Henan and Yan'an Street, in a former bank, is the **Shanghai Museum**, which has one of the best and most comprehensive collections in China. The presence of the Museum contradicts the cliche of Shanghai being a consumer's paradise bereft of culture.

The well-known modern authors, the theatres, cinemas and operas and, above all, the Acrobatic Theater on Nanjing Xilu 400 also contradict this prejudice.

The exhibition of bronzes on the ground floor is of historic interest. Objects from the 17th to 14th century B.C. are exhibited here. On the first floor, the entire range of Chinese ceramic art is shown, and on the second floor, paintings and calligraphies. A few minutes to the east, in Yan'an Street 260, is the **Natural Science Museum**. On the first floor are the remains of seven ancient human skeletons, some of them finds from Hami (3,200 years) and Mawangdui (2,100 years).

From race course to parade ground

If you go west into Yan'an Street and turn north into Xizang Street, you will reach the **People's Park** (Renmin Gongyuan) in 15 minutes. It used to be a race course of the Taipans in 1861, but part of it has been transformed into a parade ground. Today, rallies and demonstrations take place here, such as in the winter of 1987, when Shanghai students demanded an improvement in their material conditions and freedom of expression. In the former race course club, which is on Nanjing Street, is the well-stocked, recently renovated **Shanghai Library**.

On the other side of the street is another piece of colonial history, the **Park Hotel**, where in the past glamorous festivals were held under its glass dome. On the corner of Nanjing/Xizang Street is the former casino, the **Great World** (Dashijie). This was a department store for many years, then a

For the Chinese, Shanghai is the Mecca of consumerism

Youth Palace, and now has been resurrected as a pleasure centre.

Not far from the Park Hotel are two **Friendship Shops** as well as an **antique shop** for foreigners (Nanjing Xilu 694). If you feel in need of a snack, you can get one in the excellent vegetarian **Gongdelin Restaurant** in Huanghe Street 43, just behind the Park Hotel. Note the early meal times in Shanghai: lunch from 11 a.m., and in the evening the restaurant gets crowded from 5 p.m. Just two bus stops away, farther along Nanjing Street is **Cafe Kayserling**, which after numerous changes of name and ideology has regained its old name. The journey in an over-crowded bus is worth it.

Or if you walk along Henan Street for ten minutes from the Shanghai Museum in a southerly direction, you will get to Renmin Street which, together with Zhonghua Street, is on the edge of the old city. This is where the old city walls

stood until 1912. They were knocked down during the first republic, the moats were filled in and the two streets were built. The **Temple of the Town God** (Chenghuang Miao) was at the heart of the old city. Today it is used as a bazaar and is directly by the **Garden of Joy** (Yuyuan). Here, as befits a bazaar, you can find tens of thousands of trinkets, and don't be put off by the exterior of the various restaurants, give them a try. The best one is certainly the **Huxinting tea house** which, as the name confirms, lies in the middle of the small lake and whose famous zigzag bridge leads directly to Yuyuan Gardens. A bit of traditional China is preserved here, but increasingly young people come to chat or read the newspaper. On one afternoon in the week, various musicians meet here to play traditional Chinese music. Legend has it that the **Yuyuan Gardens** were built in the 16th century by the eccentric and gifted landscape architect Zhang Nanyang for the governor Pan Yunduan. The Garden of Joy covers an area of almost 12 acres (four hectares); it has artificial hills, lakes, and pavilions connected by zigzag bridges. One can well imagine how this park served as the home base for the rebels of the "Society of Small Swords" during the Taiping revolution. Today, an exhibition about this secret society is located in their former headquarters, the Spring Hall.

The alleys around Yuyuan Gardens show a different side of colonial Shanghai. If you don't succumb to the picturesque aspects of poverty, you can get a realistic impression of the normal living and housing conditions of the people in this city.

From Yuyuan you can take the bus to the culturally most important temple in Shanghai, the **Jade Buddha Temple** (Yufosi) in Anyuan Street. The journey includes a tour of half the city. The

Shanghai is a young city in every way.

258

temple is famous for its two Buddha statues made of white jade, brought back by the monk **Huigen** from Burma to China in 1882 as a gift. It was brought from Jiangwan to Shanghai in 1918, when the temple was completed. The figure of the Sleeping Buddha, which shows his entry into Nirvana, is a special rarity. However, the statue of the Seated Buddha, which is six feet (1.9 metres) tall and also made of white jade, decorated with jewels and weighing 1,000 kilos, is more famous of the two.

In addition to these two treasures the temple has other valuable items such as icons, scrolls from the Tang period and a complete edition of the Buddhist canon *Tripitaka* from the year 1890. The temple was renovated in 1979 and is now again inhabited by about 70 monks, who oversee the religious and tourist activities and have even opened a restaurant.

Right in the south of the city, on the road with the same name, is the **Longhua Temple**, built in 242 and since destroyed and rebuilt several times. The temple site consists of seven halls which, since the end of the Cultural Revolution, are increasingly being used for religious purposes again.

The former French Concession, founded in 1862 and adjacent to the old city in the south west of the town, has kept its own character with its French-inspired architecture and the many avenues. Huaihai Lu, formerly Avenue Joffre, the counterpart of Nanjing Street, with its shade-giving plane trees, is perhaps the more pleasant choice for shopping or just strolling. It has as many shops and cafes, which still reflect the French or Russian influence. This is because many White Russian emigrés used to live here.

Many famous people lived here, since it was so close to the Old City. Sun Yatsen lived in Rue Moliere 29 (today Xiangshan Lu), which is south of Huaihai Lu near Fuxing Park. Mao Zedong and Zhou Enlai also lived and worked here. In the former Rue Wantz

106, today Xingye Lu 76, east of Fuxing Park, is the founding place of the Chinese Communist Party. And, last but not least, perhaps the most important man of Shanghai before 1949 lived here: Du Yuesheng, the boss of the "Green Gang", who after the victory of the rival "Red Gang" was one of the most powerful personalities in Shanghai. He lived in the former Rue Wagner, today Ninghai Lu, between Yan'an and Jingling Lu. The "Greens", a mafia-type organisation, controlled the opium trade, prostitution, gambling halls and anything else that was part of the crime in the underworld. They made sure of official backing. Without Du Yuesheng it is unlikely that Chiang Kaishek could have carried out his bloody struggle against the communists in 1927. The Who's Who of 1937 lists all his positions and services, and he is described as a "well known benefactor"; he died in 1951 in Hongkong.

Shanghai artists are amongst the best in the country.

HANGZHOU, SUZHOU, WUXI – THE EAST

"In heaven above there is paradise, on earth there are Suzhou and Hangzhou". A popular line from a poem by Yang Chaoying during the Yuan Dynasty (1271-1368) expresses the fame, dating from the Southern Song period (1127-1279), of the towns of Hangzhou, Suzhou, Wuxi and Shaoxing, which lie along the Emperor Canal.

At the beginning of the 12th century, the Chinese court was defeated in its battle against the "northern barbarians" and fled south from Nuzhen. In 1138, the newly-formed empire of the Southern Song Dynasty perforce accepted Hangzhou as "Temporary Residence" (*Xingzai*). As the seat of the dynasty, the town flourished as officials, writers and scholars moved there with the dynasty. It had already been a fortified town since the Tang period, when in the 7th century the building of the Grand Canal had strengthened her presence.

The origins of this famous canal go back to the period of the Eastern Zhou Dynasty (770-256 B.C.). Since the end of the 13th century, this waterway has stretched over a distance of more than 1,114 miles (1,794 km); it crosses the provinces of Zhejiang and Jiansu towards Beijing and connects the rivers Qiantangjiang, Yangzijiang, Huaihe and Huanghe. The king of the state of Wu had a canal built from Suzhou to the Yangzi river when preparing for war. It was completed in 495 B.C., and was 53 miles (85 km) long.

A few years later the canal was extended to Yangzhou and the two rivers Yangzi and Huaihe in the north were linked. Numerous myths and legends exist around the building of the canal system. One tells of how the Sui emperor or Yangdi, who reigned between 605-618, had ordered a link to Yangzhou be built to enable him to admire the heavenly *qiong* flower, which, however, thwarted his desire by wilting. The Emperor's fascination created a link from the then capital Luoyang to Beijing in the north and to the Huaihe river in the south west and, subsequently, from Zhenjiang to Hangzhou. As a result, the capital Luoyang was connected with the north and with the economically important southern region by a canal system of 1,678 miles (2,700 km). From here, the customs tribute collected in the area was transported to the capital. Also transported were cereals – the Zhenjiang/Jiangsu region can produce three rice harvests per year – silk, porcelain and other items for the court. Rare wood and bricks, used for the Emperor's Palace in Beijing, were transported on the canal system.

The Yuan Dynasty (1271-1368), which made Beijing the capital, built the canal system, thus connecting the capital directly with Hangzhou and shortening the distance by about 621 to 1,114 miles (1,000 to 1,794 km). At present a study is being carried out to see if the canal can be improved to alleviate the permanent water shortage in the north.

For travellers, the Emperor Canal is not only an interesting tourist sight but it also offers an interesting boat journey. You can get a close impression of life away from the centres and enjoy the many experiences in peace.

Hangzhou was the subject of many poems in the Tang period (618-907), for instance in the work of the poet Bai Juyi (772-846). He became governor of the town in 822 and had a dam built at the **West Lake** (Xihu) which still bears his name (Baidi). The poetess Li Qingzhao, who lived from 1084 to around 1151 and had escaped to the south, was inspired by the colourful background of Hangzhou to write many poems. Hangzhou became world famous during the Southern Song period (1127-1279); its population increased from less than half a million to over one million; consequently, Hangzhou became one of the largest cities in the world. It was almost completely destroyed in the second half of the 19th century, during the Taiping Revolution. Not much remains of the once world famous town. The city walls and gates have disappeared, and the numerous canals have been filled in.

Today, Hangzhou is the capital of **Zhejiang Province**, one of the most prosperous regions in China. Its products such as silk and Dragon Well tea (Longjingcha) are famous, and its pharmaceutical industry and academy of arts are well known, at least in China. A total of 1.2 million people live in the town, which covers an area of 165 sq miles (429 sq km). The town, and particularly **West Lake**, the main tourist attraction, has many visitors, especially as West Lake is a popular excursion spot for Shanghai residents who can get there in four hours by train.

Legend has it that West Lake (Xihu) was created from a pearl dropped by a phoenix and a dragon. Originally it was only a bay on Qiantang river, but since the Tang period has been extended into a lake which now covers two sq miles (5.6 sq km). Its eastern shore is close to the town, while the other shores are surrounded by usually mist-covered mountains and forests.

The **Su Causeway** (Sudi), named after the poet Su Dongpo (1037-1101) who was governor from 1071 to 1089, leads from the northern shore, near Hangzhou Hotel, to Flower Bay Park (Huagang Guanyu) in the south west. The large site goes back to the Southern Song period. Today the park, which contains rare flowers, peonies, rocky landscaped areas, pavilions and numerous small fish ponds, is about twice its original size.

Across the Bai causeway (Baidi), also named after Bai Juyi, you will reach the largest island in the lake, **Solitary Hill** (Gushan) Island. On its southern side is **Sun Yatsen Park** (Zhong-

The Emperor Canal connects the Yangzi delta with the capital in the north.

shan Gongyuan), which was originally part of the palace gardens of emperor Qianlong (who ruled between 1735-1796). The palace from the Song period was destroyed during the Taiping revolution. To the west of the park is the **Zhejiang Museum**, founded in 1929, which exhibits the oldest rice finds in China, over 7,000 years old. They were discovered in 1973 in Yuyao. To the north west is the **Pavilion of Literary Waves** (Wenlange). Adjacent to the east, are pavilions and a small pagoda of the Xiling-Die Culting Company (Xilingyinshe), founded in 1903.

At the end of Gushan Street you come to **Xiling Bridge**, which connects the island with the mainland. In the southern part of the lake is the **Island of the Small Seas** (Xiaoyingzhou), which was created in 1607 as an artificial coral reef. It was constructed as a generously arranged garden with pavilions and bridges in such a way that it encloses four lakes which contain lotus flowers and goldfish. The island can only be reached by boat; they depart from four places: **Seashore Park** (Hubin Gongyuan) on Hubin Street near the city, the observation point "**Listening to the orioles' swaying tunes**" (*Liulangwenying*) on the east side of the lake near the Children's Palace, at the **Flower Bay Park** (Huagang Guanyu), and at the **Sun Yatsen Park** on **Solitary Hill** (Gushan).

Almost the entire shore is lined with observatories, pavilions and tea houses; the **Baochu Pagoda** to the north east stands out against the sky. It is the symbol of the city. It was built in 968, and destroyed and rebuilt several times. The present pagoda dates from 1933 and is 147 ft (45 metres) high. Slightly to the west is **Geling Hill**, which has a tea house where the older male population meets amidst bird cages – a worthwhile destination for an early

morning stroll.

On the north western shore of the lake is the **Mausoleum** and **Ancestors Temple of General Yue Fei** (Yuefen). This symbolic figure of Chinese patriotism, who is still mentioned in modern Chinese literature, was executed in 1142 as a result of intrigues, was rehabilitated shortly afterwards and is honoured at this burial site.

The temple site was built in the 13th century; in the hall of honour are paintings which depict the life and fate of the General; there is also a statue of him. This temple, too, was badly destroyed during the Cultural Revolution, but some original artefacts from the Song period have been preserved, including some of the figures which protect the path to the funeral mound. In front of the vault, the general's opponents are depicted in a kneeling position; these statues, made from iron, are from the early 19th century. Chinese visitors still spit on them in fury, which shows how strongly the General remains in the Chinese consciousness.

In the west of the town, at the end of Lingyin Street which is easily reached by bus, is the beautifully situated **Monastery of the Hidden Souls** (Lingyinsi), from where you can see the **Peak that Flew From Afar** (Feilaifeng). The monastery was founded in 326 by the Indian Buddhist Hui Li. He thought he saw in the "Peak that Flew from Afar" a part of the **Gradhrakuta Mountain** in India, and gave it that name.

The rock walls of the mountain have been carved with about 300 sculptures and inscriptions since the second half of the 10th century; the earliest figure is thought to date from 951. A group of three Buddhist deities are at the right hand entrance to the Qinlin cave. By going past these figures, you reach the monastery, one of the ten most famous Buddhist monasteries in China. The

Below and **right**, West Lake near Hangzhou and its surroundings, one of the most beautiful landscapes in China.

most popular figure is at the foot of the mountain; the fat-bellied Buddha from the Song period, one of the most touched and photographed figures because it is believed to bring luck. Up to 3,000 monks used to live in the structures on the mountain peak, in 18 pavilions and 75 temple halls. Behind the entrance gate to the temple and two stone columns inscribed with Buddhist texts is the **Hall of Heavenly Kings** (Tianwangdian), where another statue of the Maitreya Buddha can be seen, guarded by the two Heavenly Kings standing at its side. In the **Precious Hall of the Great Heroes** (Daxiongbaodian), which lies behind two nine-storey pagodas from the 10th century, is the gilded statue of the Buddha Sakyamuni which is more than 30 ft (nine metres) high and made of precious camphor wood. It is the tallest figure made from this material in China.

About five and a half miles (nine km) south west of West Lake, near the **zoo** (Dongwuyuan) is the **Spring of the Running Tiger** (Hupaoquan) whose origin or discovery is surrounded with various legends. The water of this spring has extremely high surface tension, and floating coins on it has become a national sport. The water tastes good, and can be sampled in a nearby tea house located in a temple from the Tang period (Dinghuisi)

Towards the north west is the **Dragon Well Tea Village** (Longjing) which is often acclaimed as a sight worth visiting. But it is very tourist-oriented, with the obligatory introductory speech and a guided tour through the sales rooms. The peasants went back to private agriculture some years ago, and the vessels used communally in the past for drying the tea leaves are only set in motion when the tourist buses arrive. An excursion to one of the surrounding villages is more worthwhile, for in-

stance to **Meijiawu**, about 20 minutes by car south of Hangzhou. If you are fit enough you can make the trip through the lovely landscape with its famous bamboo grove by bicycle (on hire in town). This village also grows tea, and the peasants, who have not yet been overrun by tourists, are very hospitable and willing to explain and show you everything about tea production.

South west of the Lake, on the **Moon Mountain** (Yuelunshan), near the Qiantang river, is the **Six Harmonies Pagoda** (Liuheta). It was first built in 970 to protect the town from flooding. It served as a lighthouse and was meant to pacify the dragons brought in by the floods. The Pagoda, which today is 197 ft (60 metres) tall, has seven inner and thirteen outer storeys, whose original bricks are from the 12th century, while the outer wooden parts have been renovated around the turn of this century.

In the town itself, where the tea houses and cafes have reopened and daily life carries on in the little alleys, the **Mosque Temple of the Phoenix** (Fenghuangsi) in Zhongshan Zhonglu 225 is of historical and cultural significance. It was originally built in the Tang period and, after several destructions, was restored in 1984. It is one of the four preserved mosques in China and contains numerous Arabic inscriptions.

As in all towns, a visit to the open market is worth it, as well as to the silk factories, for instance the Hangzhou Du Jinsheng Silk Factory in Youdian Lu 200. This gives you an idea of the complexity of silk production as well as of the working conditions in a Chinese factory. One way to avoid the summer heat and the crowds is to head for **Moganshan**, 37 miles (60 km) to the north. Buses go from Hangzhou to this very beautiful mountain with waterfalls and bamboo groves, which is almost 2,625 ft (800 metres) above sea level.

A laughing Buddha on a rock face opposite Lingyin monastery near Hangzhou.

Shaoxing

Shaoxing, located 42 miles (67 km) to the east of Hangzhou, is accessible directly by train. The town is known throughout the world for its rice wine. Every year the Shaoxing brewery produces about 37,000 tons of wine and has been receiving praises for its excellent quality since the 7th century.

Shaoxing was once the "Temporary Residence" of the emperor for twenty months during the Southern Song period, and is linked to the Emperor Canal. But it has never enjoyed the same importance as Hangzhou. The town has hardly been discovered by tourism, which in no way detracts from the charm and atmosphere of this small, but very lively and beautiful little provincial town.

Lu Xun, the most famous modern Chinese writer, was born in Shaoxing in 1881. Both his birth place and the **Lu Xun Museum** can be visited in Duchangfang Street. They show an example of the traditional Chinese style of living, as well as photographs and documents from the life of Lu Xun. Another known writer and revolutionary grew up in Shaoxing: Qui Jin (1875-1907), one of the first feminists in China. She was executed in 1907 after an abortive uprising against the imperial house. The house where she lived in Hechangtang 18, near the crossroads of Jiefang Nanlu and Yan'an Lu, gives an impressive picture of the life of a civil servant's family during the late Qing Dynasty and exhibits photographs and documents from her life.

Nearly two miles (three km) east of the town is the **East Lake** (Donghu), an artificial lake created towards the end of the Qing period. The boats which are typical of this area, with black canopies, are steered through the bizarre seascape by the boatsmen with their feet. Caves

The Moon Gate, typical architecture in southern Chinese gardens.

with calligraphies can be seen. Nearly three miles (four km) south east of the town, at the foot of Mount Kuaiji, is the **Tomb of the legendary emperor Yu**, who is said to have tamed the water by building dams and changing the course of rivers. A temple was first built on the mountain in 545; the present site is, however, from the Qing Dynasty. It comprises several large and small halls and pavilions which hold numerous mythical figures and a tombstone of Yu.

Lake Taihu

Between the two provinces of Zhejiang and Jiangsu is Lake Taihu, which, with 934 sq miles (2,420 sq km) and a total of 48 islands, is the third largest lake in China. Here, similar to West Lake, you get a view of a landscape in green and blue, veiled with fine mist, which has been described in many poems. The residents use the lake to catch fish, breed ducks and geese as well as lotus and water chestnuts; however, the most important economic factor is the cultivation of mulberry trees and silk worms.

The most interesting place to visit is the largest island, Dongting Xishan, which covers 34 sq miles (90 sq km), and whose highest elevation, the **Blurred Peak** (Piaomiaofeng), reaches 1,102 ft (336 metres). Also of interest is the **peninsula Dongting Dongshan**, to the south of Piaomiaofeng. On this island is a cave which is an old Daoist sacred centre and lies in the Linwu Mountain, and is worth seeing. It was only freed from the mud of Lake Taihu in 1985. A large number of religious artefacts and utensils were discovered, some of which are now exhibited in the museum in Suzhou.

In the west of the mountainous peninsula Dongting Dongshan, whose highest elevation is the 961-ft (293-

Chinese garden in Suzhou.

270

metre) high Mulifeng, is the **Purple-Gold Monastery** (Zijin'an), which dates back to the Tang period. After being destroyed it was rebuilt in the second half of the 14th century. The 16 Luohan statues and the statue of the goddess of mercy (Guanyin), a special attraction in this particular monastery, are said to have been made by the Hangzhou sculptor Lei Chao and his wife, who both lived during the Southern Song period.

The island Dongting Xishan can be reached from Xiaomenkou on the southern bank of Lake Taihu, from Wuxi in the north and from Suzhou by boat; there is also a boat connection to the peninsula. The boats leave Suzhou at 7 a.m. and return in the afternoon.

Suzhou

Even if Hangzhou has overtaken its sister town of Suzhou as the most popular destination for the Chinese on honeymoon, this city, known as the town of gardens and canals, is at least as charming as its rival town on the West Lake. Suzhou is mentioned in 484 B.C., since it was for a few years the capital of the state of Wu during the period of the Warring Kingdoms (475-221 B.C.).

Suzhou flourished as a trading and silk centre when, in the early 6th century, it was linked with the capital through the Grand Canal. Its most prosperous period was during the Ming and Qing Dynasties, when many officials, scholars and artists settled here and the local traders grew rich. This wealth was largely invested in the 150 gardens which make Suzhou so famous. The principle of Chinese garden construction – creating an illusion of the universe in a small space – can be clearly seen in these gardens: water flowing between bizarre, rocky shores, connected by canals and zigzag bridges, winding paths and craggy rock formations.

A walk through the small alleys in the town, along the canals and through the gardens has a special charm on a slightly misty autumn morning, when the tourist noise hasn't started yet.

In the north east of the town, on Qimen Street, is the **Garden of the Foolish Politician** (Zhouzhengyuan), which covers nine acres (four hectares) and is the largest garden in Suzhou. Wang Xiancheng, a retired court official, had it built in 1513 on the spot where, during the Tang period, the poet Lu Guimeng lived. It is said that Wang's son, who was a gambler, lost the property through gambling.

During the Taiping Revolution, when Suzhou was substantially destroyed, the Taiping Clan made this garden its headquarters from 1860 to 1864. The largest part of the area is covered in ponds, close to pavilions which are connected by zigzag bridges. The ponds are full of lotus flowers; one pavilion is consequently called "You see lotus everywhere" (*Hehua Simian Ting*).

A rare architectural style: the Pagoda on Tiger Hill near Suzhou.

Paths wind along willow-tree lined shores to the various viewing points.

Directly next to this garden is the **History Museum** (Lishi Bowuguan), where the history of Jiangsu Province is depicted. Farther west, on Xibei Lu, is the **North Temple Pagoda** (Beisita) which is said to have been built in the fifth century B.C. The present pagoda dates from the Southern Song period, although two thorough restorations have taken place in the second half of the 17th century. You can get a view of Suzhou from the top of the 249 ft (76 metres) high, nine storey tower which is built in octagonal shape. There is a tea house behind the pagoda offering refreshments.

On the western edge of the town, in the street of the same name, is the **Garden for Lingering in** (Liuyuan). A garden was first created here in the 16th century, but this one was newly created in 1800 by its then proprietors. The Garden for Lingering in is considered a prime example of a southern Chinese garden of the Qing era and belongs to the gardens protected as national cultural monuments. Here too, a pond forms the centre of the garden; it is lined with many paths, halls and pavilions.

There are some interesting pieces of furniture and some especially beautiful artefacts in the halls. Another speciality is a 21-ft (6½-metre) high stone from Lake Taihu which has been erected in the north eastern courtyard.

Opposite Liuyuan is the **West Garden** (Xiyuan): they used to form one large area owned by the imperial official Xu Shitai. His son had a temple built here which, after being destroyed by the Taiping, was reconstructed. At the back of the **Precious Hall of the Great Hero** (Daxiongbaodian), the Goddess of Mercy (Guanyin) is portrayed. Further west is the Hall of the Luohan (Luohantang), where 500

Suzhou, city of canals, the Venice of the East.

gilded Luohan representations are exhibited; all their faces have individual features. Particularly fascinating is the depiction of the monk Jigong, whose facial expression changes depending on where you stand.

About half a mile (one km) further to the west, in the village of Fengqiao, is the **Monastery of the Cold Mountain** (Hanshansi), named after the monk Han Shan, who became famous as an eccentric poet and a Zen Buddhist fond of drink. His poems have been translated into Western languages and are still worth reading. Han Shan is thought to have lived in the 7th century.

The monastery was built in the 6th century, though the buildings now standing were rebuilt after being destroyed during the Taipeng revolt. In the monastery are statues of Han Shan and his companion Shi De. You can buy stone rubbings and poems of the two monks. The Monastery of the Cold

Mountain is a popular place for the festival of the Chinese New Year, and if you like noise and festivities you shouldn't miss it.

In the south west of Suzhou are remnants of the old city wall and the **Panmen Gate** from the year 1351, whose origins are thought to date back to the fifth century B.C. Towards the city in a northerly direction, directly behind the wall, you pass the **Happy View Pagoda** (Ruiguangta) and the **Confucius Temple** (Kongmiao); opposite this, on Renminlu, is the **Garden of the Blue Wave Pavilion** (Canglangting). This relatively small garden was built in 1041 by the poet Su Shenqing. In the centre is the Blue Wave Pavilion which has been built on an artificially created hill. The harmonic structure of the winged roofs is impressive; they are partly covered in leaves and look as if they merge into the bamboo and Cyprus trees.

The Huishan clay figures from Wuxi are known throughout China.

Further northwards in the direction of the town, on Renminlu, is the **Garden of Harmony** (Yiyuan), which was created in 1876 when an imperial official acquired the former property of the minister Wu Kuan (1435-1504) and transformed it into this garden. In the eastern part are the pavilions and buildings, in which paintings and calligraphies are exhibited. The western part is designed to enhance the natural landscape features. Opposite the Garden of Harmony begin the alleys of the **old city**; at the northern edge of Guanqianjie is the Daoist **Temple of Mysteries** (Xuanmiaoguang) which is now partly occupied by a bazaar. The temple is thought to have been founded around 270; only the **Hall of the Three Pure Ones** (Sanqingdian) dating from the year 1180 has remained of the 31 halls. The gilded statues of the Three Pure Ones are in the Hall. Around the Temples are lots of small shops, food stalls, restaurants and many of the sweet shops for which Suzhou is famous.

North east of this busy scene, between Lindunlu and Yuanlinlu, is a garden called **Lion Grove** (Shizilin) which was landscaped by a Buddhist monk in the mid-14th century around a temple. The rock shapes of Taihu stone are worth stopping for a look. The biggest one is the **Lion Peak** (Shizifeng), which has a labyrinth of narrow paths and many caves.

Wuxi

The town can be reached from Suzhou either by railway in 40 minutes or by boat on the Emperor Canal, which takes about six hours. Wuxi's history goes back to the early centuries B.C., but the town was then called Youxi; literally: there is tin. The tin reserves must already have been exhausted during the Han Dynasty because since

Old and new meet on Emperor Canal.

274

that time it is called Wuxi; literally: there is no tin. Wuxi's importance grew with the completion of the Emperor Canal, and its modest wealth was achieved, as in the whole region, through agriculture and silk production.

Today there are nearly 800,000 people living in Wuxi, and tourism plays an increasingly important role for the town. The mild climate, the fertile soil and sufficient water make the region around Wuxi one of the most fertile ones in China. The Chinese call it "Land of fish and rice". The town itself offers few sights, but its charming landscape and its close proximity to Lake Taihu means it is a popular destination for excursions and daytrips. One special attraction is the **Emperor Canal** which flows through the town, and its arched bridges. Qingming Bridge in the south east of the town is architecturally interesting.

In the western part of the town is **Xihui Park**, an area of 111 acres (44 hectares) whose name comes from the **Tin Mountain** (Xishan), an approximately 246-ft (75-metre) high hill, and the 984-ft (300-metre) high Hui Mountain. The park was created between the two mountains in 1958. On top of the Dragon Mountain is the octagonal **Dragon Light Pagoda** (Longguangta) from the Ming period, where one can get a wonderful view over the town and Taihu Lake. Hui Mountain is famous for its water, which comes from the **Second Spring under Heaven** (Tianxia Di'erquan). There are pavilions and temple halls under ancient trees; they have inscriptions from Tang and Song times. Hui Hill is known for the small figures which have been made from the hill's clay. The material has been popular since the Ming period because of its malleability and hardness after firing. From Xihui Park you come to the adjacent **Garden of Delight** (Jichengyuan). This garden, which covers barely a hectare, was constructed about 500 years ago.

In the south west of the town is the

Plum Garden (Meiyuan) which was constructed at the end of the last century. In its centre is a rock garden with thousands of plum trees around it. In spring, the garden is one big sea of blossoms – and of visitors. Another site, the **Shell Garden** (Liyuan), is in the south west of the town by **Five Li Lake** (Wulihu), an offshoot of Lake Taihu. West of Liyuan, Baojie Bridge leads to **Tortoise Head Island** (Yuantouzhu), whose artificially created shape with many small hills is supposed to remind one of the head of a tortoise. In the past, court officials and rich families lived in the 49 acre (20 hectares) area, and there are the pavilions, pagodas and tea houses typical for this region, all in a lovely landscape. Excursions from Wuxi into the surrounding area are worthwhile, either on a daytrip by bicycle, which can be hired virtually anywhere, or a trip lasting several days. Some villages now offer tourist programs, which in some cases include accommodation in usually very good hotels with equally good food, but there is also at times the possibility of staying with a family. In any case this is not only a chance to see the lovely countryside, but also to get an impression of the peasants' life in this wealthy region.

For almost 1,500 years, the area around Wuxi has produced silk. Most peasants cultivate silk worms as a popular and very profitable sideline. The young worms, spread out on rice straw mats, are fed with juicy mulberry leaves and are then put on bundles of rice straw, where they spin a cocoon within five days. If you travel around the area between April and November, you can observe this activity on many farms. The cocoon is then washed in silk spinning mills and then the silk thread is pulled. A thin silk thread can measure more than 3,280 ft (1,000 metres). Several threads are then spun into a yarn that can be woven. You can watch the work of the weavers. In Hangzhou, Suzhou and Wuxi silk embroidery is a special art.

CHINA'S SOUTH-EASTERN COAST

A journey along the southern east coast takes you mainly through Fujian Province which consists mostly of mountains. The landscape is a rich green, the coastline is often harsh and rugged. Of particular interest in this region is the Taoist religion avidly practised by the people. The towns, which have yet to be opened up to mass tourism, offer a number of interesting sights. Almost each of the open cities can also be reached by boat, but it is best to travel by plane or overland bus.

The first stop is Shantou, a port in the eastern part of Guangdong Province, reachable by daily flights from Guangzhou. You can get an impression of its rich vegetation and the simple country life during the eleven-hour bus journey from Guangzhou (Canton). The town spreads over 94 sq miles (245 sq km) and has 700,000 inhabitants. Western influence on the city from the 18th century is noticeable in the town. However, in contrast to Shanghai with its mostly well-preserved colonial buildings, Shantou looks somewhat neglected.

The town offers little of historic interest, though it too has a **Sun Yatsen Park** (Zhongshan Gongyuan) which is worth a visit. The park lies by the bank of the **Plum River** (Meixi) which flows through the town, not far from Zhongshan Street on its southern flank.

The park, which has been constructed on an island and is linked to the town by three bridges, consists of a generous combination of water and green areas. In the south west of the park is the **Botanical Garden** (Yuemei Huayuan); the **zoo** (Dongwuyuan) is in the south eastern part, to the east of the entrance gate and the **Artificial Mountain** (Jiashan).

The real tourist destinations are on two islands which can easily be reached from the harbour in the south of the city (bus no. 3, stop at Xidi). To the south east of the town is the small island of Mayudao, which has a stony shore in the east as well as a sandy beach. In the southern part a pavilion with the poetic name Sea View (Guanhaiting) has been built. In the north of the island is the **Temple of the Sea God** (Tianhaigumiao), not far to the north is the **Maguang Temple**. Shantou is one of the five Special Economic Zones of China, and the smallest. It has started attracting overseas Chinese investment and is developing fast today.

There are flights or buses from Shantou to Xiamen in Fujian Province. This province, which lies opposite Taiwan, has become famous mainly as an area of emigrants; a large number of overseas Chinese had come from Fujian, as well as from Guangzhou.

Zhangzhou, a two-hour ride by bus from Xiamen, on the Nine Dragon River (Jiulongjiang), has been recorded

279

in historic documents since the 7th century, and has long been well known as a centre for foreign trade and as a port. Around 300,000 people live in an area of 102 sq miles (264 sq km). The most important sight in the town is the **Southern Mountain Temple** (Nanshansi). It was built during the Tang Dynasty, then destroyed and rebuilt several times. The present site originates from the Qing Dynasty. The **Precious Hall of the Great Hero** (Daxiong Baodian), in the middle of the site, houses three gilded seated Buddha statues; the huge copper bell from the Yuan Dynasty, which weighs almost 700 kilograms, is of special interest.

There are various places for excursions to the north of the town which have an interesting landscape and have many stories and legends attached to them, as for example Mount Zhishan in the north east. However, of the temples built during the Tang Dynasty, only a few pavilions have been preserved.

Xiamen

It takes about two hours to get from Zhangzhou to Xiamen. Reachable by air or bus from Guangzhou or Shantou, Xiamen, also known under the name of Amoy (Fujian dialect), is probably the best known town of the province, which in 1387 achieved the status of a city. It had long been an important port, which in the 17th century became a centre of historic battles. The last loyal supporters of the Ming dynasty sought refuge here from the new rulers, the Manchus, and the notorious Ming general Koxinga (Chinese: Zheng Chenggong) fled from here to Taiwan. The island Gulangyu, in front of the town, became a foreign enclave as a result of the Treaty of Nanking in 1842.

Since 1980, Xiamen has been a Special Economic Zone, and Chinese

The fishermen near Fuzhou use narrow bamboo rafts.

abroad, in particular, are encouraged to invest here. One of the worthwhile places for an excursion is the **Garden of the Ten Thousand Rocks** (Wanshi Gongyuan), which is to the east at the top of Huyuanlu. The area covers 202 acres (82 hectares) and includes a lake, large green areas and a pavilion. There is also a botanical garden. In the east are **Mount Taiping** (Taipingshan) and **Taiping Rock** (Taipingyan) with a small temple from the Tang period. In the south of the park, on **Mount Lion Head** (Shitoushan), are the **Temple of the Sweet Dew** (Ganlusi) and the **Temple of the Heavenly Kingdom** (Tianjiesi), dating from the second half of the 17th century. South of the park is the **Mountain of the Five Elders** (Wulaoshan), which is to be connected to the park by a tunnel. It is still possible, however, to walk across the mountain to the **Nanputuo Temple** in the south. It lies north of Siming Nanlu, on whose

opposite side is the campus of Xiamen University. The temple was founded during the Tang period, but in its present structure it belongs to the Qing period. It is dedicated to the Goddess of Mercy (Guanyin) – there are three statues of the goddess in the third hall, the Hall of Great Mercy (Dabeidian). The pavilion behind the temple houses not only valuable old Buddhist scriptures but also specimens of calligraphy from the Ming period, bells from the Song period, a Guanyin statue with eight heads and 24 arms from the Ming period, made of white porcelain, and Buddha statues made from jade. A **Lu Xun Memorial Hall** has been built on the university campus. Lu Xun was one of the sponsors of the Anthropological Museum which opened in 1952 and is located towards town on Siming Nanlu. It contains a reproduction of Peking Man as well as oracle bones from the Shang period and early bronzes.

Southern Chinese junk at the coast near Xiamen.

The most popular excursion spot is the small **island of Gulangyu**, which can easily be reached in five minutes from the mooring point near Lujiang Hotel. You can swim or sunbathe on the island, which is only half a square mile (1.64 sq km) in size and has two landmarks: **Dragon Head Hill** (Longtoushan) and **Tiger Head Hill** (Hutoushan). East of the southern beach is Shuzhuang Huayuan, a garden which was created in 1913 by a Taiwanese who was fleeing from the Japanese. It has been designed in the style of the gardens of Suzhou. The **Lotus Nunnery** (Lianhua'an), which is directly behind the gate to Dragon Head Hill, is also worth visiting. There are a number of memorials to Zheng Chenggong on the island, for whom a memorial hall (Zheng Chenggong Jinianguan) was built in 1962.

Three hours by bus north of Xiamen is Quanzhou. It was founded in 700 and was for a long time one of the biggest and most important ports in China. During the Song Dynasty it had about half a million inhabitants, while today only 400,000 people live on an area of 205 sq miles (530 sq km). In addition to Islamic traders who came in the 7th century to Quanzhou, two Muslim missionaries also settled here. The **Holy Islamic Graves** (Yisilanjiao Shengmu) on **Soul Mountain** (Lingshan) bear witness to their presence. The mountain is in the east of the town and can easily be reached on foot. The Muslim **Temple of Calm and Clarity** (Qingjingsi) in Tumenjie is another example of the strong Islamic influence. It is supposed to be a copy of a mosque in Damascus and was built in black and white granite in 1009 on commission from Arab traders. North west of this mosque, in Xijie, and easily recognisable by its two richly decorated pagodas from the 10th century, is the **Kaiyuan Temple**. It was erected in 686 and substantially extended in subsequent centuries. At 17 acres (six hectares), it is one of the largest temple sites in China today.

There are five Buddha statues in the **Precious Hall of the Great Hero** (Daxiong Baodian). The middle one, Buddha Sakyamuni, is said to be a present from the Tang emperor Xuanzong. East of the Kaiyuan temple is the **Foreign Trade History Museum** (Haiwaijiaotongshi Bowuguan). Its main exhibit is an ocean-going junk from the Song period which was discovered and lifted from the Bay of Quanzhou in 1974. A lovely two mile (three km) walk to the north leads to the **Mountain of the Clear Spring** (Qingquanshan), which was a Daoist centre. The only remnant is a 16-ft (five-metre) high figure of Laozi (or Laotse) from the Song period, which is said to have stood in the centre of a Daoist temple. From here, a path leads to **Amitabha Rock** (Mituoyan) with a 16-ft (five-metre) tall statue of the Buddha Amitabha from the Yuan period. On the way to the highest point, the 1,608-ft

Sleeping monk at Putuoshan monastery.

(490-metre) high Wutaiding, you pass the temple **Rock of Granted Grace** (Cienyan) which has a special attraction in the form of a statue of Guanyin from the 11th century. Other sights worth seeing are the **Stony Bamboo Shoots** (Shisun) on the **Tortoise Mountain** (Guishan) to the west, and the **Mountain of the Ninth Day** (Jiurishan), which is nearly four miles (five km) north west of the town on the banks of Jinjiang river. Apart from the landscape, the many inscriptions on the rocks are worth seeing.

Fuzhou

Kaiyuan Temple in Quanzhou is one of the largest in China.

Three hours by bus from Quanzhou is the capital Fuzhou, situated by the banks of the river Minjiang. Its history goes back to the 2nd century B.C. when it was the residence of the Kingdom of Yue. Its importance as a port grew from the 10th century onwards. It was opened in 1842 as a result of the Opium Wars. The town, which has over a million inhabitants today, was occupied by the Japanese from 1940 to 1945, as was Taiwan. You can get a first view of the town from the 194-ft (60-metre) high Yushan Hill in the centre.

At the north westerly edge of the hill is the **White Pagoda** (Baita) which was built in 904 and has been restored several times. A library is housed in the temple of the same name (Baitasi). East of Baitasi is the temple **Qigongci**, which was built in honour of the Ming general Qi Jiguang (1528-1587) who had successfully fought against Japanese pirates. Opposite Yushan rises the 282-ft (86-metre) high Wushi Mountain with its seven storey **Wushi Pagoda** dating to 941. **West Lake** (Xihu) in the north west of the town is a popular spot for excursions. It was constructed in the 3rd century, but has been considerably enlarged this century. The

Provincial Museum is on the northernmost of the three islands in the lake; the south western part offers the opportunity to swim and/or visit the zoo.

Another worthwhile sight in the town itself is the **Splendid Forest Temple** (Hualinsi), dating from the year 965, which lies at the foot of the 148-ft (45-metre) high Pingshan Hill in the north of the town. Only the main hall remains of the original construction; the other buildings are from the Qing period. Excursions around Fuzhou are very worthwhile; the **Drum Mountain** approximately nine miles (15 km) to the east is particularly interesting and can be reached by bus. There are numerous religious buildings set in a lovely landscape, for instance the **Temple of the Sparkling Spring** (Yongquansi) from the year 908, of which 25 halls are still preserved. Two other temples outside the town are worth visiting: **Linyang Temple**, which stands 12 miles (19 km) away on Beifengshan, and **Chongfu Temple** at the foot of Beilingshan five miles (eight km) away, built in 977, though its preserved buildings date from the second half of the 19th century.

The next stop is in Zhejiang Province. The harbour towns of Wenzhou and Ningbo are the largest in the province after the capital Hangzhou. Wenzhou lies on the south bank of the Oujiang River, 19 miles (30 km) from its estuary. Wenzhou's importance as a port has grown since 1949 and is of greater importance now since it has become an open city. The many different directions of Chinese development is clearly seen in this ancient, 2,000 year old city. The **Island at the Heart of the River** (Jiangxin), easily reached by ferry, in the town's north is the main attraction for tourists. Pagodas stand on the two hills of the island, which was originally two islands but were joined during the

View of Xiamen.

Song period. The **Eastern Pagoda** was built in 869, the western one in 969. The **Temple at the Heart of the River** (Jiangxinsi) dates from the 9th century, while the **Temple of Wen Tianxiang** (Wen Tianxiangsi) was built in 1482 in honour of a general of the Southern Song Dynasty. However, the buildings today date from the Qing period. The city museum is also on the island.

Almost a day's trip away is **Ningbo**, which is also connected to the railway network. Ningbo first became an important port during the Tang period, and flourished during the period of the Southern Song (1127-1179), when Hangzhou, 93 miles (150 km) away, was the capital. Most of the big fortunes of Shanghai before 1949 came from Ningbo. Today, 600,000 people live in the town, which continues to be an important junction. The **Private Library Tianyige** on Changchunlu, to the west of Moon Lake (Yuehu), is worth a visit.

View of the Buddha altar in Nanputuo Monastery in Xiamen.

It was installed in the 16th century by the scholar Fan Qin and used to hold about 70,000 valuable manuscripts, of which a good 15,000 are still preserved. In the south of the town rises the 98-ft (30-metre) high **Tianfeng Pagoda**, which was first built in the Tang Dynasty but in its present form dates from 1330. In the centrally situated **Sun Yatsen Park** (Zhongshan Gongyuan) is the Qita temple (Qitasi), which is again used for religious purposes and inhabited by monks.

Another worthwhile excursion is to the **Protection of the Land Temple** (Baoguosi), more than nine miles (15 km) to the north west. It was built during the Song Dynasty (960-1127). The **Precious Hall of the Great Hero** (Daxiong Baodian) is the oldest preserved wooden structure in the province. The most interesting excursion, both in terms of the landscape and culture, is the **Temple of the Heavenly Child** (Tiantongsi), 22 miles (35 km) to the east. It was built in 757 and was an important centre of Chinese Zen Buddhism.

Putuoshan Island

The island, which is one of the four sacred Buddhist mountains in China, is accessible by boat from Ningbo. Before 1949, over 2,000 monks and nuns lived here in 218 monasteries whose origins go back to the 11th century. The **Monastery of Complete Redemption** (Pujisi) was built in this century, while the **Monastery of the Law** (Fayusi) dates from the 16th century. The **Poplar Branch Convent** (Yang-shi'an), situated to the west, with its six-ft (two-metre) high stone picture of Guanyin dates from the year 1608. The third largest is the **Convent of the Enlightened Redemption** (Huijisi). Lying on Buddha Hill in the north of the island, it was founded during the Ming period, and was considerably extended in the following centuries. Numerous pilgrims come here on the 19th day of the second moon month to celebrate the birthday of Guanyin.

GUANGZHOU –
SOUTHERN GATE
TO THE WEST

Once upon a time, five celestial beings came flying on five goats, and founded Guangzhou (Canton); tracing back to its origination, it is easy to understand the zest for criticism shown by the citizens of Guangzhou to these plaintively bleating founders. They have left the name "Goat City" (Yangcheng) as a legacy to Guangzhou. Relevant reminders are frequently found in the city on the Pearl River (Zhujiang). The city's evening paper is called *Yangcheng Wanbao* (Goat City Evening News).

Guangzhou lies 28 miles (45 km) upriver from **Tiger Gate** (Humen, also called Bocca Tigris on old maps) and has around 5 million inhabitants, of whom 2.2 million live within the city's boundaries. Guangzhou is a tropical town; the Tropic of Cancer runs a few miles to the north. For a few days in July, the sun lies directly above the city. The climate is subtropical. Average temperatures are around 22°C, rising to 28°C during the hottest month (July) and falling to 13°C during the coldest month (January). It never freezes in winter. Extreme temperatures vary between 39°C in summer and 0°C in winter. The rainy season is during the hot summer months.

Guangzhou was probably founded in 214 B.C. by the armies of the Qin emperor, Shi Huangdi (221-210 B.C.), as an encampment. At first the town was called Panyu, the name **Guangzhou** first appeared during the period of the Three Kingdoms (222-280). During the Tang period (618-906), the city was already an international port, but remained second to **Quanzhou** (the Zaytun of Marco Polo) for centuries.

In 1514 the Portuguese flotilla commanded by Tome Pires reached Guangzhou. The province's name in Cantonese is Guangdong from which

the Portuguese derived the name of Cantão, the origin of Canton, a name which gradually came to be used in all European languages.

From 1757 to 1842, Guangzhou held the monopoly as the only Chinese trade port opened to the foreigners. Foreign traders were obliged to cooperate contractually with Chinese merchant guilds; this laid the seeds for the subsequent *comprador* bourgeoisie.

After the overthrow of the Ming Dynasty by the Manchu in 1644, nationalist ideas survived longer in Guangzhou than in other parts of China, and close contact with overseas Chinese (*huaqiao*) ensured the continuation of openness to the world and a desire for reform in the city. The increasingly intensive trade with the East India Company, the opium imports forced by the company (which was used to finance the colonial expansion of India), and the resulting net loss of silver reserves were

instrumental in promoting revolutionary ideas and organisations. The secret societies, especially, preserved the ideals of the Ming period and a determination to restore this last Chinese dynasty.

In 1839, the Chinese Commissioner Lin Zexu ordered the confiscation and destruction of 20,000 chests of opium, leading to military intervention by Great Britain (**First Opium War 1840-1842**). The resulting Treaty of Nanjing imposed on China led to the opening of Guangzhou (in addition to Shanghai, Xiamen, Fuzhou and Ningbo) to foreign trade and the cession of Hongkong. In 1858, foreign traders were obliged to be based on the **Island of Shamian**. After the Second Opium War (1856-1860), they were permitted to settle in other parts of Guangzhou and to continue trading.

The first significant armed rebellion against the alien rule of the Manchu emperors took place on 29 March 1911. About 72 rebels were taken prisoner and executed. After the overthrow of the Qing Dynasty in October 1911, Guangzhou became the centre of the Republican Movement led by Sun Yatsen (Sun Zhongshan) and the founding place and centre of the Guomindang (KMT, Kuomintang), the first modern party in China. In the period of cooperation between the KMT and the Communist Party, Mao Zedong worked and taught at the Institute of Peasant Movements, and Zhou Enlai and Lin Biao at the Republican Military Academy on Huangpu (Whampoa). A second workers' rebellion was brutally suppressed in 1927.

The **modernisation of Guangzhou** began in the early 1920s: most of the main streets dominating the city today were built from 1919 onwards; it took only 18 months to build 25 miles (40 km) of road. The remainder of the city wall was pulled down. In particular, the "swimming slum area", a collection of junks in the Pearl River and its side rivers, was removed.

General information

The population of Guangzhou is very different from that of the north. While it is urban, it has been marked more by trade than industry (in contrast to Shanghai), although light industry is now quite strongly represented in Guangzhou. The language is incomprehensible to northern Chinese: Cantonese has nine instead of four different tones like in the Manchurian language, and it has retained the end consonants which have disappeared from modern northern Chinese. Written Cantonese even has characters that are not used in Mandarin. Guangdong Province was already overcrowded 200 years ago, and many peasants emigrated to South-East Asia, the United States and Europe. As a result, the Cantonese language became the most commonly used among overseas Chinese.

The same is true for Cantonese cuisine; it is the most varied of all Chinese culinary trends, but is often mocked by other Chinese. According to a local joke, "the Cantonese eat anything that flies, except planes, and anything with four legs, except tables and chairs". You can get a better impression of the variety of dishes in the many restaurants and numerous snack bars around the market area as well as in the hotels. Many offer their own specialities, such as snake meat.

Shamian Island in the south west of the city is a relic of the colonial past which has been preserved. The island, which extends 656 yds (600 metres) from east to west and almost 437 yds (400 metres) from north to south was divided in 1859 into several concessions, the main ones being French and British. After 10 p.m. the Chinese population was locked out of the island, which was fortified by two iron gates and could only be reached by crossing two narrow bridges.

The former Catholic and Anglican churches have been reopened for worship. Most of the former **trade and**

consular buildings are used as government offices and schools. The formerly charming **River Road** along **Zhujiang** (Pearl River) lined with tall trees has been joined by a highway which links it to **White Swan Hotel** (Baitian'e Binguan). Opposite the canal which separates Shamian Island from the town itself, and where houseboats are occasionally moored, begins the Bund, which continues along the waterfront to Haizhu Bridge, the oldest steel bridge across the Zhujiang, built in 1933. About 109 yds (100 metres) to the east near the bridge, which connects the eastern end of Shamian with the mainland, is the **Memorial of the Martyrs of the Shaji Massacre**. Here, Chinese demonstrators died on 25 June 1925 in a hail of bullets fired by the foreign troops guarding the Concession. About a mile (two km) further east, to the north east of Haizhu Bridge, you can see the 160-ft (49-metre) high double towers of

the Roman Catholic **cathedral**. It was built in 1860-1863 based on a design by the French architect Guillemin, was left to decay after 1949 and especially during the Cultural Revolution, and was restored in the 1980s. It holds services under the auspices of the "Patriotic Catholic Church" but has no contact with the Vatican as yet.

To the north of the bridge, half way down Shamian towards the mainland on Qingpinglu, is the Qingping market occupying the side alleys around the main road Renmin Nanlu and Nürenjie. This district has flourished since the reformist policies of 1978 and is always very crowded. Attractions include meat and vegetable markets, souvenir stalls, tourist trinkets and snack stands with Cantonese specialities. To the east is the **Culture Park** (Wenhua Gongyuan) which offers roller-skating rinks, open-air theatre, theatre halls, art exhibitions and performances by the School of

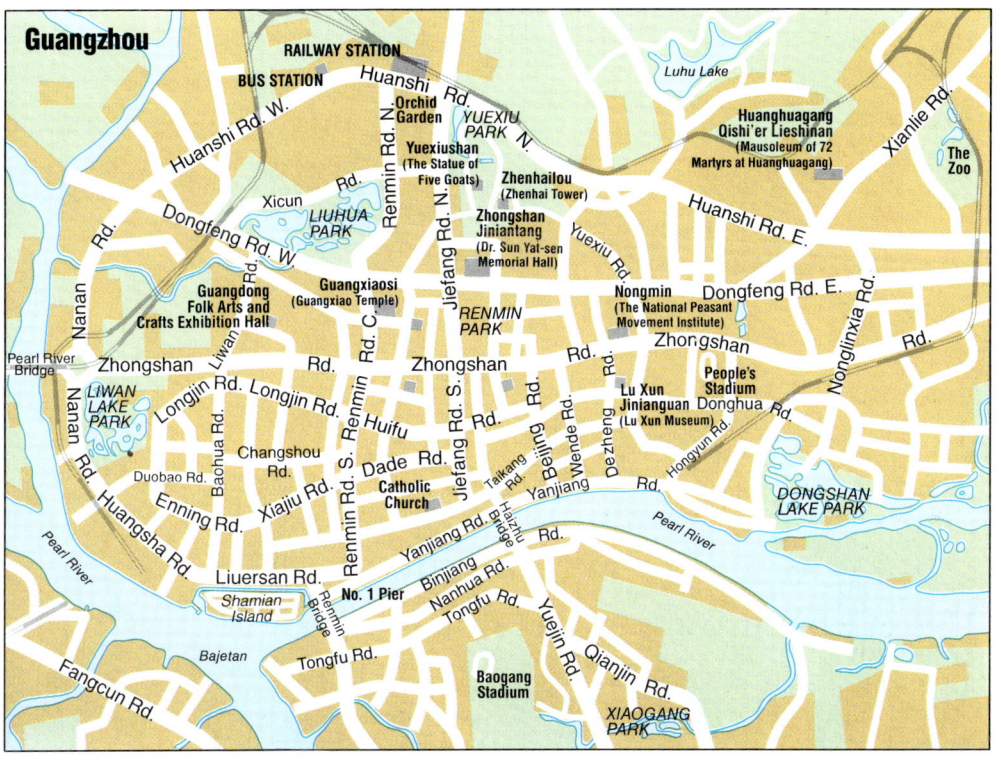

Acrobats from Guangzhou. It is like a mixture of the Tivoli and a museum garden. Close by is the well-stocked **Department Store of the South** (called Nanfang Department Store on maps for foreigners). It is on the corner of the lively main road, Renmin Nanlu (also known as Taipinglu in honour of the Taiping Revolution of 1850-1864), which is lined with numerous shops. (Street names are laid out in the following manner: the most important traffic arteries in Guangzhou are divided into sectors (as they are in Shanghai) and are laid out in grid fashion: *nan* = south, *bei* = north, *dong* = east and *xi* = west. The middle section is called *zhong*. A main road is *lu,* an alley *jie*.)

By taking Xiajiulu, which turns off to the east from the northern edge of the pedestrian zone, you get to the restaurant **Guangdong**. Behind it, in a narrow side alley (Shangxiajie), is the **Hualin Temple** (Hualinsi). It is said to have been founded by an Indian monk in 526, although the existing buildings date from the Qing period. There are 500 statues of Luohan (pupils of the Buddha) in the main hall. One of them, said to be Marco Polo, recognisable by his brimmed hat, was lost in the Cultural Revolution.

Near the crossroads of Renmin Zhonglu and the 6th section of **Zhongshanlu** (Sun Yatsen Street), in Guangtalu south of Sun Yatsen Street, is the **Mosque** (Huaishengsi) which is supposed to date back to 627. Apparently an uncle of Mohammed, who is said to have come to Guangzhou as a trader, was its founder. At that time, Arab traders could safely reach China, so the legend may well contain some truth, although it does not give sufficient evidence for an exact date of the foundation of this first mosque. The 82-ft (25-metres) high minaret (*Guangta*, literally *Naked Pagoda)* dominates the area which is still devoid of modern sky-

A floating banana market by the bank of the Pearl River.

scrapers. The mosque is a cultural centre for the approximately 4,000 Chinese Muslims who live in Guangzhou.

Northern districts

To the north of Zhongshanlu, a fairly narrow street leads to the **Temple of the Six Banyan Trees** (Liurongsi), whose "Decorated Pagoda" or "Flower Pagoda" (Huata) is a symbol of the city. The temple, said to date back to the year 479, got its name in 1099 in a calligraphic tribute from the poet Su Dongpo (1031-1101); it is the local seat of the Chinese Buddhist Association. The main hall contains a statue of the Buddha, eight Luohan, the God of Medicine, and (on the reverse side), the Goddess of Mercy (Guanyin), who in the Buddhist context is a female incarnation of the Bodhisattva Avalokiteshvara and in the traditional Chinese context, the Goddess of Fortune. The statues date from the Qing period. You can climb up the nine-storey pagoda behind the main hall; unfortunately, the view, which was once renowned, has today been spoilt by numerous new skyscrapers.

A few hundred yards north east, is the **Guanxiao Temple** (Guanxiaosi), preserved during the Cultural Revolution on orders from Zhou Enlai. Local legend has it that the temple is older than the town; it dates from the time between 397 and 401. Most of the present buildings were, however, built after a big fire (1269), and the majority probably only after 1832. The **Western** and **Eastern Iron Pagodas** (Dongtieta, Xitieta) date from the Founding Period.

There is a 23-ft (seven-metre) high stone pagoda behind the main hall, with sculptures of the Buddha placed in eight niches. It is thought to date from 967, but was only put in its present location at the beginning of Mongolian rule. The halls represent a mixture of all the styles

in different epochs.

To the north west, in a formal garden near Jiefang Beilu, is the **Sun Yatsen Hall** (Zhongshan Jiniantang) with its eye-catching blue roof tiles. The hall, which was built shortly after the death of Sun Yatsen in 1925, now houses a large theatre and lecture hall which can seat 5,000.

Yuexiu Park (Yuexiu Gongyuan), due north, is a beautiful example of a landscaped park. It is dominated by the **Tower Overlooking the Sea** (Zhenhailou), which is a memorial to the seven great sea journeys undertaken by the eunuch Zheng He between 1405 and 1433, when he travelled to East Africa, the Persian Gulf and Java. Today, the tower houses a museum on the history of Guangzhou.

Restored after the Cultural Revolution, the **Chen Family Temple** (Chenjiasi) dates from 1894 and lies in the western part of Zhongshanlu. It has six courtyards and a classic layout, and is decorated with friezes manufactured in Shiwan.

The name Chen is one of the most common in Guangdong Province. The families of that name from throughout the province donated money to build this temple dedicated to their ancestors. It serves to honour the forebears they have in common, and for the education of the children of the Chen Clan. Today, it is used as an exhibition area for handicrafts (Guangdong Minjiang Gongyiguan). The north of the town is dominated by **White Cloud Mountain** (Baiyunshan) four miles (six km) away, accessible by cable-car.

Eastern districts

In the east of the city, at the 4th section of Zhongshan Street (Zhongshan Silu), is the former **Confucius Temple** (Kongzimiao). It lost its reli-

gious function during the "bourgeois revolution" in 1912. In July 1924, the Peasant Movement Institute (Nongmin Yundong Jiangxisuo) was opened here, practically the first party school of the Chinese Communist Party. This is where the elite of the CP taught: Mao Zedong (from 1926; his work and bedroom can be viewed), Zhou Enlai, Qu Qiubai, Deng Zhong, Guo Moruo and others. This is also where Mao developed his Theory of Peasant Revolution. His tract "Class Analysis of Chinese Society" was written in this temple. After the collapse of the workers' uprising from 11 to 13 December 1927, the CP was forced to retreat for a time from the cities. A park and memorial were created in 1957 (Qiyi Lieshi Lingyuan) in memory of the uprising and its 5,000 victims. The temple is also worth visiting because of its 16th-century (Ming period) construction.

Directly next to it, eastwards, is the

The ancestral temple, Zumiao, near Foshan.

Provincial Museum of the Revolution (Guangdong Geming Bowuguan), which is a reminder of the role of the Guomindang and its predecessors since the First Opium War.

South of Zhongshan Ganlu are the old buildings of **Guangdong University** where China's first modern author, Lu Xun, lectured in 1927. There is an exhibition dedicated to him. Until 1927, the **All Chinese Trade Union Federation** was located nearby; the revolutionary and later President of the People's Republic and a victim of the Cultural Revolution, Liu Shaoqi, worked there. He wrote his work *Organisational Methods of Trade Unions* here, which is being increasingly quoted again.

In the north east, near the **zoo** on Xialielu, is a park created along Western lines. In it is a Memorial, built in 1918, to the 72 victims of the uprising of 29 March 1911.

The town of Foshan in Guangdong, ("Buddha Mountain") with one million inhabitants, is worth mentioning. It has a famous temple, the **Daoist Ancestor Temple** (Zumiao), whose history goes back to the Song Dynasty (emperor Yuanfeng, 1078-1085). It was renovated in 1372 and contains a 2½-ton (2,540-kg) bronze statue of the Northern God, Zhenwu, from the year 1452. There is also a small **museum** on the grounds, which has relics dating back to the Han period. The buildings – most of which were built during the Qing Dynasty – have been decorated with ceramics produced in the factory of **Shiwan** which is located in a suburb. Shiwan ceramics were also used in the Ancestor Temple of the Chen Family in Guangzhou.

The former **Renshousi Temple** is today a factory producing arts and crafts such as lanterns and papercuts. A visit to the 700-year-old Shiwan factory is permitted; it is famous for its porcelain and produces industrial ceramics as well as knick-knacks and crockery. On the journey from Guangzhou to Macau you pass the county of Zhongshan, with Sun Yatsen's birthplace in **Cuiheng**.

GUILIN – AMAZING LANDSCAPE

Flying into the hilly karst landscape of Guilin at sunset is one of the most breathtaking approaches in China, and it confirms that the town by the banks of the Li River (Lijiang) in southern China is justifiably considered to be one of the most beautiful in China. The view confirms the poem by the Tang scholar Han Yu (768-834): "The river is like a green silk belt, and the hills are like turquoise jade hairpins".

Chinese artists have immortalised their impression of this bizarre landscape with its round mountain tops in countless poems and paintings. Today, Guilin attracts innumerable tourists because of its unique landscape; together with Beijing, Shanghai and Xi'an, it is one of the main tourist destination in China. Until the end of the 1970s, it was a quiet, sleepy area. Since then, Guilin and the settlements along the Li River have undergone an incredible development through tourism. This was made easier because of the relatively good connections; there are daily flights to and from Shanghai, Beijing, Guangzhou and to Hongkong. Other parts of Guilin can also be easily reached by train and overland bus.

The autonomous region of Guangxi

The Guangxi region is in the subtropical part of China. Summers are long, hot and humid; the best times to visit are spring and autumn. Guilin is in the north eastern part of the Autonomous Region of Guangxi-Zhuang. The 152 million Zhuang are the largest national minority in China. More than 40 million people live in Guangxi, which borders on Vietnam in the south. Of these, 34 percent are Zhuang, and 5 percent belong to various small minorities, including the Yao, Miao, Yi and Dong. These minorities are predominantly settled in the more backward areas in the west and north of the Autonomous Region. The area around Guilin owes its beauty to a geological process over time: the amazing karst formations were forced up from the limestone seabed more than 300 million years ago. Erosion then shaped the bizarre hills and globe-shaped peak tops of the area and also left numerous subterranean caves in the eerie and fantastic rock formations.

The scented town of Guilin

The town, which today has over 400,000 inhabitants, acquired its name from the Cassia trees whose blooms carry their sweet scent through the whole town in autumn. Guilin literally means "Cassia Tree Forest". According to historic records, Guilin is said to have been founded in 214 B.C. At that time, the Lingqu Canal was built under the

regency of the first Chinese emperor, Qin Shi Huangdi. It still connects the central Asian plain with southern China and South-East Asia, via the Yangzi, the Lijiang and the Pearl river. The first Europeans who arrived in A.D. 1550 captured the Portuguese seafarers. In 1647 the Ming established a temporary settlement here during their flight from the Manchus. Hundreds of thousands of northern Chinese sought refuge from the Japanese in Guilin during World War II. Guilin was one of the last towns to be taken by the Chinese communists in 1949.

Guilin and its surroundings are still mostly agricultural, but this is limited by the numerous mountains which pose a problem in the whole of Guangxi. The landscape is characterised by terraced rice paddies, water buffalos and bamboo groves, and peasants with turned up trousers and cone-shaped straw hats. Jujube, a type of date, is harvested here, and Guilin is famous for its spicy Guilinjiang, a type of pepper sauce.

The town of Guilin itself is not particularly attractive; there is still many old, somewhat run-down houses, but that is compensated for by the wonderful surroundings. A building boom has started with the arrival of tourism. Many modern hotels have sprung up, and the face of Guilin has changed considerably in recent years.

In the centre of town and around Zhongshanlu are many large and small souvenir shops, clothes shops, small hotels, and, in between, an increasing number of snack bars and small restaurants which offer specialities such as snakes, frogs' legs or pangolin.

North of the centrally situated **Lijiang Hotel** in Ronghu Beilu is the 499-ft (152-metre) tall Duxiufeng, the **Peak of Unique Beauty**, with 300 steps leading to the top. Nearby, in the grounds of

Cormorant fishermen in the evening.

the Pedagogic Institute, are the **ruins of the Royal Residence** (Wang Cheng) from the late 14th century. A bit further west, by the bank of the Li River, at the corner of Binjianglu and Fengbeilu, **Mount Fuboshan** rises. It is named after a general from the Han period who had defended the inhabitants against attackers. On the way up to Fuboshan you pass a 2½-ton bell and a huge cooking pot from which more than 1,000 people could apparently be served. Both are from the former temple site. On the south slope is the **Returned Pearl Grotto**. This is where a dragon, who had a beautiful pearl to light his cave, is supposed to have lived . A fisherman stole it one day but brought it back quickly when he discovered to whom it belonged. On the eastern slope of the mountain is the **Thousand Buddha Rock** (Qianfoyan) with around 300 Buddhist sculptures from the Tang and Song period.

Further north is the **Mountain of Coloured Layers** (Diecaishan). You can get a wonderful view of Guilin and Lijiang from the 732-ft (223-metre) high mountain. There are also Buddhist sculptures and Chinese calligraphies in the **Caves of Diecaishan**. At the foot of the mountain, tourists can have their picture taken with living cormorants.

On the eastern bank of Lijiang – which can easily be reached by crossing Jiefang bridge – is the **Seven Star Park** (Qixing Gongyuan). Its seven hills are laid out according to the star pattern of the Ursa Major (Big Dipper) constellation. There are several illuminated caves in the mountain; the most famous one is the **Seven Star Cave** with its inscriptions and poems. The **Camel Mountain** (Luotuoshan) has an interesting shape, resembling a seated dromedary. There is also a bonsai-exhibition and a small zoo in the park.

Almost four miles (six km) north

A village by the Li River.

west of the city centre is the **Reed Flute Cave** (Ludiyan) which goes 787 ft (240 metres) into the mountain. It takes its name from the reeds growing at the entrance of the cave which were once used to make flutes. There are many bizarre stalagtites and stalagmites along the way which resemble pagodas, people, lions, mushrooms etc. There is no limit to the imagination. The most beautiful spot of the tour is the **Crystal Palace of the Dragon King** and a subterranean water landscape which resembles the landscape around Guilin and the Li River.

Li River – a green band of silk

A boat trip on the peaceful Li River is the absolute high point of any visit to Guilin. The boats leave by Jiefang Bridge near the Lijiang hotel. Smaller boats leave from **Elephant Trunk Hill** (Xiangbishan). The cruise from Guilin to Yangshuo, about 37 miles (60 km) away on the winding and twisting Li River, goes past the many bizarre mountains whose shapes have inspired and fired the Chinese imagination: Elephant Trunk Mountain, Old Man Mountain, Pagoda Mountain, Hole Mountain etc.

Cormorant fishermen in narrow bamboo boats, bathing children, water buffaloes, small settlements and women doing their washing on the banks of the river can be seen along the way. Sometimes the water level is so low that the boats can only go from the settlement of **Yangdi**.

The second part of the journey is the more interesting one. **Yangshuo**, the end of the boat journey, is today a developed village which thrives mainly on tourism and seems to have nothing but tourist shops. But when the tourists have departed, the village streets become tranquil again.

The boat trip usually ends in the small town of Yangshuo.

From Yangshuo, there is a bus back to Guilin (about two hours' journey). You can get an impression of the varied landscape and an insight into Guilin agriculture, as well as see many traditional graves from the bus.

The region around Guilin

North east of Guilin is **Sanjiang**, a settlement of the Song people. **Changyong Bridge** is an architecturally unique sight. South west of Guilin, in the centre of the Autonomous Region of Guangxi, is **Liuzhou** (600,000 inhabitants), an expanding industrial town, picturesque and typically southern Chinese. The main attraction is the **Dule Rock** (Duleyan) with its numerous karst caves. Another area with a beautiful landscape is the settlement of **Guiping** (80 miles/130 km from Liuzhou south eastwards).

The capital of the Autonomous Region of Guangxi is **Nanning**. It is located deep in the south and is only 99 miles (160 km) from the Vietnamese border. Here, you can visit a Museum of the Autonomous Region, an Institute for National Minorities, a Cultural Centre where the villages of eleven national minorities have been reconstructed in an open air museum.

South west of Nanning, near the Vietnamese border by the river **Zuojiang** is a landscape as fantastic as that in Guilin. In Ningmeng county you can see a 1,700-year-old, mysterious rock painting along a steep rock face by taking a boat on Zuojiang river.

If you travel from Guilin via Liuzhou towards Guangzhou (or the other way by boat), you pass **Wuzhou**, a small town which is also surrounded by a magnificent landscape. The coastlines of Guangxi by the Gulf of Tongking, however, have so far hardly been opened up to tourism.

The "Crystal Palace of the Dragon King" in the Reed Flute Cave.

THE YANGZI RIVER – CHINA'S LIFELINE

The source of Changjiang (Long River), as the longest river in China (3,915 miles/6,300 km) is called in Chinese, is in the south west of the Qinghai plateau on Geladandong, the main peak of the Tanggula Mountains. Its estuary is north of Shanghai, where it is eight miles (13 km) wide when it flows into the Yellow Sea.

The river flows through nine provinces and, with its 700 tributaries, covers an area of 694, 985 sq miles (1.8 million sq km), that is, 19 percent of the total area of China and 25 percent of the agriculturally viable area. The river flows through most of the important industrialised area in China – industries such as silk weaving, embroidery, lacquer work and carving. It also forms a delta where the density of the poulation is the highest in the South. This paints a picture of how important a role this river has played for the whole of China.

Wuhan

Since the Hollywood film *Gunboat up the Yangtse,* it has become generally known in Europe and the US that large boats can navigate the Yangzi river as far as Hankou. Hankou is one of three formerly independent municipalities of what is today the industrial city of Wuhan. The two other districts are Wuchang and Hanyang.

After the Treaty of Tianjin (1860) made Hankou into a Free Port, the colonial powers quickly established themselves here, including Great Britain, France, Germany, Russia and Japan. They divided the former village into concessions and tried to use it as a base from which to colonise the provinces of Inner China. Wuhan district, which has become the largest district, is still characterised by colonial architecture.

There is, for instance, an old house with a sign saying that this is where the Siemens company had a branch.

Today Wuhan, which has 4 million inhabitants, is better known as a starting or finishing point for excursions through the three Yangzi gorges, and tourist groups tend to stop only for a short time. But even though the capital of Hubei province has not been very attractive and had a poor reputation – an industrial centre with its associated negative aspects – restoration works carried out in the last few years have definitely improved the old city centre. A boat trip here will immediately take you back in time to the era of the Three Kingdoms.

The **Yellow Crane Tower** (Huanghelou) on **Snake Mountain** (Sheshan), for instance, has been restored with a great deal of effort, and the surrounding buildings have been rebuilt in the traditional Chinese style, thus preserving a

popular destination in Wuchang district.

The first Yellow Crane Tower is said to have existed in the 3rd century. It was destroyed and rebuilt several times, and it was last burnt down in 1884. Today, there are exhibitions of calligraphy and paintings in the pagoda-like building, and you can still see the famous **Yangzi bridge** from different viewing points located on every floor.

Changjiang Daqiao, as the bridge is called in Chinese, is 3,793 ft (1,156 metres) long with eight piers. It was the first bridge across the Yangzi, and was built for rail and road traffic. Its completion was important for the Chinese economy. Its construction, which was carried out quickly (1955-1957), created the urgently needed communications link between the north and south of China, and henceforth Wuhan became a junction for north-south and east-west connections.

On the edge of the town is a large lake area, the **East Lake** (Donghu), situated in a huge park which has a number of other sights. There is a lovely view across the entire lake and park area from the **Sparkling Lake Pavilion** (Huguangge). The lakes are a popular spot for members of the many institutes situated in this part of the town. But despite the many visitors, particularly in the hot summer months when temperatures in Wuhan rise to around 40 degrees centigrade, it is a quiet and pleasantly cool place because of its enormous size.

Near **East Lake Park** (Donghu Yuan) is the restored **Hubei Provincial Museum**, worth a visit particularly because of its unique set of well-preserved chimes from 433 B.C.

The **Guiyuan Temple** (Guiyuansi), a Buddhist temple from the 16th century, is in the centre of Hanyang. It has not yet been restored, although it was not destroyed during the Cultural Revo-

Yangzi Bridge in Wuhan.

lution. A walk through the halls and courtyards adds an air of certain nostalgic charm to it. The painting of the bodhisattva *Guanyin* shows the Goddess of Mercy standing on a tortoise; the picture has given the temple its name.

Yangzi Cruise

The liners which go daily at various times from Wuhan to Chongqing used to be called *Dongfanghong* (the East is red) during the days of the Cultural Revolution. Today they have been renamed after their home ports Chongqing, Hankou or Shanghai. For reasons which are not clear, there is still no first class section on the boats; the best class is second class with two-bed cabins, toilets and showers, a day room and the privilege of better food in a separate dining room. There is also third class (four to eight bed cabins), fourth class

The Yangzi is navigable for ocean-going ships as far as Wuhan.

(24 bed cabins), and fifth class (a floor space on the lower deck).

For several years, tourist excursion boats have been operating as well, stopping where the various sights are and running boat trips up the Daning tributary. The **Three Small Gorges** there have been judged by many travellers to be even more beautiful than the big gorges. The cost of a trip on one of these boats is about ten times the price of regular boats.

The first stop on the trip from Wuhan to Chongqing by regular boat is the town of **Yueyang**. Located in Hunan Province on the southern edge of Hubei Province, Yueyang is on the eastern shore of **Lake Dongting**.

The best-known sight in the town, which has around 200,000 inhabitants, greets the traveller south of the Yangzi. This is the **Yueyang Tower** (Yueyang-lou), one of the most famous pavilion towers. Numerous songs have been

composed about it since the Tang period (618-907). The newly restored building, however, dates from the last century. The tower is flanked on both sides by two pavilions, the **Plum Blossom of the Immortal Pavilion** (Xianmeiting) and the **Three Drunks Pavilion** (Sanzuiting).

Lake Dongting, one of the largest inland lakes in China, is linked to the Yangzi by several rivers, canals and lakes and serves as a natural water reservoir for the river. During the rainy season, it takes up to 40 percent of the waters from the Yangzi; in droughts, it returns its water to the river, and its expanse is reduced by almost a third. It contains a wealth of fish, is a breeding place for rare water birds, and in the summer months, its shores are covered in the red and green hues of blooming lotus plants.

About 124 miles (200 km) west of Wuhan is the next stop, still in Hubei Province, the town of **Shashi** (Sand Town). This town, which by Chinese standards is small – with only about 200,000 inhabitants – has few sights to offer. The **Zhanghuasi Temple** is worth mentioning. It was founded in 535; its present structure is from the Ming period (1368-1644), and it contains two beautifully worked jade Buddhas. There is also a seven storey, 31-ft (40-metre) high **Pagoda of Eternal Life** (Wanshoubaota).

Yichang, the last stop before reaching the Yangzi Gorges, is a predominantly industrial town. The completion of the Gezhouba coffer-dam has made the town increasingly important for the Chinese economy.

If you want to break your journey here, you could enjoy a short excursion by bus to see how the Yangzi emerges from the gorges at the **Nanjing Pass**, three and a half miles (six km) away.

The famous battle between the state

armies of Shu and Wu (A.D. 221) took place in Yiling, as Yichang used to be called in the past. The leader of the army, the king of Shu, Liu Bei, lost the battle. It is vividly remembered in Chinese history as a victory of a weak army over a numerically much stronger army by the use of tactical skills. After his defeat, Liu Bei was forced to flee through the gorges of the Yangzi to Baidichen (*see below*).

The Three Gorges

Just behind Yichang, the canalized right part of the river takes the boats to an enormous lock. In front is the biggest coffer-dam in China, 8,202 ft (2,500 metres) wide and 154 ft (47 metres) deep. It was completed in 1986 and supplies electricity to the surrounding provinces. A new town has grown up in recent years along its right and left banks. However, its installation was not

uncontroversial since the dam has raised the water level of the upper course and has possibly increased the danger of flooding.

West of Yichang, work has begun on what will, if completed, be one of the world's largest dams. The **Three Gorges Dam** has already proved controversial, because it will be enormously costly, over a million people will have to be moved, it could cause environmental problems, and it will create a reservoir 370 miles (600 metres) long and up to 575 ft (175 metres) deep in one of China's premier scenic areas. But the scheme has boosted tourism to the Three Gorges, with visitors arriving to see them before the transformation.

The floodgate of the dam near Yichang opens to let several boats through at a time; they negotiate a difference in height of up to 98 ft (30 metres). Soon after the coffer-dam, four rockfaces, resembling silhouettes, emerge on the

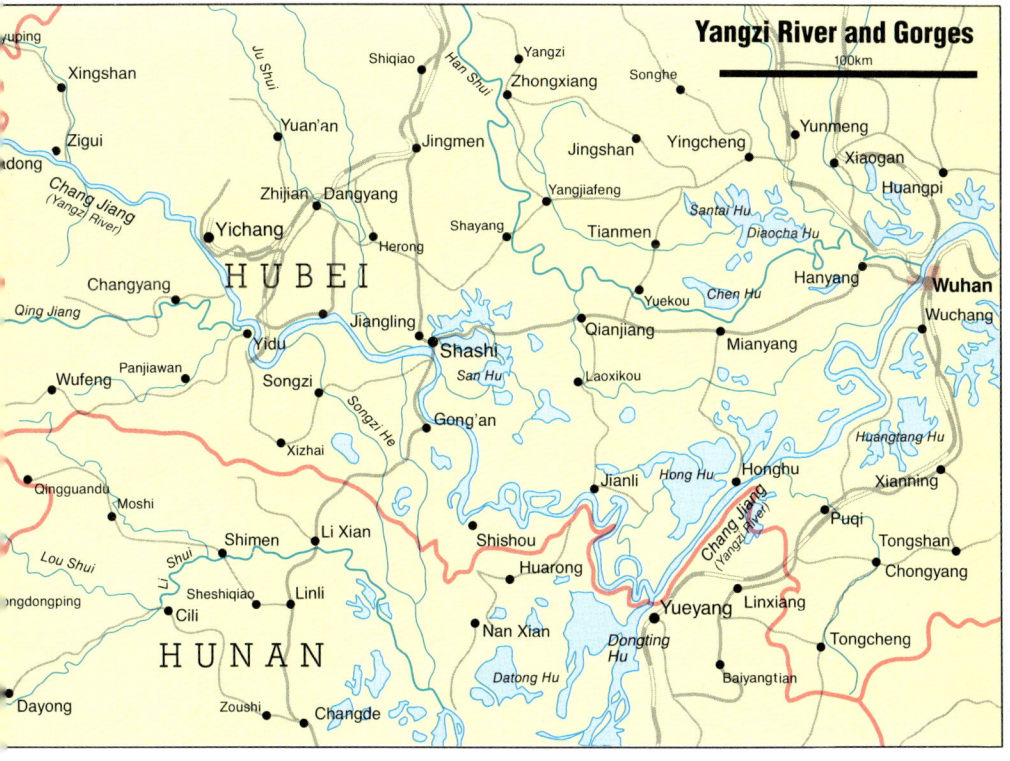

southern bank of the river. With a bit of imagination you can recognise the four famous heroes from the novel *The Journey to the West*, which is known throughout China. They are the ape king *Sun Wukong*, the Buddhist master *Xuanzang*, the pig *Zhu Bajie* and the monk *Sha*. The trip through the Yangzi gorges, which stretch to a total length of 120 miles (193 km), starts here with the **Shadow Play Gorge**. The first and longest gorge, which includes the Shadow Play Gorge, is the **Xiling Gorge** (Xilingxia). This 48-mile (78-km) long gorge really consists of several smaller gorges. From the north, the river is overlooked by the **Yellow Hill Temple** (Huanglingmiao). The main hall of the temple, which is said to originate in the Han period (202 B.C.-A.D. 220), is dedicated to the ruler Yu.

About half way into the Xiling Gorge, the river is divided by a sand bank. The peculiar shape of the next small gorge earned it the name **Horse-Lung and Ox-Liver Gorge** (Niugan Mafei Xia); hidden behind it is the 394-ft (120-metre) long abyss of the **Blue Cliff** (Qingtan). The **Book on the Art of War and the Precious Sword Gorge** (Bingshu Baojian Xia) also got its name from its appearance – a rock which juts up like a sword – and from legend. Zhuge Liang, a famous military leader from the period of the Three Kingdoms (220-280), and brother-in-arms of Liu Bei, is said to have written a military manual which he locked into the rock because he couldn't find anyone worthy of becoming his successor. Since then, the Chinese have waited for a military commander who has the capabilities of moving the rock and freeing the valuable book.

The mouth of the Fragrant River (Xiangxi) on the northern bank signals the end of Xiling Gorge. You pass **Zigui**, the home of the famous poet Qu

The water acquires a yellow colour during the rainy season.

Yuan (approx. 332-295 B.C.) who, according to legend, drowned himself in despair over the occupation of his home state Chu by the armies of the Qin empire. The whole of China still celebrates the Dragon Boat Festival in his honour, which is very popular both with the Chinese and tourists.

Despite its name, the 25-mile (40-km) long **Witches Gorge** (Wuxia) is relatively calm. As with so many places in China, the gorge, surrounded by twelve mountain peaks, is steeped in legend, and the loudspeaker on board the ship hardly stops, recounting all the lore: the story of the youngest daughter of the Western Heavenly Mother (Xi-wangmu), who helped the legendary Emperor Yu conquer the water and who now keeps watch – and one can really visualise her – over the river from the highest peak, the **Fairy Peak** (Shennü-feng) with her eleven sisters. A Chinese Lorelei, which, however, does not bring

Chinese travellers on a Yangzi riverboat.

misfortune to the seafarers but protects them. The border between the provinces of Hubei and Sichuan runs here, through the Witches Gorge.

The entry to the third gorge, **Bellows Gorge** (Qutang Xia) is breathtakingly-beautiful . Although it is only five miles (eight km) long, it is probably the most fascinating one. Perpendicular walls rise up from the river, narrowing it to a width of 30 ft (100 metres). You almost seem to be able to touch the rock face, and begin to admire the skill of the helmsman. It requires great concentration and a lot of experience to steer through this narrow gap. It is difficult to know what is more fascinating, the perpendicular rock face or the swirling, brown water which reveals underneath its expansive, smooth circling surface, the treacherous maelstroms.

Travel reports from the 1920s and 30s give an exciting account of the journey through the gorges with cargo boats and

junks. The boats had to be towed upstream, and the coolies carried out heavy work which could at times end in death if one of the men lost his footing on the paths hewn into the rock and pulled his mates, who were all chained together, down into the abyss.

The crossing of the Qutang Gorge in a normal cargo boat required more than a hundred trackers who were hired from among the peasants in the surrounding areas. But even then, the relatively short distance took several days, depending on the water level. The saying "To reach Sichuan is more difficult than to reach heaven" now acquires a specific meaning. Until this century, this passage was almost the only way to get from eastern China to Sichuan Province, which is surrounded by impassable mountain ranges.

After passing through Qutang Gorge, the settlement of **Fengjie** now appears. To the east of Fengjie is **Baidicheng**,

the City of the White Emperor. Legend has it that a ruler from the time of the eastern Han Dynasty (A.D. 25-220) saw a white dragon emerge from a well outside his palace. He considered it a good omen and henceforth called himself "White Emperor".

In the main hall of the **White Emperor Temple** are figures of the above mentioned army generals of Shu from the time of the Three Kingdoms (221-263): Liu Bei and Zhuge Liang. After the military defeat at Yichang mentioned above, Liu Bei was forced to flee to Baidicheng and, on his death bed, named Zhuge Liang as his successor.

The next large town is **Wanxian**, which has, for a long while been a trading centre and port for transport ships going through the gorges. An impressive steep staircase leads upwards to the city near the mooring. The steps lead into the market street where at almost any time during the day or night,

traders offer the local produce, bamboo goods and fruits, to buyers coming from the boats. Wanxian is particularly famous for its oranges and pomelos (fruit similar to grapefruit). It is also the place where Chinese travellers like to get their provisions.

About five hours from Wanxian, on the northern bank of the river, is the **Stone Treasure Stronghold** (Shibaozhai). During the reign of emperor Qianlong (1736-1797), a temple was erected on a rock which rose up 98 ft (30 metres) from the northern bank of the Yangzi. According to legend, there was a small hole in the temple wall, from which enough rice trickled to feed the monks – thus the name "Stone Treasure". However, when the monks became greedy and thought they could get even more rice if they made the hole bigger, the treasure dried up.

As the ascent to the temple was very tiring, a pagoda-shaped pavilion was built against the rock at the time of emperor Jiaqing (1796-1820). Its eleven storeys reach as far as the temple, and so you can easily climb up to the temple from inside the pavilion.

Fengdu, which is also on the northern bank of the Yangzi, has been named after a dam and the mountain range surrounding the town. It is really called the Ghost or Devil Town, because from the Tang Dynasty (618-907) onwards, statues of demons and devils have been housed in numerous temples.

Chongqing – mountain city on the river

The journey up the river, which has covered nearly 435 miles (700 km), ends in Chongqing. During the Tang period (618-907), Chongqing was called Yuzhou, and it is still called Yu for short today. The emperor Zhao Dun of the Southern Song Dynasty (1127-1279) had renamed it "Twin Fortune",

eft, Shibaozhai Pagoda, clinging to the rock. Right, old stone pagoda by the river.

i.e. Chongqing, after two lucky events. First, he had become prince of the prefecture, and later emperor. It has always been an important trading centre due to its location at the confluence of the Yangzi and Jialing rivers. Chongqing is one of the few cities in China built on a rocky promontory. It has little to offer in the way of interesting architecture.

There is a proverb which says, "when the sun shines in Sichuan in winter, the dogs bark". This is particularly apt for Chongqing, because through most of the winter, that is from around October to March, when temperatures can fall to 4 degrees centigrade, the town is shrouded in fog which rises from the rivers. This fog depresses the spirit. During the war, when the Japanese had occupied parts of the country and the Guomindang government under Chiang Kaishek had fled to Chongqing, the town was bombed for several summers by the Japanese. Then, people were grateful for the winter fog because no enemy reconnaissance planes flew over the city and people could recover from the summer bombings.

The mountain city, as the town with a population of 13 million is also called, is the only Chinese metropolis not located in a flat area and not constructed on grid lines; it has been built against the hills by the confluence of the Yangzi and Jialing rivers. The houses in the old city centre are typical of the architecture in this region. They cling on to the slopes, their black roofs resembling swallows nests; the top floor has a door to the street and the lower floors overlook one of the two rivers. The city, at present, is threatening to burst at the seams. To alleviate this problem, rather ugly looking skyscrapers are being cheaply built in the centre, which houses about 2 million inhabitants.

The palace-like Renmin Hotel, built in the 1950s, rises from this maze of

Early morning arrival in Chongqing Harbour.

houses. Its central hall, which is used as the Town Hall, has been modelled on the Heavenly Temple in Beijing. Two cable cars link the river banks, and the Yangzi Bridge, completed in 1982, has relieved the pressure on the ferries.

Another bridge, supplementary to the existing one across the Jialing is being built farther north, creating a link between the districts of Shapingba and Jiangbei and is intended to lead to the new international airport which is also being built. The old airport, which is only suitable for internal flights, is more than an hour's drive outside the city behind Mount Gele. There are landing difficulties because of its location between the mountain peaks. Moreover, the frequent bad weather conditions can often lead to flight delays.

The old city area around **Liberation Square** (Jiefangbei) is full of small meandering alleys and seems to be one big free market. Steep steps lead from the tip of the peninsula down to the river banks studded with moorings. At the tip of the peninsula is a small pavilion, the **Door facing Heaven** (Chaotianmen). The flood level is marked here, as a reminder of the last big flood in 1982 which swamped a large area and caused great devastation.

Not far from the Chaotianmen pavilion, hidden in a narrow side street, is a small Buddhist temple, known as **Luohansi**. It has been restored in recent years, and although it doesn't contain any particular treasures, it is worth visiting this relatively small construction, crammed in between the residential houses. In the evening, you can get a brilliant view of the whole city from the **Pipa Mountain**.

A bus journey takes you past numerous industrial buildings and some paper factories – whose waste emissions create a lot of pollution problems on Jialing River – out of town towards the **Northern Springs** (Beiquan). The journey takes one and a half hours. The idyllic park on the river bank is very refreshing after the hurly-burly of the town. You can bathe in the warm spring, whose temperature is 35 degrees centigrade. Some 15 miles (25 km) further on are the **Southern Springs** (Nanquan), which are also in a park and where you can swim or row a boat.

Buddhist caves in Dazu

An excursion to **Dazu** is definitely recommended. The former county town, 99 miles (160 km) west of Chongqing, can be reached by bus in around five hours. The bus journey there, through lovely countryside, is in itself an experience. In addition, thousands of Buddhist sculptures and reliefs are scattered along the nearly 40 hills. Construction had begun in the 9th century, when many Buddhists had fled from persecution to Sichuan and had found patrons in Dazu who facilitated the building of these places of worship. At present, two hills are open to visitors. On **North Mountain** (Beishan), which is within walking distance of the town, is a site called "Amitayus-Dyana-Sutra" with more than 600 figures which depict the teachings relating to Buddha Amitabha, who was worshipped as Master of the Western Paradise. A white stone pagoda stands on the opposite hill.

The even more impressive **Treasure Mountain** (Baodingshan) is nine miles (15 km) north east of Dazu. The sculptures cut into the mountain are larger and more colourful. They show scenes which represent the teachings of Buddhism. One hall contains a Guanyin sculpture with exactly 1,007 arms; nearby is the Sleeping Buddha, a 102-ft (31-metre) long, prostrate figure which symbolises the passing of Buddha into nirvana. The adjacent rock faces represent Heavenly Paradise and Hell. A notable aspect in these scenes is that ethical principles of both Buddhist and Confucian origin are interwoven. They represent the efforts made by the Buddhists at that time to present their teachings as compatible with the Confucian teachings of the state.

SICHUAN – THE INNERMOST PROVINCE

Sichuan is the most populous Chinese province; around 10 percent of the Chinese population, more than a hundred million people, live on a land area of 218,920 sq miles (567,000 sq km), including national minorities such as the Yi, Tibetans, Miao, Hui and Qiang, who are predominantly settled in the three autonomous regions of the province.

The plain, which is surrounded by high mountain ranges to the north, east and west, has a climate which is very favourable to agriculture. It has warm summers and not very cold winters with high humidity, allowing cultivation throughout the year. Even during the winter months of January and February, the peasants supply the market with fresh fruit and vegetables

The picturesque terraced plots, typical of the "Red Basin" at the centre of the province, can produce up to three harvests in a year. The farmhouses, often built in a timber-frame style, are scattered prettily between the fields and are surrounded by shade-giving bamboo groves.

The main grain of the region is rice; a large amount of rape seed is also grown, which supplies most of the cooking oil used in China. Towards the end of March, the plain glows yellow with the blooming rape seed fields. Along the edges of many of the terraced fields are mulberry trees, the food for the silk worm industry which many peasants have as a lucrative sideline. Other agricultural products in the relatively wealthy province are citrus fruit such as oranges, mandarins and pomelos, oil, sugar cane, camphor, raw lacquer, wax, tea and bamboo which amongst other things is used as raw material for the intricate Sichuan wickerworks.

The forests in the western mountain region are rich in fir and deciduous trees

and rare animals. This is the home of the Giant Panda, which has increasingly been pushed into ever higher mountain regions by human settlements, and is now threatened with extinction. Unfortunately, the ruthless economic exploitation and environmental pollution are visibly affecting these regions. Some areas have been put under special environmental protection to maintain the flora and fauna at its present level at least, and to carry out research.

Today, the province, which in past centuries was not easily accessible, and which as a result has preserved a rich tradition, is linked to the rest of China through numerous routes. Chengdu is the centre for air traffic, and can be reached easily and quickly from towns and cities including Beijing, Shanghai, Wuhan, Guangzhou, Xi'an, Kunming, Lhasa and Hongkong.

There are numerous direct railway links between Sichuan and almost all

Preceding pages: rice paddies in Sichuan. **Left**, the hanging bridge across Minjiang near the irrigation system, Dujiangyan. **Right**, a Mao statue in Chengdu.

other Chinese provinces, and the stretch between Chengdu and Kunming counts amongst the most beautiful train journeys in the country. The link between Chongqing and Xi'an goes in hairpin bends through many tunnels and across many bridges, crossing the Qingling Mountains to the north beyond Sichuan.

The two regions Shu and Ba were part of the area of present-day Sichuan under the first emperor of a united China, Qin Shi Huangdi. These prefixes still appear as abbreviations for Sichuan. Around the year 1,000, during the Northern Song Dynasty, four districts were created to facilitate administration. They were called Chuan Xia Si Lu (four districts of Chuanxia), and were later abbreviated to the modern name Sichuan.

Capital Chengdu

The capital of the province, Chengdu, lies in the centre of the Sichuan plain, the Red Basin. The town, which is more than 2,000 years old, now has around 3.7 million inhabitants. In contrast to some other Chinese metropolises, it has preserved a special atmosphere – it is how we imagine China to have been in the past. Chengdu was already the political, economic and cultural centre of West Sichuan in 400 B.C. During the Five Dynasties (907-960), Meng Chang (935-965), a ruler of the later Shu, had numerous hibiscus trees planted on the city walls, so the town became known as the "City of Hibiscus". The famous brocade manufacture earned it another name: Brocade Town.

Built on flat ground, the town can easily be explored on foot or by bicycle. It has almost a southern aspect with its colourful old streets which are lined by many small restaurants and are crowded till late into the evening with traders, buyers or people out for a stroll. You could eat your way through the countless specialities by visiting the snack bars or tea houses, which often have free performances of Sichuan operas or other songs, or instrumental pieces to entertain guests having the popular jasmine tea.

The Temple of the Duke of Wu (Wuhousi) in the southern suburb of Chengdu was built by the king of the Cheng empire in the last years of the Western Jin Dynasty (265-316). It was built in memory of Zhuge Liang, the Prime Minister of Shu and Duke of Wuxiang. During the Ming period (1368-1644), the temple was merged with the site of Zhaomieliao, a temple dedicated to the memory of Liu Bei (Zhuge Liang and Liu Bei; see also the chapter "The Yangzi River – China's Lifeline").

The temple site as it can be seen today was rebuilt in the 11th year of the Kangxi era of the Qing Dynasty (1672). There are more than 40 sculptures of famous personalities from the Shu and Han period, as well as numerous memorial stones, scrolls and various sacral implements.

In the south western suburb of Chengdu, by the Huanhua stream is the park which contains the so-called **Straw Hut of the Poet Du Fu** (Du Fu Caotang). Du Fu, a poet from the Tang Dynasty (618-907) had sought refuge in Chengdu with his family from a disturbance. He had built a straw hut on the land of a helpful friend, where he lived for three years in very modest circumstances. He is said to have written more than 240 of his popular and much-read poems while here.

The memorial to this famous poet, Du Fu has been renovated or rebuilt several times during the subsequent dynasties. The present site in the park dates from two different periods: the governing period Hongzhi of the Ming Dynasty and the governing period Jiaqing of the Qing Dynasty. They include the **Gongbu Temple**, the **Shishi Pavilion** and the study in the straw hut (*Caotang Shuwu*). Next to the straw hut is the Straw Hut Temple. Handwritten and printed examples and various editions of the poet's works are on display here.

The **River View Tower** (Wangjiang-lou) stands on the southern bank of Jinjiang (Brocade River), in the south eastern part of the town. It was built during the Qing Dynasty in memory of Xue Tao, a famous poetess of the Tang Dynasty. Today, this area is a public park with several towers and pavilions.

The **Chongli Pavilion**, which is 98 ft (30 metres) tall and has four floors, is particularly noticeable because of its striking ornaments, green glazed tiles and red lacquered columns. More than a hundred varieties of bamboo have been planted here in honour of Xue Tao, who is said to have loved bamboo. It includes such rare varieties as spotted bamboo or square bamboo. The poetess is said to have fetched the water from the well on the site for making the paper that she used.

It is worth visiting the **Tomb of Wang Jian** (Wangjianmu) in the west of the town. Wang Jian (847-918) was a general in the last days of the Tang emperor Lizhu (who ruled between 904-907), and was the first ruler of the newly founded state of Shu in present-day Sichuan Province. The building, which is 33 ft (10 metres) high, has three burial chambers. The center chamber contains a sarcophagus between two rows of stone figures, with a frieze running along three walls depicting musicians and dancers.

Try not to forget a visit to Chengdu **zoo**. Although the old buildings and the way animals are kept do not generally make Chinese zoos very pleasant, Chengdu zoo has several pandas, including some young ones.

Around Chengdu

Eleven miles (18 km) north of Chengdu, in the county town of Xindu, is the famous Buddhist **Precious Light Monastery** (Baoguangsi). It is thought to have been founded during the Eastern Han Dynasty and to have housed more than 3,000 monks in the 10th and 11th centuries. The site was burnt down during the Ming period and rebuilt in 1670. The oldest building on the monastery site is the 98-ft (30-metre) tall pagoda (Shelita) in the front courtyard; the only one to have survived the fire. A Buddha relic is kept in the abbot's rooms. The 500 relatively well preserved Luohan statues from the Qing Dynasty are well worth seeing.

Dujiangyan Dam, on the upper course of the Minjiang, west of Guanxian county and 31 miles (50 km) from Chengdu, is an over 2,000-year-old irrigation structure. The project was built under the guidance of the prefect, Li Bing, and his son, from 306 to 251 B.C. The irrigation network was capable of irrigating over 494,200 acres (200,000 hectares) of land shortly after its completion; today, 600,000 acres (242,820 hectares) of agricultural land are supplied with water. The **Two Kings Temple** (Erwangmiao) was built in honour of its architects. There is a

Boddhisattva with a thousand arms in Baoguangsi Monastery.

1,900-year-old, 9-ft (2.9-metre) tall stone statue of Li Bing in the **Pavilion of the Dragon's Defeat** (Fulongguan). You can get a wonderful view over the whole site from here.

Holy Mount Emei Shan

The Emei mountain range is to the south west of the Sichuan basin, 99 miles (160 km) from Chengdu. The county town Emeixian at the foot of the mountain range can be reached either by bus or train from Chengdu. The journey takes about three hours, or you can get off at Emeixian on the Kunming-Chengdu line. There are minibuses from Emeixian to the **Emei Mountain Gate**, the Baoguo Temple (Baoguosi) which dates from the 16th century. The temple, built on a slope, comprises four halls, each one built in a more elevated position than the previous one. There are also various exhibition halls with artefacts, calligraphies and paintings.

The Emei Shan mountain was named after its shape, a curved eyebrow. The Baoguosi Temple is only one of the many temples scattered around the mountain range. The Daoists had started erecting their temples here in the 2nd century, and from the strengthening of Buddhism in the 6th century onwards, the mountain became a sacred place of Buddhism. It is one of the four sacred Buddhist mountains; 151 monasteries are said to have been built here over the centuries, but many have decayed when they were no longer inhabited, or have been destroyed. Today, you can only visit twenty.

Near Baoguosi, by a small pond under some trees is the former rest house for political cadres, now Hotel Hongzhushan. You can make day trips to the mountain from here, or an excursion lasting several days. Several

The mountainous region of Sichuan is the home of the giant panda.

guest houses have been built next to the hotels in recent years.

There are steps leading from Baoguosi Temple up to the peak. A road was built some years ago to the Jieyindian Pavilion, which lies at an altitude of 8,789 ft (2,670 metres), and you can go by bus to within four miles (six km) of the 10,170-ft (3,100-metre) high **Golden Peak** (Jinding). About 72 ft (22-metres) below the summit is the **Golden Peak Temple** (Jindingsi), with a 66-ft (20-metre) long bronze hall, the so-called Gold Hall.

In favourable weather conditions, you can experience a remarkable, unique natural phenomenon on the peak: if the sun is in the right position, the shadow of the onlooker is cast onto the clouds beneath the peak, and an aura in the colours of the rainbow forms around the silhouette. The Buddhist pilgrims, of whom there are still many, interpret it as a special sign when they experience this natural phenomenon. In the past, some pilgrims would throw themselves from the peak, believing or rather imagining that this led directly to the longed-for Nirvana.

If you descend the stone steps, you can get food and shelter in some of the larger monasteries during the two and a half day descent. The further up on the mountain you stay, the more expensive the food is, since everything, including the coal for the kitchen stoves, has to be carried up by porters. It is recommended that you plan your day's walking in such a way that you arrive before 5 p.m. at a monastery offering shelter. This will give you the opportunity to get a bed in a separate room rather than to sleep on the floor in the temple halls with the many other hikers.

About six miles (10 km) below the Jieyindian Pavilion is the **Elephant Bathing Pool** (Xixiangchi), a relatively large temple built against a rock. It offers a lovely view of the surroundings. According to legend, this is where the elephant of Bodhisattva Samantabhadra (Puxian), whom we'll meet again below, took his bath. You can take part in the religious ceremonies at 5 a.m. when the sky is still dark.

Below the Xixiangchi, the descent divides into a relatively steep but shorter path to the **Temple of Eternity** (Wanniansi) or a longer, but more beautiful path to **Pure Sound Pavilion** (Qingyinge). While on the upper third of the path to the pavilion, you will usually find a troop of monkeys who will demand a toll in the shape of peanuts or fruits. The brochures sold in the settlements at the foot of the mountain warn that these monkeys should not be teased, as they can be aggressive and there are cases where the monkeys have grabbed cameras and clothes from people. But if you approach them, they tend to keep their distance.

Further along the path is a small gorge, **Yixiantian** (A Thread of Sky), through which winds a stream called "Black Dragon". It is lined by very lush

Porters offer their services at the sacred Mount Emeishan.

vegetation. There are rare animal and bird species on Emei Shan, and up to 200 different types of butterfly.

The **Temple of Eternity** (Wannian-si) stands at the lower end of the steeper path, at about 3,937 ft (1,200 metres). It was built in the 4th century and is said to have consisted of seven halls. Today, only one 52-ft (16-metre) high hall remains. The structure, made of bricks without rafters, is typical of the architecture of the Ming Dynasty. The square building has a domed roof. It contains a bronze figure of Bodhisattva Samantabhadra from the year 918, riding on a white elephant. According to legend, this bodhisattva came to Emei Shan riding on a white elephant.

The northern and southern path join again at the **Pavilion of Pure Sound** (Qingyinge), and the two streams "Black Dragon" and "White Dragon" also join. The pavilion serves as a rest house now, with proper meals being served on two floors. A few miles further along the Dragon Stream is a picturesque little settlement, Lianghekou, where you can catch a bus, which runs every hour, back to Baoguosi Temple.

The Grand Buddha of Leshan

Leshan can be reached by bus from Emeixian railway station in less than an hour. The town, which is over 1,300 years old, lies at the confluence of the Qingyi, Min and Dadu rivers.

The most important sights are on the mountains **Lingyun** and **Wulong**. On the cliff face of Lingyunshan (Mountain which reaches to the clouds), Buddhist monks in the 8th century spent 90 years carving a huge, seated Buddha figure. The head of the 233-ft (71-metre) high Buddha is 48 ft (14.7 metres) long and three ft (10 metres) wide, and is covered with more than 1,000 snail-shaped hair knots. Over 100 people could stand on

The Sleeping Buddha at Treasure Peak Mountain in Dazu.

his 28-ft (eight and a half-metre) wide foot. According to legend, the Buddha was built by monks from Lingyun monastery to tame the swift currents of the river. The reason that the figure is so well preserved is that inside its hollow body, invisible from outside, gutters were carved to drain the rain water.

Lingyun Monastery lies on the mountain above the Buddha figure. Its buildings originally date from the Tang period (618-907), but have been renovated several times in the course of the centuries. Next to it rises the 125-ft (38-metre) high **Soul Pagoda** (Ling-baota) from the Song period (960-1270), a square brick building which has five floors inside, but thirteen storeys outside, each decorated with a Buddha statue.

Wuyou Temple, which also dates to the Tang period, stands on the mountain of the same name, and is very well preserved. You can see the gold-plated,

The Buddha of Leshan, the tallest statue in China, is 233 ft high.

wooden figures of Buddha Sakyamuni, Manjusri and Samantabhadra inside.

Jiuzhaigou Nature Reserve

The **Jiuzhaigou Nature Reserve** (Nine Villages Valley) in the north west of Sichuan, situated very close to the border with the Gansu Province, has been open to tourists for some years. It is advisable to join an organised tour led by a reputable travel agency, since travel into this area can be extremely difficult. This is especially the case during the rainy summer months, when torrential rain and mud slides often make the way impassable to traffic.

Jiuzhaigou is about 311 miles (500 km) from Chengdu. It lies about 8,200 ft (2,500 metres) above sea level, and covers an area of 148,260 acres (60,000 hectares), framed by forested mountains and high mountain peaks covered with eternal snow. Lush vegetation alternates with grass steppes, lakes, rivers and bizarre water falls. The Tibetan population in the region has a legend about the creation of Jiuzhaigou: An immortal called Dage and a fairy called Wunuosemo are said to have lived deep in the mountains. They fell in love. One day, Dage gave Wunuosemo a mirror as a present, which he had polished to a high shine with the wind and the clouds. Unfortunately, she dropped the mirror and it broke into 108 pieces, which changed into the 108 lakes of the Nine-Village-Valley.

The area stretches from the Demon Cliffs, via the Shuzheng Waterfalls and the Five Flower Lake to Lake Panda or, along a different way to an altitude of 10,170 ft (3,100 metres), where the highest lake, Changhai (the Long Sea) is located. About 80 miles (130 km) before Jiuzhaigou, the road forks off towards the area around the Yellow Dragon river. There, at Five Colour Lake, the lime-containing water deposits residues which make the lake look like terraced fields, reflecting the sky in all shades of blue and green.

YUNNAN – THE SOUTH-WEST OF CHINA

"Behind the clouds" could be a loose translation of the name of China's south western Province, Yunnan. It borders on Burma in the west, and on Laos and Vietnam in the south. South west China is said to have been ruled by six princes in the 8th century. The story goes that one of these princes made the long journey to the imperial court of the Tang dynasty for an audience with the emperor. When asked where he came from, he replied that his home was even farther to the south than the rainy area in southern Sichuan. In response, the emperor created the name Yun Nan, which in literal translation means "Cloud-South...where freedom is without frontiers". The Ming emperors (1368-1644) used Yunnan mostly to banish critical intellectuals or bureaucrats who opposed them. While the Chinese imperial dynasties didn't consider the region to be outside their territory, they did see it as outside of Chinese culture; only barbarians lived there, on the edge of what they saw as the flat, saucer-shaped earth. Whoever was banished there was usually forgotten.

Modern promoters of tourism are keen to have tourists in south west China, though the people living in the former banishment area may still find it difficult to acknowledge a foreigner as a traveller. The locals may well think that Western travellers have taken a wrong turning or at least are crazy to travel into this remote corner of the Middle Kingdom.

Yunnan is a Chinese province with a great variety of peoples. There are 26 different nationalities on the Yunnan Guizhou high plateau, mostly peasants in the mountain villages, while in the towns Han Chinese predominate. The Yi, Naxi, Bai and Dai are amongst the most populous groups in the province.

There are no grand buildings, archaeological finds or cultural artefacts to be viewed by the traveller; it is the unspoilt countryside, rare animals, rich flora and the variety of ethnic groups and their cultural traditions which attract.

On the way to Yunnan

Many towns and regions in south west China have been opened to foreigners recently. And while, until a short while ago, the few accessible towns could only be reached via **Kunming**, it has now become possible to travel through the area in various directions. The town of **Dukou** (recently renamed **Panzhihua**) has been newly opened. It lies on the railway line from Chengdu to Kunming.

The railway journey from the plain of Sichuan takes you gradually to the Yunnan Guizhou Plateau which on average lies at an altitude of 6,560 ft (2,000 metres). The landscape is unspoiled; bare mountains rise majestically, the few trees pointing their green foliage defiantly skywards. Calm rivers dominate the valleys and only where nature permits it, in narrow valleys hemmed in between river and mountain slope, can people settle. The railway itself looks like a foreign object from a distant century. Nevertheless it is increasingly becoming a lifeline for an almost forgotten region.

The town of **Dukou** on the Sichuan border is an artificial creation; constructed out of nothing and as uninviting as many of the Siberian settlements which probably served as an example in the 1950s. The pioneers of Chinese industrialisation are attracted by the lucrative ore deposits rather than by the beauty of the area. All the inhabitants are strangers from other provinces. The indigenous people, particularly the Yi, live as they have always done, in the mountain villages. You have to travel quite a long way into the mountains to find villages where the old traditions still survive.

Visitors are usually greeted at the entrance of the village, where people will do a circle dance around a fire, in simple, rhythmical steps to the sounds of the Lusheng, a reed flute. The plain houses are sparsely furnished, almost without any furniture. The fireplace is in the middle of the large room on the floor, surrounded by three stones which symbolise the presence of a deity and must not be touched. Hospitality is shown mainly by offering plenty of spirits, and older inhabitants will sing spontaneously improvised texts of old tunes to greet the guests.

With the Naxi in Lijiang

The road from Dukou to Lijiang, the area of the Naxi peoples, crosses several mountain passes and narrow gorges. Huge rocks, tumbling waterfalls and wild streams make you powerfully aware of the force of nature.

There is a proverb in the *Dongba* scriptures of the Naxi people, preserved in an old picture scroll, which says: "When the sky and the earth were not yet separated, trees could walk and stones could speak". The scripts aptly recount the mythology and history of the Naxi as much as astronomy, magic and exorcism.

The number of *Dongba shamans* still alive is estimated at approximately 30 to 40, some work in the Lijiang Institute which was founded only a few years ago. They are helping to decode the Naxi picture script. A fire and knives dance is often performed by old *shaman* priests at cultural events.

The origin of the Naxi is still not clear. It is thought that they settled many thousands of years ago in the north west of China in the modern provinces of Qinghai, Gansu and Sichuan before being driven south by central Asian invaders and settling here.

The snow-covered peak of Jade Dragon Mountain.

The Naxi have for some decades attracted a lot of interest from ethnologists worldwide. They are interested both in the Naxi hieroglyphs and in their customs and social structures. The Naxi are amongst the very few people in the world where remnants of matriarchal structures are still clearly recognisable. Women carry out both the heavy and the important tasks and are dominant in family life.

The costume of the Naxi women serves as a cushion on the back to ease the pressure of heavy loads. Two large and seven small, circular ornaments adorn the back, symbolising the sun, moon and stars – the firmament. It demonstrates that the shoulders of Naxi women, bent by heavy work, are turned skywards day and night.

It is women who choose their partners in festive rituals. The chosen man only spends the nights with "his" woman over many years; he continues to work and live in his mother's house. Female members of the family have the privilege of their own room where they can receive their lovers, while the male members of the family have to make do with a shared room.

Where women are in charge, the men naturally seek escape in entertainments: they are considered to be keen singers, dancers and musicians.

You should visit the **Black Dragon Pond** (Heilongtan) in Lijiang, which offers a marvellous view of the Jade Dragon Mountain. In the small park is the **Five Phoenix Pavilion** (Wufenglou) which exhibits Naxi cultural artefacts. The small institute dedicated for research into Naxi culture is also located in this park.

The sky and the earth are still in close proximity in Lijiang. **Jade Dragon Mountain** (Yulongshan), whose highest peak Shanzidou (18,360 ft/5,596 metres) dominates the open Lijiang plain, gives credence to the proverb from the Dongba scripts of the Naxi. Jade Dragon Mountain has so far resisted any human attempts to conquer

it. No expedition has yet succeeded in reaching its summit.

In summer, the slopes below the snow line bloom with azaleas of all colours, and countless medicinal herbs attract collectors. Cattle, goats, as well as yak and the Tibetan oxen, graze on the pastures at the foot of the mountain. One of the biggest gorges in the world, the 10-mile (16-km) long **Tiger Leap Gorge** (Hutiaoxia) is located in Yulongshan. The canyon itself is between 8,202 ft and 9,843 ft (2,500 and 3,000 metres) deep and, at its narrowest point, it is 98 ft (30 metres) wide. The Jinshajiang (the upper course of the Yangzi River) flows at the bottom of the gorge.

Dali at Lake Erhai

Many of the more than twenty different minority peoples in south west China still show traces of matriarchal social structures. This is also the case

A scroll painting of the Naxi people.

with the Bai, who are predominantly settled in the area around Lake Erhai.

The town of Dali takes its name from a proud and powerful empire which ruled in south west China from the 10th to the 13th century, before Kublai Khan, the great Mongol emperor, conquered this remote corner of the empire. The Bai had already created the first kingdom called Nanzhao (738-902) three centuries before. The last, well preserved relics of that culture can be seen in the **caves of the Stone Bell Mountain** (Shizhongshan) in **Jianchuan** on the way from Lijiang to Dali. They contain both religious sculptures and several depictions of the kings of Nanzhao.

The **Nanzhao stele**, a 10-ft (three-metre) high monolith from the year 766 can still be seen at the site of the former capital Taihe of the Nanzhao kingdom. Its inscriptions give an indication of the political and economic system of the Nanzhao state.

The symbols of Dali, which is known in the whole of China, are the **Three Pagodas** (Dali Santa). The central pagoda, which at 226 ft (69 metres) is the highest, dates from the 9th century and used to stand in the centre of a temple. During restoration work in 1978, more than 600 different artefacts were discovered, hidden in the buildings. They date from the 7th to 10th century and included bronze mirrors, medicines, Buddha sculptures of gold and a phoenix made of silver.

The Pagodas of Dali are painted white. Bai means "white"; but its real significance is still not known. The Bai call their ancestor "White King", and their language, which resembles Mandarin Chinese, is called "white language". However, Bai women prefer strong, bright colours, particularly red, in their costume, which is amongst the most colourful in south west China.

Bai girls in Dali, Yunnan province.

The culture and religion of the Bai synthethises in a unique way its own traditions with Chinese, Indian and Tibetan influences.

In the numerous small temples the Buddha, Laozi, the founder of Daoism, Guandi, the War God, and lama deities are equally worshipped. The day before the full moon is celebrated with food and drink in the temple, and the monks feel no scruples about practising fortune-telling and producing horoscopes for a donation.

The charm of the landscape, the mild climate, even in winter, and the hospitality of the people have made Dali a favourite soon after its opening to foreigners. The enterprising inhabitants of Dali have quickly developed a knowledge of the needs and wishes of the foreigners. There are now a few restaurants in backyards which offer coca cola, coffee and hot chocolate as well as pizzas and hamburgers. Thus they have made sure that travellers need not feel banished.

The City of Spring - Kunming

The capital of Yunnan province, with its nearly two million inhabitants, is situated on a 6,562-ft (2,000-metre) high plateau. Its protected location favours a mild climate; with an average temperature of 18 degrees centigrade, making it spring all year round.

The great variety of nationalities in Yunnan can be seen in the streets of Kunming. The southern atmosphere, the variety of cultures and customs can best be enjoyed by strolling through the market streets away from the big avenues in this city.

Green Lake (Cuihu) is in the north west of the town. With its lovely promenades, small temples and pavilions, it is amongst the favourite excursion spots of the local residents. You can see cul-

A satisfied fisherman on Lake Erhai near Dali.

tural artefacts from the different nationalities in the Yunnan **Provincial Museum**. If you have a special interest in the different nationalities of south west China, you should visit the **Institute for National Minorities**. South east of the town, two brick pagodas, both square and with thirteen storeys, tower over the town: these are the West Temple Pagoda (Xisita) and the East Temple Pagoda (Dongsita).

On the southern edge of the town is **Lake Dianchi**. It is the sixth-largest inland lake in China, 29 miles (40 km) long and five miles (eight km) wide.

You can take a boat trip and watch the south Chinese junks on the lake from a vantage point, and pass the West mountains, where you can spot a small Daoist temple high up in the rock face. Climbing up to this rock temple to the **Pavilion of the Three Pure Ones** (Sanqingge) may seem a little precarious, since it involves following paths carved into the rockface and through tunnels. There are two monasteries worth visiting at the foot of the West mountains: **Taihua** and **Huating** monasteries. The wonderful Luo figures in the Hall of the 500 Luohan in the latter monastery are particularly worth seeing.

In the north, about nine and a half miles (15 km) away, is the Black Dragon Pond (Heilongtan), situated in a lovely park. The Black Dragon Hall (Heilonggong) is the last remaining memorial of a former Daoist temple, which dates from the time of the Mongolian Yuan dynasty.

Some six miles (10 km) in a north westerly direction is the **Bamboo Temple** (Qiongzhusi) which was built during the early Ming Dynasty and has been renovated several times since then. The temple is particularly interesting because of its either very surrealistic or realistic Luohan figures in the Hall of the 500 Luohan. The often brazen, absurd or amusing depiction of the Luohan is in sharp contrast to the otherwise customary, serious and respectful presentation of the Luohan figures in most Buddhist monasteries found all over China.

The 17th-century **Golden Hall** (Jindian) in the north eastern suburb is made entirely of bronze. The rafters, columns, tiles, statues and wall decorations, which imitate a wooden hall, have been entirely made of bronze; only the staircases and the balustrade are made of marble. The hall alone weighs more than 200 tons (203,210 kg).

The main attraction of Kunming is the **Stone Forest** (Shilin), located 74 miles (120 km) south east of the town in the Autonomous District of Lunan of the Yi. The "trees" in this almost 64,250 acres (26,000 hectare) forest consist of narrow, bizarrely shaped rock needles which are between 16 ft and 98 ft (five and 30 metres) tall. This karst formation goes back about 200 million years when the earth crust rose and the waters from a lake receded. A huge rock carved with the two symbols, Shi and Lin, greets the visitor at the entrance to the approximately 198-acre (80-hectare) area usually toured. If you follow the 1,312-yd (1,200-metre) long, marked path, you will come across all sorts of peculiarly shaped rock formations which would require either considerable climbing skills or just an ability to tell some fascinating stories.

One of the best-known rocks amongst the locals is Ashma rock: it represents a legend which is popular with the Sani: The beautiful Ashma had been kidnapped by a rich landowner. Her lover Ahai set off, armed with magic weapons, to free her. Unfortunately, she died through some misfortune during her escape and was transformed into a rock. Even to this day, she is still waiting for her lover, Ahai. On special days, the Sani from the nearby villages gather for their traditional festivals by Ashma Rock.

Tropical Xishuangbanna

The tuneful name, Xishuangbanna, unfortunately has a more prosaic meaning: It means Twelve Administration Units in the Dai language. However, nature provides what the name lacks. The evergreen landscape in this tropical region is still the home to many wild animals which elsewhere have long been extinguished: elephants, tigers, pythons, Malay bears, leopards and rare birds are just a few examples. The lush tropical jungle covers more than 247,100 acres (100,000 hectares) of land. Exotic fruits such as kiwi, mangoes, bananas and papayas grow in abundance in the hilly countryside with its deep valleys. In the forests are precious woods: mahogany, teak, camphor and sandal wood.

Xishuangbanna is most easily reached by flying from Kunming to Jinghong, the capital of the Autonomous District. This Chinese-looking town gets crowded with peasants from the outlying villages, particularly on Sundays, which is the traditional market day. They are mostly Dai, who make up one third of the population, but also Hani who live in the very remote mountain villages, Jinuo and members of other nationalities.

There are few sacral buildings to see in the area. The most striking and beautiful pagoda is the **White Pagoda of Damenglong**, located about 31 miles (50 km) south of Jinghong, close to the borders of Myanmar (formerly Burma). Legend has it that the feet of the Buddha are buried in this pagoda, which has been built in the very distinct South-East Asian style.

The ochre coloured Manlei Pagoda in Mengzhe, in Menghai district, has been built in the shape of a Tibetan stupa. The Octagonal Pavilion of Jingzhen (Jingzhen Baijiaoting), about eight and a half miles (14 km) to the west of the county town of Menghai, has a striking and unique roof construction, a sight not to be missed.

The splendid pagoda of Damenglong in the south of Yunnan.

TIBET – THE ROOF OF THE WORLD

Tibet – for a long time the mysterious, legendary and unknown Roof of the World, hidden and almost unreachable behind the highest mountains in the world, the dream of innumerable explorers and adventurers. Many tried to travel to and explore the roof of the world, but only few succeeded in penetrating as far as the strictly guarded, holiest place of Tibetan Buddhism, the capital Lhasa, residence of the Dalai Lama. Heinrich Harrer is one of those who succeeded, while the great explorer of Asia, Sven Hedin, failed in his repeated attempts and only got as far as Xigaze, to the Tashi Lhunpo Monastery of the Panchen Lama.

Unfortunately, a journey to Tibet has no longer anything in common with the adventures of the past. Instead of strong nerves, energy and privations, it just costs a lot of money today, which allows the traveller to travel comfortably in about two hours from Chengdu, the capital of Sichuan province, to Lhasa. This is the safest way to get to Tibet, which is called Xizang by the Chinese, and has the status of an Autonomous Region. If you are looking for adventure and feel physically fit, you can travel overland from Nepal or from Lanzhou via Xining and Golmud, taking the overland bus or a jeep to Lhasa. Western Tibet was also opened to foreigners a few years ago. There is a highway from Kashgar in Xinjiang province leading through this border area in the extreme west, in a southerly direction past Mount Kailas and Lake Manasarovar, via Xigaze to Lhasa. You should expect this route to take at least six days.

The Himalayas are the youngest folded mountains in the world. Before the south Indian land mass began to shift northwards about 40 million years ago, the Tethys Ocean, one of the largest oceans in the history of the earth,

occupied the area. Today, the Tibet-Qinghai Plateau is, at an average altitude of 13,120 ft (4,000 metres), the most elevated plateau on earth, covering 25 percent of the entire Chinese territory. It is closed off on three sides by the highest mountain chains in the world: to the south, the Himalayas, in the west the Karakorum, and in the north the Kunlun and Tanggula mountain ranges. The Indus and Sutlej rivers have their source in the sparsely populated west, on the sacred Kailas Mountain; the source of the Brahmaputra (*Yralung Zangbo*) is to the east. It crosses Tibet in an easterly direction, before flowing through huge gorges southwards into the Gulf of Bengal. Further north, in Qinghai province, are the sources of the two big Chinese rivers: the Yellow River (Huanghe) and the Yangzi River (Changjiang).

The Tibetans have been nomads for centuries, crossing the highland pastures in the south with their herds of sheep, goats and yak. In contrast, the north is an uninhabited desert. The Tibetans are thought to be the descendants of Turan and Tangut tribes from Central Asia who reached Tibet through the Qaidam Gate from the north and mixed with the local population. The Tibetans settled in the Yarlung Zangbo valley where nature was kind to human beings and provided everything necessary to engage in agriculture. Today, 2.2 million people live in the autonomous region of Tibet, of whom about 1.7 million are Tibetans. Tibetans also live in Qinghai, Sichuan and Yunnan provinces as well as in exile in India and Nepal; the total number of Tibetans is estimated to be six million.

Tibetan history

The 31st king of the Yarlung empire, Namri Songtsen, succeeded in A.D. 607 to unify the Tibetan tribes. He founded the Thufo empire. However, Songtsen Gampo (620-649) is considered historically to have unified the empire. He created a powerful military state, conquering a vast territory and even threatening the Chinese capital. He transferred his residence from the Yarlung valley to Lhasa. Conflicts with the powerful Chinese neighbour continued into the 9th century, when Tibet broke up into numerous small statelets. In 866 the western Tibetan kingdom of Guge was founded. In the 12th century, the abbots of the biggest monasteries became powerful rulers, challenging the worldly rulers. In 1207 the first Mongol armies invaded Tibet; Kublai Kahn gave secular powers to the powerful abbots of the Sakya monastery.

In the 14th and 15th centuries, the great reformer Tsongkhapa (1357-1416) revived Buddhism and founded new monasteries which became centres of religon and secular power. He founded the Gelugpa Sect (Virtue Sect), still called "Yellow Hat Sect" after the colour of the monks hats), which be-

came the dominant religious and secular power and whose highest representatives became the Dalai Lama and the Panchen Lama, incarnations of the highest gods of Tibet. The Great Fifth Dalai Lama founded the theocracy of the Yellow Church, supported by the Mongol Khan Gusri who simply subjected the Tibetan kings and followers of the ancient Tibetan Bon religion.

Chinese rule over Tibet began in the 18th century. In 1720 the Qing emperor Kangxi chased the Dsungar invaders out of Tibet and took over control; Chinese functionaries, so-called Ambane, controlled and headed the local government. Finally, in the late 19th century the British began to penetrate Tibet, and the country quickly became a centre of big power conflicts. In additon to the British, the Chinese and Tsarist Russia made claims on the country. China, torn by war and revolution in the early 20th century, lost control of Tibet for a long

time, until barely a year after the foundation of the People's Republic. On 7 October 1950, the Chinese People's Liberation Army entered Tibet.

The early hopes Tibetans had for a better life and more freedom under the Chinese were quickly crushed. In 1959, a Tibetan uprising was brutally repressed; the Cultural Revolution in the 1960s and 70s resulted in brutal suppression of religious life and destruction of Tibet's cultural treasures. After liberalisation in the early 1980s, demonstrations and violent clashes followed in 1988. To this day, Tibet is still waiting for peace and autonomy.

Lhasa – Seat of the Gods

Statue of the Tibetan King Songstsen Gampo in the oldest chapel in the Potala.

The capital of the province and centre of Tibetan Buddhism, Lhasa, lies at an altitude of 12,001 ft (3,658 metres) on the banks of the river Kyichu (also called Lhasa River), a tributary of Yar-

lung Zangbo river. You reach Lhasa by plane from Chengdu, Xi'an or on an irregular basis from Golmud, or via the above-mentioned overland routes. The airport is situated on the southern bank of the Yarlung Zangbo, a two-hour journey from the city.

The gold-clad roofs of the **Potala** greet you from afar. A palace built by King Songtsen Gampo stood on the Marpori, the "Red Mountain" in the 7th century. Since the construction of the Potala Palace in 1645 at the time of the Great 5th Dalai Lama, the Dalai Lamas resided here as religious and secular rulers. The section called **White Palace** was constructed first; half a century later, the **Red Palace** was completed. It rises like a huge tower from the sea of white painted buildings. That is also where the private residence of the Dalai Lama is located. The entire palace covers an area of almost 437 yds (400 metres) from east to west, and 383 yds

(350 metres) from north to south. It rises 384 ft (117 m) above the Lhasa valley; the thirteen floors hold almost 1000 rooms, whose ceilings are supported by more than 15,000 columns.

In the **Red Palace** are the great ceremonial halls, 35 small chapels, four meditation halls and eight vaults for deceased Dalai Lamas. The most splendid and valuable one is for the 5th Dalai Lama: It is 48 ft (14,85 metres) high, and is decorated with 3,7 tons of gold, innumerable diamonds, turquoises, corals and pearls. The vault for the 13th Dalai Lama is 46 ft (14 metres) long. In the north eastern part of the Palace you find the **Avalokiteshvara Chapel**, which is considered the oldest part of the structure and is said to have been preserved from the original palace of Songtsen Gampo. The chapel, which is also called the brides chamber, contains a statue of the king Songtsen Gampo with his Chinese wife Wen Chen, and his Nepalese wife Bhrikuti.

You can look down into the valley and the old city from the roof of the Potala. The holiest temple of all Tibetans is in the city centre. In the central building, surrounded by buildings of the **Tsuglagkhang**, the offices of the Tibetan government administration used to be located.

You arrive at the **Jokhang** Temple by walking through a prayer hall which is supported by red columns. The main buildings of the Jokhang, built on a square Mandala foundation, date from the mid-7th century. The temple had been built as a shrine for a Buddha statue which the Chinese princess Wen Cheng had brought to Lhasa as a wedding gift from the Chinese emperor. This Buddha, called Jobo in Tibetan, gave the temple its name: Jokhang - the hall of the Jobo Buddha. The centre of the temple is occupied by a light courtyard; four gilded roofs mark the holiest

Heavy clouds hang over Jokhang temple in the old part of Lhasa.

halls: the chapel of the Jobo Buddha, the Avalokiteshvara Chapel, the Maitreya Chapel and the Chapel of King Songtsen Gampo. The golden Jobo statue is richly decorated with jewels and usually covered with brocade and silk bands. At the feet of the Buddha, butter lamps made of heavy silver and filled with yak oil burn continually. It is not quite certain whether the statue really is the original from the year 641.

Other statues and paintings were destroyed during the Cultural Revolution and replaced with newly-made copies. From the roof of the Jokhang, you can get a view of Potala Palace and of the Barkhor, the sacred ritual path which surrounds the Jokhang and the Tsuglagkhang.

Numerous pilgrims and traders are crowded on the 875-yd (800-metre) long path. The pilgrims constantly prostrate themselves in the dust and circle in this manner around the Jokhang temple; others continuously turn their prayer hats. On both sides of the path, traders offer their wares. Travelling monks meditate at the side of the road and will offer special prayers in return for a donation. There used to be a longer ritual path, the four-mile (seven-km) long Lingkhor, which surrounded the town, but it has today been broken up by new buildings. In those times, the pilgrims had to measure the path with the length of their bodies before they were allowed to enter the city.

At the entrance of the Jokhang temple, a willow tree planted in 1985 on the **Barkhor** marks the spot where the Chinese princess planted a willow tree as a symbol of friendship between the two peoples on her arrival in A.D. 641. A floor tile in front of the temple entrance has an inscription of the 821 Tibetan-Chinese friendship treaty.

About four miles (seven km) from the city centre you arrive at **Norbulingkha**

The monasteries have reopened their doors.

(Precious Stone Garden), which was built on the orders of the 7th Dalai Lama in the second half of the 18th century. Since then, it served as a summer residence for the Dalai Lamas. The New Summer Palace, which was built for the 14th Dalai Lama and completed in 1956, is the best preserved of the whole site. On the top floor of the building, which is decorated with numerous wall murals, is an audience hall with paintings of episodes from the history of the Tibetan people. You can also visit the meditation room and bedroom of the Dalai Lama. There is a throne for the God King in the reception hall, and the wall paintings tell of the various experiences in the life of the 14th Dalai Lama, framed by legends from the lives of the Buddha and Tsongkhapa.

Other buildings in the park include the palaces of the 8th and 13th Dalai Lamas and the Drunzig Palace with a library and study.

In the north of the town, near the Barkhor, is the **Ramoche Temple**, probably the oldest monastery in Lhasa. It is said to have been constructed in the first half of the 7th century and served as a shrine for a statue brought to Tibet by the Nepalese wife of king Songtsen Gampo. Later, after the arrival of the Chinese princess Wen Cheng, the Jobo Buddha was housed here before it was transferred to the Jokhang Temple. The temple was only restored and reopened in 1958; it had been destroyed during the Cultural Revoluton and used as a residence. Now there are some monks living here again.

The three great monasteries near Lhasa are considered as important centres of the Yellow Hat sect and as pillars of the theocratic state: Sera, Drepung and Ganden.

Sera Monastery was built in 1419 by a pupil of Tsongkhapa at a place where his great master had spent many years

View of Gyantse with the Kumbum memorial in the fore-ground.

studying and meditating in a small hut. During its most active period, almost 5,000 monks lived in the monastery, which had a brilliant reputation throughout Tibet because of its famous academy. Today, nearly 300 monks live in the monastery, whose main buildings were saved from the destruction of the Cultural Revolution. Sera monastery is about three miles (five km) north of Lhasa, at the foot of the mountains dominating the Lhasa valley.

On the way to Drepung Monastery, six miles (10 km) west of the town centre, you pass the small **Netschung Monastery**, which used to house the Tibetan state oracle: both monks and lay people could become oracle priests. Before each decision, the oracle was consulted, after the priests had put themselves into a trance. The last oracle priest went into exile in India with the Dalai Lama and died there in 1985.

Drepung Monastery, which was built in 1416, also by a pupil of Tsongkhapa, was for a long time the political headquarters of the Yellow Hat sect. Before the Potala palace was completed, the predecessors of the Great 5th Dalai Lama resided here before moving to Potala; the tomb stupas of the second, third and fourth Dalai Lama are housed in Drepung Monastery. Drepung is probably the largest monastery in the world. At the height of its activities, nearly 10,000 monks are said to have lived here. Walking around the cloistered city is somewhat tiring, particularly walking up the slight slope in the thin air. The lower part of the site is occupied by monks' hermitages, numerous store rooms and similar facilities. Further up are the prayer halls, the *dukhangs*, which contain valuable statues and Thangkas.

The third big monastery of the Gelugpa sect is **Ganden Monastery**, 25 miles (40 km) north east of Lhasa. The

Lake Yamdrok, at almost 13,125 ft altitude.

monastery, which was founded in 1409 by Tsongkhapa, the reformer and founder of the Yellow Hat sect, is one of the most sacred places of Tibetan Buddhism where 5,000 monks once lived. It made the almost total destruction of the site during the Cultural Revolution even more tragic. Hardly any of the monastery's treasures were preserved, the buildings were torn down to their foundations. Only in 1985 was the rebuilding of the monastery finally completed, and that was limited to the most important buildings, including the Mausoleum of Tsongkhapa which is recognisable from a distance by its red walls. Meanwhile, some 300 monks have returned to the monsatery.

Valley of the Kings - Yarlung Valley

After a two-hour bus ride from Lhasa airport in an easterly direction you reach **Tsetang**. This small country town

has two hotels for tourists; from here, you can undertake excursions to the Yarlung valley to see the Tibetan kings' graves, the old Samye and Mindroling monasteries. The old town of Tsetang is said to have been built on the spot where bodhisattva Avalokiteshvara descended from heaven in the shape of a monkey and, with a female demon, produced the first Tibetan.

Four miles (seven km) south of Tsetang, on the road to the Yarlung valley, is Khrabrug Monastery, one of the first Buddhist monasteries in Tibet which is said to have been built under the rule of king Songtsen Gampo. Since the Cultural Revolution, the buildings are being used as a farm and agricultural storage places; the site has still not been completely restored.

Eighteen and a half miles (30 km) from Tsetang lies the **Yarlung Valley**, where the kings of the Yarlung dynasty who reigned between 627 and 842 were buried. The tombs are only discernible as small mounds of earth. The biggest mound, which has a small temple built on it, is said to be the burial ground of Songtsen Gampo. **Yumbulhakhang Citadel** is said to be one of the few early Tibetan buildings; it looks as if it literally grew out of the peak of a hill. The citadel had already been changed into a chapel in early times. Since the Cultural Revolution reduced it to a ruin, the buildings were rebuilt in 1982.

You can visit the oldest monastery of Tibet, **Samye Monastery** from Tsetang. First you cross the Yarlung Zangbo in a ferry, which takes about one and a half hours. On the opposite bank you get into a lorry or tractor with a trailer which takes you to the monastery in about 30 minutes. It is said that Samye was founded by the Indian teacher Padmasambhava around A.D. 767. He is considered to be the founder of Tibetan Buddhism who, so it is said, succeeded in winning over the demon gods of the Bon religion. Many of the demon gods in the Tibetan monasteries refer back to such Bon gods. The site

A travelling monk with drums and bell.

348

has been built on a Mandala foundation and reflects the cosmic view of Tibetan religion. The main temple stands in the centre; it symbolises Mount Meru. Four smaller chapels were erected on the four cardinal points of the compass. The whole site is surrounded by a wall which is still partly preserved.

About 37 miles (60 km) west of Tsetang is Mindroling Monastery, which can also be visited on an excursion to or from Lhasa. It is a monastery of the **Nyingma School**, the oldest order which was founded by Padmasambhava. It was built in 1676.

The journey from Lhasa, via Gyantse to Xigaze is a breathtaking experience. First the route takes you along the banks of the Yarlung Zangbo, up to the Kampa-La pass (15,728 ft/4,794 metres). If you look back, you see the valley of Yarlung Zangbo below and, in front of you, a few hundred feet further down, the deep blue-green colours of Lake Yamdrok. The road continues for several miles along the shores of the lake. Travellers usually stop at the lake for a picnic. From the opposite shore, a hairpin road hewn into the steep mountain face leads up to the next pass, the 16,552-ft (5,045 metres) high Karo-La. Up there, one of the glaciers goes down as far as street level. On the way to Gyantse you pass small villages, fertile valleys, cattle herds and many yaks, the Tibetan oxen who climb up the steepest slopes with surprising skill, to graze.

Gyantse, which lies by the northern bank of Nyangchu River 165 miles (265 km) south west of Lhasa is, after Lhasa and Xigaze, the third largest of the old Tibetan towns. The exposed location of the town, on the road from Xigaze to Lhasa and on the trading route to India, Sikkim and Bhutan, makes it into one of the most important trading centres. You can see the Dzong, a fortification on a hill, from far away. This citadel was

Headdress with ornament made of amber, silver and coral.

attacked, taken and destroyed in 1904 by an English military expedition led by Colonel Younghusband. The fortification has only been open to visitors since 1985. In 1910, an English diplomat compared the market of Gyantse with Oxford Street in London; apparently, one could buy Scottish whisky and Swiss watches there in addition to silk, brocade, wool and jade.

The most important structure in Gyantse is however Palkhor Tschöde. The circle-shaped monastery site, which is enclosed by a wall, used to have several monasteries belonging to different sects. The 105-ft (32-metre) tall Kumbum dagoba in the centre of the monastery site is a unique example of Tibetan architectural skill. The layout of this dagoba is in the shape of a three dimensional Mandala and symbolises Mount Meru. The central structure at the tip of the dagoba is a chapel for the original Buddha; again there are four chapels at the four cardinal points of the compass. Other shrines are located on the four floors, and you walk along it as if in a trance. The path to the centre is thus a symbol of the spiritual path of salvation. The stupa erected in the first half of the 15th century has survived all historical turbulence.

Xigaze, 224 miles (360 km) west of Lhasa on the southern bank of Yarlung Zangbo is traditionally the seat of the Panchen Lama, the second head of Tibetan Buddhism. In ancient Tibet the town, which today has less than 50,000 inhabitants, was the capital of Tsang province. The Great 5th Dalai Lama bestowed the title of Panchen Lama on his teacher from Tashi-Lhunpo Monastery. While the Dalai Lama is an incarnation of the Tibetan deity bodhisattva Avalokiteshvara, the Panchen Lama is worshipped as the reincarnation of the Buddha Amithaba and is therefore higher up in the heavenly hierarchy. In

Tashi Lhunpo Monastery in Xigaze, seat of the Panchen Lama.

the rivalries between the Russians, British and Chinese this latent conflict was constantly being used by each for their own advantage. The 10th Panchen Lama died in early 1989 in Beijing. In 1993, the Chinese government invited the Dalai Lama to help in the search for the next Panchen Lama.

The residence of the Panchen Lama, **Tashi-Lhunpo Monastery**, was founded in 1447 by a pupil of Tsongkhapa. The monastery site was substantially enlarged during the 17th and 18th centuries. Nearly 4,000 monks used to live here; today there are 600. The most important building is without doubt **Maitreya Chapel**, built by the 9th Panchen Lama in 1914. An 86-ft (26.2-metre) tall golden Maitreya statue (Maitreya is the Buddha of the Future) is housed in the 98-ft (30-metre) high, red stone building.

The memorial of the 4th Panchen Lama is also worth seeing. It is 36 ft (11 metres) tall and was erected in 1662. It is decorated with 3,000 ounces of gold, 15 tons of silver and innumerable precious stones. The gilded roofs of the chapels for the deceased Panchen Lamas tower over the entire site. A high stone wall stands on the slope behind the monastery. On feast days, huge Thangkas are revealed there. To the west of the town, in a large park, is the Palace of the 7th Panchen Lama. While it was easy to visit in the early 1980s, when it was still a protected building, this has become more difficult in recent years because the palace had been returned to the 10th Panchen Lama, and the resident monks were not keen on tourist visits.

About 90 miles (145 km) south west of Xigaze is Sakya. The road to Sakya goes across two high mountain passes. On a clear day you can see the summit of Mount Everest from Tso-Lakann. **Sakya Monastery** has a special place in Tibetan history. Its foundation in 1073 also saw the creation of a new order, the Sakyapa School. In some ways the Sakya abbots were the predecessors of the Dalai Lamas. Since 1247, when the Mongol Kahn Göden made the abbot Pandita of Sakya vice-king of Tibet, the Sakya Trizin, an incarnation of the bodhisattva Manjusri, ruled over the region to the west of Xigaze. The Sakya monastery buildings are striking because of their dark grey colour and the white horizontal stripes under the roof, as well as the red vertical stripes on the corners. While the southern monastery was left alone during the struggles of the Cultural Revolution, the northern Monastery was almost completely destroyed. Some buildings have since been rebuilt.

On the way back to Lhasa, unless you plan to leave by overland route towards Nepal, it is worth taking the northern route. There are many pastures here and consequently you will come across the nomads. The route takes you across a 17,388-ft (5,300-metre) high mountain pass, past the glacier covered summit.

Hayagriva – the deity dancing a mask dance at Kumbum monastery near Xining (Qinghai province).

INSIGHT GUIDES
Travel Tips

So, you're getting away from it all.

Just make sure you can get back.

AT&T Access Numbers
Dial the number of the country you're in to reach AT&T.

AMERICAN SAMOA	633 2-USA	**INDIA**◆	**000-117**	NEW ZEALAND	000-911
AUSTRALIA	0014-881-011	**INDONESIA**◆	**00-801-10**	*PHILIPPINES	**105-11**
*CAMBODIA	**800-0011**	*JAPAN	0039-111	SAIPAN†	235-2872
CHINA, PRC◆◆	**10811**	**KOREA**	**009-11**	SINGAPORE	800-0111-111
COOK ISLANDS	09-111	**KOREA**◇◇	**11 ✱**	SRI LANKA	430-430
GUAM	018-872	MACAO	0800-111	*TAIWAN	**0080-10288-0**
HONG KONG	**800-1111**	*MALAYSIA	**800-0011**	THAILAND◆	0019-991-1111

Countries in bold face permit country-to-country calling in addition to calls to the U.S. *Public phones require deposit of coin or phone card. ◆ Not available from public phones. ◆◆ Not yet available from all areas. ◇◇ From public phones only, push the red button, wait for dial tone and then dial. †May not be available from every phone. ©1993 AT&T.

Here's a travel tip that will make it easy to call back to the States. Dial the access number for the country you're visiting and connect right to AT&T **USADirect**® Service. It's the quick way to get English-speaking operators and can minimize hotel surcharges.

If all the countries you're visiting aren't listed above, call 1 800 241-5555 before you leave for a free wallet card with all AT&T access numbers. International calling made easy—it's all part of **The *i* Plan.**℠

TRAVEL TIPS

GETTING THERE

BY AIR

The number of direct flights from Europe to Beijing has increased considerably in recent years. Since 1988, no less than 12 European airlines have been flying direct to Beijing. Finnair holds the record with 7 hours 55 minutes flight time from Helsinki to Beijing. The average flight time from Heathrow, for instance with British Airways or Air China, takes 12 hours. The cost of a ticket from Frankfurt to Beijing is considerably lower in the winter months of December, January and February than the rest of the year.

One possibility for a tour itinerary would be to fly to Beijing, go on a sightseeing journey from northern China to the south, and fly home from Hong Kong. This can also be arranged in the reverse order, and everyone can follow their own inclination, whether to travel direct from Europe to the "centre of China", to Beijing, or to choose the more Western oriented metropolis of Hong Kong as a way into Chinese culture.

Hong Kong is an important hub for travel to the mainland, with flights to some 18 cities. If you want to travel to China via Hong Kong, there is a daily flight direct from Frankfurt with Cathay Pacific, the Hong Kong airline. The flight takes about 12 hours.

Beijing is the main destination for international flights to China. There are also some long-haul flights to Shanghai, while an increasing number of mainland cities are served by flights from countries and territories close to China.

Some airlines now also offer Shanghai as a destination. It is to be expected that other airlines will in future decide to offer this destination as well.

International airline telephone numbers
Aeroflot, Beijing: 5002412
Air China, Beijing: 6016667; Shanghai: 727763
Air France, Beijing: 5051818; Shanghai: 2558866
Alitalia, Beijing: 5014861
All Nippon Airways, Beijing: 5053311; Dalian: 239744; Shanghai: 2797000
Asiana, Beijing: 5061118
British Airways, Beijing: 5124070/75
Canadian Airlines, Beijing: 5001956
China Eastern Airlines, Beijing: 6017589; Shanghai: 2587830, 2558899
China Northern Airlines, Beijing: 6024078; Shenyang: 444490

China Southern Airlines, Beijing: 6016899; Guangzhou: 6678901
Dragon Airlines, Beijing: 5054343; Changsha CITS: 433355; Chengdu CITS: 582222 ext 363; Dalian: 2638238 ext 2011/601; Guilin: 225588 ext 8895; Haikou: 773088 ext 1743; Hangzhou: 577903; Hong Kong: 5901188; Kunming: 3138592; Nanjing: 454888 ext 1902; Shanghai: 4336435; Tianjin: 301556; Xiamen: 225389; Xian: 742988
Ethiopian Airlines, Beijing: 5050314
Finnair, Beijing: 5127180/1
Garuda Indonesia, Beijing: 5052905
Iran Air: 5104040
Japan Airlines, Beijing: 5130888; Shanghai: 4336337, 4333000
Korean Air, Beijing: 5051047; Shanghai: 2588450
Lufthansa, Beijing: 4654488, 5123636
Malaysian Airlines, Beijing: 5052681; Guangzhou: 3358828
Northwest Airlines, Beijing: 5053505; Shanghai: 2798068/88
Pakistan International, Beijing: 5052256
Philippines Airlines, 12-53 Jiangoumenwai, Tel: 5323992
Polish Airlines, Beijing: 5050136
Qantas, Beijing: 4674794, 5002481
Romanian Air Transport, Beijing: 5002233 ext 109
Scandinavian Airlines System, Beijing: 5120575/6
Silkair, Kunming: 3138888
Singapore Airlines, Beijing: 5004138/342, 5052233; Guangzhou: 3358999; Shanghai: 2798000
Swissair, Beijing: 5123555
Thai International, Beijing: 5123881; Kunming: 3160156
United Airlines, Beijing: 5128888; Shanghai: 2483333
Xinjiang Airlines, Beijing: 4562803; Ürümqi: 3137888

The Hong Kong agent for Chinese airlines flying charter flights from the territory to China is China Travel Air Service Hong Kong Limited, Tel: 8533888.

BY SEA

If you travel by boat to China from Hong Kong, the choice of destinations includes Guangzhou, Xiamen, Shantou and Shanghai.

There is an overnight steamer between Hong Kong and Guangzhou, which takes 8 hours; also a daytime catamaran service, which takes just 3 hours 15 minutes.

Ferry journeys to Shantou take 14 hours, to Xiamen 20 hours, and to Shanghai 60 hours. All steamers have restaurants on board.

There are now numerous possible cruises from Hong Kong to China. They usually stop at Xiamen, Shanghai, Yantai, Nanjing, Qingdao and Dalian. The final event, or, if the programme is reversed, the first event, is a tour of Beijing, which is reached by train from the port of Qinhuangdao at the Gulf of Bohai or from Tianjin.

THE NOBLE TIME

JUVENIA

—— 1860 ——

Mystere ®

C O L L E C T I O N

STEEL - STEEL/GOLD - 18KT GOLD AND WITH PRECIOUS STONES

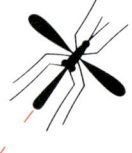

AUTAN®

– makes biting insects keep their distance.

Effective for 6-8 hours indoors and outdoors.

Autan for protection against
mosquitoes, gnats, midges,
and other insects. For external
use only. Do not apply to
the eyes, nose or mouth.

BY RAIL

By Trans-Siberian Railway: A journey on the Trans-Siberian Railway from or to Beijing is no doubt one of the most attractive possibilities of covering the huge distance between Europe and China. If you want to travel there by rail, you should contact an experienced travel agent or go directly to the official Russian travel agency, Intourist. Getting all the necessary visas and the ticket can be a complicated business. You should allow at least six weeks, and up to three months, for this procedure.

First, you travel by train or plane to Moscow, where you have a day to look around (the official Russian travel agency usually requires you to spend at least one night in Moscow). The next day, you take the train for Beijing at Jaroslavskij station.

There is a choice of two routes: taking the Chinese train – which is better equipped and looked after – for 5 days via Ulan Bator through Mongolia, entering China via Erlian. Or you can choose the Russian train, which goes through Manchuria and takes a day longer. Entry into China is at Manzhouli. Both trains leave once a week from Moscow.

Depending on the type of train, there are two or three classes ranging from 2-bed compartments with washing facilities or "soft" 2 or 4-bed compartments to "hard" 4-bed compartments. Food is not included in the ticket price. Initially the food on the train is fairly reasonable, but it gets increasingly monotonous as the journey continues. The stops at the railway stations become welcome interruptions when you can not only stretch your legs but stock up with fruit and biscuits. There is usually hot water available so you can prepare your own tea or coffee.

Preparation for the journey in the opposite direction, from Beijing to Western Europe, is quicker and cheaper. A train leaves Beijing twice a week for Moscow: train No. 3 goes through Mongolia (5 days) and train No. 19 through Manchuria (7 days). You should allow 4 to 10 days for getting the necessary visas and the ticket in Beijing. First, you need a ticket reservation. The international ticket office of CITS in Beijing is in Chongwenmen Dajie next to the restaurant "Maxim's". Then take your confirmed ticket reservation and sufficient passport photos to the Russian and – if you will travel through Mongolia – Mongolian embassies (also, if you will be travelling on through Poland and Hungary, the Polish and Hungarian embassies). Only the Russian transit visa may take a while; if you are unlucky, it can take up to 10 days.

If you want to interrupt the train journey in Russia for longer than 24 hours, you need a tourist visa and you have to show a hotel booking (bookings can be made at the state tourist office, Intourist, at the Russian embassy in Beijing). The fees for the visa have to be paid mostly in foreign currency certificates (FEC) or at the Mongolian embassy in dollars. Once you have all the visas, you can then get your reserved ticket at the international ticket office at CITS.

A hint for photographers: Public and military installations must not be photographed. Infringement of these rules can result in the film being confiscated.

From Kazakhstan: There are twice-weekly trains between Alma-Ata in Kazakhstan and Ürümqi in Xinjiang province. If you plan to take the train in the other direction, you may apply for your visa for Kazakhstan before arriving in China; CITS Xinjiang is one source of tickets.

From Hong Kong to Guangzhou: If you want to start your journey in the southern part of China, you would normally take the train from Hong Kong to Guangzhou. For the time being, the airport in Guangzhou can only cope with a limited number of foreign flights.

The comfortable express train from Hung Hom station in Kowloon takes you through the New Territories and Shenzhen, an area of special economic status. There are three trains a day, and the journey takes about three hours. There are also frequent KCR (Kowloon to Canton Railway) trains to the border at Lo Wu. From here, you can cross the border to Shenzhen, and take onward transport to Guangzhou. Note, however, that the border crossing may be congested, especially at weekends and on public holidays.

BY ROAD

Over the last four years, several possibilities of travelling to China overland have opened up:

Via Nepal: Crossing via Nepal by bus or taxi has been possible since 1985. You can get an entry visa for Nepal, valid for seven days, at Kathmandu airport. You should already have procured your Chinese visa in Europe since the Chinese embassy in Nepal will only issue one in exceptional cases.

The road from the Nepalese capital takes you to the Friendship Bridge on Khodari Pass, at a distance of 81 miles (130km). You should allow a full day's travel by bus because of the difficult terrain; sometimes the road is completely closed because of recurring landslides. You may have to make part of the journey on foot. All passengers have to leave the bus at the Friendship Bridge and walk the rest of the way to the border town of Khodari. From here, buses go at irregular intervals via Xigaze to the Tibetan capital Lhasa. The journey takes six to seven days, including stops. You shouldn't expect the overnight accommodation and washing facilities to be very comfortable, and it is best to ensure that you have taken sufficient food. The journey is only suitable for anyone who feels physically fit . The high altitude makes even short walks, with or without luggage, very strenuous.

Via Pakistan: Since 1986, it has been possible to enter China from Pakistan via the Karakorum Highway. You can get an entry visa for Pakistan at the Pakistani embassy, and remember that you need to have a Chinese visa as well.

The Karakorum Highway links Rawalpindi and Islamabad with the Chinese province of Xinjiang and has recently been completed as a joint, 15-year project between Pakistan and China. The journey takes you via the towns of Besham, Pattan, Sazin, Chilas, Gilgit and Hunza to the Chinese border at the Khunjerab Pass at an altitude of more than 13,123ft (4,000m). From Sust, on Pakistan territory, you carry on to the Chinese border town of Pirali. From there, you can continue by bus to Kashgar, 267 miles (430km) away.

On both the Pakistani and Chinese side of the border, the roads may be blocked by landslides, and you may have to walk a fair distance, carrying your luggage. Accommodation along the journey is very modest.

From Kazakhstan: A direct bus route between the two border towns of Panfilow, east of the Kazakh capital Alma-Ata, and Yining on the Chinese side, was opened in February 1989.

From Hong Kong: Citybus operates services from Hong Kong to Shenzhen; for information, Tel: (Hong Kong) 7363888.

Travel Essentials

VISAS & PASSPORTS

All travellers need an entry visa for the People's Republic of China. If you go as part of a group, the tour operator will obtain this. Group visas will usually be issued for groups with at least 10, and the courier accompanying your group will keep the visas. Individual travellers can approach the embassy of the People's Republic of China in their country. The visa will be stamped in your passport, and – if it is a tourist visa – will probably be valid for three months from the date of issue (the duration depends on current regulations, and on your country's regulations for visiting Chinese citizens).

The embassy requires your passport, valid for at least two months after the trip, a passport photograph, a completed visa application form and a cheque to cover the fee. Please enclose a stamped self-addressed envelope as well. It takes about three weeks to get the visa. If your visa runs out while you are in China, you can have it extended by the local security police (Gong-anju) on submission of your passport.

The addresses of the embassy of the PR of China in the UK and USA are:

UK, 31 Portland Place, London W1N 3AH, Tel: 071-6365726; (visas) 071-6365637

USA, 2300 Connecticut Avenue N.W., Washington D.C. 20008, Tel: 202-3282515

In Hong Kong, you can obtain a visa in just three days or, if you are prepared to pay a premium, within a working day. Visas are issued by the Visa Office of the Ministry of Foreign Affairs, 26 Harbour Road, Wanchai; they can also be obtained through travel agents.

The visa permits entry to and departure from all official border crossings and visits to more than 400 towns and places in China. The local security police in China can extend the visa.

Further information is available from:

China National Tourist Office, 4 Glenworth Street London NW1, Tel: 071-9359427; Fax: 071-4875842

China National Tourist Office, 60 East 42nd Street, Suite 3126, New York NY 10165, Tel: 212-867-0271/72/73; Fax: 212-5992892

MONEY MATTERS

The Chinese currency is called Renminbi (literally: people's currency); the basic unit is the Yuan (also called 'Kuai'). One Yuan is worth 10 Jiao – also called 'Mao' – or 100 Fen. So 1 Jiao (Mao) is worth 10 Fen. All units are in the form of banknotes; there are 1, 2, 5, 10, 50 and 100 Yuan notes, 1, 2 and 5 Jiao notes, and 1, 2 and 5 Fen notes. There are also Fen coins in 1, 2 and 5 Fen pieces.

The standard Chinese currency, Renminbi (RMB), is not readily convertible.

China has, effectively, a second currency. Called Foreign Exchange Certificates (FEC), it too is denominated in yuan, jiao and fen. As its name suggests, it can be exchanged for foreign currency. When you change cash or travellers cheques, you will be given FECs (keep one or more of the receipts for when you leave China you can exchange your remaining FECs). The exchange rate is fixed by the Central Bank. You can find the rate in the *China Daily*, or from the information boards at banks. Recent years have seen a downward trend in the yuan; at time of press, the rate was around 5.8 yuan to US$1.

Officially, FECs are the same in value as RMB. In practice, because they can be readily converted to foreign currency, they are more valuable. In the big towns, it is quite common to be asked to 'change money' outside hotels by Chinese wanting FECs in exchange for RMB. The rate can be attractive (if you are interested in changing money, it is wise to first check the rate with other tourists), but be aware that there are heavy penalties for doing this, and that some money changers swindle tourists through sleights of hand and other trickery. Also, while RMB is useful in, say, shops and restaurants along the street, many hotels and other tourist-related businesses will only accept FECs from foreigners.

The import and export of RMB were formerly prohibited. But individuals are now permitted to take up to 6,000 RMB in or out of China. Accompanying this easing of restrictions, money changers in Hong Kong have begun exchanging RMB and Hong Kong dollars; since the rates are better than the official rate for the yuan, this can be a useful way of obtaining local currency before you enter China.

When you leave China, banks will only change FECs. It is therefore advisable to ensure you have a little or no RMB remaining at the end of your trip.

Many tourist places such as hotels, Friendship Shops etc., take the usual credit cards such as American Express, Visa, Diner's Club, Master Charge, JCB Card, Federal Card, East Americard etc. You can also use credit cards to obtain cash from major branches of the Bank of China, including the head office of the Bank of China, 410 Fuchingmennei Dajie, Tel: 6016688, or the Beijing branch at 19, Dong An Men St, Tel: 5199115/4.

Lately, China has been suffering from inflation – at time of press the rate is about 20 percent per year in urban areas.

HEALTH

On entering China, you will be asked to fill in a Passenger's Health Declaration, giving details about your state of health. Unless you are coming directly from an area which has recently had an epidemic, you do not need inoculations for smallpox, cholera or yellow fever. For visits to some areas of southern China, the World Health Organisation recommends taking an anti-malaria prophylactic. There were several outbreaks of hepatitis A particularly in Shanghai in 1988. Although the number of cases has in the meantime declined to "normal" proportions (hepatitis also occurs in Europe, especially in the Mediterranean countries), a preventive gammaglobulin injection is advisable as it increases the body's immune system.

Travellers with active tuberculosis and carriers of the AIDS virus are banned from the country.

You can get detailed information from medical centres in most cities in Europe, and from the London School of Hygiene and Tropical Medicine, Keppel St., WC1, Tel: 01-636-8636.

The best prevention is to ensure maximum hygiene while travelling, especially in restaurants and roadside snack bars, and never to eat raw, uncooked or partially cooked food. As much as you may crave fresh food such as salad, you shouldn't eat this outside of the hotels (in any case, it is rarely on offer and hardly ever eaten by the Chinese). Animal or human nightsoil is still frequently used for manure, so that bacteria on uncooked vegetables can easily enter the human intestine. This advice is especially

important for individual travellers; travellers in a group are usually fed in hotels and restaurants which do not present such risks.

Also advisable for individual travellers: make sure you acquire some chopsticks and a tin bowl with lid at the start of your trip, so that you are well equipped for the train journey and meals in small restaurants at the side of the road where the crockery appears "suspicious". You should also only drink boiled water, even though the tap water is drinkable in some places and hotels. All hotels and restaurants in China keep a stock of boiled water in large thermos flasks or cans. The adjustment to a different climate and different food frequently leads to colds or digestive problems which, although they are rarely serious, can nevertheless spoil your enjoyment when travelling. It is advisable to take some appropriate medicines with you.

Tibet, the Silk Road in north west China, and the tropical province of Yunnan make particularly high demands of your physical fitness. It is wise to consult your doctor beforehand. Heart disease and high blood pressure can lead to serious problems when travelling in Tibet. On the Silk Road, you have to expect very high temperatures and dry conditions; you may need to counteract the loss of moisture by taking salt or mineral tablets. If you intend to spend a prolonged period in Yunnan, it is advisable to take anti-malaria pills.

WHAT TO WEAR

Much has changed in China in recent years, including the style of dress, which is now less uniform than it used to be. Simple and appropriate clothing is equally advisable for foreign travellers. In the summer months, you should take enough light cotton clothes that are easily washed and not too delicate. While the laundries in Chinese hotels are very thorough, they tend not to be very careful with the clothes. You should take at least one jumper or a warm shawl even for the hottest season, because the air conditioning in the hotels is often more than effective and you may otherwise catch the obligatory cold on your first stop.

Most Chinese wear their ordinary clothes to evening performances at the Beijing opera, the theatre or circus. It is best to follow this custom, especially at some of the venues. Sometimes the floor is simply made of compressed mud which makes high heeled shoes very uncomfortable.

You should generally make sure that your footwear is comfortable and strong, not only because of the long distances you'll be walking when sightseeing, but also because in the towns, you may often come across areas which are difficult to pass or have numerous building sites. Sturdy walking shoes are, of course, necessary for walks up the sacred mountains of China; the same is true for journeys to Tibet or along the Silk Road.

In contrast to the past, there are now some

possibilities of showing off your evening finery, since most of the new joint ventures or luxury hotels have bars, dance halls, conference rooms and sometimes even discos.

Clothes for rainy and windy weather should definitely be packed, particularly for travelling on the Yangzi river and for walks in the sacred mountains. This is especially necessary during the summer months because China's rainy season is from May to August.

In the north, winters tend to be very dry and cold. Temperatures during the day of between -15° to -20° centigrade are not rare. It is advisable to kit yourself out with thick quilted jackets, lined trousers and boots. Although you can buy quilted jackets in the larger cities at quite a low price, trousers may present some difficulties, especially for women. Cut and design often differ quite considerably from Western conceptions.

WHAT TO BRING

It is best to take your usual toilet articles and medicines with you. Sometimes, hotel shops will have quite a good choice of Western goods, though some items, such as tampons or sanitary towels, are still rarely used in China and are, therefore, not often available.

Accessories for cameras are rarely available in China and it is best to bring sufficient quantities of film – especially slides. Your preferred make could well be sold out in the hotel shops, and the quality is often inferior due to inappropriate storage. Batteries are available (1.5 volt) though they generally tend to have a short life.

It is worth taking a torch, especially for individual travellers who may stay the night in modest hostels. An adapter may be useful too; many of the older hotels have sockets which require a three pin plug and the hotel service often only has a limited number of adapters available.

ON ARRIVAL

You will have to fill in a Customs Declaration listing all items of value, such as camera, tape recorder, watches and money. Another form asks for details of your health (Health Declaration). A third requirement is the Entry Card, on which you fill in details about the length of your stay in China. It will be put with your passport. You need to keep the customs declaration safe because you need to hand it in at the end of the trip. The Chinese customs officers may check, when you hand in your customs declaration, whether you are taking out all the items you had declared. The loss of the customs declaration can incur a high fine from the customs administration.

There are exchange bureaux at the arrival halls of the airport, railway station and harbour where you can change your money into Chinese currency, i.e. Foreign Exchange Certificates. You can also find taxis which will take you to your hotel. The Chinese airlines provide buses which will take travellers from the airport, which is often a long way outside the city, to the airline offices in town. The fare is generally modest.

Be wary of people offering taxis before you reach taxi ranks. Before setting off in a taxi, agree on a price for the journey, or ensure the driver will use the meter.

CUSTOMS

On arrival, each traveller will have to fill in a form, declaring any cash, travellers cheques, credit cards as well as all valuables such as cameras, tape recorders, walkmans etc. There is no restriction on normal camera and film equipment, except for professional film and video equipment, 16 and 35 mm equipment and 1 inch video recorders which require a special permit. The declaration must be handed in on departure; if required, the listed objects must be shown so that it can be ascertained that they haven't been sold during the trip.

Tourists can freely import four bottles of alcoholic beverages and 600 cigarettes, as well as foreign currency and valuables for personal use without restrictions. The import of weapons, ammunition, drugs and pornographic literature is prohibited. Please note on departure that antiques such as porcelain, paintings, calligraphies, carvings, old books etc. which do not carry the red lacquer seal of an official antique shop may not be exported and should in any case not be in your possession. Such objects can be confiscated by the customs officials without any compensation.

LUGGAGE SERVICE

Luggages are generally not treated with care by the airlines and rail transport companies within China. It is advisable to take a sturdy suitcase. When travelling in a group, it is best to have only one piece of luggage per person such that the number of passengers equals the number of pieces of luggage. Suitcases should be locked, otherwise the Chinese luggage handling service can refuse to transport them. On arrival, the luggage will be taken to the hotel separately and left either in the hotel lobby or on the appropriate floor. On the morning of departure, leave your suitcase outside your door; it will then be transported to the hotel of your next destination.

The best luggage for individual travellers is a rucksack or something similar, because storing a suitcase when travelling on an overcrowded train or bus is often difficult.

RESERVATIONS

It is now possible to reserve rooms in certain hotels direct from Europe. This is particularly the case for joint venture hotels, i.e. hotels belonging to an international chain; but it is also possible in some Chinese hotels. Reservations are best made by telex or fax or through a suitable travel agency.

Unfortunately, this is not the case for travelling inside China. Reservations for air and train tickets can only be made in China, either via a travel agency or direct with an airline or at the station. Travel agents charge a small fee for making the reservation, but this is the safest and easiest way since not all airline agencies or stations have a special counter for foreigners where English is spoken, as it is at Beijing railway station.

You usually have to decide between taking an express train, an inter-city train, or a slow train; and buy a seat reservation at the same time, otherwise you cannot demand a seat or couchette.

ON DEPARTURE

Before leaving, by train or plane, you must first hand in your customs declaration, and, on request from the customs official, show the valuables you declared on entry. You will be given cash in the requested currency for the Foreign Exchange Certificates although, sometimes, this is limited by the stock held by the exchange bureau. It can happen that you'll get part of your money in Pound Sterling and another part in US Dollars. You could also be asked to produce all the receipts showing what money or travellers cheques you changed into FEC's.

For passengers leaving China by plane, there is departure tax of 60 FEC.

GETTING ACQUAINTED

GOVERNMENT & ECONOMY

The People's Republic of China is, according to its constitution, a socialist state. It was founded on 1 October 1949. The national flag is red with five stars. The large star at the centre symbolises the Chinese Communist Party, while the smaller stars represent the four main social classes who participated in the revolution. The state emblem is the Gate of Heavenly Peace (Tiananmen), illuminated by five stars, on a red background. It is surrounded by a corn wreath with a cog-wheel below. The capital of the PR of China is Beijing.

China is administratively divided into 23 provinces (including Taiwan), five Autonomous Regions (Inner Mongolia, Xinjiang, Tibet, Ningxia and Guangxi), and three locally governed cities (Beijing, Tianjin and Shanghai). The island of Hainan in southern China, which was part of Guangdong province, became a self-governing province in 1989. The provinces and autonomous regions are further subdivided into autonomous districts, counties and towns, the counties are composed of local authorities and parishes. The towns are further subdivided into districts and counties. On a district level, there were 151 districts and 183 towns not belonging to a district, on the county level there were 1,936 counties, 644 city districts and 248 towns not belonging to a county.

The autonomous regions are mostly populated by members of national minorities who have the right to determine their own affairs autonomously within the framework of a central state policy. They can follow their own customs and traditions and use their own language.

The structure of the Chinese People's Republic has no federal aspects, that is, all provinces and autonomous regions are strictly subordinate to the central government. Most of the important companies and enterprises are directly accountable to the central ministries in Beijing. The policies of modernisation and reform introduced in recent years have aimed to change this by strengthening the rights and competence of the lower levels of industrial units through decentralisation.

The National People's Congress is the highest state organ, with the local people's congresses of the provinces, districts and counties being subordinate to it. Only the people's congresses at the lowest level are directly elected, though the method of election can be called neither free nor secret as the party retains the right to propose candidates. As yet, there are no democratic elections for all citizens in China. The higher people's congresses are elected by the lower people's congresses, also upon proposals from the party. The delegates are given a five year mandate. The People's Liberation Army, overseas Chinese and the national minorities send their own representatives.

The National People's Congress meets annually. In between its sessions, its tasks are carried out by the Permanent Committee of the National People's Congress, whose present chairman is Wan Li. The State Council is the central government organ, led by a Prime Minister and deputy Prime Minister. Below the State Council are the central ministries. From 1949–1976, Zhou Enlai was Prime Minister, followed by Hua Guofeng. The position was then held from 1980 to 1987 by Zhao Ziyang; today, Li Peng holds the post.

The Communist Party of China has the leading role within the Chinese state and society. With more than 45 million members, the Chinese CP is the largest communist party in the world. It was founded on 1 July 1921. Since the Cultural Revolution, the Chinese CP has been held in low esteem among the population (because of privileges for high functionaries, misuse of power and bureaucracy), which it is aiming to improve by introducing changes. Mao Zedong led the Chinese CP from 1935–1976; after his death, Hua Guofeng became party leader. But by 1978, Deng Xiaoping had virtually consolidated his position as China's effective ruler in the post-Mao era. Two potential successors to Deng have come and gone – Hu Yaobang, who took over as party general secretary in 1981, and was forced to resign, dying soon afterwards, and his successor, Zhao Ziyang, who was sacked after the 1989 democracy movement – but Deng has remained. Even after officially retiring from politics by 1993, Deng Xiaoping has held on as China's *de facto* leader. He is the real strongman who, although retired from all official positions, has kept the important office of chairman of the Central Military Commission of the Party. Thus, he is still the commander in chief of the army. Today, all leading organs are filled with supporters of the reforming faction centred around Deng Xiaoping, although there are strong differences amongst them about the extent of reform, especially in the political arena. These differences became clear during the student unrest in May 1989. With no mechanism in place for an orderly succession of power, there is great uncertainty over what will happen once Deng dies.

Since the adoption of the new constitution on 4 December 1982, the government of the PR of China has made efforts to build a socialist legal system which is to guarantee constitutional civil rights, such as freedom of expression, to all citizens. Many of these still remain only on paper. However, the constitution of 1982 which formally obliges each Chinese citizen to follow the "four basic principles – socialist path, democratic dictatorship of the people, leading role of the Chinese Communist Party, Marxism-Leninism and Mao Zedong Thought", considerably restricts the guaranteed freedoms. Generally though, the present party leadership follows a pragmatic line which wants to combine economic growth with a broadening of democracy and of the legal system. The Four Modernisations, which are official party policy, are: modernisation of agriculture, industry, science and technology, and defence. China is aiming to transform itself from a backward agricultural country into an industrial nation by the year 2000. This target is to be reached with structural reforms in the economic and political sectors which are intended at loosening the centralised and bureaucratic economic and government system. Socialist planning is to be combined with a market economy. Since the end of the 1970s, China has encouraged foreign capital within the framework of opening the country to the outside world. One manifestation of this opening are the five Special Economic Zones along the coast where foreign companies can operate under special conditions.

Reforms are most advanced in agriculture. Peasant families now predominantly work privately on land over which they have guaranteed usage. Reform in industry, which is aimed at giving greater independence to companies from the state planning bureaucracy, is progressing sluggishly. The backward technology of many industrial concerns, the energy shortage, the poor infrastructure, growing environmental problems and inflation all create economic problems. In addition, the emphasis on promoting the coastal regions threatens to leave the backward areas in the west and northwest even further behind. Another problem which cannot be underestimated in terms of modernising the country is the continuing low level of education and training. Despite all these problems, the Chinese economy has shown relatively high levels of growth in recent years. It has also been successful in raising the standard of living in the countryside considerably. Today, the average life expectancy in China is over 70 years.

GEOGRAPHY & POPULATION

China is the third largest country in the world after Russia and Canada. Topographically, the country divides into 35 percent mountain regions, 27 percent high plateaus, 17 percent basin regions, 8 percent hilly areas and 13 percent plains. Only about 11 percent of the land area is agriculturally viable. The Chinese borders comprise 17,398 miles (28,000km) on land and 11,166 miles (18,000km) along the coasts. The largest of the more than 5,000 islands are Taiwan and Hainan. The highest population densities are found along the coast, while the population decreases in the west.

The People's Republic of China is the most populous nation on earth. Around 1.2 billion people live in China, that means every fifth person in the world is Chinese. About 20 percent of the population live in the towns; to curb further movements into the towns, a restriction has been put on migration to the cities. China is a country of many peoples: 93 percent of the population are Han Chinese; the remaining 7 percent, or around 68 million people, include 55 national minorities who differ fundamentally in their customs, traditions, languages and culture from the Han Chinese. The government has tried to introduce strict population control for the Han Chinese: every family should only have one child. The minorities have been exempted from this strict population control.

TRAVELLING IN HUNGARY

ADVENTURE IN STYLE

◆ Paris ◆ Munich ◆ New York ◆ Beverly Hills ◆ Japan ◆ Singapore ◆ Taipei ◆ Jakarta ◆ Auckland

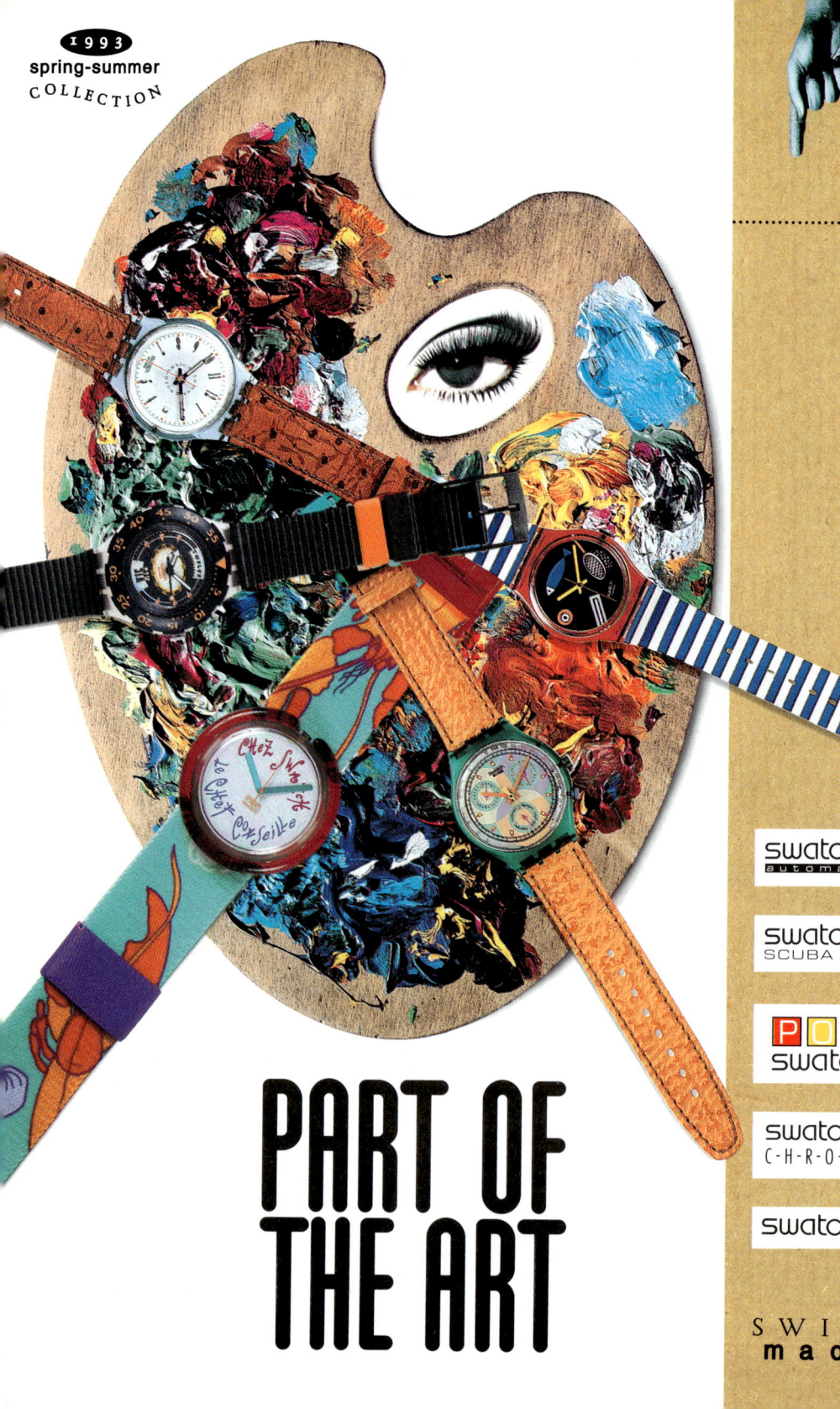

PROVINCES, AUTONOMOUS REGIONS & DIRECTLY ADMINISTERED TOWNS

Province	Area		Population (1990)
Beijing	6,489sq m	(16,807sq km)	10.87 million
Shanghai	2,388sq m	(6,185sq km)	13.51 million
Tianjin	4,363sq m	(11,300sq km)	8.83 million
Hebei	69,499sq m	(180,000sq km)	60.28 million
Shanxi	60,657sq m	(157,100sq km)	28.18 million
Inner Mongolia	463,324sq m	(1,200,000sq km)	21.11 million
Liaoning	58,302sq m	(151,000sq km)	39.98 million
Jilin	72,201sq m	(187,000sq km)	25.15 million
Heilongjiang	178,766sq m	(463,000sq km)	34.77 million
Shaanxi	75,676sq m	(196,000sq km)	32.47 million
Gansu	173,746sq m	(450,000sq km)	22.93 million
Ningxia	23,166sq m	(60,000sq km)	4.66 million
Tibet	471,046sq m	(1,220,000sq km)	2.22 million
Qinghai	278,380sq m	(721,000sq km)	4.43 million
Xinjiang	635,834sq m	(1,646,800sq km)	15.37 million
Shandong	57,915sq m	(150,000sq km)	83.43 million
Zhejiang	39,305sq m	(101,800sq km)	40.84 million
Jiangsu	41,313sq m	(107,000sq km)	68.17 million
Anhui	53,668sq m	(139,000sq km)	56.29 million
Jiangxi	63,321sq m	(164,000sq km)	38.28 million
Fujian	47,491sq m	(123,000sq km)	30.61 million
Henan	64,479sq m	(167,000sq km)	86.14 million
Hubei	72,394sq m	(187,500sq km)	54.76 million
Hunan	81,082sq m	(210,000sq km)	60.60 million
Guangdong &	84,943sq m	(220,000sq km)	63.21 million
Hainan	(area combined)		6.42 million
Guangxi	88,803sq m	(230,000sq km)	42.53 million
Sichuan	219,692sq m	(569,000sq km)	106.37 million
Guizhou	66,410sq m	(172,000sq km)	32.37 million
Yunnan	150,580sq m	(390,000sq km)	36.75 million

LOCAL TIME

The time difference between China and Britain is eight hours. Chinese time is in advance of British time. When it is midnight in London, it is 8am in Beijing. The same time operates throughout China since there are no time zones

CLIMATE

The largest part of China is in a moderate zone with clearly recognisable seasons. The country has great climatic differences resulting from the monsoon, the expanse of the land mass, and the considerable differences in altitude. While it is generally warm and humid in south-eastern and central China, the north and north east are relatively dry. The best time for travelling is spring (May) and autumn (September and October). China stretches across 35° of latitude, resulting in a great variation of regional climates. In many areas, the summer is hot and rainy, with a high level of humidity, while the winter is dry. In northern China, more than 80 percent of rainfall occurs in the summer months; but only 40 percent of the annual rainfall occurs in southern China during this season. There are frequent typhoons in south east China during the rainy season, between July and September. North of the Yangzi, the winter can be extremely cold. The northern regions, particularly, show a clear alteration of the four seasons.

The north east has hot, dry summers and long, cold winters. Summer in the desert regions of Xinjiang and Inner Mongolia is also hot and dry, while winter is cold and dry. On the Tibet Qinghai Plateau (average altitude – 13,100ft/4,000m), summer is short and moderately warm, while winters can get very cold. There is little rainfall throughout the year. The differences in day and night temperatures are very great. In central China, the summers are hot and humid, with a lot of rainfall in the late summer months. In the low lying regions of the Yangzi, winter is somewhat milder than in the central Chinese loess mountain regions or in Sichuan, which is enclosed by mountains. In the regions around Beijing, Xi'an and Zhengzhou, there are occasional sand storms in winter and spring. A mild climate with warm summers and cool winters generally prevails on the Yunnan Guizhou High Plateau, with little rainfall, and very rare frosts. Southern China has a sub-tropical climate. Rainfall is distributed around the year; the summers are long, humid and hot, and the winters are short with cooler temperatures.

TABLE OF CLIMATE

Climatic Zone	Regions	Frost-free Period
Tropical zone	Taiwan, Guangdong, Southern Yunnan	12 months
Subtropical zone	South of Qingling mountains, north of tropical zone	8-12 months
Warm-temperate zone	North of Qingling mountains and Huaihe, Gansu, Shaanxi, Hebei, Shandong, Henan, Tarim Basin in Xinjiang	5-8 months
Temperate sone	North east China, Inner Mongolia, Junggar Basin in Xinjiang	4-7 months
Cold-temperate zone	Northern-most part of Heilongjiang province and Inner Mongolia	3 months
Qinghai-Tibet-Plateau	Highland Plateaus in Qinghai, Tibet, West Sichuan	0-2 months

Town	Jan	Mar	May	July	Sept	Nov
Harbin	-19.7	-5.1	14.3	22.7	14.3	-5.8
Hohhot	-13.5	-0.4	15.2	21.8	13.8	-3.0
Beijing	-4.7	4.4	20.2	26.0	19.5	4.0
Taiyuan	-7.0	3.6	17.5	23.7	16.1	1.8
Jinan	-1.7	7.3	21.9	27.6	21.7	7.8
Qingdao	-2.6	4.6	16.7	24.7	20.5	7.4
Nanjing	1.9	8.4	20.0	28.2	22.9	10.7
Shanghai	3.3	8.3	18.8	27.9	23.8	12.5
Hangzhou	3.6	9.2	20.3	28.7	23.5	12.1
Fuzhou	10.4	13.4	22.2	28.7	26.0	17.8
Nanchang	4.9	10.9	22.0	29.7	25.1	13.1
Wuhan	2.8	10.0	21.3	29.0	23.6	11.2
Changsha	4.6	10.9	21.7	29.5	24.5	12.5
Guangzhou	13.4	17.7	25.7	28.3	27.0	19.7
Guilin	8.0	13.1	23.1	28.3	25.8	15.2
Nanning	12.9	17.3	26.0	28.3	26.7	18.9
Chongqing	7.5	14.0	22.2	28.6	24.0	13.9
Chengdu	9.1	16.6	25.3	29.7	24.9	15.4
Kunming	7.8	13.2	19.3	19.9	17.6	11.5
Lhasa	-2.3	4.3	12.6	14.9	12.8	1.9
Xi'an	-1.3	8.0	19.2	26.7	19.4	6.5
Lanzhou	-7.3	5.3	16.7	22.4	15.9	1.6
Turpan	-9.5	9.6	25.9	33.0	23.6	1.5
Ürümqi	-15.2	0.7	18.9	25.7	17.4	-2.6

Town	Spring Beginning	End	Summer Beginning	End	Autumn Beginning	End	Winter Beginning	End
Harbin	26.4	25.6	26.6	15.8	16.8	10.10	11.10	25.4
Hohhot	26.4	15.7	16.7	25.7	26.7	30.9	1.10	25.4
Taiyuan	21.4	10.6	11.6	20.8	21.8	20.10	21.10	20.4
Beijing	1.4	25.5	26.5	5.9	6.9	25.10	26.10	31.3
Qingdao	11.4	5.7	6.7	15.9	16.9	15.11	16.11	10.4
Jinan	26.3	15.5	16.5	20.9	21.9	15.11	16.11	25.3
Nanjing	21.3	25.5	26.5	20.9	21.9	20.11	21.11	20.3
Shanghai	23.3	5.6	6.6	25.9	26.9	25.11	26.11	25.3
Hangzhou	21.3	25.5	26.5	30.9	1.10	30.11	1.12	20.3
Wuhan	16.3	15.5	16.5	30.9	1.10	30.11	1.12	15.3
Changsha	6.3	10.5	11.5	30.9	1.10	30.11	1.12	5.3
Chongqing	21.2	5.5	6.5	30.9	1.10	5.12	6.12	20.2
Chengdu	26.2	10.5	11.5	15.9	16.9	30.11	1.12	25.2
Kunming	1.2	10.12					11.12	31.1
Guangzhou			21.4	5.11	6.11	24.4		
Guilin	21.2	30.4	1.5	20.10	21.10	5.1	6.1	20.2
Nanning			16.4	10.11	11.11	15.4		
Xi'an	21.3	25.5	26.5	5.9	6.9	10.11	11.11	20.3
Ürümqi	16.4	5.7	6.7	20.7	21.7	5.10	6.10	15.4

362

Chinese people have a reputation abroad as a people of high culture and extreme politeness. This politeness has, however, always been a very formal one which followed very strict rules. Chinese people can, in fact, be very impolite and show their contempt for the "long noses" quite clearly. It does happen, particularly in the area of travel, that no information or even lies are told about such problems as late trains or flights. In all cases, travellers are best advised to remain polite towards their Chinese counterparts and refrain from shouting or even being insulting. Stay calm in all situations but indicate politely and firmly what your problem or inquiry is about.

Politeness is definitely a foreign word when it comes to public transport. Whether on the underground or the bus, the overcrowded conditions always engender a struggle. No priority is given to pedestrians on the roads. Pedestrians do not even have priority on zebra crossings; basically, the pedestrian has to give way to the car. You should therefore be careful when crossing the road. No car, with some exceptions, will stop for you.

It is still very important in China to save face. For a Chinese, it is very bad to lose face, especially in front of a foreigner. Therefore, don't put a Chinese person in a position where they lose face. If you want to criticise, do so discreetly and tactfully and, if possible, not with other Chinese people present.

Chinese names are in reverse order to ours. For instance, Deng Xiaoping's second name is Deng, and his first name is Xiao-ping; and Mrs. Li Yuelan has Li as her second name, and Yuelan as her first name. Only among family and very good friends is it usual to use first names. You should therefore address Chinese men or women whom you may meet by their second name, and in the polite form of address, for instance Mr. Deng or Mrs. Li, or in Chinese, Deng Xian-sheng and Li Furen – with the title after the name. The same goes for the form of address referring to the person's position, which is sometimes used in China. For instance, Manager Li in Chinese is Li Jingli, and Professor Wang is Wang Jiaoshou. The term comrade, common until a few years ago, is less used now.

It is usually not the custom in China to greet people with a handshake, though it is commonly used with foreigners. However, to embrace or kiss when greeting each other or saying goodbye, is highly unusual. Even though the atmosphere has become more relaxed in some of the Chinese cities and one can see courting couples embracing, this is certainly not so in many other parts of the country. Chinese people generally do not show their emotions and feelings in public. Consequently, it is better not to behave in too uninhibited a fashion in public. And despite the recent trend towards more openness, it is still advisable to be fairly cautious in political discussions.

If you have been invited to a Chinese family's home, it is not customary to take flowers for the lady of the house, though this could well become a custom. If you feel it would be suitable, please remember that in China, the colour of mourning is white, therefore white chrysanthemums would be unsuitable for the occasion. A gift of a bottle of spirits would be more appropriate. The Chinese are good hosts and the visitor is usually served an excellent meal.

It is very important for Chinese people to have good connections; one could indeed say that someone who has no connections (*Guanxi*) is only half Chinese. It is very important for the Chinese to make contacts and keep them. This is equally important to foreigners on business. One should expect lots of invitations and gifts. The obligations are mutual. *Qingke*, the wining and dining of guests, is an old Chinese tradition and is still used today to thank friends for a favour or make new business contacts. If you are invited by Chinese people, you are obliged to return the invitation. The same is true the other way round; Chinese people would feel, bound to invite you to return your hospitality. You should make sure that you are on time as the Chinese value punctuality, particularly for business appointments.

Many Chinese people like a glass of liquor, particularly the good and strong Chinese spirits. Drinks are mainly consumed with a meal, and it is bad manners to be drunk in public. Women drink very little, usually no alcohol at all. Smoking continues to be taboo for women.

It is considered quite normal in China to eat noisily and belch during a meal. This doesn't mean that the foreign guest has to follow suit. An increasing number of Chinese, particularly in the big cities, don't find it very pleasant either. In many simple restaurants, bones and other remnants just get thrown on the table or the floor. It is also quite common for people to spit, despite official campaigns to try and restrain this and other such habits. It is important for foreign visitors to know that this is customary and that in simple restaurants, noisy eating and belching are quite common and not at all bad manners. You don't, however, have to accept dirty or unhygienic conditions such as dirty glasses; a complaint would be quite appropriate.

TIPPING

Officially, it is still illegal to accept tips in China. It has, however, become the custom for travel groups to give a tip to the Chinese travel guides and bus drivers. If you are travelling with a group, ask your guide, who is responsible for the "official" contacts of the group, whether you should tip and how much. On the other hand, tipping is still not usual in most restaurants and hotels although it is accepted in the modern top hotels and restaurants. Small gifts such as paperbacks, cassette tapes and Western cigarettes continue to be appreciated. Note that it is part of the ritual that any gift or tip will at first be firmly rejected.

WEIGHTS & MEASURES

Both the local and international standards for weights and measures are used in China:

ft.	chi	metre
3.28	3	1
1.09	1	0.33
1	0.91	0.3
acre	**mu**	**hectare**
0.62	15	1
0.31	1	0.5
1	3.22	1.61
pound	**jin**	**kilo**
2.20	2	1
1.10	1	0.5
1	0.91	0.45
gallon	**sheng**	**litre**
0.22	1	1
1	4.55	4.55

The Chinese use their own system for measuring shoe size (size 39, for instance, is 26.5 in China). However, international sizes are also used.

ELECTRICITY

Electricity is 220 volts, 50 cycles AC. Most modern hotels will have international standard two pin sockets, while elsewhere the three pin plugs are frequently found. Adapters will be available in the big hotels. You could bring American-style adapters. If you are travelling in areas away from the tourist centres, it is worth taking battery-operated equipment. Since Chinese batteries tend not to be very good, it is best to bring enough of your own.

BUSINESS HOURS

Shops are open on all days of the week, including public holidays. Opening hours are usually from 8.30am (or 9am) to 8pm. Government offices and banks are usually open from Monday to Friday, 8.30am to 5.30pm, with a lunch break from 12pm to 1.30pm. This does not necessarily apply to the banks in the big hotels.

HOLIDAYS

School holidays in China are between 1 August and 30 September. This also applies to higher education institutions such as universities etc. The Chinese do not have a legal right to holidays, but there are some free days during the great festivals, particularly the Spring Festival.

FESTIVALS

The most important Chinese festival is the Spring Festival (*chunjie*), the New Year Festival following the traditional Chinese lunar calendar. The date changes each year; usually it is in February. Its importance is comparable to that of Christmas for the Westerners. The Chinese have three days holiday for the Spring Festival; it is a family celebration and all members of the family come home. You should expect a reduction in services during the Spring Festival since many offices, including CITS, work restricted hours. Some means of transport get overcrowded during this time, particularly the traffic between Hong Kong and Guangzhou. The main focus of the festival is the great family meal, visits to relatives and throwing crackers. Traditionally, sacrifices were offered to the ancestors and gods – a custom that is still frequently followed in the countryside. Other festivals in the traditional calendar are the Lantern Festival, the Remembrance Day for the Dead (*Qing-ming*), the Dragon Boat Festival and the Moon Festival. The Chinese still eat moon cakes during the Moon Festival. They are stuffed with meat, spices, melon kernels, almonds, orange peel, sugar etc. In contrast to the Spring Festival, the Chinese do not get holidays for these festivals. They are usually celebrated within the family. There are various local traditional festivals in the regions where the national minorities live; for instance, the Water Festival of the Dai (a traditional New Year's festival celebrated by this national minority), or the Nadamu Festival of the Mongolians, the Tibetan New Year Festival or the Torch Festival of the Yi nationality.

In contrast to the traditional festivals, the most important official celebrations and memorial days are held according to the Gregorian calendar:

1 Jan	New Year's Day	1 day holiday
8 Mar	International Women's Day	½ day holiday
5 April	Qingming Festival (Remembrance Day for the Dead)	
1 May	International Labour Day	1 day holiday
1 July	Founding day of the CPC	
1 August	Day of the People's Liberation Army	
1 Oct	National Day	2 days holiday

Most shops are open on holidays and there are often public performances in the parks. Traditional Western holidays such as Christmas are not celebrated officially in China.

RELIGIOUS SERVICES

Officially, the PR of China encourages atheism. However, the dominant religion in China is Buddhism. There are Buddhist temples and places of worship throughout the country. Daoist institutions can also be found. There are also mosques in the Muslim areas and in all big cities, which have regular

K P M

KÖNIGLICHE
PORZELLAN
MANUFAKTUR
Berlin

BERLIN MASTERPIECES

ROCAILLE,
Breslauer Stadtschloß
The unusual reliefs and
opulent embellishments
of this rococo design
places extremely high
demands on the artistic
abilities of the craftsmen.

SCHINKEL Basket
Design: app. 1820
by Karl Friedrich Schinkel.

KURLAND, *pattern 73*
The first classicistic service
made by KPM was created
around 1790 by order of
the Duke of Kurland.

KPM BERLIN · Wegelystraße 1 · Kurfürstendamm 26a · Postal address: Postfach 12 21 07, D-10591 Berlin · Phone
(030) 390 09 - 226 · Fax (030) 390 09 - 279 · U.K. AGENCY · Exclusif Presentations, Ltd. · 20 Vancouver Road
Edgware, Middx. HA8 5DA · Phone (081) 952 46 79 · Fax (081) 951 09 39 · JAPAN AGENCY · Hayashitok Co., Ltd.
Nakano-Cho. Ogawa. Marutamachi · Nakagyo-Ku. Kyoto 604 · Phone (075) 222 02 31 / 231 22 22 · Fax (075) 256 45 54

No-one appreciates the special needs of business travellers more than Thai. We were, after all, the first Asian airline to offer a business class.

Thai's Royal Executive Class fulfils every wish of the business traveller. From bigger, wider seats to more leg room between your seat and the one in front.

This extra room gives you generous space to wo or relax. And, of course, Thai's fabled inflight serv is always at your beck and call.

Our Royal Executive Class passengers savo

SM

MNC&H/THA1907A

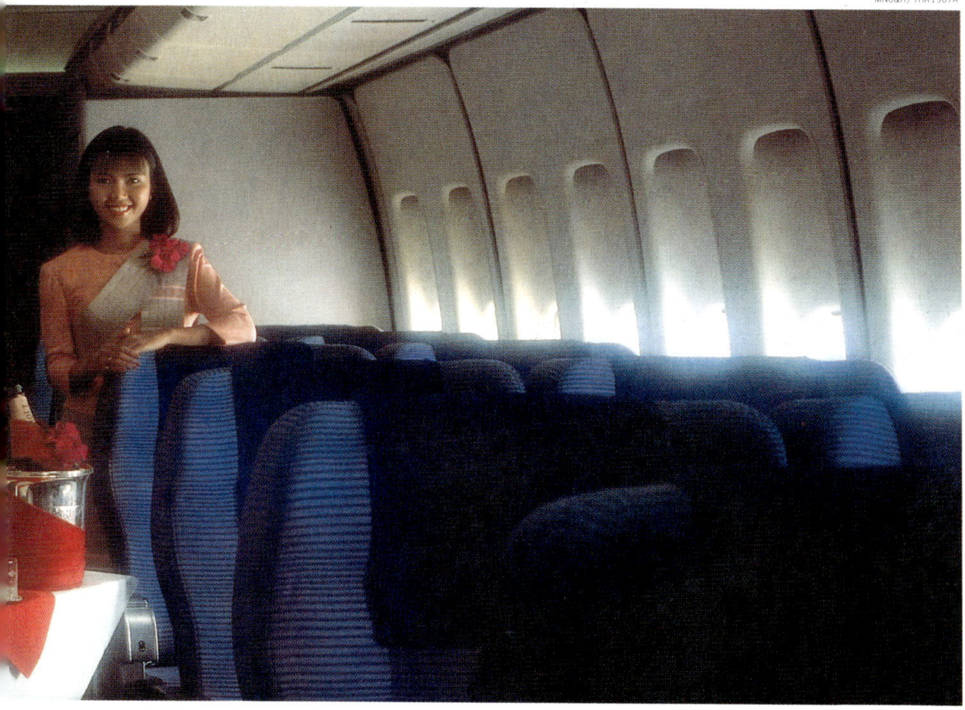

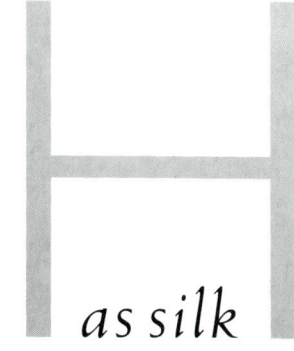

ecially selected champagnes and vintage wines from arkling crystal. Meals are served from fine china on isp table linen.

Speedy check-ins at special Royal Executive ass counters together with lounge facilities at most airports are yours for just a small premium over the full economy fare.

Where business takes you, Thai probably can too. In fact, for business travel that's smooth as silk, it's really an open and shut case.

Thai

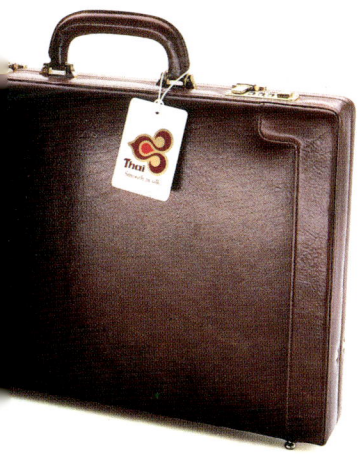

TH

as silk

THE WORLD IS FLAT

Its configuration may not be to Columbus' liking but to every other traveller the MCI Card is an easier, more convenient, more cost-efficient route to circle the globe.

The MCI Card offers two international services—MCI World Reach and MCI CALL USA—which let you call from country-to-country as well as back to the States, all via an English-speaking operator.

There are no delays. No hassles with foreign languages and foreign currencies. No foreign exchange rates to figure out. And no outrageous hotel surcharges.

If you don't possess the MCI Card, please call the access number of the country you're in and ask for customer service.

The MCI Card. It makes a world of difference.

MCI

With MCI CALL USA and MCI WORLD REACH services, reaching around the world has never been easier.

To reach around the world, use your MCI Card or call collect.° Just select the number next to the country you're calling from. An English-speaking operator will put your call through to anywhere in the 50 States as well as a growing list of participating World Reach countries.#

Australia	0014-881-100	Malaysia	800-0012
China**	108-12	New Zealand	000-912
Guam	950-1022	Philippines	102-612
Hong Kong	800-1121	Saipan	950-1022
Indonesia	00-801-11	Singapore	800-0012
Japan†	0039-121 (KDD)	Taiwan	00801-34567
	0066-55-121 (IDC)	Thailand	001-999-1-2001
Korea	009-14		
Phone Booth+:	Red Button 03 then press ∗		
Military Bases:	550-2255		

#Country-to-country calling may not be available to & from all MCI CALL USA locations. Certain restrictions apply. **Available from most major cities. †KDD & IDC are international telecommunications carriers in Japan. +Limited availability. °Collect calls to U.S. only. In some countries, public phones may require deposit of coin or phone card for dial tone. © MCI International, Inc., 1993. MCI, its logo, and all other MCI products and services mentioned herein, are proprietary marks of MCI Communications Corporation.

prayers at the prescribed times. Catholic and Protestant churches can also be found in most big cities. You can get information of the church services available from the big modern hotels. Some of these hotels conduct their own services as well.

COMMUNICATIONS

MEDIA

An English language newspaper is published in China daily except on Sundays. It is informative and takes a relatively critical position. Often obtainable from the big hotels for free, it contains the television programme and a diary of cultural events in Beijing. The sports section is good and informative. Unfortunately, you can only get the day's edition in the big cities; in other places, it often comes several days late. Several other foreign language papers are published in China which contain information for tourists about the country and its people. They can also be obtained by subscription abroad.

Many of the big hotels sell foreign language newspapers and journals, including the *South China Morning Post, International Herald Tribune, The Times, Asian Wall Street Journal, Time, Newsweek,* the *Far Eastern Economic Review,* and many more.

You can usually get the overseas edition of the party newspaper *Renmin Ribao* (*People's Daily*) in the hotels. Chinese newspapers are sold at newsstands or at the post office.

POSTAL SERVICES

You will find postal facilities in all Chinese hotels. Letters and postcards to and from China take around six days. A postcard costs 1.6 yuan, a letter 2 yuan. You can also send small parcels from all these postal facilities. Small and large parcels must be packed and sealed at the post office. The post office for *poste restante* mail and for mailings abroad is in Yong'an Lu, near Qianmen Hotel.

TELEPHONE, TELEX & FAX

Telephone: Local calls in China, including in the hotels, are usually free of charge. More and more telephone boxes have been put up in recent years. You can also make local calls from the so-called public telephones (*gongyong dianhua*), which, however, are often difficult to find for foreigners because they are located in courtyards, apartment blocks etc. Connections inside China are often poor, and long distance calls can take quite a long time.

You can make calls abroad from hotels during the day or night, in some cases even by dialling direct, but first check the current rates for overseas calls – China's IDD rates are among the highest in the world. Otherwise, book your call through the operator or at the hotel reception (where English is spoken). Calls through the operator are charged at a minimum of three minutes. The connections are usually very good and waiting time is short.

Telex and fax: Most of the big hotels have telex and fax facilities to help business people. Alternatively, you can telex from the central telegraph or the post offices.

Telegrammes: Sending telegrammes abroad is relatively expensive; at least 1.20 yuan per word. Express telegrammes are double the price. There is usually a telegramme counter at the hotel; otherwise, go to the central telegraph or post office.

EMERGENCIES

SECURITY & CRIME

There is still less crime in China than in many other countries. You can walk around safely in Chinese towns and cities without being pestered – this goes for women as well. However, criminal activities against tourists have increased in recent years. There have been thefts in tourist hotels, and money, valuables or photographic equipment have been stolen from foreigners. Don't leave your money, jewellery or valuables lying around in your hotel room, and try to keep your money safely on you.

THEFT/LOSS

If you noticed that money or objects have been stolen or lost, immediately contact the hotel reception and/or the police. If you are travelling with a group, inform your courier. In serious cases, if all your money and documents have been stolen, contact your embassy or consulate.

MEDICAL SERVICES

There is a big difference in China between medical services in the towns and in the countryside. It is possible that, if you are travelling in the countryside, there will be no appropriate medical services. Some of the hospitals in the big cities have a special section for foreigners where English is spoken. In Beijing, there is even a separate hospital for foreigners. Many of the big modern hotels have their own ambulance section or doctors. If you want to get treatment from a traditional Chinese doctor, you will have to make a special request. Normally, foreigners are treated with Western medicines. You can get the addresses of the hospitals from CITS or your hotel. Payment has to be made straightaway for treatment, medicine, transport and interpreter. In Beijing, it is possible, in serious cases, to consult the doctor at some of the embassies.

LUGGAGE

It is definitely advisable to take sturdy, strong suitcases as the frequent transport can easily damage them. If your luggage gets damaged, immediately contact the appropriate authority (for instance at the airport or railway station) so that you may get recompense. Unfortunately, this often fails to materialise. You should immediately notify your insurance company at home (group travellers will have had insurance cover as part of their booking, while individual travellers should take out their own). Give exact details and cite witnesses. The same goes for loss of luggage. It is important that your suitcase is locked, otherwise your luggage may not be accepted for transport.

GETTING AROUND

ORIENTATION

The main means of public transport in the PR of China are the railways, buses and airplanes. In the regions along the big rivers, boats play an important part. All main cities can be reached by plane and train. The road network has been improved in recent years but is still very poor in many areas.

DOMESTIC TRAVEL

By Air: The following list shows the time needed for flight connections from Beijing to other domestic destinations.

Flight connections from Beijing to	Travel time hrs/min
Chengdu	2.35
Chongqing	2.30
Dalian	1.10
Guangzhou	2.40
Guilin	2.35
Hangzhou	1.50
Harbin	1.40
Hohhot	1.15
Kunming	2.55
Lanzhou	2.10
Nanjing	1.50
Qingdao	1.15
Shanghai	1.50
Taiyuan	1.35
Ürümqi	3.55
Wuhan	1.45
Xi'an	2.00

By Rail: The distance and time needed to travel from Beijing to other domestic destinations are as given below:

From Beijing to	Distance miles (km)	Travel time hrs
Chengdu	1,273 (2,048)	34
Chongqing	1,586 (2,552)	40
Datong	249 (400)	8
Dalian	770 (1,239)	19
Guangzhou	1,437 (2,313)	33
Guilin	1,326 (2,134)	31
Hangzhou	1,026 (1,651)	26
Harbin	862 (1,388)	17
Hohhot	423 (680)	14
Kunming	1,975 (3,179)	59
Lanzhou	1,169 (1,882)	33
Luoyang	509 (819)	12
Nanjing	719 (1,157)	15
Qingdao	551 (887)	17
Shanghai	908 (1,462)	17
Suzhou	855 (1,376)	21
Taiyuan	319 (514)	9
Ürümqi	2,345 (3,774)	73
Wuhan	764 (1,229)	16
Wuxi	829 (1,334)	17
Xi'an	724 (1,165)	17

WATER TRANSPORT

There are regular ferry and boat connections between the large coastal cities in China. The same is true for some of the big rivers, particularly the Yangzi and the Pearl River (but not the Yellow River). Both the ocean liners and the inland river boats have several classes. You can find out the exact timetable from travel agents or the shipping agencies.

Railways: The Chinese rail network covers 32,467 miles (53,400km), of which 2,734 miles (4,400km) are electrified. Average train speed is not very high, mainly due to poor construction. There is no first or second class on Chinese trains, but four categories or classes: *ruanwo* or soft-sleeper; *ruanzuo* or soft-seat; *yingwo* or hard-sleeper, and *yingzuo* or hard-seat. The soft-seat class is usually only available for short journeys. Long distance trains normally only have soft-sleeper or hard-sleeper facilities. The soft-sleeper class has 4-bed compartments with soft beds. It is to be recommended particularly for long journeys. The hard-sleeper class has open, 6-bed compartments. The beds are not really hard, but are not very comfortable either. While you can reserve a place for the first three classes (you always buy a ticket with a place number), this is not essential for the lowest class.

There is always boiled water available on the trains. There are washrooms in the soft-sleeper and hard-sleeper classes. The toilets, regardless of which class, are usually not very hygienic, and it is a good idea to bring your own toilet paper. There are dining cars on long distance trains which can vary in quality. If you can't get a reservation for the soft-sleeper you may find that you can book one directly with the soft-sleeper guard if there are any vacant ones. However, Chinese trains are usually fully booked and it is advisable to get a ticket well in advance. This is particularly so during the main travel season. There are special ticket counters for foreigners at several big railway stations. Fares are usually higher for foreigners than for the Chinese. The price also depends on both the class and the speed of the train; there are slow trains, fast trains, express trains and inter-city trains. Reservations can be made at ticket offices in the town centre or through travel agencies. The China Publishing House in Beijing will send timetables in Chinese or English. Be on time as Chinese trains tend to be very punctual.

Buses (*gongonqiche*): Overland buses are the most important means of transport in many parts of China, especially where there is as yet no railway line. In most towns and settlements, there are main bus stations for overland buses. They are certainly the cheapest means of transport, but are also correspondingly slow. There are regular breaks during bus journeys; on journeys lasting several days you will usually find simple restaurants and overnight accommodation near the bus stations. Many overland buses have numbered seats and it is advisable to book a ticket and seat well in advance.

Modern buses with air conditioning are frequently available in the tourist centres.

Motorcycles or cars: Private car or motorcycle journeys were until recently not possible in China, but this has slowly begun to change. You need to investigate the actual possibilities through the tourist office of the PR of China or other information offices. You may also join travel agencies which organise car or motorcycle trips on a regional basis. It is also possible to hire a car with driver for a specific time through the travel agencies in China or the taxi companies.

Hiking tours are now possible in China. You need to study what's on offer from the tour operators. Chinese travel agencies can arrange such tours.

The visitor can choose between taxis, buses or bicycles for transport in the towns. In Beijing, there is also the underground. Taxis are certainly the most comfortable form of transport, and can be hired for excursions.

Buses in Chinese towns are always overcrowded. The fare depends on distance, and should be paid to the conductor. Buses are usually easy to use, and timetables or town maps are available everywhere. In some Chinese cities such as Beijing, there are also minibuses for certain routes. They carry a maximum of 16 people. They are a bit more expensive but will stop at any point you want along the route.

You can now hire bicycles in many Chinese towns, either at the hotels or at special hiring shops. It is advisable to park the bicycle at guarded parking spaces for a small fee. Parking is not very expensive, but usually a deposit is required. China too has bicycle thieves and there is a fine for illegal parking.

WHERE TO STAY

The years since the early 1980s have seen a huge building boom in the hotel sector in China's big cities. Particularly in Beijing, Guangzhou and Shanghai, there are now hotels comparable in standard to those in Hong Kong or Western cities. Most belong to international hotel chains, and their management and staff have been trained abroad.

Often, the prices of these better hotels are in line with hotel prices in the West. But thanks to the glut of rooms in, say, Beijing, competition is fierce, and there are bargains to be found, with discounted room rates and special offers.

Most members of tourist groups are accommodated in good tourist hotels. These are quite luxuriously furnished. Rooms have two beds, a sitting area, desk, telephone, air conditioning, a separate bathroom and, sometimes, a fridge. They always have thermos flasks with boiled water. Many of the modernised hotels of the old style offer numerous facilities which guarantees a pleasant stay. Usually, they have several restaurants offering Chinese, Western, or sometimes, Japanese cuisine as well. In addition to a bank, post, telex and telegramme counter, there is a floor service on each floor which keeps the room keys and offers a laundry service. You should be cautious about the laundry service, particularly with delicate clothes, except in the first class hotels. If you give your washing to the express service, it will be returned within a few hours, washed and ironed. It is advisable to find out first from the floor service how long it will take.

Almost all hotels have one or several small shops selling souvenirs, cigarettes, drinks, and often clothes or artefacts. The bigger hotels have cafes and bars, which are popular meeting places after 8pm. Many hotels also have a hairdresser who frequently offers massage and acupuncture as well; and there is usually a medical emergency service which can give first aid in emergencies.

In some hotels, there is a travel service office, which handles bookings and other queries (see *Tour Operators*). Hotels may also offer tour itineraries in the local area.

It is usually not a problem for individual travellers to book a room in the first class and luxury hotels, even at the last minute. Bookings with hotels of a medium and cheap range tend to be more difficult, particularly during the main summer season in May, September and October, when they are hopelessly booked up. If you have pre-booked your accommodation in each town as part of a mini-package or a full package tour, you will not usually have any problems – hotels are rarely overbooked.

Until recently, hotels, airports and railway stations used to be the only places where a tourist could be sure of getting a taxi. Nowadays, it is becoming increasingly easy to hail a taxi in the street (see *Town Transport*).

Some small hotels, which are really only accessible to Chinese guests (called Lüguan in Chinese), offer the possibility of a cheap night using sleeping bags. The cost varies between 10 and 30 Yuan. It is advisable to arrive at the hotel in good time.

Worth mentioning are the few well preserved hotels built in some Chinese towns by the colonial powers and later by Russia. They include the Peace Hotel (*He-ping*) in Shanghai, the People's Hotel in Xi'an (*Renmin Dasha*) and the Friendship Hotel (*Youyibinguan*) in Beijing. While the interior has been modernised, the outside of these buildings and such fixtures as the "Oldtimer Jazzband" at the Peace Hotel in Shanghai give a flavour of the past.

The following list is a short survey of the most important hotels in the towns which are of greatest interest to tourists. It cannot, of course, be complete, if only because in many towns, new hotels are currently being planned, under construction or just opened. We have chiefly listed star-rated hotels. Prices for standard rooms in 5-star hotels are around US$80–180 upwards; for 4-star hotels around US$60–110; for 3-star US$35–70; for 2-star US$20–40; and for 1-star under US$25. Several of the hotels listed here without star ratings are recently built.

BEIJING

☆☆☆☆☆
Beijing Hotel, 33 East Chang'an Ave. Tel: 5137766, Fax: 5137703, 5137307, Tlx: 222755 BHCRD
China World Hotel, 1 Jianguomenwai Ave. Tel: 5052266, Fax: 5053167-9, Tlx: 211206 CWH
Daioyutai Star Guest House, Sanlihe Road, Haidian District. Tel: 80331188, Fax: 8013362, Tlx: 22798 DYTSG
Grand Hotel Beijing, 35 East Chang'an Ave. Tel: 5137788, Fax: 5130049, Tlx: 210454 BHPTW
Great Wall Sheraton Hotel, North Donghuan Road. Tel: 5005566, Fax: 5001919, Tlx: 22002
Holiday Inn Crown Plaza, 48 Wangfujing Dajie. Tel: 5133388, Fax: 5132513, Tlx: 210676 HICPB
Jing Guang New World Hotel, Hu Jia Lou, Chaoyang District. Tel: 5018888, Fax: 5013333, Tlx: 210489 BTJGC
Kempinski Hotel (Beijing Lufthansa Centre), Xiao Liangmaqiao, Chaouyang District. Tel: 4653388, Fax: 4653366, Tlx: 21062 KIRV
Kun Lun Hotel, 2 Xinyuannan Road, Chaoyang District. Tel: 5003388, Tax: 5003228, Tlx: 210327 BJKLH
New Otani Chang Fu Gong Hotel, 26 Jiangoumenwai St. Tel: 5125711, Fax: 5139811, Tlx: 210465 BCFGH
Palace Hotel, 8 Goldfish Lane, Wongfujing. Tel: 5128899, Fax: 5129050, Tlx: 2222696 PALBJ
Shangri-La Hotel, 29 Zizhuyuan Road. Tel: 8412211, Fax: 8418006, Tlx: 222231 SHABJ
Swissotel Beijing (Hong Kong Macau Centre), Dong Si Shi Tiao, Li Jiao Qiao. Tel: 5012288, Fax: 5012501, Tlx: 222527 HMC

☆☆☆☆
Beijing Continental Grand Hotel, 8 Bei Chen Dong Street, North Sihuan Road, Anding Men Wai. Tel: 4915588, Fax: 4910106, Tlx: 210564 ICH
Beijing International Hotel, 9 Jianguomennei Ave. Tel: 5126688, Fax: 5129961, Tlx: 211121 BIH
Beijing Mandarin Hotel, 21 Che Gong Zhuang Road. Tel: 8319988, Fax: 8322135, 8311818, Tlx: 221042 XDDH
Beijing Movenpick Hotel, Xiaotianzhu Village,

Shunyi County, PO Box 6913. Tel: 4565588, Fax: 4565678, Tlx: 222986

Beijing-Toronto Hotel, 3 Jianguomenwai St. Tel: 5002266, Fax: 5002022, Tlx: 210012 JLH

Capital Hotel, 3 Qian Men Dong Ave. Tel: 5129988, Fax: 5120309, 5120323, Tlx: 222650 CHB

Central Plaza Hotel, 18 Gaoliang Qiao Lu, Xizhimenwai. Tel: 8318888, Fax: 8319887, Tlx: 222988 ZYH

China Resources Hotel, 35 Jianguo Road, Chaoyang District. Tel: 5012233, Fax: 5012311

Fragrant Hills Hotel, Fragrant Hill Park, Haidian District. Tel: 2565544, Fax: 2566794, Tlx: 222202 FHH

Friendship Hotel, 3 Baishiqiao Road. Tel: 8498888, Fax: 8498866, Tlx: 222362 FHBJ

Grace Hotel, 8 Jiangtai Road West. Tel: 4362288, Fax: 4361818, Tlx: 210599 BJGH

Holiday Inn Downtown Beijing, 98 Beilishilu, Xichengqu. Tel: 8322288, Fax: 8320696, Tlx: 221045 HIDTB

Holiday Inn Lido, Jiang Tai Road, Jichang Road. Tel: 4376688, Fax: 4376237, Tlx: 22618 LIDOH

Jianguo Hotel, 5 Jianguomenwai Ave. Tel: 5002233, Fax: 5002871/5010539, Tlx: 22439 JGHBJ

New Century Hotel, 6 Southern Road, Capital Gym. Tel: 8492001, Fax: 8491107, Tlx: 222375 NCH

Peace Hotel, 3 Jinyu Hutong, Wangfujing. Tel: 5128833, Fax: 5126863, Tlx: 222855 PHB

Tianlun Dynasty Hotel, 50 Wangfujing Ave. Tel: 5138888, Fax: 5137866, Tlx: 210574 TLX

Traders Hotel, 1 Jianguomenwai Ave. Tel: 5052277, Fax: 5050818, Tlx: 222981 THBBC

Xi Yuan Hotel, 1 Sanlihe Road. Tel: 8313388, Fax: 8314577, Tlx: 22834 XYH

Yuyang Hotel, Xinyuan Xili, Chaoyang District. Tel: 4666610, Fax: 4081101, Tlx: 4666601

Zhaolong Hotel, 2 Worker's Stadium Road North, Chaoyang District. Tel: 5002299, Fax: 5003319, Tlx: 210079 ZLH

☆☆☆
Beijing Asia Hotel, 8 Xinzhong Xijie, Gongti, Beilu. Tel: 5007788, Fax: 5008091, Tlx: 210597 AHR

Chains City Hotel, 4 Gongti East Rd. Tel: 5007799, 5007668, Tlx: 210530 NWTBJ

CVIK Hotel, 22 Jiangoumenwai Ave. Tel: 5123388, Fax: 5123542, Tlx: 210689 CSTNT

Dongfang Hotel, 11 Wanming Road, Xuanwu District. Tel: 3014466, Tlx: 222385 DFH

Dragon Spring Hotel, North Shuizha Road, Mentougou. Tel: 9843366, 9843362, Fax: 9844377, Tlx: 222292 DSHBJ

Exhibition Hall Hotel, 135 Xizhimenwai. Tel: 8316633, Fax: 8327450, Tlx: 222395

Friendship Hotel, 3 Baishiqiao Rd. Tel: 8498888, Fax: 8498866, Tlx: 222362 FHBJ

Grand Hotel, 20 Yumin East Region, Deshengmenwai, West City District. Tel: 2010033, Fax: 2029893, Tlx: 222227 YSH

Guangming Hotel, Liangmaqiao Rd, Chaoyang District. Tel: 4672613, Fax: 4081682, Tlx: 210383 BGC

Huadu Hotel, 8 South Xin Yuan Road. Tel: 5001166, Fax: 5001615, Tlx: 22028 HUADU

Huilongguan Hotel, Huilongguan, Deshengmenwai. Tel: 2913931, Fax: 2913376, Tlx: 210083 BHLGH

Jin Lang Hotel, 75 Chongnei Street, Dong Cheng District. Tel: 5132288, Fax: 5125839

Landmark Towers, 8 North Dongsanhuan Road. Tel: 5016688, Fax: 5013506, Tlx: 210616 LMH

Media Hotel, 11B Fuxing Road. Tel: 8014422, Fax: 8016288, Tlx: 22836 MEDIA

Minzu Hotel, 51 Fuxingmennei Street. Tel: 6014466, Fax: 6014849, Tlx: 22990 MZHTL

Olympic Hotel, 52 Baishiqiao Road, Haidian. Tel: 8316688, Fax: 8315985, Tlx: 222859 OLHTL

Park Hotel, 36 Huang Yu Road South. Tel: 7212233, Fax: 7211615, Tlx: 22968

Qianmen Hotel, 175 Yongan Road. Tel: 3016688, Fax: 3013883, Tlx: 222382 OMHTL

Rainbow Hotel, 11 Xijinglu, Xuanwu District. Tel: 3012266, Fax: 3011366, Tlx: 222772 RBH

Taiwan Hotel, 5 Jinyu Wutong, Wangfujing North. Tel: 5136688, Fax: 5136896, Tlx: 210543 TWHTL

Twenty-First Century Hotel, 40 Liang Ma Qiao Lu. Tel: 4663311, Fax: 4664809, Tlx: 210615 SJYEC

Xinqiao Hotel, 2 Dongjiaomin Xiang, Chongwenmen. Tel: 5133366, Fax: 5125126, Tlx: 222514 XQH

Yanjing Hotel, 19 Fuxingmenwai Ave. Tel: 8326611-7, Fax: 8326130, Tlx: 20028 YJHTL

Yan Shan Hotel, 138A Haidian Road. Tel: 2563388, Fax: 2568640, Tlx: 211203 YSHBJ

Yanxiang Hotel, A2 Jiang Tai Road, Dongzhimenwai. Tel: 5006666, Fax: 5006231, Tlx: 210014 YXH

☆ **rating not available for the following:**
Beiwei Hotel, Xijing Lu 13, Xuanwu District

China Merchants Beijing Hotel, 2 Yangjingxili, Hongmiao Chaoyangmenwei. Tel: 5005599, Fax: 5001386. Tlx: 210243 JYHPK

Chongwenmen Hotel, 2 Chongwenmenxi Dajie. Tel: 5122211

Dadu Hotel, 21 Chegongzhuang St. Tel: 890981, Tlx: 222477 DDH

Garden View Hotel, Nancaiyuen St, Xuanwu District. Tel: 3268899, Fax: 3263139

Gloria International Hotel, 2 Jianguomenan Ave. Tel: 5158855, Fax: 5158533

Jinfeng Hotel, 71 Fengtai Road, Fengtai District. Tel: 372411

Novotel Beijing, 88 Deng Shi Kou, Dong Cheng. Tel: 5138822, Fax: 5739088

Parkview Tian Tan Hotel, 1 Tiyuguan Road, Chongwen District. Tel: 7012277, Fax: 7016833, Tlx: 221034 TTH

Plaza Hotel, B45 Dong Zhong St, Dongcheng District. Tel: 482490, Fax: 4082231, Tlx: 211262 ICEC

Qiao Yuan Hotel, Dongbinhe Road, You'anmenwai, Fengtai District. Tel: 338861

Ritan Hotel, 1 Ritan Park, Jianguomenwai.
Tel: 5125588
SAS Royal Hotel, 6A East Beisanhuan Road. Tel:
4663388, Fax: 4653186, Tlx: 211241 SASZH
Sara Hotel Beijing – Hua Qiao Da Sha, 2 Wangfujing
Dajie. Tel: 550604, Fax: 5130064
Wannianqing Hotel, Zizhuyuan Lu.
Xuanwumen Hotel, Xuanwumen Dondajie.
Universe Building, 14 Dongzhimen Nandajie,
Dongcheng District. Tel: 5001188, Fax: 5010268,
Tlx: 211262
Xisanqi Hotel, Xisanqi, Desheng Menwai. Tel:
2913966, Tlx: 22755 XSQ
Yuanwanglou Hotel, 13 West Beihuan Road. Tel:
2013366, 222501 YWLH
Yue Xiu Hotel, 24 East Xuansumen. Tel: 3014499
Yulong Hotel, 40 Fucheng Road, Haidian District.
Tel: 8415588, Fax: 8413108, Tlx: 222729 YLHCH

CHENGDE

☆☆☆
Yun Shan Hotel, 6 East Nanyuan Road. Tel: 224657,
Fax: 224551, Tlx: 27727 YSHCD

Star rating not available
Chengde Diplomatic Missions Guest House, Wuli
Road. Tel: 221982, Fax: 221967
Mongolian Yurt Hotel, Wan Shu Yuan, Inside
Mountain Summer Resort. Tel: 223094
Mountain Villa Hotel, 127 Lizhengmen. Tel: 223501
Qiwang Building Chengde, North 1 East Road of
Bi Feng Gate. Tel: 223528

CHENGDU

☆☆☆☆
Jinjiang Hotel, 36 Renmin Road South. Tel: 582222,
Fax: 581849, Tlx: 60109 JJH
Minshan Hotel, 17 Section 2 Reminnan Road. Tel:
583333, Fax: 582154, Tlx: 60247 MSH

☆☆☆
Chengdu Hotel, East Section of Shudu Road. Tel:
444112, Fax: 441603, Tlx: 60164 CDHOT
Sichuan Hotel, 31 Zongfu Jie. Tel: 661115, Fax:
665263, Tlx: 6000029 SCHTL
Tibet Hotel, 10 Renmin North Road. Tel: 334001,
Fax: 333526, Tlx: 60309

☆☆
Zhufeng Hotel, 107 Shuncheng Street, Shangxi. Tel:
662441, Fax: 760949, Tlx: 600023 ZHGHO

CHONGQING

☆☆☆☆
Holiday Inn Yangtze Chongqing, 15 Nan Ping Bei
Road. Tel: 203380, Fax: 200884, Tlx: 62220 HIYCQ

☆☆☆
Chongqing Guest House, 235 Minsheng Road. Tel:
354491, Fax: 350643, Tlx: 62122 CQGH
Chongqing Hotel, 41-43 Xinhua Road. Tel: 349301,
Fax: 343085, Tlx: 62193
Renmin Hotel, 175 Renmin Road. Tel: 351421,
Fax: 351387, Tlx: 62224 WTCCQ
Shaping Grand Hotel, 84 Xiaolongkan New Street.
Tel: 663194, Fax: 663293, Tlx: 62194 SCGE

DALIAN

☆☆☆☆☆
Furama Hotel, 74 Stalin Road. Tel: 230888, Fax:
804455, Tlx: 86441

☆☆☆☆
Dalian Regent Hotel, 12 Hutan St, Zhongshan
District. Tel: 282811, Fax: 282100, Tlx: 86352
DLRH
Holiday Inn Dalian, 18 Sheng Li Square, Zhong Shan
Ward. Tel: 808888, Fax: 809704, Tlx: 86383 DJZH

☆☆☆
CAAC Mansions, 143 Zhongshan Road. Tel: 333111,
Fax: 338211, Tlx: 86277
Dalian Hotel, 4 Zhongshan Square. Tel: 2333111,
Fax: 234363, Tlx: 86238
Dalian Inn Fine Hotel, Changchun Road, Econ &
Tech Dev. Tel: 712888, Fax: 711322, Tlx: 86054
INFIN
Grand Hotel Dalian, 1 Jiefang St. Tel: 806161, Fax:
806969, Tlx: 86338
Nan Shan Hotel, 56 Fenglin St, Zhongshan District.
Tel: 238751, Fax: 804898, Tlx: 86446 DNSH
Xiuyu Hotel, Fujiazhuang. Tel: 282484

☆☆
Jinzhou Hotel, 412 Stalin Road, Jinzhou. Tel:
792172, Fax: 790146
Lushan Blue Sea Hotel, 36 Bayi Jie, Lushun. Tel:
3841, Tlx: 3950

☆ **rating not available for the following:**
Bangchui Island Hotel, 1 Bangchui Island. Tel:
235131, Tlx: 86236
Dalian International Hotel, 9 Stalin Road. Tel:
238238, Fax: 230008, Tlx: 86363 DIH

DATONG

☆ **rating not available for the following:**
Datong Hotel, 8 West Yingbin Road. Tel: 232476
Yungang Hotel, 21 East Yingbin Road. Tel: 521601,
Fax: 522046, Tlx: 290006 DTTLX

DAZU

☆
Dazu Hotel, 47 Gongnong Jie, Longgang Zhen.
Tel: 22967

☆☆
Feitian Hotel, Dingzhi Road. Tel: 2606, Tlx: 72076 DHFTW
Silk Road Hotel, 2 Dongdajie. Tel: 2371
Taiyangleng Hotel, Beidajie. Tel: 2134, Tlx: 72077 DHTYZ

☆ **rating not available for the following:**
Dunhuang Hotel, 1 Dongdajie. Tel: 2415, 2538, Fax: 2415, Tlx: 72078 DHBGS

☆ **rating not available for the following:**
Hong Zhu Shan Hotel, Emeishan. Tel: 33888, Fax: 33788

☆☆☆☆
Fujian Foreign Trade Centre, May Fourth Avenue. Tel: 550154, Fax: 550358, Tlx: 92158 FTC
Fuzhou Lakeside Hotel, 1 Hu Bin Road. Tel: 839888, Fax: 839752, Tlx: 92255 FLHBC
Hot Spring Hotel, May Fourth Avenue Middle. Tel: 551818, Fax: 535150, Tlx: 92180 HSHFZ

☆☆☆
Donghu Hotel, 44 Dongda Road. Tel: 557755, Fax: 555519, Tlx: 92171 DHHFZ
Haishan Hotel, May Fourth Road. Tel: 557766, Fax: 534473, Tlx: 92177 HSG
Min-Capital Building, Gu Tian Road. Tel: 557720, Fax: 535060, Tlx: 92187 MCB
Minjiang Hotel, May Fourth Ave. Tel: 557895, Fax: 551489, Tlx: 94146 MJHT
Overseas Chinese Hotel, May Fourth Road. Tel: 557603, Fax: 550648, Tlx: 92275 OCHTZ

☆ **rating not available for the following:**
Taiwan Hotel, 28 Hualin Road. Tel: 570570, Fax: 571409, Tlx: 92253 TWHF

☆☆☆☆☆
China Hotel, Liuhua Rd. Tel: 6666888, Fax: 6677014, Tlx: 44888 CHLGZ
Dongfang Hotel, 120 Liuhua Road. Tel: 6669900, Fax: 6662775, Tlx: 44439 GZDFH
Garden Hotel, 368 Huanshi Road East. Tel: 3338989, Fax: 3350467, Tlx: 44788 GDHTL
White Swan Hotel, 1 Southern St, Shamian Island. Tel: 8886968, Fax: 8861188, Tlx: 44688 WSH

☆☆☆☆
Central Hotel, 33 Jichang Road, Sanyuanli. Tel: 6678331, Fax: 6662316, Tlx: 44664 GICSO

Equatorial Hotel, 931 Renmin Bei Road. Tel: 6672888, Fax: 6672583, Tlx: 44168
GITIC Riverside Hotel, 298 Yanjiang Road Central. Tel: 3329888, Fax: 3318714
Holiday Inn City Centre, Guangzhou, Huanshi Dong, Overseas Chinese Village, 28 Guangming Road. Tel: 7766999, Fax: 7753126, Tlx: 441045 HICCG
Plaza Canton Hotel, 348 Jiang Nan Da Road. Tel: 4418888, Fax: 4429645, Tlx: 441032 PLZCT
Ramada Pearl Hotel, 9 Ming Yue Yi Road, Dong Shan District. Tel: 7772988, Fax: 7767481

☆☆☆
Aiqun Hotel, 113 Yanjiang Xi Road. Tel: 8866668, Fax: 8883519, Tlx: 44706 AQHTL
Baiyun Hotel, 367 Huanshi Rd East. Tel: 3333998, Fax: 3336498, Tlx: 44327 BYHTL
Dong Shan Hotel, 44 San Yu Rd, Dongshan. Tel: 7773722, Fax: 7758288, Tlx: 44733 DSHCN
Guangzhou Hotel, Haizhu Square. Tel: 333168, Fax: 3330791, Tlx: 44336 KCHTL
Guangzhou Ocean Hotel, 412 Huanshi Rd East. Tel: 7765988, Fax: 7765475, Tlx: 44638 GOHOL
Liuhua Hotel, 194 Huanshi Rd West. Tel: 6668800, Fax: 6667828, Tlx: 44298 GZLHH
Mei Hua Cun Hotel, 28 Mei Dong Rd. Tel: 7766668, Fax: 7766262
Nanhu Hotel, Tonghe, Sha He. Tel: 7706706, Fax: 7706160, Tlx: 44511 NANHU
New Mainland Hotel, 70 Zhanqian Rd. Tel: 6678638, Fax: 6676880, Tlx: 44763 MAINL
Overseas Chinese Hotel, 63 Zhan Qian Road. Tel: 6663488, Fax: 6663230, Tlx: 44217 CTS
Victory Hotel, 54 Shamian St. Tel: 8862622, Fax: 8862413, Tlx: 441163

☆ **rating not available for the following:**
Furama Hotel, 316 Changdi Lu. Tel: 8863288, Fax: 8863388
GITIC Plaza, 339 Huanshi East Rd. Tel: 3311888, Fax: 3311666, Tlx: 44556
Guangdong Building, 309 Dongfeng Road Central. Tel: 3339933, Fax: 3339723, Tlx: 44503 GDDSD
Guangzhou Binjiang Tower, 2-6 Hongde Road. Tel: 449709, Fax: 8861109, Tlx: 4434 GUITN
Guangzhou Hutian Hotel, 156 Dongfeng Rd West. Tel: 8871888, Fax: 8877988
Parkview Square, 960 Jiefang North Rd. Tel: 6665666, Fax: 6671741, Tlx: 441088 PVSQ
San Yu Hotel, 23 San Yu Rd. Tel: 7756888, Fax: 7766136, Tlx: 441065 SYHTL
Sino Trade Centre, 63 Pan Fu Road. Tel: 3336622, Fax: 3338669, Tlx: 44833 STC
UNIC International Hotel, 96 Xianlie Zhong Road. Tel: 7758888, Fax: 7758618, Tlx: 441061
Yue Xiu Hotel, 198 Xiaobei Road. Tel: 3330680
Zhu Dao Hotel, 443 Yanjiang Rd East. Tel: 7750725, Fax: 7750725

GUILIN

☆☆☆☆
Guilin Plaza, 20 Lijiang Lu. Tel: 512488, Fax: 513323, Tlx: 48449
Guilin Royal Garden Hotel, Yuanjiang Road. Tel: 442411, Fax: 445051, Tlx: 48445
Guishan Hotel, Chuan Shan Road. Tel: 443388, Fax: 444851, Tlx: 48443 GSHTL
Holiday Inn Guilin, 14 South Ronghu Rd. Tel: 223950, Fax: 222101, Tlx: 48456 GLHCL
Sheraton Guilin Hotel, Bing Jiang Nan Rd. Tel: 225588, Fax: 225598, Tlx: 48439 GLMAN

☆☆☆
Guilin Osmanthus Hotel, 451 Zhongshan South Rd. Tel: 334300, Fax: 335316, Tlx: 48455 GLOSH
Guilin Park Hotel, 1 Luosi Hill, Laoren Shan Qian. Tel: 228899, Fax: 222296, Tlx: 48498 GLPKH
Guilin Riverside Resort, Anjiazhou. Tel: 332291, Fax: 334973, Tlx: 73945
Guilin Seven Star Hotel, 7 Lijiang Rd East. Tel: 512311, Fax: 512288, Tlx: 48491 GLWSS
Hong Kong Hotel Guilin, 8 Xihuan Yi Rd. Tel: 333889, Fax: 332752, Tlx: 48454 GLXJH
Lijiang Hotel, 1 North Shanhu Rd. Tel: 222881, Fax: 222891, Tlx: 48470 GLLIR
Pine Garden Resort, 9 Lijiang Road. Tel: 442311, Fax: 445893, Tlx: 48447
Ronghu Hotel, 17 Ronghu Rd North, Tel: 223811, Fax: 225390, Tlx: 48467
Tailien Hotel, 102 Middle Zhongshan Rd. Tel: 222888, Fax: 226251, Tlx: 48453 GLTLH
Universal Guilin Hotel, 1 Jiefangdong Rd. Tel: 228228, Fax: 223868, Tlx: 48475 GLHUG

☆ rating not available for the following:
Beauty Swallow Hotel, 5 Tao Huajiang Rd. Tel: 222986, Fax: 224011

HANGZHOU

☆☆☆☆☆
Shangri-La Hotel, 78 Beishan Road. Tel: 777951, Fax: 773545, Tlx: 35005/6 HOTCH

☆☆☆☆
Dragon Hotel, Shu Guang Rd. Tel: 554488, Fax: 558090, Tlx: 351048 DRAGN

☆☆☆
Friendship Hotel, 53 Ping Hai Rd. Tel: 777888, Fax: 773842, Tlx: 35068 FRISH
Hangzhou Huagang Hotel, 4 Xi Shan Rd. Tel: 771324, Fax: 772481, Tlx: 35007 HUAJQ
Hangzhou Linping Hotel, Linping Town. Tel: 553559, Fax: 351169 HSSDC
Hangzhou Overseas Chinese, 15 Hubin Rd. Tel: 774401, Fax: 774978, Tlx: 35070 HOCH
Wanghu Hotel, 2 Huanchen Rd West. Tel: 771024, 771942, Fax: 771350, Tlx: 351029 OLWH

Xin Qiao Hotel, 176 Jiefang Rd. Tel: 776688, Fax: 722768, Tlx: 351028 XQH

☆ rating not available for the following:
Hangzhou International Mansion, 157 Tiyuchang Rd. Tel: 553697, Fax: 574201, Tlx: 35029 HZIB
Hangzhou Building, 1 Wu Lin Square. Tel: 553911, Fax: 570062, Tlx: 351008 HZB
Hangzhou Xi Hu State Hotel, 7 Xi Shan Road. Tel: 776889, Fax: 772348, Tlx: 35004 BTHXH
Hangzhou Zhijiang Hotel, 84 Moganshan Road. Tel: 866888, Fax: 864966
Huajiashan Hotel, Xishan Rd. Tel: 771224, Fax: 773980, Tlx: 35063 HJSGH
Jingxiu Hotel, 103 An Le Road, Tonglu. Tel: 22267, Tlx: 2795 TONGLU
Zhejiang Guest House, 68 San Tai Shan Road. Tel: 777988, Fax: 771904, Tlx: 351044 ZIGH

HARBIN

☆☆☆
Harbin Friendship Palace, 57 Youyi Road. Tel: 416146, Fax: 417132, Tlx: 87124 HFP
Harbin Modern Hotel, 129 Zhongyang Street. Tel: 415846, Fax: 414997, Tlx: 87075 MDR
Overseas Chinese Hotel, 52 Hong Jun Street, Nangang. Tel: 341420, Fax: 329429
Swan Hotel, 73 Zhongshan Road. Tel: 220201, Fax: 224895, Tlx: 87080 TIANE

☆☆
Beiyuan Hotel, 8 Chunshen St, Nangang District. Tel: 338261, Fax: 322921, Tlx: 87144
Jinxing Guest House, Wangzhaoxinchun, Dongli District. Tel: 224729

☆ rating not available for the following:
Daqing Hotel, 13 Guomin St. Tel: 337241, Fax: 343079, Tlx: 887167
Harbin International Hotel, 124 Dazhi Street. Tel: 341441, Fax: 325651, Tlx: 87081 GUOLU
Milky Way Hotel, 230 Zhongshan Road. Tel: 220707, Fax: 228375
Peace Hotel, 109 Zhongshan Road. Tel: 220101, Fax: 220124, Tlx: 87079

HOHHOT

☆☆☆
Inner Mongolia Hotel, Hulun South Rd. Tel: 25754, Fax: 85016
Zhaojun Hotel, 11 Xinhua Ave. Tel: 662211, Fax: 668825, Tlx: 85053 ZJHPT

JINAN

☆☆☆☆
Qilu Hotel, 86 Jingshi Rd. Tel: 616688, Fax: 613524, Tlx: 39142

Ming Hu Hotel, 398 Beiyuan Road. Tel: 556688, Fax: 551634, Tlx: 390008

Shungeng Mountain Villa, 1 Shun Geng Rd. Tel: 615901, Fax: 615288, Tlx: 39184 MTCJN

KAIFENG

☆☆

Dongjing Hotel, 14 Yingbin Road. Tel: 31075, 33155, Tlx: 46110 KFFAO

Kaifeng Hotel, 64 Zhongduan, Ziyou Rd. Tel: 33115, Fax: 33798

KASHGAR

☆☆

Kashgar Hotel, 7 Tawuguzi Rd. Tel: 22367-941

Seman Hotel, 170 Seman Rd. Tel: 22179

KUNMING

☆☆☆☆

Green Lake Hotel, 6 South Cuihu Road. Tel: 5157867, Fax: 5157867, Tlx: 64073 GLHTL

Holiday Inn Kunming, 25 Dongfeng East Rd. Tel: 3165888, Fax: 3135189

King World Hotel, 28 Beijing Rd South. Tel: 3138888, Fax: 3131910, Tlx: 64143 KIWH

Kunming Hotel, 145 East Dongfeng Rd. Tel: 3162063, Fax: 3138220, Tlx: 64149

☆☆☆

Golden Dragon Hotel, 575 Beijing Rd. Tel: 3133015, Fax: 3131082, Tlx: 64060 GHKM

☆☆

Camellia Hotel, 154 East Dongfeng Road. Tel: 3163000, Tlx: 64135 KMCH

Friendship Hotel, Renmin Dong Rd Kou. Tel: 3162286, Fax: 3132533

Golden Flower Hotel, 143 Huangcheng West Road. Tel: 5156900, Fax: 5156893, Tlx: 64020 JHHT

Golden Peacock Hotel, Right of Daguan Park. Tel: 4141334, Fax: 4141087, Tlx: 64017 GDHKM

Tea Gardens Hotel, Yongping Road. Tel: 3139208, Fax: 38313, Tlx: 64148 TGHTL

☆ rating not available for the following:
Begonia Hotel, End of Donghuan Rd. Tel: 3138749, Tlx: 64051

LANZHOU

☆☆

Friendship Hotel, 14 West Xijin Rd. Tel: 33051, Tlx: 72143 LFSHL

Lanhua Guest House, Welfare District, Xigu. Tel: 55981

Shengli Hotel, 127 Zhongshan Road. Tel: 465221, Fax: 461531

☆ rating not available for the following:
Jincheng Hotel, 363 Tian Shui Rd. Tel: 27931, Fax: 418438, Tlx: 72121 BTHHC

Lanzhou Hotel, 204 Donggang West Rd. Tel: 28321, Tlx: 72131 FANDN

Zhongchuan Airport Hotel, Zhongchuan Airport. Tel: 23415

LHASA

☆☆☆☆

Holiday Inn Lhasa Hotel, 1 Minzu. Tel: 22221, Fax: 35796, Tlx: 68010, 68011 HILSA

☆☆

Tibet Hotel, 221 Beijing West Rd. Tel: 33738, Fax: 36787, Tlx: 68013 TGSIH

LUOYANG

☆☆☆

Peony Hotel, 15 Zhong Zhou West Road. Tel: 413699, Fax: 413668, Tlx: 473047 LYPH

☆☆

Friendship Guest House, 6 Xiyuan Rd, Jianxi District. Tel: 412780, Fax: 413808, Tlx: 473041 LYFGH

Garden Hotel, Nanchang Rd. Tel: 221681

Orient Hotel, 182 Jianshe Rd. Tel: 221691, Fax: 413228

NANJING

☆☆☆☆

Jinling Hotel, Xin Jie Kou Square. Tel: 454888, Fax: 714695, Tlx: 34110 JLHNJ

Nanjing Central Grand Hotel, 75 Zhongshan Road. Tel: 400888, Fax: 414194, Tlx: 34083 VHNJ

☆☆☆

Ding Shan Hotel, 90 Chahaer Rd. Tel: 805931, Fax: 636929, Tlx: 34103 DSHNJ

Mandarin Chamber Hotel, 9 Zhuang Yuan Jing. Tel: 202555, Fax: 201876

Nanjing Hotel, 259 North Zhongshan Road. Tel: 302302, Fax: 306398, Tlx: 34102 NKHNK

Rainbow Hotel, 202 North Zhongshan Road. Tel: 301466, Fax: 635756, Tlx: 342203 HQHNJ

Shuangmenlou Hotel, 185 North Huju Road. Tel: 805961, Fax: 801421, Tlx: 34118 SMLNJ

Xuan Wu Hotel, 193 Zhongyang Road. Tel: 303888, Fax: 639624, Tlx: 34026

☆ rating not available for the following:
Grand Hotel, 208 Guangzhou Road. Tel: 311999, Fax: 315385

NANNING

☆ rating not available for the following:
Mingyuan Hotel, 59 Xinmin Rd. Tel: 28923, Fax: 28583, Tlx: 48143 MIYUH
Nanning Hotel, 38 Minsheng Rd. Tel: 21023
Xiyuan Hotel, 38 Jiang Nan Rd. Tel: 29923, Fax: 24864, Tlx: 48137 XIYUH
Yongjiang Hotel, 41 Jiangbin Rd. Tel: 23695, Fax: 20535, Tlx: 48151 YJHNG
Yongzhou Hotel, 59 Xinmin Rd. Tel: 202338, Fax: 225032, Tlx: 48145 GNYZH

QINGDAO

☆☆☆☆
Haitian Hotel, 39 Zhanshan Da Lu. Tel: 371888, Fax: 371777, Tlx: 321014 QDHTH CN
Huiquan Dynasty Hotel, 9 Nanhai Road. Tel: 279279, Fax: 279220, Tlx: 32178 HQDTY

☆☆☆
Huanghai Hotel, 75 The First Yanan Yi Rd. Tel: 270215, Fax: 279795, Tlx: 32151 BOOTH
Stone Cliffs Beach Hotel, Stone Old Man Tourism Dev District. Tel: 597888, Fax: 597052, Tlx: 32168 QSCBH

QUFU

☆☆☆
Que Li Hotel, 15 Zhong Lou St. Tel: 411300, Fax: 412002, Tlx: 3990044 BTHQS

☆☆
Xingtan Hotel, South Xue Quan Lu. Tel: 411420

QIQIHAR

☆☆
Crane City Hotel, 4 Wenhua Street. Tel: 472669, Fax: 475836, Tlx: 880006

☆
Longjiang Guest House, 57 Longhua Rd. Tel: 27981
Nenjiang Guest House, 7 Fengheng St. Tel: 72686

☆ rating not available for the following:
Hubin Hotel, 4 Wenhua Street. Tel: 472081, Tlx: 87125 QHRGL

QUANZHOU

☆☆☆
Quanzhou Hotel, 22 Zhuang Fu Rd. Tel: 229958, Fax: 212128
Zaitun Hotel, 1 Yinbin Rd, Donghu. Tel: 213248, Fax: 213028

☆ rating not available for the following:
Golden Fountain Hotel, Bai Yuan Rd. Tel: 225078, Fax: 224388, Tlx: 93083 CTSQZ
Overseas Chinese Hotel, Qingchi Xi, Baiyuan District. Tel: 22192, Fax: 23311

SHANGHAI

☆☆☆☆☆
Garden Hotel Shanghai, 58 Maoming Rd South. Tel: 433111, Fax: 4338866, Tlx: 30157 GHSH
Jin Jiang Tower, 161 Changle Rd. Tel: 4334488, Fax: 4333265, Tlx: 33652 FOJJT
Portman Shangri-La, 1376 Nanjing Road West. Tel: 2798888, Fax: 2798999, Tlx: 33272 PSH
Shanghai Hilton International, 250 Hua Shan Rd. Tel: 2480000, Fax: 2553848, Tlx: 33612 HILTL
Shanghai Jin Cang Mandarin, 1225 Nanjing Rd West. Tel: 2791888, Fax: 2791822, Tlx: 33939
Sheraton Huating Hotel, 1200 Caoxi Rd North. Tel: 4396000, Fax: 2550830, Tlx: 33589 SHHTH
Westin Tai Ping Yang Hotel, 5 Zun Yi Rd South. Tel: 2758888, Fax: 2757576, Tlx: 33345 PASHC

☆☆☆☆
Equatorial Hotel, 65 Yanan Road Rd West. Tel: 2791688, Fax: 2581773
Galaxy Hotel, 888 Zhang Shan Rd West. Tel: 2755888, Fax: 2750201, Tlx: 33176 SGHRD
Holiday Inn Yin Xing Shanghai, 388 Panyu Rd. Tel: 2528888, Fax: 2528545, Tlx: 30310 SFAC
Jinjiang Hotel, 59 Maoming Rd South. Tel: 2582582, Fax: 2155588, Tlx: 33380 GRJJH
Nikko Longbai Shanghai, 2451 Hongqiao Rd. Tel: 255911, Fax: 2559333, Tlx: 30138
Peace Hotel, 20 Nanjing Rd East. Tel: 3211244, Fax: 3290300, Tlx: 33914 BTHPH
Rainbow Hotel, 2000 Yanan Rd West. Tel: 275152, Fax: 2757244, Tlx: 30330 SRHF
Regal Shanghai (FT) Hotel, 1000, Qu Yang Rd. Tel: 5428000, Fax: 5448400
Yangtze New World Hotel, 2099 Yan'an Rd West. Tel: 2750000, Fax: 2750750, Tlx: 33675 YNWHR

☆☆☆
Baolong Hotel, 70 Yi Xian Rd. Tel: 5425425, Fax: 6632710, Tlx: 30908 BSFSC
Bao Shan Hotel, 2 Mudanjiang Rd, Baoshan. Tel: 6646944, Fax: 6601924, Tlx: 33901
City Hotel, 5-7 Shaanxi Rd South. Tel: 2551133, Fax: 2550611, Tlx: 33532 SYTS
Donghu Hotel, 70 Donghu Rd. Tel: 4370050, Fax: 4331275, Tlx: 33453 BTHDH
Hengshen Hotel, 534 Hengshen Rd. Tel: 4377050, Fax: 4335732, Tlx: 33933 SHS
Huaxia Hotel, 38 Cao Bao Rd. Tel: 4360100, Fax: 4333724, Tlx: 30345 HXH
Jianguo Hotel, 439 Caoxi Rd North. Tel: 4399299, Fax: 4398588
Jing'an Hotel, 370 Huashan Rd. Tel: 2551888, Fax: 2552657, Tlx: 30022 BTHJA

Jin Sha Hotel, 801 Jin Sha Jiang Rd. Tel: 2578888, Fax: 2574149, Tlx: 33454 BTHJD

Lantian Hotel, 2400 Siping Rd. Tel: 5485906, Fax: 5485931, Tlx: 33913 BTHLT

Longhua Hotel, 2787 Longhua Rd. Tel: 4399399, Fax: 4392964

Longmen Hotel, 777 Hengfeng Rd. Tel: 3170000, Fax: 3172004

Magnolia Hotel, 1251 Siping Rd. Tel: 5456888, Fax: 5459499, Tlx: 30331 MHP

New Asia Hotel, 422 Tiantong Rd. Tel: 3242210, Fax: 3269529, Tlx: 30034 SNA

New Garden Hotel, 1900 Hong Qiao Rd. Tel: 4329900, Fax: 2758374, Tlx: 33918 BTHNW

Novotel Shanghai Yuanlin, 201 Bai Se Road. Tel: 4701688, Fax: 4700008, Tlx: 33680 SYLHR

Ocean Hotel, 1171 Dong Da Ming Rd. Tel: 5458888, Fax: 5458993, Tlx: 30333 OCHTL

Park Hotel, 170 Nanjing Rd West. Tel: 3275225, Fax: 3276958, Tlx: 33932

Qianhe Hotel, 650 Yishan Rd. Tel: 4700000, Fax: 4700348

Qing Nian Hui Hotel, 123 Tibet Rd South. Tel: 3261040, Fax: 3201957, Tlx: 33920 QNHSH

Shanghai Hotel, 505 Wulumuqi Rd North. Tel: 4712712, Fax: 4331056, Tlx: 33295 SHR

Shanghai Huaqiao Hotel, 104 Nanjiang Rd West. Tel: 3276226, Fax: 3269620, Tlx: 33909 BTHH

Shanghai International Airport Hotel, 2550 Hongqiao Rd. Tel: 2558866, Fax: 2558393, Tlx: 30033 SIAHA

Shanghai Mansion, 20 Suzhou Rd North. Tel: 3246260, Fax: 3269778, Tlx: 33921 SMH

Shanghai Olympic Hotel, 1800 Zhongshan Rd South. Tel: 4391391, Fax: 4396295, Tlx: 33413 SSSC

Shanghai Pacific Hotel, 104 Nanjing Rd West. Tel: 3276226, Fax: 3269620, Tlx: 33909 BTHHF

Swan Cindic Hotel, 111 Jiang Wan Rd. Tel: 3255255, Fax: 3248002, Tlx: 30023 BTHSC

Tianma Hotel, 471 Wuzhong Rd. Tel: 2758100, Fax: 2757139, Tlx: 30901 BTHTM

Windsor Evergreen Hotel, 189 Bai Se Rd. Tel: 4700888, Fax: 4704832

☆☆

Yangzhi Hotel, 740 Hankou Road. Tel: 3207880, Tlx: 3206974

☆ rating not available for the following:

Cherry Holiday Villa, 77 Nonggong Road. Tel: 2758350, Fax: 2756457, Tlx: 33908 BTHYH

Cypress Hotel, 2419 Hongqiao Rd. Tel: 2558868, Fax: 2756739, Tlx: 33288 CYH

Da Hua Guest House, 914 Yanan Rd West. Tel: 2512512, Fax: 2512702, Tlx: 30029

Hongqiao Guest House, 1591 Hongqiao Rd. Tel: 4372170, Fax: 4372170, Tlx: 30024 BTHGH

Huating Guest House, 2525 Zhongshan Rd West. Tel: 4391818, Fax: 4390322, Tlx: 30192 HTGHS

Ruijin Guest House, 118 Ruijin Er Rd. Tel: 4331076, Fax: 4374861. Tlx: 33003 BTHRJ

Sofitel Hyland Hotel, 505 Nanjing Rd East. Tel: 3205888, Fax: 3205762, Tlx: 30386 SHLSO

SHANTOU

☆☆☆☆

Shantou International Hotel, Jinsha Rd. Tel: 251212, Fax: 252250, Tlx: 45475 STIH

☆☆☆

Longhu Hotel, Longhu Industrial District. Tel: 260706, Fax: 260708, Tlx: 45458 LHHTL

☆☆

Jinshan Hotel, Zhongduan, East Jinsha Road. Tel: 231700, Fax: 231267

☆ rating not available for the following:

Golden Gulf Hotel, Jinsha East Rd. Tel: 263263, Fax: 265163

Overseas Chinese Hotel, Shanzhang Rd. Tel: 319888-2003, Fax: 252649

SHENYANG

☆☆☆

Liaoning Hotel, 97 Zhongshan Road. Tel: 339104, Fax: 339103, Tlx: 80083 LNH

Phoenix Hotel, 109 South Huanghe Ave. Tel: 646501, Fax: 665207, Tlx: 80045 FHFD

Rose Hotel, 201 Zhongjie Road. Tel: 441001, Fax: 449546, Tlx: 80084 SHYRH

☆ rating not available for the following:

Liaoning Mansion, 105 South Huanghe St. Tel: 462536

Zhongshan Hotel, 65 Zhongshan Road. Tel: 333888, Fax: 339189, Tlx: 804088 SYZSB

SUZHOU

☆☆☆☆

Bamboo Grove Hotel, Zhu Hui Road. Tel: 225601, Fax: 238778, Tlx: 363073 BGHSZ

New World Aster, 156 San Xiang Road. Tel: 731888, Fax: 731838, Tlx: 363023 ASTER

☆☆☆

Nanlin Hotel, 20 Gun Xiu Fang. Tel: 222808, Fax: 231028, Tlx: 363063 NLHSZ

Nanyuan Guest House, 249 Shiquanjie. Tel: 227661, Fax: 238806

Suzhou Hotel, 115 Shiquan Street. Tel: 224646, Fax: 231015, Tlx: 363002 SZTLX

Xucheng Hotel, 120 Sanxiang Road. Tel: 334855, Fax: 731520, Tlx: 363037 XCHSZ

☆☆

Gusu Hotel, 5 Xiang Wang Road. Tel: 224689, Fax: 779227, Tlx: 34401 SZTLX

TAIYUAN

✩✩✩
Shanxi Grand Hotel, 5 South Xinjian Road. Tel: 443901, Fax: 443525, Tlx: 282037

✩✩
Bingzhou Hotel, 32 Yingze Ave. Tel: 442111, Tlx: 28125
Yingze Hotel, 51 Yingze Street. Tel: 443211, Fax: 442941-731

TIANJIN

✩✩✩✩
Crystal Palace Hotel, Youyi and Binshui Rds. Tel: 310567, Fax: 310591, Tlx: 23277 TCPH
Hyatt Tianjin Hotel, Jiefang Rd North. Tel: 318888, Fax: 310021, Tlx: 23270 HYTJN
Sheraton Tianjin Hotel, Zi Jin Shan Road, Hexi District. Tel: 343388, Fax: 358740, Tlx: 23353 SHTJH

✩✩✩
Astor Hotel, 33 Taierzhuang Rd. Tel: 311688, Fax: 316282, Tlx: 23266 ASHTL
Friendship Hotel, 94 Nanjing Rd. Tel: 310372, Fax: 310616, Tlx: 23264 FRHTL
Geneva Hotel, 32 Youyi Road, Hexi District. Tel: 342222, Fax: 349855, Tlx: 234075 TWTC
Tianjin View Hotel, 1 Zhabei Road, Donggu, Tanggu. Tel: 511301, Fax: 771322, Tlx: 23376
Victory Hotel, 11 Jintang Rd, Tanggu District. Tel: 985833, Fax: 984470, Tlx: 23375 TJVH

✩✩
Intertech Mansion, 25 Youyi Rd, Hexi District. Tel: 359115, Fax: 359391, Tlx: 23332 ISTCC

Star rating not available
Tianjian Grand Hotel, Binshui Dao, Hexi District. Tel: 359000, Fax: 359822, Tlx: 23276 TJHOT

TURFAN

✩✩
Turfan Oasis Hotel, 41 Qingnian Rd. Tel: 22491

✩
Turfan Hotel, Qingnian Rd. Tel: 22301

ÜRÜMQI

✩✩✩✩
Holiday Inn Ürümqi, 168 North Xinhua Rd. Tel: 218788, Fax: 217422, Tlx: 79161
Xinjiang Hotel World Plaza, 2 South Beijing Rd. Tel: 336360, Fax: 339007

✩✩
Friendship Hotel, 62 Yan'an Road. Tel: 264222, Fax: 264219

Kunlun Hotel, 38 North Youhao Rd. Tel: 412411, Fax: 412411-3302, Tlx: 79131
Overseas Chinese Hotel, 51 Xin Hua Rd South. Tel: 260845, Fax: 260622, Tlx: 79164

WUHAN

✩✩✩
Jianghan Hotel, 245 Shengli Jie, Hankou. Tel: 516076, Fax: 514342, Tlx: 40150
Lijiang Hotel, 1 Tiyuguan Road, Wuchang. Tel: 713668, Fax: 713638, Tlx: 400282
Qingchuan Hotel, 88 Ximachang St, Hangyang. Tel: 441141, Fax: 564964, Tlx: 40134 QCH
Xuangong Hotel, 57 Jianghan Yi Rd. Tel: 321023, Fax: 516942
Yangzi Hotel, 361 Jiefang Dadao, Hankou. Tel: 562828, Fax: 554110, Tlx: 40205 YGHTE

WUXI

✩✩✩✩
Wuxi Grand Hotel, 1 Liangqing Road. Tel: 606789, Fax: 200991, Tlx: 362055 WXGHL

✩✩✩
Hubin Hotel, Li Yuan, Hubin Rd. Tel: 601888, Fax: 602637, Tlx: 362002 WXHB
Milido Hotel, 2 Liangxi Road. Tel: 665665, Fax: 601668, Tlx: 362029 WMLD
Taihu Sunshine Hotel, Meiyuan. Tel: 607888, Fax: 602771, Tlx: 362012

✩✩
Shuixiu Hotel, Hubin Road. Tel: 601888, Fax: 602637, Tlx: 362002

✩ **rating not available for the following:**
Tiahu Hotel, Meiyuan. Tel: 607888, Fax: 602771, Tlx: 362012 WXTUH

XIAMEN

✩✩✩✩✩
Holiday Inn Crowne Plaza Harbourview Xiamen, No 12-8 Zhenhai Road. Tel: 223333, Fax: 236666, Tlx: 93138

✩✩✩✩
Xiamen Mandarin Hotel, Foreigners Residential Area, Huli. Tel: 623333, Fax: 621431, Tlx: 93028 MANDA
Xiamen Plaza Hotel, 908 Xiahe Road. Tel: 558888, Fax: 558899

✩✩✩
East Ocean Hotel, 1 Zhongshan Road. Tel: 221111, Fax: 233264, Tlx: 93164
Jinbao Hotel, 124-6 Dongdu Rd. Tel: 626888, Fax: 623122, Tlx: 93034 JINBO

Lujiang Hotel Xiamen, 54 Lujiang Rd. Tel: 222922, Fax: 224644, Tlx: 93024 LUTEL

Miramar Hotel, Xinglong Rd, Huli District. Tel: 631666, Fax: 621814

Overseas Chinese Building, 70-74 Xinhua Rd. Tel: 225602, Fax: 238236, Tlx: 93029 CTSXM

Xiamen Singapore Hotel, 113-121 Xi An Rd. Tel: 223973, Fax: 225950, Tlx: 93069 SINGA

Friend Hotel, Xiamen, Hu Bin S. Rd. Tel: 555888, Fax: 557335, Tlx: 93175 UFHXM

Xiamen Xindeco Hotel, Xinglong Rd, Huli. Tel: 621666, Fax: 621814, Tlx: 93027 INFRM

Xin Qiao Hotel, 444 Zhong Shan Rd. Tel: 238883, Fax: 238765, Tlx: 93166 XMXQH

☆☆

Jimei Hotel, 174 Yinjiang Road, Jimei. Tel: 668560, Fax: 668279

Xiamen Aviation Hotel, 5 South Rd, Lianhua New Village. Tel: 554888, Fax: 553774, Tlx: 93096 XAHCL

☆ **rating not available for the following:**
Gulang Hotel, 24 Gu Sheng Rd, Gulangyu. Tel: 225280, Fax: 230165

Jinghua Hotel, Shuanghan. Tel: 554471, Fax: 554481

Seaview Garden Tourist Village Gulangyu Xiamen, 8 Taiwan Rd, Gulangyu. Tel: 269519, Fax: 26950

Xiamen Hotel, 16 Huyuan Rd. Tel: 225275, Fax: 221765, Tlx: 93065 GUEST

XI'AN

☆☆☆☆☆
Sheraton Xi'an, 12 Feng Gao Rd, West Suburb. Tel: 741888, Fax: 742983, Tlx: 70032 GAHL

☆☆☆☆
Dynasty Hotel, 55 Huanchengxi Rd North. Tel: 712718, Fax: 712728, Tlx: 700233 DHX

Grand New World Hotel, 48 Lian Hu Rd. Tel: 716868, Fax: 719754, Tlx: 700215

Holiday Inn Xi'an, 8 South Sec, Huancheng East Rd. Tel: 333888, Fax: 335962, Tlx: 70043

Hyatt Regency Xi'an, 158 Dongda St. Tel: 712020, Fax: 716799, Tlx: 70048 AFPH

Shangri-La Golden Flower, 8 Chang Le Rd West. Tel: 332981, Fax: 335477, Tlx: 70145 GFH

Xi'an Garden Hotel, 4 Dongyanyin Rd, Dayanta. Tel: 75111, Fax: 751998, Tlx: 70027 GAHTL

☆☆☆
Bell Tower Hotel, South West Corner of Bell Tower. Tel: 779200, Fax: 718767, Tlx: 70195

China Merchants Hotel, 131 Heping Rd. Tel: 718988

Empress Hotel, 45 Xing Qing Rd. Tel: 331229, Fax: 714152, Tlx: 70148 CTSSP

Jiangou Hotel, 20 South Jin Hua Rd. Tel: 338888, Fax: 335145, Tlx: 700209

New World Hotel, 5 Nan Da St. Tel: 719988, Fax: 716688, Tlx: 70042 NWH

Orient Hotel, Xiaozhai West Rd. Tel: 752242, Fax: 751768, Tlx: 700228

People's Hotel (Renmin Dasha), 319 Dongxin Rd. Tel: 715191, Fax: 718152, Tlx: 70176 RMHTA

Tangcheng Hotel, 3 South Lingyuan Rd South. Tel: 55920, Fax: 751164, Tlx: 70013 TCH

Wan Nian Hotel, 11B Chang Le Rd Central. Tel: 331932, Fax: 335460, Tlx: 70033 XWNH

Xi'an Hotel, 36 North Section, Changan Rd. Tel: 751351, Fax: 751796, Tlx: 70135 XAHTL

☆ **rating not available for the following:**
Concord Hotel, 28 East Fenggao Road. Tel: 742811, Fax: 741939, Tlx: 70024

JZ Regency Hotel Xi'an, 15 Changle Middle Rd. Tel: 332009, Fax: 332180

Royal Xi'an, 334 Main Street East. Tel: 710305, Fax: 710798

Scarlet Peacock Hotel, 26 West Xiao Zhai Rd. Tel: 53311, Fax: 711590, Tlx: 70186 TSBHL

Shaanxi Guest House, Zhang Ba Gou. Tel: 713831, Fax: 713834, Tlx: 70181 SXHTA

Xi'an Lee Gardens Hotel, 8 Loadong South Rd. Tel: 743388, Fax: 743288

XIGAZE

☆☆
Jiangzi Hotel, Gyange, Gyange County. Tel: 356

Xigaze Hotel, Xinjie. Tel: 2530

XINING

☆☆
Xining Hotel, 215 Qiyi Rd. Tel: 45901

☆ **rating not available for the following:**
Qinghai Guest House, 20 Huanghe Road. Tel: 44365, Fax: 44145

ZHENGZHOU

☆☆☆
Dukang Hotel, 178 Tongbai Road. Tel: 776888, Fax: 775371, Tlx: 460124

International Hotel, 114 East Jinshui Rd. Tel: 556600, Fax: 551526, Tlx: 46061 HNZIH

☆☆
Huanghe Hotel, 106 Zhongyuan Road. Tel: 771006, Fax: 772235, Tlx: 46020

Zhengzhou Guest House, 115 Jin Shui Ave. Tel: 24255

GUESTHOUSES

Individual travellers may find accommodation in guest houses in smaller towns off the beaten tourist track. Guest houses usually have rooms with two or more beds, and often dormitories are available; there are usually shower and washing facilities as well. It is not always possible to have breakfast there. They are recommended as cheap accommodation for backpackers.

Some guest houses or simple hotels refuse to take foreign guests. This is usually because of the rules of the Chinese travel agency or the local security police, who decide which places may lodge foreigners.

OTHERS

It is practically impossible for foreigners in China to find accommodation outside of hotels and guest houses. Private lodgings are unknown because of the crowded living conditions. At times, some universities and institutes have guest houses where foreign visitors can find good and cheap accommodation. Advance booking is not possible. It helps to know the Chinese language.

If you are going on a long trip or on a hike in the countryside, for instance in Tibet or in the areas around the sacred mountains, you will come across various types of "long distance travellers lodgings". Often, you can spend the night in monasteries or temple halls. These very basic lodgings offer no luxuries, often no washing facilities as well, and it is advisable to carry a sleeping bag.

FOOD DIGEST

CHINESE CUISINE

Speaking of Chinese cuisine generally does not, of course, do justice to the great variety of Chinese food, its ingredients and different ways of preparing it. For most of us, our experience of Chinese restaurants in Europe has determined our ideas. The dishes on offer are mostly Cantonese, adapted to the taste and preference of the host country.

The main symbol of Chinese food is the use of chopsticks, which are practical because the food is cut into small pieces. This illustrates the common denominator of the different types of Chinese cuisine. Due to the short supply of fuel over the centuries, it has been necessary to prepare food using a minimum of fuel – consequently, ingredients are chopped into small pieces.

Only about 11 percent of the total land mass of China is suitable for agriculture. This explains why, for example, beef does not figure as large as in Europe. The need to cultivate intensively means cattle grazing is neither possible nor common, except

in the extreme north and northwest. Thus, until recently, milk and dairy products were not widely known, though yoghurt and other dairy products have come into fashion following Western examples. However, they are quite expensive in comparison with other Chinese products such as foodstuff made of soy bean which supply protein requirements.

The ingredients in Chinese meals are not all that different from ours, except that in China, everything from the animal is used and made palatable. Traditionally, food should not only fill you up but also have a healing effect. Such a combination is possible as some foods are considered to have healing powers. A Chinese meal is based on balance; at large banquets the individual courses should combine to harmonise and create a total balance.

There are roughly four main styles of Chinese cuisine (this does not take into account the often completely different cooking and eating traditions of the national minorities):

– The northern cuisine, with Beijing at the centre. The soil around Beijing is fairly poor, thus the food it produces is unvaried. In contrast to the south, where rice is preferred, noodles and pasta dishes predominate here. The main vegetable used is Chinese cabbage: boiled, steamed, fried, preserved, with a variety of different spices. A side dish, or breakfast, often consists of steamed or fried dough pieces, either plain or stuffed with sweet pudding, or meat and vegetables. Special mention should be made of Peking duck and the Mongolian hotpot – feasts which you shouldn't miss if you are in Beijing. The quality of Peking duck restaurants is variable, and it is definitely worth finding out about them first.

– In the eastern coastal areas around Shanghai, the predominant food is fish (particularly freshwater fish), and shellfish, though you should perhaps avoid the latter because of health risks. There is a greater choice of vegetables here than in the north.

– The southern cuisine around Guangzhou is probably the most varied. The Cantonese have a reputation for eating anything with four legs except the table, bed and chair. Here, even the most exotic gourmets can eat to their heart's content. The markets offer everything a Chinese palate desires; cats, monkeys and snakes are considered as delicacies. You can try all of them in one of the restaurants specialising in such foods.

– The cuisine of Sichuan province in mid-west China is famous for its highly spiced foods. Sichuan pepper, chilli and pepperoni ensure that the guest warms up even in the often humid and cold winters. The dish called *mapo doufu* comes from this province. It is a strongly spiced soy beancurd dish which you must try.

The food that is usually served in the hotels is only a weak reflection of the number of courses offered at a classic Chinese banquet. This includes platters of cold hors d'oeuvres, with pieces of meat and vegetables colourfully arranged. The main course, or rather courses, follow, consist of freshly cooked hot

OYSTER *GLX*

Samsonite*

Our Strengths Are Legendary*

*Trademarks of Samsonite Corporation

GlobalAccess

GlobalAccess means just what its name says: instant access to your money, wherever and whenever you need it. 24 hours a day. In over 60 countries around the world.

At HongkongBank's ATM network throughout Asia and the Middle East, you can conduct all your usual ATM transactions. You can also withdraw cash and make balance enquiries at Midland Bank ATMs in the UK, and Marine Midland Bank ATMs in the USA. Simply look for the GlobalAccess logo. And, of course, you can get cash from the Plus ATM network worldwide.

It's easy, it's instant and it's fast becoming indispensable for anyone who travels.

For more details on GlobalAccess contact your nearest HongkongBank office. Then you can keep in constant contact with your cash, no matter how far you are from home.

HongkongBank
The Hongkong and Shanghai Banking Corporation Limited

Our history could fill this book, but we prefer to fill glasses.

When you make a great beer, you don't have to make a great fuss.

dishes of various types of meat, chicken, duck and fish, which are placed on a round table. Your eyes are feasting as well because of the lovely presentation. Rice is served afterwards, and right at the end, a soup rounds off the meal. Desserts are not generally known in China. Sweets are often served in between courses to counteract a particularly spicy or sour dish.

The Chinese tend to eat quite early; lunch is often served in Chinese restaurants from 11am (the hotels and restaurants for foreigners have, of course, adjusted to the habits and sightseeing schedules of travel groups). In the evenings, you won't easily find any food after 8pm, though this is different in the south where social life continues until the late evening, as in Europe and US.

Chinese restaurants are usually quite reasonably priced and you should, from time to time, be brave and go out for a "real Chinese meal". Even if you can't read the menu, since it is written in Chinese, you can always point to the dishes on a neighbour's table to show what you would like.

Breakfast in hotels usually consists of coffee or tea, toast, eggs and jam. If you want to change your diet occasionally, you should order a Chinese breakfast. In the north, this consists of rice porridge with salted vegetables; in the south, breakfast is usually small snacks (*dianxin*).

WHERE TO EAT

Hotel restaurants in China are usually clean and serve relatively good food. These days, group travellers don't have their meals exclusively in hotel restaurants. They may be out sightseeing all day and have lunch while out; in the evening, they may eat at a restaurant which serves specialities.

Chinese meals are best eaten in a group, with each person taking their pick from a variety of dishes – Chinese restaurants are not well suited to individual diners. Costs may be as low as 10 to 20 yuan per person in restaurants along the street; or well over 100 yuan in better restaurants.

The individual traveller is more likely to have the opportunity of frequenting one of the typical Chinese restaurants at the roadside. While you may be attracted by the tasty food on offer, you should make sure the restaurant is clean and the food has been freshly prepared and is hot. Bringing your own chopsticks isn't seen as an insult at all. In addition to the large, state-owned restaurants, there are also many small, privately-run ones which give more attention to cleanliness, offer better services and good food.

One hint: Chinese restaurants are not heated even during the cold season, nor are theatres or concert halls, so it is advisable to dress warmly.

We have limited the list of restaurants to a few well-known ones in some towns, giving only an impression of the great variety of Chinese cuisine:

BEIJING

Cuihualou, 60 Wangfujing. Tel: 554581. Shandong cuisine
Donglaishun, 16 Jinyu Hutong (northern exit of Dongfeng market on Wangfujing). Tel: 550069. Muslim cuisine: Mongolian hotpot, Peking duck
Fanshan, Beihai Park. Tel: 4011889. Emperor's cuisine
Fengzeyuan, 11 Beili, Fengtaiqu. Tel: 7211331/6. Shandong cuisine
Hongbinlou, 82 Chang'an Jie. Tel: 657947. Lamb specialities, hotpot, Peking duck
Quanjude, 32 Qianmen Dajie. Tel: 5112418. Peking duck restaurant
Tingliguan, In the Summer Palace. Tel: 2581608. Emperor's cuisine

CHENGDU

Chengdu Restaurant, Chengli Zhonglu. Tel: 25338. Sichuan cuisine
Furong Restaurant, Southern part of Renmin Lu. Tel: 24004. Regional Sichuan cuisine
Shaanxi Huiguan, Shaanxi Lu.

GUANGZHOU

Banxi Jiujia, Xiangzang Yi L. Cantonese cuisine
Beiyuan Jiujia (North Garden), 439 Dongfeng Lu. Tel: 3333365
Datong Jiujia, 63 Yanjiang Lu. Tel: 8888988
Taotaoju, 288 Xiuli Yi Lu. Tel: 8816111

NANJING

Dasanyuan Jiujia, 38 Zhongshan Lu. Tel: 649027
Jiangsu Jiujia, 26 Jiankang Lu. Nanjing specialities
Liuhuachun Caiguan, 248 Shaoshan Lu. Shanghai cuisine
Qingzhen Maxianxing Caiguan, 5 Zhongshan Beilu. Nanjing specialities

SHANGHAI

Dongfeng Restaurant, 3 Zhongshan Lu. Suzhou and Cantonese cuisine
Gongdeling Sucaiguan, 43 Huanghe Lu. Tel: 3271532. Vegetarian specialities
Meilongzhen, 1081 Nanjing Xilu. Tel: 2551157. Yangzi cuisine, Sichuan cuisine
Shanghai Lao Fandian, Near Yuyuan garden. Tel: 3282782. Shanghai cuisine
Sichuan Fandian, 457 Nanjing Lu. Tel: 3222247. Spicy Sichuan cuisine
Yangzhou Restaurant, Nanjing Donglu. Yangzhou specialities

Bell Tower Dumpling Restaurant (Zhonglou Jiaozi Guan), Beidajie.

Wuyi Restaurant (Wuyi Fandian), Dongdajie.

Xi'an Restaurant, Dongdajie. Tel: 23821. Shanxi dishes

Yu Jiang Chun Restaurant, Jiefanglu. Dishes from the imperial court

DRINKING NOTES

As soon as you arrive at your hotel room you will notice thermos flasks with hot and cold water, and bags with green or black tea (called *hong* = red in Chinese). A cup of hot tea, or just "white tea" – hot water – as the Chinese usually drink it, is the most effective way of quenching your thirst. At mealtimes, Chinese beer, which contains less alcohol than European beer, mineral water or lemonade (often very sweet) are offered as well as green tea.

While you will hardly ever see an obviously drunk Chinese man on the streets (for women, drinking alcohol is still not acceptable), there is a surprisingly large choice of Chinese spirits on offer. The most famous are *maotai jiu*, a 55 percent spirit made of wheat and sorghum which for centuries has been produced in Maotai in Guizhou province, and *wuliangye jiu*, a spirit made from five different grains. You'll either take to it immediately or not at all. Chinese wine, both red and white, tend to be very sweet, tasting a bit like sherry. Wine for foreign tastes is also being produced now.

Things to Do

GROUP TRAVEL

The simplest and most comfortable way of travelling to China at a reasonable price is in a group. Participants will have their to and fro passage, their hotel accommodation and full board, and their sightseeing programme booked from Europe. There are hardly any additional costs apart from drinks and shopping. Sometimes, additional excursions may be on offer once you have arrived, but they are generally not too costly. At some places a charge is made for taking photographs.

The local courier is supplied by the Chinese tourist office and is in charge of taking you to the sights. A short introduction plus any additional information will usually be given on the tour.

There are now a lot of tour operators offering group travel. You should ensure that you book with a specialist. While almost all travel in China is handled by the headquarters of the Chinese state travel office, the specialists will have better knowledge of places of special interest when planning a particular route. Also, the pitfalls of a journey through China have increased rather than diminished in recent years; an experienced tour operator can avoid many difficulties.

Another decisive factor for a successful group trip is the courier. While each group with more than ten participants is allocated a permanent Chinese guide in addition to the local guides, their qualifications vary considerably, both in terms of organising the trip and in their knowledge of the country and its sights, and their ability to communicate. The importance of the courier employed by the tour operator shouldn't be underestimated.

A number of tour operaters now offer trips around a theme as well as the traditional routes. A few offer courses in shadow boxing, calligraphy or acupuncture; some even offer language courses.

INDIVIDUAL TRAVEL

There are three ways of travelling in China for the individual traveller. The most comfortable, and of course, most expensive way, is to book a full package tour through an experienced travel agent. Everything is pre-booked from Europe, including flights and journeys, accommodation, full board, transfers etc., with the difference that the traveller can choose a route according to their preference. The same is the case for sightseeing: a courier from a China travel agency is available in each town and will help with putting together and arranging a sightseeing programme. The traveller is completely taken care of.

The second possibility is booking a mini-package tour. The agent pre-books the flights, accommodation with breakfast, transfers and transport of luggage in China while the traveller is responsible for organising a programme of sightseeing. The traveller is met at the airport or railway station of each town and taken to the hotel. Each hotel has a travel agency counter where you can discuss your plans for sightseeing and have them arranged for a fee. You can usually have lunch and dinner at your hotel or maybe try a Chinese restaurant while out and about.

For the individual tourist, this way of travelling is the most pleasant. The most essential bookings have been made (to make them yourself requires a lot of time and strong nerves), and with thorough preparation, you have a good chance of getting to know China beyond the usual tourist routes. You should get a definite booking with an experienced travel agent three months before departure at the latest.

Then, there is also the completely independent travel, without any pre-booking from Europe. This form of travelling in China has increased in recent years. The Chinese travel bureaux have partially adapted to it and can help, in the large towns, with buying air and train tickets. You have to arrange your own air and train tickets at each place you visit; unless you speak Chinese, you will probably find it easiest to do this through a travel agency, where it is more likely you will find English-speaking staff. At airports and stations, you will often find that information about destinations is given in Pinyin, or sometimes only in Chinese characters. You shouldn't expect short term plans to come through; it can easily happen that you have to wait several days for your railway or air ticket or abandon your chosen destination and choose a different town for your next visit. You should try and reserve air or rail tickets as soon as you arrive. Tickets cost more for foreigners than for Chinese, and only in rare cases might you succeed (for instance if you have a student card) in getting a ticket at the cost that overseas Chinese pay.

Travel agencies will book hotels for a relatively small fee, though this is typically only the case with hotels in the more expensive range. It is best to approach cheaper hotels or guest houses directly; here, a knowledge of Chinese is an advantage.

TOUR OPERATORS

In tandem with China's opening to the rest of the world, the number of travel agencies had mushroomed. At the time of press, there were 160 category A, 676 category B and 1,240 category C travel agencies.

The category A travel agencies can both tout for business abroad and receive overseas tourists. Category B agencies can receive overseas tourists. Category C agencies are restricted to handling domestic tourists.

Prominent among the agencies is China International Travel Services (CITS), which formerly was virtually the sole agency handling overseas tourists. It now has many branches throughout China, which can operate independently.

China Travel Services (CTS) is a similar, parallel organisation, originally responsible for domestic tourists and overseas Chinese, but now also catering to overseas tourists.

Other agencies may be specialised – China Rail Express Travel Service arranges railway-linked tours, including the Chinese *Orient Express*, and Changjiang Cruise Overseas Travel Corporation specialises in Yangzi cruises. But agencies may operate tours that seem outside the spheres their names suggest – an advertisement for Fujian Youth Travel Service, from southeast China, includes a photograph of a mostly middle-aged group of Westerners at the Temple of Heaven in Beijing.

Agencies may also have business interests extending beyond simply arranging tours and bookings – for instance, they may own or partly own hotels.

An agency which arranges a tour for you may do so by contacting agencies in places you will visit, and asking them to deal with local bookings. This means that, if you go direct to an agency in the area you plan to visit (rather than, say, first approaching a travel agent in Europe or the US), you may well save money, yet receive the same service.

Also, there is competition between agencies; it may be worth contacting more than one agency, and checking the prices and services they offer. If possible, try to gauge the interests and abilities of agency staff; just one or two enthusiastic and capable tour organisers/guides can be a boon to your travels.

Sometimes, agencies such as CITS may hold tickets for rail journeys, operas, acrobatic performances and concerts even when they are sold out at the stations or venues.

There are also small-scale unlicensed tour operators. Reportedly, some of these use unroadworthy vehicles, take their customers to shops and restaurants that give the guides 'backhanders' (though perhaps this can also happen with licensed operators), and demand markups of 100 percent or more for tickets to tourist sites. Others may be trustworthy, and cheap.

National Travel Agencies

China Civil International Tourist Corp, Jingdo Hotel, Beijing, Worker's Stadium, Beijing 100027. Tel: 5018869, Fax: 5018870, Tlx: 210673 CCT
China Comfort Travel Head Office, 57 Di'anmen-Xi Dajie, Beijing 100009. Tel: 6035423/6016288; Fax: 6016336, Tlx: 222862 KHT
China Cultural Tours Inc, 1 Tiyuguan Rd, Chongwen District, Beijing 100061. Tel: 7013887, Fax: 7013884, Tlx: 22013
China Everbright Travel Inc, 9/F East Bldg, Beijing Hotel, 33 Chang'an Avenue East, Beijing 100004. Tel: 5137766-9022, Fax: 5120545, Tlx: 222285 CETI
China Golden Bridge Travel Service Corp Head Office, 171A Di'anmen Street West, Beijing 100035. Tel: 6015933, Fax: 2018939/6032628, Tlx: 222367 CGBT
China Goodwill Travel Service, Rm 20116, Bldg No. 2, Friendship Hotel, 3 Baishiqiao, Beijing 100873. Tel: 8499135/849888-20116, Fax: 8498388, Tlx: 222869 CGTS
China International Sports Travel Co, 4 Tiyuguan Rd, Chongwen District, Beijing 100061. Tel: 7017364, Fax: 7017370, Tlx: 222283 CIST
China International Travel Service Head Office, 103 Fuxingmen-Nei St, Beijing 100800. Tel: 6012055/6011122, Fax: 5122068/6012013, Tlx: 22350 CITSH
China M&R Special Tours, A7 Bei-Sanhuan Road West, Beijing 100088. Tel: 2026611-4166/2022399, Fax: 2010865/2010802, Tlx: 222880
China Merchants International Travel Corp, Tiandi Building, 14 Dongzhimen-Nan Street, Beijing 100027. Tel: 5019198/5062228, Fax: 5011308, Tlx: 210390 CMITC
China Nation Travel Service, 51 Fuxingmen-Nei Street, Beijing 100046. Tel: 6014466-2190, Fax: 6023906

China Rail Express Travel Service, Blk 3, Multiple Service Bldg, Beifengwo Rd, Haidian District, Beijing 100038. Tel: 3246645, Fax: 3261824, Tlx: 222224 YTSRB

China Rainbow Travel Service, 5-A Agricultural Exhibition Rd North, Chaoyang District, Beijing 100026. Tel: 5017901, Fax: 5017901, Tlx: 211177 YAAH

China Supreme Harmony Travel Servcie, Rm 944, Media Hotel, B-11 Fuxing Rd, Beijing 100859. Tel: 8014422-3944, Fax: 8016218

China Swan International Tours Inc, Rm 2018-2020 East Building, Beijing Hotel, Beijing 100004. Tel: 5137766-2020, Fax: 5138487, Tlx: 222517 CSIT

China Travel Service Head Office, 8 Dongjiaominxiang, Beijing 100005. Tel: 5129933-216, Fax: 5129008, Tlx: 22487 CTSHO

China Women's Travel Service, 103 Dongsi-Nan St, Beijing 100010. Tel: 553307/5136311, Fax: 5129021, Tlx: 21160 CWTS

China Workers' Travel Service Head Office, 1 Ritan Rd, Chaoyang District, Beijing 100020. Tel: 5128657/5128379, Fax: 5128680, Tlx: 211129 RTH

China Youth Travel Service Head Office, 23B Dongjiaominxiang, Beijing 100006. Tel: 5127770, Fax: 5120571/5138691, Tlx: 20024 CYTS

CITIC Travel Inc, 19 Jianguomen-Wei Dajie, Beijing 100004. Tel: 5005920, Fax: 51275144, Tlx: 22967 CTI

National Tourism Administration of the People's Republic of China, 9A Jianguomennei Ave. Tel: 5138866, Fax: 5122096

Category A Travel Agencies in Provinces and Directly Administered Cities

The following abbreviations are used:
CITS – China International Travel Service
CTS – China Travel Service
OTC – Overseas Tourist Corporation

BEIJING

Beijing CTS, Beijing Tourism Building, No. 28 Jianguomen-Wai St. Tel: 5158844-2802, Fax: 5158557, Tlx: 22032 BCTS

Beijing Divine Land Travel Service, 19 Xinyuan Nan Rd, Dongzhimen-Wai. Tel: 4677619/4666887, Fax: 4677307, Tlx: 210347 DLTS

Beijing OTC, 6/F Beijing Tourist Building, 28 Jianguomen-Wai St. Tel: 5158262, Fax: 5158381, Tlx: 20052 BOTC

Beijing Travel Service, 13 Xiagongfu. Tel: 5122441/5124306, Fax: 5122219, Tlx: 211168 BTS

Beijing Xinhua Tours Corp, A23 Fuxing Rd. Tel: 8214880, Fax: 8214880/8213066

Beijing Youth Travel Service, Building 3, 96 Andingmen-nei St, Dongcheng District. Tel: 4033521, Fax: 4033560, Tlx: 210098 BYTS

CITS Beijing, 28 Jianguomen-Wai St. Tel: 5158562, Fax: 5158602, Tlx: 22047 CITSB

China Peace International Travel Corp, 14/F Yatai Dasha, 8 Yabao Rd. Tel: 5122504, Fax: 5125860, Tlx: 222354 CLTI

Huayuan International Travel Service Beijing, Huitongci, Deshengmen Street West. Tel: 6014841, Fax: 6014154, Tlx: 222872 HYITS

New Ark Travel Service, 3 Zaoying Rd, Chaoyang District. Tel: 5004385, Fax: 5004118, Tlx: 211229 BNATS

North Star International Tourist Corp, 10 Third Block, Anhuili, Chaoyang District. Tel: 4910682/4910683, Fax: 4910684/4910691, Tlx: 210303 NSITC

FUJIAN

CITS Fujian, 44 Dongda Rd, Fuzhou. Tel: 555506, Fax: 537447, Tlx: 92201 CITSF

CTS Fujian, May 4th Rd, Fuzhou. Tel: 556304/539202, Fax: 553983, Tlx: 92123 FJKTS

CTS Xiamen, 70-74 Xinhua Rd, Xiamen. Tel: 225602/225701, Fax: 31862, Tlx: 93029 CTSXM

China Youth Travel Service Fujian Branch, 20/F International Mansion, Wusi Rd, Fuzhou. Tel: 810001/810011, Fax: 810021/810022, Tlx: 92254 FCYTS

China Youth Travel Service Xiamen, 65 Bailu Rd, Xiamen. Tel: 253188, Fax: 220024, Tlx: 93077 XCYTS

Fujian Overseas Tourist Enterprises Co, 44 Dongda Rd, Fuzhou. Tel: 550111, Fax: 523456, Tlx: 02131 FCITS

Xiamen CITS, Zhenxing Bldg, North Hubin Rd, Xiamen. Tel: 551822, Fax: 551819, Tlx: 93148

Xiamen OTC, Dong Yuan Estate, Dongdu Rd, Xiamen. Tel: 630750-755, Tlx: 93179 XMOTC

GANSU

Gansu OTC, 361 Tianshui Rd, Lanzhou. Tel: 25374, Fax: 418442, Tlx: 72160 GSOTC

GUANGDONG

China Comfort Guangdong Travel Service, 3/F, 367 Huanshi Rd East, Guangzhou. Tel: 3333998, Fax: 3351341

China Comfort Shantou Travel Service, 52 Changping Rd, Shantou. Tel: 240231, Fax: 230230

CITS Guangdong, 179 Huanshi Rd, Guangzhou. Tel: 6677271/6671453, Fax: 6678048, Tlx: 44450 CITS

Dongfang Tourist Company Guangzhou, Room 2266, Dongfang Hotel, Liuhua Rd, Guangzhou. Tel: 6669900-2266/6661646, Fax: 6669900-2200, Tlx: 44439-2266

Guangdong CTS, 10 Qiaoguang Rd, Guangzhou. Tel: 3336888, Fax: 3332247, Tlx: 44217 CTS

Guangdong China Youth Travel Service, 3rd Floor, 509 Huanshi Rd East, Guangzhou. Tel: 7760105/773471/7781645, Fax: 7765112, Tlx: 44302 CYTS

Guangdong Railway China Youth Travel Service, 69 Dadao Rd, Dongshan, Guangzhou. Tel: 7752407, Fax: 7762509, Tlx: 44761
Guangzhou Tourist Corp, 155(4), Huanshi Rd West, Guangzhou. Tel: 6665182, Fax: 6677563, Tlx: 44575 GTC
Guangdong OTC, 179 Huanshi Rd, Guangzhou. Tel: 6668856, Tlx: 6668859
Shantou Tourist Corp, 136 Yuejin Rd, Shantou. Tel: 293555, Fax: 293678

GUANGXI

CITS Guilin, 14 North Ronghu Rd, Guilin. Tel: 224833, Fax: 222936/227205, Tlx: 48460 GLITS
Guangxi China Youth Travel Service, 10 Yucai Rd, Guilin. Tel: 442115/442336, Fax: 443974, Tlx: 48468 GLYTS
Guangxi Tourist Corp, 40 Xinmin Rd, Nanning. Tel: 202042, Fax: 204105, Tlx: 48142 CITSN
Guilin OTC, 8 Zhishan Rd, Guilin. Tel: 334999, Fax: 335395, Tlx: 48463 GLTRA

HEBEI

CITS Chengde, 6 Nanyuan Rd East, Chengde. Tel: 226827, Fax: 227484, Tlx: 27720 BSSZT

HEILONGJIANG

CITS Heilingjiang, 73 Zhongshan Rd, Harbin. Tel: 222476, Fax: 222476, Tlx: 87034 HCITS
Harbin OTC, 129 Zhongyang Avenue, Daoli District, Harbin. Tel: 414259, Fax: 414259, Tlx: 87028
Heilongjiang OTC, 124 Dazhi St, Harbin. Tel: 342671, Fax: 321088, Tlx: 87187 OTC

HENAN

CITS Henan, 15 Jinshui Rd, Zhengzhou. Tel: 552072, Fax: 557705, Tlx: 46041 CITSZ
CITS Louyang, 6 Xiyuan Rd, Louyang. Tel: 413701, Fax: 412200, Tlx: 473011
Henan Tourist Corp, 16 Jinshuihe Rd, Zhengzhou. Tel: 226637, Fax: 552273

HUBEI

Changjiang Cruise Overseas Travel Corp, 89 Yanjiang Ave, Wuhan. Tel: 216412, Fax: 211049, Tlx: 40132 HBICB
Hubei OTC, 48 Jianghan Yilu, Wuhan. Tel: 235018, Fax: 211891, Tlx: 40211 CITWH
Wuhan OTC, 332 Jeifang Rd, Wuhan. Tel: 556473, Fax: 554601, Tlx: 400262

INNER MONGOLIA

CITS Inner Mongolia, Inner Mongolia Hotel, Hohhot. Tel: 24494, Fax: 661479

Inner Mongolia OTC, Inner Mongolia Hotel Office Building, Hohhot. Tel: 26774, Fax: 667924, Tlx: 85054 OTCIM

JIANGSU

CITS Wuxi, 7 Xinsheng Rd, Wuxi. Tel: 200416, Fax: 201489, Tlx: 362025 WCITS
Jiangsu CTS, 313 North Zhongshan Rd, Nanjing. Tel: 801502, Fax: 801533, Tlx: 34051 CTSJS
Jiangsu OTC, 255 North Zhongshan Rd, Nanjing. Tel: 342328, Fax: 306002, Tlx: 34119 JTTBN
Nanjing CITS, 202-1 North Zhongshan Rd, Nanjing. Tel: 341980, Fax: 308954, Tlx: 34024 ITSNJ
Nanjing OTC, 5/F Zhongshan Hotel, 200 Zhongshan Rd, Nanjing. Tel: 362959, Fax: 714353, Tlx: 342228 JSBNJ
Suzhou CITS, 115 Shiquan St, Suzhou. Tel: 223063, Fax: 23593, Tlx: 363028 ITSSU
Suzhou CTS, 115 Shiquan St, Suzhou. Tel: 221918, Fax: 225931, Tlx: 363065 CTSSZ
Suzhou OTC, 115 Shiquan St, Suzhou. Tel: 226280, Fax: 235535, Tlx: 363028 ITCSU
Wuxi CTS, 59 Chezhan Rd, Wuxi. Tel: 207584, Fax: 202743
Wuxi OTC, 7 Xinsheng Rd, Wuxi. Tel: 204134, Fax: 203851, Tlx: 362025 WCITS

JILIN

Changchun OTC, 45 Jiefang Rd, Changchun. Tel: 845610, Fax: 845608
CITS Jilin City, 4 Jiangwan Rd, Jilin City. Tel: 459204, Fax: 453773
CITS Jilin Province, 10A Xinmin St, Changchun. Tel: 642401, Fax: 645069, Tlx: 83085 CITSC
Jilin OTC, 6F, 10A Xinmin St, Changchun. Tel: 646800, Fax: 642419, Tlx: 83028 CITSC

LIAONING

CITS Dalian, 1 Changtong St, Dalian. Tel: 337956, Fax: 337631, Tlx: 86485 DCITS
CITS Liaoning, 113 South Huanghe St, Shenyang. Tel: 646037, Fax: 64772/654833
Dalian OTC, 1 Changtong St, Xigang Dist, Dalian. Tel: 339859/331080, Fax: 337831, Tlx: 86460 OTCDL
Liaoning OTC, 1 Huanghe St North, Shenyang. Tel: 600276, Fax: 600897, Tlx: 804065 LNTB
Shenyang OTC, 8 Bei-Erjing St, Shenhe District, Shenyang. Tel: 729979/220286, Fax: 729737, Tlx: 80132 SYTTA

NINGXIA

Ningxia OTC, 117 West Jiefang Rd, Yinchuan. Tel: 41783, Fax: 41783, Tlx: 750010 BOTY

Qinghai Tourist Corp, 215 Qiyi, Xining. Tel: 45901-1307, Fax: 42721, Tlx: 77

China Comfort Travel Xian, Tancheng Hotel, Xian. Tel: 55550, Fax: 751507, Tlx: 70049 XAKHT
CITS Xian, 32 Chang'an Rd (N), Xian. Tel: 752066, Fax: 751558, Tlx: 70115 CITSX
CTS Shaanxi, 272 Jiefang Rd, Xian. Tel: 712658, Fax: 714152, Tlx: 70148
Xian OTC, 158 East Youyi Rd, Xian. Tel: 754547, Fax: 751530, Tlx: 700210 OTCXA
Shaanxi OTC, 15 North Chang'an Rd, Xian. Tel: 751516, Fax: 751660, Tlx: 700201 OTCSX

CITS Shandong, 86 Jingshi Rd, Jinan. Tel: 265858, Fax: 266210, Tlx: 390001 CITSJ
CITS Taishan, 46 Hongmen Rd, Tai'an. Tel: 333259, Fax: 332240, Tlx: 397005 STSGTA
Jinan OTC, 137 Jingqi–Weisi Rd, Jinan. Tel: 612804, Fax: 611037, Tlx: 39123 OBCJN
Qingdao OTC, 9 Nanhai Rd, Qingdao. Tel: 270830, Fax: 270983, Tlx: 32202 QCITS
Shandong Tourist Corp, 86 Jingshi Rd, Jinan. Tel: 265858, Fax: 265870, Tlx: 39144 SDTJN

China Comfort Travel Shanghai Branch, 15/F Chang'an Mansion, 100 Chang'an Rd. Tel: 3174049, Fax: 3174751
CITS Shanghai, 33 Zhongshan Rd E1. Tel: 3217200, Fax: (021) 3291788, Tlx: 33277 SCITS
China Merchants International Travel Co Shanghai, 277 Wuxing Rd. Tel: 4317100, Fax: 4316992, Tlx: 30362 SCMIT
Oriental International Travel & Transport Corp Ltd, 549 Shaanxi Rd (N). Tel: 2477972, Fax: 2470585, Tlx: 33646 OITT
Shanghai CTS, 881 Yan'an Rd (M). Tel: 2478888, Fax: 2475521, Tlx: 33301 COTOS
Shanghai China Youth Travel Service, 2 Hengsan Rd. Tel: 4331826, Fax: 4330507, Tlx: 30241 CYTS
Shanghai Crane International Tours Inc, Nanying Hotel, 1720 Huaihai Rd (M). Tel: 4333375, Fax: 4338409, Tlx: 33536 SAL
Shanghai Great World International Travel Service, 220 Xizang-Zhong Rd. Tel: 3204293, Fax: 3224210, Tlx: 30320
Shanghai Huating OTC, 505 Ürümqi Rd (N). Tel: 4712322, Fax: 4375470
Shanghai Jinjiang Tours, 27/F, 100 Yan'an Rd East. Tel: 3262910, Fax: 3200595, Tlx: 33429 SJJTC
Shanghai Spring International Travel Service, No. 2027 Yan'an Rd (W). Tel: 2517777, Fax: 2518617, Tlx: 30307 SSST

Shanghai Tourist Corp, 33 Zhongshan Rd E1. Tel: 3217200, Fax: 3291949, Tlx: 33411 SCITS
Shanghai Workers' International Travel Service, 60 Huangpu Rd. Tel: 3247724, Fax: 3243282, Tlx: 33603 SISC

Shanxi OTC, 6 Pingyang Rd, Taiyuan. Tel: 441155, Fax: 441155

Chengdu OTC, 45 Shang Xishuncheng St, Chengdu. Tel: 662399, Fax: 660617, Tlx: 600098 OTCCD
Chongqing OTC, 175 Renmin Road, Chongqing. Tel: 350806, Fax: 350095, Tlx: 62126 CCITS
Sichuan CTS, 31 Zongfu St, Chengdu 610016. Tel: 677473, Fax: 660957
Sichuan OTC, 19 Sec 2, South Renmin Rd, Chengdu. Tel: 672369, Fax: 672970, Tlx: 600085 OTCSC

Tianjin OTC, 22 Youyi Rd, Hexi District. Tel: 380821, Fax: 312619, Tlx: 23281 TJITS

Tibet Tourist Corp, 208 Beijing Rd West, Lhasa. Tel: 26315, Fax: 26315

CITS Kashgar, 93 Seman Rd, Kashgar. Tel: 23156, Fax: 23087, Tlx: 79051 CITS
CITS Ürümqi, 51 Xinhua Rd North, Ürümqi. Tel: 221427, Fax: 210689, Tlx: 79108 CITSW
CTS Xinjiang, 51 South Xinhua Rd, Ürümqi. Tel: 261970, Fax: 262131
China Youth Travel Service Xinjiang, 9 Jianshe Rd, Ürümqi. Tel: 227172, Fax: 217078, Tlx: 79023 CYTSX
Xinjiang Ili Travel Service, 63 Jiefang Rd, Yining. Tel: 20042, Fax: 24939, Tlx: 79171 YLTS
Xinjiang Nature Travel Service, 64 Dongfeng Rd, Ürümqi. Tel: 227791, Fax: 217174, Tlx: 79049 XJTCA
Xinjiang OTC, 51 North Xinhua Rd, Ürümqi. Tel: 225913, Fax: 218691, Tlx: 79108 OTCXJ

Yunnan OTC, 154 East Dongfeng Rd, Kunming. Tel: 3163018, Fax: 3132508, Tlx: 64135 KMCH
CITS Kunming, 218 Huancheng Rd South, Kunming. Tel: 3132594, Fax: 3169240, Tlx: 64027

China Hangzhou West Lake, 220 Yan'an Rd, Hangzhou. Tel: 571962, Fax: 555585

CITS Zhejiang, 1 Shihan Rd, Hangzhou. Tel: 552888, Fax: 556667, Tlx: 351110

China Youth Travel Service Zhejiang, 32 Wen Er Rd, Hangzhou. Tel: 871212, Fax: 877326, Tlx: 351097 ZYTS

Hangzhou Overseas Tourist Corp, 8/F Hangzhou Tower, 1 Wulin Square, Hangzhou. Tel: 573888, Fax: 574393, Tlx: 351039 CHTS

Ningbo OTC, Lane 3-5, Xinchangchun Rd, Ningbo. Tel: 364451, Fax: 364481

Zhejiang CTS, 215 Fengqi Rd, Hangzhou. Tel: 557479, Fax: 556746, Tlx: 351033 CTSZJ

Zhejiang OTC, 2 Huanchengxilu. Tel: 771501, Fax: 722837, Tlx: 35031 HZT

TOUR GUIDES

Each travel agency has a number of guides who accompany a group or are responsible for looking after a group locally. Each group with at least ten members has a permanent courier allocated to it who is responsible for the well-being of the visitors throughout the journey, and for arranging the various connections – not an easy task in China today. The local couriers are responsible for arranging the sightseeing programme in the place where the group is staying, ensuring accommodation, board, and other items. Obviously, the qualifications of the couriers vary considerably. They have generally been trained at a foreign language institute which sometimes also has a department of tourism, and they will have a good knowledge of the language the group speaks. But Chinese students still only rarely ever have a choice over the profession they want to follow, which of course has an effect on motivation and initiative. But you will frequently come across guides who enjoy showing their country to visitors and are constantly trying to improve their foreign language skills.

CULTURE PLUS

MUSEUMS

There are a great variety of museums in China. From the revolution to Natural History, everything is captured in exhibitions at various places. Many Chinese museums are not very well administered and not easy for the visitor to appreciate. Recommended below are mainly museums in the field of art and culture which are really worth visiting. Opening hours are usually between 9am and 5pm.

BEIJING

Museum of Chinese History (Zhongguo Lishi Bowuguan), Tiananmen Square. Tel: 558321. On Tiananmen Square. It is one of the most comprehensive and best museums in China covering the entire Chinese history.

Military Museum, Fuxingmenwai Dajie. Tel: 8014441

Museum of the Revolution (Zhongguo Geming Bowuguan), Tiananmen Square. Tel: 558321

Palace Museum in the Imperial Palace (Gugong Bowuguan). Tel: 5132255. The Imperial Palace is one huge museum; occasionally it has special exhibitions.

Lu Xun Museum, Fuchengmennei Dajie. Tel: 6037617

Xu Beihong Memorial Hall, Xinjiekou Beidajie. Tel: 661592

Museum of Chinese Art (Beijing Meishu Zhanlanguan), 1 Wusi Dajie, Chaoyangmennei. Tel: 4017076

The Beijing Agricultural Exhibition Hall (Nongye Zhanlanguan), Sanlitun. Tel: 582331

CHANGSHA

Hunan Provincial Museum. The museum contains mainly objects which were discovered in a Han tomb near Man-wangdui, ½ miles (3km) east of the museum. They include the perfectly preserved corpse of a 50-year-old woman.

LANZHOU

Gansu Provincial Museum (Gansu Sheng Bowuguan), The museum, which unfortunately is badly kept, has many beautiful neolithic pots and sacrificial jars from the Zhou period as well as the "Flying Horse of Gansu".

NANJING

Nanjing Museum. 321, Zhongshan Donglu. The most precious exhibit, in addition to pottery, porcelain (including some from the Ming Dynasty), bronzes, tortoise shells and jewellery from various dynasties, is a 2,000-year-old shroud made of 26,000 jade pieces.

SHANGHAI

Shanghai Museum of Art (Yan'an Lu). West of Xizang Lu. It houses one of the best collections of Chinese art history. It has bronzes, pottery, stone figures, weapons as well as an excellent collection of Chinese painting from the Tang dynasty to the end of the Qing dynasty.

ÜRÜMQI

Xinjiang Provincial Museum (Xinjiang Bowuguan). It contains an archaeological exhibition about the Silk Road as well as an exhibition about the minorities in Xinjiang.

WUHAN

Hubei Provincial Museum. It is located on the western shore of Lake Donghu and has finds from a tomb of a prince from the 5th century BC. They include unique bronze chimes with 65 well perserved bronze bells which can still be sounded. Other bronzes and musical instruments were also found in the tomb.

XI'AN

Shaanxi Provincial Museum. The museum is located in the former Confucian temple found in the south of the town. It has three departments: the history of Xi'an and its surroundings to the end of the Tang Dynasty, Stele forest, and stone sculptures. It also regularly holds special exhibitions.
Museum of the Terracotta Soldiers of the First Qin Emperor. In Lintong county near the tomb of Emperor Qin Shi Huangdi.

CONCERTS

There are regular concerts of Western classical or traditional Chinese music in various cities. Indigenous or foreign songs and musical performances are often part of the programme. Dance performances are also common. In many areas – particularly in those of the national minorities – you can admire performances of local dances and songs on the stage. Ballet is also performed. Young people – though not only them – are very keen on concerts by various pop stars, whether from the PR of China, Hong Kong or even Taiwan. You can find out about time and place of performances in each town from the hotel or through travel agencies.

OPERAS

There are more than 300 types of opera in China. You can attend performances of traditional opera in virtually every town. The most famous one is the Beijing Opera. The address of the opera and theatre is available from the hotel or from travel agencies. A visit to the Chinese opera is a relaxed affair and occasionally quite noisy. You can leave your evening dress and tie at home; normal day clothes are fine.

THEATRES

The spoken theatre has become more important in recent years. There are indigenous modern pieces and increasingly, foreign plays as well, on offer. If you are interested, you can get details in the towns themselves. There is no need for formal dress in these theatres.

ACROBATICS

Acrobatics is popular throughout China. Almost every large town has its own troupe of acrobats. Many of the troupes tour the country. You can get details of time and place of performances locally. In big cities such as Beijing, Shanghai and Guangzhou, there are permanent performances. In China, acrobatics means a mixture of proper acrobatics, magic and animal acts, and of course clowns. Circus performances are similar.

MOVIES & TELEVISION

Movies are very popular in the People's Republic of China, and has long ago taken over the viewership from traditional and modern theatre. There are cinemas all over China. The programme can be checked from the newspaper (ask at the hotel), and in Beijing, from the *China Daily*.

Television programmes in the evening are interesting and varied, ranging from news bulletins, traditional opera and Chinese to foreign films. There are two national channels as well as local ones. You can find the television programme in the *China Daily*.

Many hotels now carry feed from Star TV, a Hong Kong-based satellite broadcaster that is largely owned by News Corporation. There are English language channels with music, features and news.

NIGHTLIFE

PUBS & BARS

Night life is not particularly widespread in China. Most restaurants close early, and theatres, films etc. generally finish before 10pm. In southern Chinese towns, there is more life at night, with restaurants, bars, and cafes open till midnight or even later. Otherwise, such places are only open in the big hotels. *China Daily* has a good listing of cultural life. It lists the television programme, theatre and cinema performances in the big cities, particularly in Beijing, and notices of exhibitions, art galleries etc.

There are, of course, bars in hotels, offering both Chinese and foreign drinks. Also, in the larger cities, some places resembling pubs have opened; they tend to be meeting places for the better-off youths.

Far more common than these 'pubs' are karaoke bars. The Japanese-style singalong bars have swept China. Most are easily recognised by the letters 'OK' amongst the characters for their names. Some are relatively pricey – members of China's *nouveau riches* are happy to show off their wealth by paying, for an evening out, amounts that would seem wildly extravagant to most of the country's workers. Also, reports have surfaced that some of these bars are fronts for prostitution; note that such hostess-style bars are illegal in China, and can fleece customers.

DISCOS

Discotheques are popular throughout China nowadays and can be found in a number of towns. Many hotels have their own discos which are frequented by well-off local youths. The most fashionable dances are as well known here as anywhere else in the world. Many discotheques – particularly in the hotels – are open till midnight or slightly later.

SHOPPING

WHAT TO BUY

Typically "Chinese" goods such as silk, jade and porcelain are still cheaper and of a better quality in Hong Kong than in the People's Republic of China. The choice varies – if you are lucky, the shelves are well stocked and you can find excellent and well-cut silk articles being sold cheaply; if the supply has dried up, you will only find meagre remnants even in Hangzhou, the centre of silk production. You will usually find good quality goods which are produced for export. These are mostly sold in the "Friendship Stores" (*Youyi Shangdian*) and in the hotel shops.

Until recently, it was not usual to bargain and it is still not advisable in the state-owned shops and warehouses. But at the many souvenir stands, it is a good idea to bargain because of the greatly overpriced goods on offer. It is also worth comparing prices in the free markets (if you can read them) and watch how much Chinese customers pay.

When buying antiques, it is essential to check that the official red seal of the shop is on the product. Buying and exporting of antiques is only permitted with this official stamp, otherwise you could meet with great difficulties when leaving the country.

It is worth looking for local products in the smaller towns or in the places where ethnic minori-

ties live. These will be difficult to find anywhere else in China. The most usual articles are craft objects for everyday use or specially worked or embroidered garments.

SHOPPING AREAS

Department Stores: In every town, you will find a department store selling products for everyday use. You can buy all the essentials here, from toothpaste to a bicycle. However, as far as clothing is concerned, the quality of the fabric (artificial fibres are commonly used for shirts and blouses, skirts and long trousers), the cut and the sizes are usually not up to expectation. It is therefore not advisable to come to China expecting to buy your holiday wardrobe here.

The big department store are state-owned institutions, but many small shops and street stalls – privately owned – have sprung up as well. Here you will often find products from Hong Kong, such as jeans, silk blouses etc., which have been brought up from the south by painstaking courier networks.

Friendship Store: A visit to the "Friendship Store" (*Youyi Shangdian*) is an essential part of the programme of all tour groups. These stores usually offer a good selection of wares for export: silk fabric, craft articles, electronic devices, clothing and books. Often, there is a whole department offering traditional and modern medical products and equipment. Individual travellers, too, should take the opportunity to look round these stores from time to time. The Friendship Store in Beijing, for instance, has an excellent food department with many dairy products. A visit to the antiques department in the Friendship Store in Shanghai is also worthwhile.

Some large Friendship Store and warehouses have a delivery section which will send your purchases to your country. Shops and department stores generally open around 9am and close at 6pm or 7pm. The markets open much earlier.

Markets: Food items such as fruit, vegetables, fish and meat are sold at fixed prices in the state controlled markets. In the free markets, there are often additional useful items on offer which are even more attractively laid out, such as wicker baskets, metal and iron bits, and clothes; some small tailors have also opened up. In the big towns, numerous street traders offer their wares well into the evening; you can often find good items, such as jeans or silk blouses from Hong Kong, at such places. A visit to the free markets is definitely worthwhile, for even in the smaller towns, something interesting can often be found.

Bear in mind the caution mentioned above, about comparing and watching how much the Chinese pay; all too often, traders in free markets will happily fleece unwary customers.

IMPORT & EXPORT

When buying antique objects, make sure that they have the official red lacquer seal of the antique shop which entitles you to export it. All other antiques are the property of the Peoples' Republic of China and may not be taken out of the country.

Foreign currency can be imported and exported without restrictions. You may not export more foreign currency than you imported, unless you have a special permit.

You should not export, or even buy in the first place, objects which have been made from wild animals, e.g. ivory goods. They are subject to the Washington Species Protection Agreement.

SPECIAL INFORMATION

DOING BUSINESS

China has, since the 1970s, increasingly opened up towards other countries. Since then, economic and business contacts with foreign companies and business people have also increased. Today, many big international banks and companies have subsidiaries in China, and many Chinese import-export businesses, as well as the Bank of China, have branches abroad. Chinese companies, businesses or concerns, actively seek contact with foreign partners. Joint ventures are particularly sought after. Doing business in China continues to be complicated, and if you want to enter the Chinese market, you should first obtain detailed information. The relevant Chamber of Commerce and Industry can usually help, as can the specialist trade and interest groups. They can, for instance, tell you when, where and what trade fairs are taking place in the People's Republic of China. Various consultants also offer services in this area. The following are important contact addresses:

UK
Department of Trade and Industry
Trade Promotion with China Branch, Kingsgate House, 67-74 Victoria Street, London SW1E 6SW. Tel: (071) 2155357

USA
National Council for US-China Trade
1050 17th Street N.W., Washington D.C. 20036. Tel: (202) 4290340

CHILDREN

The Chinese are fond of children, so travelling with children in China is not difficult. If you travel with toddlers or babies, you should note that disposable nappies and baby food in jars are not normally available in China. Children travel at reduced cost on trains and planes. Big hotels supply babysitters for a fee.

DISABLED

The problems of disabled people have only in recent years received attention in China. In general, Chinese towns, institutions, public means of transport and sights do not cater for the disabled. Travelling in a group for the disabled certainly reduces these problems considerably. There is an organisation for the disabled in the People's Republic of China. It is not known whether the organisation offers a special service for foreign disabled visitors. You can contact the organisation directly to find out what services it offers. The China National Tourist Offices and the State Travel Agency Lüxingshe (CITS) have information about whether special trips for the disabled are possible and how they are organised.

STUDENTS

There are no special rules for foreign students in the PR of China. As far as is known, international student cards are not recognised in China, only student cards of foreign students who study in China.

PHOTOGRAPHY

There are few restrictions on taking photographs and filming in China. Taking photographs of military installations is prohibited. If you are unclear or uncertain, consult your courier if you are travelling with a group. By using the usual discretion and tact, you can photograph freely and without hindrance. As in other countries, some museums, palaces or temples will not allow photographs to be taken. Sometimes, it is allowed without the use of a flash. It is a good idea to take some specially sensitive films. In some places, it is possible, despite the prohibition on taking photographs, to take some pictures for a fee. These fees can reach a considerable amount (for instance in Lhasa).

Cameras must be declared on entering the country

(the Customs Declaration must be kept until departure). No special permit is necessary for video or cine cameras. Half-inch video cameras are allowed, but not ¾ inch; 16 mm cameras are not allowed at all. Most hotels sell films, but it is still difficult to get slide films. Generally, Fuji and Kodak are on offer. Some modern luxury hotels also offer film processing services.

LANGUAGE

English is increasingly being used in the People's Republic of China, but on the whole, you will still find it difficult to meet people away from the big hotels and business and tourist centres who speak English, not to mention German or French. It is therefore advisable – especially for individual travellers – to learn some Chinese. Some people joke that, apart from *meiyou* ("it doesn't exist"), the most common words in China are "change money?".

More than a billion people in China, and many other Chinese in South East Asia and the United States, speak Chinese. In the People's Republic of China, other languages in addition to Chinese – the language of the Han people, the original Chinese – are spoken in the regions where the national minorities are settled, including Tibetan, Mongolian, Zhuang or Uygur. But everywhere in the People's Republic today, standard Chinese, also called Mandarin, is more or less understood or spoken. Regardless of whether you are in Guangzhou or in Heilongjiang, in Tibet or in Xinjiang, you can get through with standard Chinese.

The Chinese language is divided into several groups of dialect. For instance, a native of Guangzhou or Hong Kong cannot understand someone from Beijing or vice versa, unless both speak standard Chinese. The different dialects have, however, the same grammar and vocabulary; but above all, the writing is the same. The pronunciation may differ, but the written symbols can be understood by all literate Chinese. Thus, a native of Guangzhou and a Beijing citizen can understand each other by simply writing down the symbols.

Since the 1950s, all schools in the People's Republic of China teach standard Chinese or Mandarin – also called Putonghua or common language. It is also used on radio and television. Young Chinese people, particularly, know standard Chinese. Consequently, one can manage throughout the People's Republic – including in Guangzhou – by using standard Chinese. You will immediately notice the difference when you go from Guangzhou to Hong Kong: in Hong Kong, the official language amongst the Chinese is Cantonese.

The transcription of Chinese symbols: Standard Chinese is based on the pronunciation of the northern dialects, particularly the Beijing dialect. There is an officially approved Latin writing of standard Chinese, called *Hanyu Pinyin* (the phonetic transcription of the language of the Han people). Hanyu Pinyin is used throughout the People's Republic; many railway stations, airports etc. show name places and street names both in symbols and in the Latin transcription.

All dictionaries use the Hanyu Pinyin system. This transcription may at first appear confusing if one doesn't see the words as they are pronounced. The capital, Peking, is shown as Beijing in transcription. It would definitely be useful, particularly for individual travellers, to familiarize yourself a little with the pronunciation of Hanyu Pinyin, as even when asking for a place or street name, you need to know how it is pronounced, otherwise you won't be understood. This travel guide, and the *Insight Cityguide: Beijing* use the Hanyu Pinyin system throughout for Chinese names and expression.

The pronunciation of Chinese: The pronunciation of the consonants is similar to those in English. b, p, d, t, g, k are all voiceless. p, t, k are aspirated, b, d, g are not aspirated. The i after the consonants ch, c, r, sh, s, z, zh is not pronounced, it indicates that the preceding sound is lengthened.

Hanyu Pinyin	English transcript	Sound
a	a	far
an	un	run
ang	ung	lung
ao	ou	loud
b	b	bath
c	ts	rats
ch	ch	change
d	d	day
e	er	dirt
e (after i,u,y)	a	tram
ei	ay	may
en	en	when
eng	eong	ng has a nasal sound
er	or	honor
f	f	fast
g	g	go
h	ch	loch
i	ee	keen
j	j	jeep
k	k	cake
l	l	little
m	m	month
n	n	name
o	o	bond
p	p	trapped

q	ch	**ch**eer
r	r	**r**ight
s	s	me**ss**
sh	sh	**sh**ade
t	t	**t**on
u	oo	sh**oo**t
u (after j,q,x,y)	as German u+	m**u+**de
w	w	**w**ater
x	**ch**	as in Scottish lo**ch**, followed by s
y	y	**y**ogi
z	ds	re**ds**
zh	dj	**j**ungle

It is often said that the Chinese language is monosyllabic. At first sight this may seem the case since, generally, each symbol is one word. However, in modern Chinese, most words are made up of two or three syllable symbols, sometimes more. Chinese generally lacks syllables, there are only 420 in Mandarin to represent all symbols in sounds. The sounds are used to differentiate – a specifically Chinese practice which often makes it very difficult for foreigners when first learning the Chinese language. Each syllable has a specific sound. These sounds often represent different meanings. For instance, if one pronounces the syllable 'mai' with a falling fourth sound (mài) it means to sell; if it is pronounced with a falling-rising third sound, mai, it means: to buy. When one reads the symbols carefully this is always clearly shown. To show this again with the simple syllable ma:

First sound *ma* mother
second sound *má* hemp
third sound *ma* horse
fourth sound *mà* to complain

The Chinese language has four sounds and a fifth, 'soundless' sound: The first sound is spoken high pitched and even, the second rising, the third falling and then rising, and the fourth sound falling. The individual sounds are marked above the vowel in the syllable in the following way: First sound -, second sound ´, third sound ˇ, fourth sound `.

The Chinese sentence structure is simple: subject, predicate, object. The simplest way of forming a question is to add the question particle 'ma' to a sentence in ordinary word sequence. It is usually not possible to note from a Chinese word whether it is a noun, adjective or another form, singular or plural. This depends on the context.

The Chinese language is a language of symbols or pictures. Each symbol represents a one-syllable word. There are in total more than 47,000 symbols, though modern Chinese only use a part of these. For a daily paper, between 3,000 and 4,000 symbols are sufficient. Scholars know between 5,000 and 6,000. Many symbols used to be quite complicated. After 1949, several reforms in the written language were introduced in the People's Republic in order to simplify the written language. Today, the simplified symbols are used throughout the People's Republic, though in Hong Kong and Taiwan, the complex ones are still used.

Many Chinese words are composed of two or more symbols or single-syllable words. For instance, the Chinese word for film is *dian-ying*, and is made up of the two words: *dian* for electricity and *ying* for shadow. To make reading easier, the Hanyu-Pinyin system joins syllables which, together, form words. Group travellers generally have translators with them to whom they can turn in case of communication problems. But if you are travelling on your own, it is worth taking a dictionary with you. Below are several language guides that are available on the market:

Chinese at your Fingertips, Don Rimming and Li Kaimin, Routledge, 1989. ISBN 0-415-00238-9.
Chinese-English Phrase Book for Travellers, John S. Montanaro, Wiley, 1981. ISBN 0-471-08298-8 (book), 0-4710-09749-7 (cassette), 0-471-87566-X (set).
Pocket Interpreter Chinese, Peking 1988.
Chinese in 10 Minutes a Day (revised edition), Kristine Kershul, Bilingual Books 1988. ISBN 0-944502-07-5.

USEFUL PHRASES

Greetings

How are you?	Nǐ hǎo	你好
How are you?	Nǐ hǎo mǎ?	你好吗?
Thank you	Xièxie	谢谢
Good bye	Zài jiàn	再见
My name is…	wǒ jiào….	我叫…
My last name is…	wǒ xìng…	我姓…
What is your name?	Nín jiào shénme míngzì?	您叫什么名字?
What is your last name?	Nín guìxìng?	您贵姓?
I am very happy…	Wǒ hěn gāoxìng …	我很高兴…
All right	Hǎo	好
Not all right	Bù hǎo	不好
Can you speak English?	Nín huì shūo yīngyǔ mǎ?	您会说英语吗?
Can you speak Chinese?	Nín huì shūo hànyù mǎ?	您会说汉语吗?
I cannot speak Chinese	Wǒ bú huì Hànyǔ.	我不会汉语。
I do not understand	Wǒ bùdǒng.	我不懂。
Do you understand?	Nín dǒng mǎ?	您懂吗?
Please speak a little slower	Qing nín shuō màn yìdiǎnr.	请您说慢一点儿!
What is this called?	Zhègè jiào shénme?	这个叫什么?
How do you say…	…..zěnmè shuō?	…怎么说?
Please/Thank you	Qing/Xièxiè	请/谢谢
Never mind	Méi Guānxì	没关系
Sorry	Duìbùqǐ	对不起

Pronouns

Who/Who is it?	Shéi?	谁
My/mine	wo/wode	我/我的
You/yours (singular)	nǐ/nǐdè	你/你的
He/his	tā/tādè	他/他的
We/ours	wǒmén/wǒméndè	我们/我们的
You/yours (plural)	nǐmen/nǐméndě	你们/你们的
They/theirs	tāmèn/tāmènde	他们/他们的
You/yours (respectful term when addressing seniors)	Nín/Nínde	您/您的

Travel

Where is it?	…zài nǎr?	…在哪儿?
Do you have it here?	Zhèr yǒu …. mǎ?	这儿有…吗?
Hotel	fàndiàn	饭店
Restaurant	fànguǎn	饭馆
Bank	yìnháng	银行
Post Office	yóujú	邮局
Toilet	cèsuǒ	厕所
Railway Station	huǒchēzhàn	火车站
Bus Station	(gōnggòngqì) chēzhàn	公共汽车站
Embassy	dàshíguǎn	大使馆
Consulate	lǐngshìguǎn	领事馆
Passport	hùzhaò	护照

Visa	qiānzhèng	签证
Medicine shop	yàodiàn	药店
Hospital	yīyuàn	医院
Doctor	yīshēng	医生
Translate	fānyì	翻译
Bar	jǐubā	酒吧
Rented car	chūzūqìzhē	出租汽车
Do you have…?	Nín yōu…. mǎ?	您有…吗?
I want/I think I want	Wǒ yào/wǒ xiǎng yào	我要/我想要
I want to buy…	Wǒ xiǎng mǎi ….. .	我想买……
Can I buy it there?	Nǎr néng mǎi ….. mà?	哪能买…吗?
This/that	zhège/nèige	这个/那个
Green tea/red tea	lǔchá/hóngchá	绿茶/红茶
Coffee	kāfēi	咖啡
Cigarette	xiāngyān	香烟
Films	jiāojuǎnr	胶卷儿
Ticket	piào	票
Post card	míngxìnpiàn	明信片
A letter	yì fēng xìn	一封信
Air mail	yì fēng hángkōngxìn	一封航空信
Postage stamp	yóupiào	邮票

Shopping

How much…?	Duōshǎo?	多少?
How much does this cost/ What is the price…	Zhègē duōshǎo qían?	这个多少钱?
Too expensive, thank you	Tài gùile, xièxiè.	太贵了，谢谢。
Very expensive	Hěn gùi.	很贵。
A little (bit)	Yìdiǎnr.	一点儿。
Too much	tài duōle	太多了
A lot	dūo	多
Few	shǎo	少

Money Matters

Cash/money	qián	钱
Chinese currency	Rénmínbì	人民币
One dollar	yì yuán	一元
Ten cents	yì jiǎo	一角
One cent	yì fēn	一分
Traveller's cheques	lǔxíngzhīpiào	旅行支票
Credit card	xìnyòngkǎ	信用卡
Foreign currency	wàihuìquàn	外汇卷
Where can one change money?	Zài nár kěyī huànqián?	在哪可以换钱?
I want to change money	Wǒ yào huàn qián.	我要换钱
What is the conversion rate?	bǐ jià shì duō shǎo?	比价是多少?
We want to rent a car for one/two/three persons	Wǒmén yào zhù yì (liǎng, sān …) tīan.	我们要住一 (俩，叁…)天。
What is the room rates for a day?	Fángjīan duōshǎo qián yì tiān?	房间多少钱一天?
Hotel	fàndiàn	饭店
Room	fángjīan	房间
Single room/double room	dānrén fángjīan/shúangrén fángjīan	单人房间/双人房间

Airport	fēijīchǎng	飞机场
Bus	gōngoǹqìchē	公共汽车
Rented car	chūzhūqìchē	出租汽车
Telephone	diànhùa	电话
Long distance call	chángtú diànhùa	长途电话
Telephone number	diànhùa haòmǎ	电话号码
Reception	fúwútai	服务台
Telegram	diànbào	电极
Telex	diànchúan	电传
Key	yàoshì	钥匙
Clothes	yīfù	衣服
Luggage	xínglì	行李

Restaurants

Waiter	fúwúyuán	服务员
Miss/Madam	xǐaojǐe	小姐
Breakfast	zǎofàn	早饭
Lunch	wǔfàn	午饭
Dinner	wǎnfàn	晚饭
Chopsticks	kùaizi	筷子
Fork	chāzi	叉子
Soup ladle	sháozi	勺子
I want	Wǒ yào …	我要…
I do not want	Wǒ bú yào ….	我不要…
I did not reserve	Zhègè wǒ meí dìng.	这个我没订。
Beer	píjiǔ	啤酒
Eat	chīfaǹ	吃饭
Coca-cola	kěkóu kělè	可口可乐
Mineral water	kúangqúanshǔi	矿泉水
Menu	càidān	菜单
Rice	mǐfàn	米饭
Noodles	miàntiáo	面条
Tea	chá	茶
Soup	tāng	汤
Dishes (food dishes)	(fàn)cài	（饭）菜
Beef/pork/lamb	níuròu/zhūroù/yángroù	牛肉/猪肉/羊肉
Fish	yú	鱼
Vegetables	shūcài	蔬菜
Fruit/fruits	shúigǔo	水果
Bread	miànbāo	面包
Toast	kaǒmiànbāo	烤面包
Butter	húangyóu	黄油
Egg	jīdaǹ	鸡旦
Cup	bēizi	杯子
Glass cup	bōlì bēizi	玻璃杯子
Hot (spicy)/sweet/sour/salty	là/tián/suān/xián	辣/甜/酸/咸
White wine/red wine	bǎi pútàojiǔ/hóng pútàojiǔ	白葡萄酒/红葡萄酒
Can we have the bill?	Qǐng sùanzhàng bǎ.	请算帐吧。

Time

When?	Shénmè shíhòu?	什么时候?

What time is it?	Jí diǎnzhōng?	几点钟?
How long?	Duōcháng shíjiān?	多长时间?
one/two/three	Yī/liǎng/sān diǎnzhōng	一/俩/三点钟
morning/early afternnon/ late afternoon	zǎoshàng/shàngwǔ/zhōngwǔ/	早上/上午/中午
Afternoon/night	xiàwǔ/wǎnshàng	下午/晚上
Monday	xīngqīyī	星期一
Tuesday	xīngqīèr	星期二
Wednesday	xīngqīsān	星期三
Thursday	xīngqīsì	星期四
Friday	xīngqīwǔ	星期五
Saturday	xīngqīliù	星期六
Sunday	xīngqītiān	星期天
Weekend	zhōumò	周末
Yesterday/today/tomorrow	zuótiān/jīntiān/míngtiān	昨天/今天/明天
This week/last week/ next week	zhège/sháng/xìaxīngqī	这个/上/下星期
Hour/day/week/month	xiǎoshí/tiān/xīngqī/yuè	小时/天/星期/月
January, February, March, April, May	yīyuè/éryuè/sānyuè/sìyuè/wǔyuè	一月, 二月, 三月, 四月, 五月,
June, July, August, September	lìuyuè/qīyuè/bāyuè/jǐuyuè	六月, 七月, 八月, 九月,
October, November, December	shíyuè/shíyīyuè/shíèryuè	十月, 十一月, 十二月,

Numbers

One	yī	一
Two	ér	二
Three	sān	三
Four	sì	四
Five	wǔ	五
Six	liù	六
Seven	qī	七
Eight	bā	八
Nine	jiǔ	九
Ten	shí	十
Eleven	shíyī	十一
Twelve	shíèr	十二
Twenty	érshī	二十
Thirty	sānshī	三十
Forty	sìshī	四十
Fifty	wǔshī	五十
Sixty	liushī	六十
Seventy	qīshī	七十
Eighty	bāshī	八十
Ninety	jiǔshī	九十
One hundred	yìbǎi	一百
One hundred and one	yìbǎilíngyī	一百零一
Two hundred	èrbǎi	二百
Three hundred	sānbǎi	三百
Four hundred	sìbǎi	四百
Five hundred	wǔbǎi	五百
Six hundred	liùbǎi	六百

Seven hundred	qībǎi	七百
Eight hundred	bābǎi	八百
Nine hundred	jiǔbǎi	九百
One thousand	yì qīan	一千
Ten thousand	yí wàn	一万
One hundred thousand	shí wàn	十万
Onc million	yì bǎi wàn	一百万
Ten million	yì qiān wàn	一千万
One billion	yí yì	一亿

FURTHER READING

OTHER INSIGHT GUIDES

This book leads you through an Asian metropolis with more excitement than any other city in the world

Other *Insight Guides* which highlight destinations in this region are:

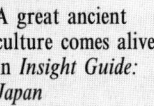

A great ancient culture comes alive in *Insight Guide: Japan*

Isle Formosa – The Beautiful Island – vividly described in *Insight Guide: Taiwan*

ART/PHOTO CREDITS

INDEX

398

G

H

A
B
C
D
F
G
H
I
J
a
b
d
e
f
g
h
i
j
k
l